HM TREASURY

Budget 2007

Building Britain's long-term future: Prosperity and fairness for families

Economic and Fiscal Strategy Report and Financial Statement and Budget Report

March 2007

Return to an Order of the House of Commons dated 21 March 2007

Copy of Economic and Fiscal Strategy Report and Financial Statement and Budget Report – March 2007 as laid before the House of Commons by the Chancellor of the Exchequer when opening the Budget.

John Healey
Her Majesty's Treasury
21 March 2007

Ordered by the House of Commons to be printed 21 March 2007

HC 342   LONDON: The Stationery Office   £45.00

HM Treasury contacts

This report can be found on the Treasury website at:

hm-treasury.gov.uk/budget2007

For general enquiries about HM Treasury and its work, contact:

Correspondence and Enquiry Unit
HM Treasury
1 Horse Guards Road
London
SW1A 2HQ

Tel: 020 7270 4558
Fax: 020 7270 4861
E-mail: public.enquiries@hm-treasury.gov.uk

This and other government documents can be found on the Internet at:

www.official-documents.co.uk

ISBN: 978-0-10-294455-6

The Economic and Fiscal Strategy Report and the Financial Statement and Budget Report contain the Government's assessment of the medium-term economic and budgetary position. They set out the Government's tax and spending plans, including those for public investment, in the context of its overall approach to social, economic and environmental objectives. After approval for the purposes of Section 5 of the European Communities (Amendment) Act 1993, these reports will form the basis of submissions to the European Commission under Article 99 (ex Article 103) and Article 104 (ex Article 104c) of the Treaty establishing the European Community.

CONTENTS

Page

Economic and Fiscal Strategy Report

Financial Statement and Budget Report

Economic and Fiscal Strategy Report

The Government's economic objective is to build a strong economy and a fair society, where there is opportunity and security for all. Budget 2007, *Building Britain's long-term future: Prosperity and fairness for families*, presents updated assessments and forecasts of the economy and public finances, and reports on how the Government's policies are helping to deliver its long-term goals. The Budget:

- shows that the economy is stable and growing and that the Government is meeting its strict fiscal rules for the public finances;

- sets out the next stage in the Government's reforms to simplify the tax system, to provide help for pensioners, support for families and make work pay, including:

  - removing the 10 pence starting rate of tax and cutting the basic rate of income tax from 22 pence to 20 pence from April 2008;

  - increasing the upper earnings limit for national insurance and fully aligning it with the point at which taxpayers start to pay the higher rate of income tax, and raising the aligned upper earnings limit and higher rate threshold by £800 a year above indexation in April 2009;

  - raising the higher personal allowances for those aged 65 or over by £1,180 above indexation in April 2008;

  - increasing further the child element of the Child Tax Credit by £150 per year above earnings indexation in April 2008; and

  - increasing the threshold for Working Tax Credit by £1,200 to £6,420 and raising the withdrawal rate on tax credits by 2 per cent to 39 per cent in April 2008, and increasing the weekly rate of Child Benefit for the eldest child to £20 in April 2010.

- sets out a major package of reforms to the corporate tax system, including reducing the headline corporation tax rate from 30 per cent to 28 per cent from April 2008, simplifying capital allowances, further enhancing research and development tax credits, and increasing the small companies' rate to tackle individuals incorporating to minimise tax;

- increases investment in education and skills in England by 2.5 per cent a year in real terms (5.3 per cent in nominal terms) on average between 2008-09 to 2010-11;

- restricts tax relief available on empty commercial properties, to encourage the supply of office, retail and industrial premises;

- introduces further reforms to modernise the tax system, and a number of measures to tackle tax fraud and avoidance; and

- takes further steps to tackle the global challenges of climate change including an increase in fuel duty rates from 1 October 2007, reforms to Vehicle Excise Duty and measures to improve the energy efficiency of homes.

1.1   The Government's economic objective is to build a strong economy and a fair society, where there is opportunity and security for all.

1.2   The long-term decisions the Government has taken – giving independence to the Bank of England, new fiscal rules and a reduction in debt – have created a strong platform of economic stability. In the UK, with low and stable inflation, interest rates set by the Monetary

Policy Committee to meet the Government's symmetric inflation target, and fiscal policy supporting monetary policy over the cycle, the economy has grown continuously throughout this period. The UK economy is currently experiencing its longest unbroken expansion since quarterly records began, with GDP now having grown for 58 consecutive quarters.

Meeting long-term global challenges 1.3   The global economy is in the midst of radical transformation with far reaching and fundamental changes in technology, production and trading patterns. Rapid technological change continues to impact on how individuals, business and communities interact with each other and how they expect to interact with the state. Global security is being reshaped as the international community responds to the ongoing threat of international terrorism, conflict and the challenges of ending world poverty. The pressures that economic and population growth are placing on the earth's natural resources and climate are increasingly apparent, presenting an urgent need for international cooperation.[1]

1.4   This transformation will present both challenges and opportunities for the UK. Individuals, businesses and communities all need to be ready to respond to the changing global environment. Stable, flexible, skilled and innovative economies will prosper. This Budget sets out further reforms to lock in stability and to invest in the UK's future including a major package of reforms to the corporate tax system to enhance international competitiveness, encourage investment and promote innovation, reducing the main rate of corporation tax to 28 percent by April 2008, the lowest in the G7.

1.5   Fairness must go alongside flexibility, providing security and support for those that need it and ensuring that everyone has the opportunity to fulfil their potential. The reforms of the welfare state, introduced since 1997, reflect the Government's aims of eradicating child poverty, supporting families to balance their work and family life, promoting saving and ensuring security for all in old age. The Government is also committed to a modern and fair tax system which encourages work and saving, and ensures that everyone pays their fair share of tax. This Budget announces the next stage in modernising the tax and benefit system, to provide support for pensioners, tackle poverty and make work pay. This includes removing the 10 pence starting rate of tax, cutting the basic rate of income tax from 22 pence to 20 pence, increasing the upper earnings limit for national insurance and aligning it with the higher rate threshold for income tax, as well as increases in Child Tax Credit and the threshold for Working Tax Credits.

1.6   This Budget describes the next steps the Government is taking to enhance its long term goals of:

- **maintaining macroeconomic stability, ensuring the fiscal rules are met and that inflation remains low**;

- **raising the sustainable rate of productivity growth**, through reforms that promote enterprise and competition, enhance flexibility and promote science, innovation and skills;

- **providing employment opportunity for all,** by promoting a flexible labour market which sustains a higher proportion of people in employment than ever before;

- **ensuring fairness,** by providing security for people when they need it, tackling child and pensioner poverty, providing opportunity for all children and young people and delivering security for all in retirement;

---

[1] Detailed analysis of these issues is set out in: *Long-term opportunities and challenges for the UK: analysis for the 2007 Comprehensive Spending Review*, HM Treasury, November 2006.

- delivering world-class public services, with extra investment alongside efficiency, reform and results; and

- addressing environmental challenges, such as climate change and the need for energy efficiency in response to rising oil prices.

MAINTAINING MACROECONOMIC STABILITY

1.7   The Government's long-term economic goal is to maintain macroeconomic stability, ensuring the fiscal rules are met at all times and that inflation remains low. Chapter 2 describes how the Government is working to achieve this goal and summarises prospects for the UK economy and public finances, full details of which are set out in Chapters B and C of the *Financial Statement and Budget Report (FSBR)*.

The policy framework   1.8   The Government's macroeconomic framework is based on the principles of transparency, responsibility and accountability, and is designed to ensure lasting stability so that businesses, individuals and the Government can plan effectively for the long term. The Bank of England has operational independence to meet the Government's symmetrical inflation target. Fiscal policy is underpinned by clear objectives and two strict rules which ensure sound public finances over the medium term. The fiscal rules underpin the Government's public spending framework which facilitates long-term planning and provides departments with the flexibility and incentives they need to increase the quality of public services and deliver specified outcomes.

Economic prospects   1.9   The UK economy is currently experiencing its longest unbroken expansion on record, with GDP now having grown for 58 consecutive quarters. Over the past 10 years, the Government's macroeconomic framework has delivered more stability in terms of GDP growth and inflation rates than in any decade since the war. This historically low volatility puts the UK in a strong position to respond to the global economic challenges of the next decade.

1.10   Overall economic developments are as forecast at the Pre-Budget Report. The UK economy grew by $2^3/_4$ per cent in 2006, as forecast in the Pre-Budget Report. The rebalancing of domestic demand gathered pace during 2006, with business investment ending the year growing at the fastest rate for eight years. Following five consecutive quarters of above-trend growth, the UK economy is estimated to have ended 2006 operating close to its trend level, although there remains evidence of some slack in the labour market. The Budget 2007 economic forecast is little changed from that of the Pre-Budget Report. GDP is forecast to grow by $2^3/_4$ to $3^1/_4$ per cent in 2007, and then at trend rates of $2^1/_2$ to 3 per cent. CPI inflation is expected to return to target in the second half of 2007.

The public finances   1.11   The Budget 2007 projections for the public finances are broadly in line with the 2006 Pre Budget Report and show that the Government is meeting its strict fiscal rules:

- the current budget shows an average surplus as a percentage of GDP over the current economic cycle, even using cautious assumptions, ensuring the Government is meeting the golden rule. Beyond the end of the current cycle, the current budget moves clearly into surplus including, by the end of the projection period, the cyclically-adjusted current budget in the cautious case; and

- public sector net debt is projected to remain low and stable over the forecast period, stabilising at a level below 39 per cent, below the 40 per cent ceiling set in the sustainable investment rule.

Table 1.1: Meeting the fiscal rules

	Per cent of GDP						
	Outturn	Estimate	Projections				
	2005-06	2006-07	2007-08	2008-09	2009-10	2010-11	2011-12
Golden Rule							
Surplus on current budget	-1.2	-0.7	-0.3	0.2	0.4	0.6	0.8
Average surplus since 1997-1998	0.2	0.1	0.0	0.1	0.1	0.1	0.2
Cyclically-adjusted surplus on current budget	-1.0	-0.5	-0.3	0.2	0.4	0.6	0.8
Sustainable investment rule							
Public sector net debt[1]	36.5	37.2	38.2	38.5	38.8	38.8	38.6

[1] Debt at end March; GDP centred on end March.

Budget policy decisions 1.12 Against this backdrop, and building on steps already taken, Budget 2007 announces further decisions to lock in stability and invest in the UK's future, including:

- reforms to simplify the tax system, to provide help for pensioners, support for families and make work pay, including:

  - removing the 10 pence starting rate of tax and cutting the basic rate of income tax from 22 pence to 20 pence from April 2008;

  - increasing the upper earnings limit for national insurance and fully aligning it with the point at which taxpayers start to pay the higher rate of income tax, and raising the aligned upper earnings limit and higher rate threshold by £800 a year above indexation in April 2009:

  - raising the higher personnal allowances for those aged 65 or over by £1,180 above indexation in April 2008;

  - increasing further the child element of the Child Tax Credit by £150 per year above earnings indexation in April 2008; and

  - increasing the threshold for Working Tax Credit by £1,200 to £6,420; raising the withdrawal rate on tax credits by 2 per cent to 39 per cent and increasing the weekly rate of Child Benefit for the eldest child to £20 in April 2010.

- a major package of reforms to the corporate tax system, including reducing the headline corporate tax rate from 30 per cent to 28 per cent from April 2008, simplifying capital allowances, further enhancing research and development tax credits, and increasing the small companies rate to tackle individuals incorporating to minimise tax;

- restricting tax relief available on empty commercial properties, to encourage the supply of office, retail and industrial premises;

- further reforms to modernise the tax system, and a number of measures to tackle tax fraud and avoidance;

- taking further steps to tackle the global challenge of climate change including an increase in fuel duty rates from 1 October 2007, reforms to Vehicle Excise Duty and measures to improve the energy efficiency of homes.

1.13 Budget 2007 also confirms the firm overall spending limits for the 2007 Comprehensive Spending Review years 2008-09, 2009-10 and 2010-11, which ensure that the

Government meets its strict fiscal rules while allowing it to increase total public spending by an average of 2 per cent per year in real terms with:

- current spending increasing by an average of 1.9 per cent per year in real terms;

- net investment rising to $2\frac{1}{4}$ per cent of GDP compared with $\frac{1}{2}$ per cent of GDP in 1997-98, locking in the step change in investment over the past decade;

- an early CSR07 settlement for the Department for Education and Skills which sees education spending in England rise by 2.5 per cent a year in real terms (5.3 per cent in nominal terms) on average between 2007-08 and 2010-11, increasing UK education spending from 4.7 per cent of GDP in 1996-07 to 5.6 per cent by 2010-11; and

- substantial additional resources to support the Government's vision for personalised education, including funding for one-to-one teacher-led tuition for over 300,000 under-attaining pupils a year in English by 2010-11 and 300,000 in Maths.

1.14 Consistent with the requirements of the Code for Fiscal Stability, the updated public finance projections in Budget 2007 take into account the fiscal effects of these and all other firm decisions announced in the Budget. The fiscal impact of Budget policy decisions is set out in Table 1.2. Full details are provided in Chapter A of the FSBR.

1.15 An analysis of long-term fiscal sustainability was published alongside the 2006 Pre-Budget Report in the *2006 Long-term public finance report,* and is updated in Annex A of the Economic and Fiscal Strategy Report. Using a range of sustainability indicators, this shows that the public finances are sustainable in the longer term, and that the UK is well placed relative to many other countries to face the challenges of an ageing population.

MEETING THE PRODUCTIVITY CHALLENGE

1.16 Productivity growth, alongside high and stable levels of employment, is central to long-term economic performance. In the increasingly knowledge-driven global economy, science, innovation and creativity are important drivers of productivity growth, backed up by a highly skilled workforce and a competitive and enterprising economy. The UK has historically experienced comparatively low rates of productivity growth. However, UK performance has improved in relation to other major economies in recent years. The Government's long term goal is for the UK to continue to close the productivity gap by achieving a faster rate of growth than its main competitors.

Action so far **1.17** The Government's strategy focuses on five key drivers of productivity performance:

- **improving competition** which promotes flexible markets and increases business efficiency and consumer choice;

- **promoting enterprise,** including through reducing the regulatory burden on business, to ensure that UK firms are well-placed to respond to opportunities in a rapidly changing global market;

- **supporting science and innovation** which is central to success in the international economy, as global restructuring focuses developed economies toward knowledge-based and high value-added sectors;

- **raising UK skills** to create a more flexible and productive workforce, and to meet the long-term challenge of rising skills levels in emerging markets; and

- **encouraging investment** to increase the stock of physical capital supported by stronger, more efficient capital markets. In the global economy, attracting international capital and investment will require macroeconomic stability and a robust and efficient investment environment.

Next steps 1.18   Building on the reforms and initiatives already introduced, Budget 2007 sets out the next steps the Government is taking to strengthen the drivers of productivity growth and meet the long-term challenges of the global economy, including:

- **a major package of reforms to the corporate tax system** to promote growth by enhancing international competitiveness, encouraging investment and promoting innovation:

  - a reduction in the main corporation tax rate from 30 per cent to 28 per cent from April 2008, making it the most competitive rate in the G7 and other major economies;

  - modernising and simplifying the capital allowance system;

  - increasing the small companies' rate, to tackle individuals incorporating to minimise tax and national insurance liabilities;

  - the introduction of a new Annual Investment Allowance (AIA) of £50,000 for all businesses who invest to grow; and

  - further enhancements to the SME and large company R&D tax credit schemes.

- **driving forward the risk-based approach to regulation** by implementing the Hampton review's risk-based approach, for example, in relation to employment tribunals; and encouraging regulatory reform in Europe based on risk;

- **maintaining the Government's commitment that private and public sector R&D investment reach 2.5 per cent of GDP**, with the announcement of early CSR settlements for the Department for Trade and Industry's science budget and the Department for Education and Skills, which together will ensure that total investment in the public science base will rise by 2.5 per cent in real terms over the CSR period; and

- **reforming empty property reliefs in business rates** alongside a wider package of land and property incentives to increase competitiveness, encourage investment and deliver sustainable increaeses in housing supply.

INCREASING EMPLOYMENT OPPORTUNITY FOR ALL

1.19   The Government's long-term objective for the labour market is to realise employment opportunity for all – the modern definition of full employment. There has been considerable progress towards this objective, particularly in those areas and among those groups of people who had previously been most disadvantaged. The Government aims to go further, however, and has set a long-term aspiration for an employment rate equivalent to 80 per cent of the working age population. This will involve reaching out to the hardest to help, moving people from inactivity to labour market participation and encouraging more individuals to take personal responsibility to move from welfare to work.

Action so far **1.20**   The Government's strategy for extending employment opportunity to all builds on the strong performance of the UK labour market over recent years. Employment in the UK reached 29 million for the first time in 2006. This is the highest figure since comparable records began in 1971. The working age employment rate is now 74.4 per cent, up from 72.7 per cent in 1997, while unemployment has fallen to 5.5 per cent. Chapter 4 describes the successful action the Government has taken to increase employment opportunity, through:

- **delivering employment opportunity to all,** to provide everyone who is able to work with the support they need to move into work as quickly as possible;

- **extending employment opportunity** to those groups and regions which have faced the greatest barriers to work;

- **enhancing skills and mobility,** to ensure that everyone can fulfil their potential in the labour market and that business has access to the skilled workforce they need to compete in the global economy; and

- **making work pay,** through the National Minimum Wage and tax credits which create a system of support that provides greater rewards from work, improving incentives for individuals to participate in the labour market.

Next steps **1.21**   Budget 2007 describes the further steps the Government is taking to build on this success and further strengthen the labour market, with a long-term vision for extending support to the inactive and those who face particular barriers to work. The Budget announces:

- **steps to provide further help to lone parents to stay in employment,** by continuing to make In-Work Credit available to eligible lone parents in the current pilot areas until June 2008, benefiting over 250,000 lone parents, and offering a higher rate of £60 across the whole of London;

- **a four-week run-on in entitlement to Working Tax Credit** from the day that a previously eligible claimant ceases to work 16 hours;

- **testing reforms to the education and training offered to participants on New Deal for young people,** and a seamless link from New Deal to in-work training delivered through Train to Gain;

- **local employment partnerships with large retail employers working in partnership with Jobcentre Plus** at a local level, to help the long-term unemployed and economically inactive back to work;

- **trialling short, work-focused approaches for English as a second or other language (ESOL) courses in the London City Strategy pathfinders** for parents on benefits or tax credits;

- **improve further the administration of Housing Benefit,** and setting out an intention to reform Housing Benefit subsidy for temporary accommodation;

- **a package of measures to align further and simplify the benefits system;** and

- following the Low Pay Commission recommendations, **raising the adult rate of the National Minimum Wage to £5.52 per hour**, the youth rate, for workers aged between 18 to 21, to £4.60 and the development rate for 16 and 17- year olds to £3.40; all from October 2007.

BUILDING A FAIRER SOCIETY

1.22 The Government's long-term economic goal is to combine flexibility with fairness. Policies that ensure fairness act to minimise the short-term costs that can be associated with the changes that are needed in flexible outward-looking economies. Fairness provides security and support for those that need it and ensures that everyone has the opportunity to fulfil their potential in the global economy, now and in the future. The Government is also at the forefront of global efforts to achieve the Millennium Development Goals for global poverty, and to reduce debt in the poorest countries.

Action so far **1.23** Chapter 5 describes the range of reforms the Government has undertaken to achieve its goals in these areas, including:

- **support for families and children** to lift children out of poverty and so ensure they have the opportunity to fulfil their potential;

- **support for pensioners** to tackle poverty and ensure security in retirement for all pensioners, with extra help for those who need it most and rewards for those who have saved modest amounts;

- **steps to encourage saving,** including through the introduction of the Child Trust Fund, stakeholder pensions and Individual Savings Accounts; and

- **measures and reforms to improve the tax system,** and to ensure that everyone pays their fair share toward extra investment in public services.

Next steps **1.24** Building on these reforms this Budget announces the next stage in modernising the tax and benefit system, as part of a rebalancing of the tax system to offer more support for work, families and pensioners:

- **removing the 10 pence starting rate and cutting the basic rate of income tax from 22 pence to 20 pence in April 2008,** creating a simpler structure of two rates: a 20 pence basic rate and a 40 pence higher rate;

- **increasing the upper earnings limit for national insurance by £75 a week above indexation in April 2008 and, from April 2009, fully aligning it with the higher rate threshold** – the point at which taxpayers start to pay the higher rate of income tax, simplifying the system;

- **raising the aligned higher rate threshold and upper earnings limit by £800 a year above indexation in April 2009;**

- **increasing the higher personal allowances for those aged 65 or over by £1,180 above indexation in April 2008,** removing 580,000 pensioners from paying tax. **By April 2011, no pensioner aged 75 or over will pay any tax until their income reaches £10,000;**

- **increasing the child element of the Child Tax Credit by £150 a year above earnings indexation in April 2008, raising the child element to £2,080 a year;**

- increasing the threshold for Working Tax Credit by £1,200 to £6,420 in April 2008, further strengthening the incentives to work for families with children and low-income working households;

- raising the withdrawal rate on tax credits by 2 per cent to 39 per cent in April 2008, helping to retain the current focus of tax credits; and

- increasing the weekly rate of Child Benefit for the eldest child to £20 in April 2010, providing support to all families in line with the principle of progressive universalism.

1.25 This Budget also announces:

- an increase in the annual Individual Savings Accounts investment limit from April 2008 to £7,200, with an increase in the cash limit to £3,600, in order to encourage savings;

- that the inheritance tax allowance will rise to £350,000 in 2010-11, to continue to provide a fair and targeted system;

- measures to support the third sector, including £80 million in small grants for community organisations, a campaign to drive up giving gift aid, and gift aid changes to facilitate relationship building with donors; and

- further reforms to modernise the tax system and protect tax revenues, including measures to tackle avoidance.

DELIVERING HIGH QUALITY SERVICES

1.26 The Government's aim is to deliver world-class public services through sustained investment and far-reaching reform. High quality education and training, a modern health service, a fair and effective criminal justice system and a fast and reliable transport network provide the essential foundations for a flexible economy and a fair society, which is well placed to prosper in the increasingly competitive global environment.

Action so far **1.27** Chapter 6 sets out the steps the Government has taken to deliver lasting improvements in the delivery of public services, including:

- a new framework for managing public spending that strengthens incentives for departments to plan for the long term;

- significant extra resources for public services, consistent with the fiscal rules. The 2004 Spending Review set departmental spending plans for the three years to 2007-08, locking in the increased resources delivered in previous spending reviews while providing for further investment in priority areas of the public services; and

- challenging efficiency targets for all departments, delivering over £21 billion of efficiency gains a year by 2007-08 to be recycled to front-line public services.

---

[2] *Stern Review on the Economics of Climate Change*, October 2006, Cambridge University Press.

Next steps **1.28**   The 2007 CSR will set departmental spending plans for the years 2008-09, 2009-10 and 2010-11. A central element of preparations for the 2007 CSR is a comprehensive value for money programme which will embed efficiency into departmental planning and release the resources needed to meet new priorities. This Budget announces further details of that programme, including:

- having established the baseline savings ambition for the 2007 CSR period of 3 per cent savings per year across central and local government, this Budget confirms that all of these savings will be net and cash-releasing, thereby maximising resources available to improve frontline services and fund new priorities; and

- an early 2007 CSR settlement for the Attorney General's Departments, which sees their budgets fall by 3.5 per cent per year in real terms and provides the early certainty needed to take forward an ambitious programme of reform and improvement across the criminal justice system.

1.29   Budget 2007 confirms the firm overall spending limits for the 2007 CSR years, 2008-09, 2009-10 and 2010-11, which ensure that the Government meets its strict rules while allowing it to increase total public spending by an average of 2 per cent per year in real terms with:

- current spending increasing by an average of 1.9 per cent per year in real terms; and

- net investment rising to $2^{1}/_{4}$ per cent of GDP compared with $^{1}/_{2}$ per cent of GDP in 1997-98, locking in the step change in investment over the past decade.

1.30   To ensure that the UK has the skills and science base it needs to prosper in an increasingly competitive global economy, alongside the early 2007 CSR settlement for the science budget announced in Chapter 3, Budget 2007 announces:

- an early 2007 CSR settlement for the Department for Education and Skills which sees education spending in England rise by 2.5 per cent a year in real terms (5.3 per cent in nominal terms) on average over the period, increasing UK education spending from 4.7 per cent of GDP in 1996-97 to 5.6 per cent by 2010-11; and

- substantial additional resources to support the Government's vision for personalised education, including funding for one-to-one teacher-led tuition for over 300,000 under-attaining pupils a year in English by 2010-11 and 300,000 in maths.

1.31   To accelerate the ongoing development of counter-terrorism capabilities, Budget 2007 announces a further £86.4 million for the Security and Intelligence Agencies.

PROTECTING THE ENVIRONMENT

1.32   The Government is committed to delivering a strong economy based not just on high and stable levels of growth and employment but also on high standards of environmental stewardship. Growth in the developed world, accompanied with the rapidly growing and highly populated economies of China and India, will place increasing demands on the world's resources and environment over the coming decade. Meeting this long-term challenge requires action at a local and national level, but crucially also through international cooperation. Climate change is a very significant challenge, and the recently published *Stern*

Review on the Economics of Climate Change[2] has highlighted how long-term global prosperity will be undermined if early and coordinated international action is not taken.

Action so far 1.33   Chapter 7 describes the steps the Government has taken to deliver its environmental objectives, including:

- **tackling climate change** and reducing emissions of greenhouse gases in line with domestic as well as international targets – in particular through the EU Emissions Trading Scheme and Climate Change Levy;

- **improving air quality** to ensure that air pollutants are maintained below levels that could pose a risk to human health – including through support for cleaner fuels and vehicles;

- **improving waste management**, so that resources are used more efficiently and waste is re-used or recycled to deliver economic value – for example through increases in the landfill tax; and

- **protecting the UK's countryside and natural resources**, to ensure that they are sustainable economically, socially and physically – in particular by increasing the aggregates levy.

Next steps 1.34   The Government is committed to delivering sustainable growth, and a better environment and to tackling the global challenges of climate change. It is using a range of economic instruments to address the challenges posed by sustainable development, whilst taking into account other social and economic factors. This Budget sets out the next stage in the Government's strategy for tackling the global challenge of climate change including:

- that the Government will launch this year a competition to develop the UK's first full-scale demonstration of the carbon capture and storage, the result of which will be announced next year;

- an increase in fuel duty rates of 2 pence per litre (ppl) from 1 October 2007, and increasing in the next two years of 2 ppl and 1.84 ppl respectively;

- announcing car vehicle excise duty rates for the next three years, including rates for the most polluting cars rising to £400 and rates for clean cars in band B falling to £35;

- a review to examine the vehicle and fuel technologies which could achieve over the next 25 years low and zero carbon cars;

- a package of measures to support biofuels including extending the 20 pence per litre biofuels duty differential to 2009-10;

- a rise in climate change levy rates from 1 April 2008 in line with current inflation;

- that from 1 October 2007 all new zero-carbon homes costing up to £500,000 will pay no stamp duty, with zero-carbon homes costing in excess of £500,000 receiving a reduction in their stamp duty bill of £15,000;

- an intention that, by the end of the next decade, all householders will have been offered help to introduce energy efficient measures with the aim that, where practically possible, all homes will have achieved their cost effective energy efficiency potential;

---

[2] *Stern Review on the Economics of Climate Change*, October 2006, Cambridge University Press

- increasing funds available through the Low Carbon Buildings Programme to a total of over £18 million to help meet demand for microgeneration technologies; and

- a £800 million international window for the Environmental Transformation Fund to finance overseas development projects that deliver both poverty reduction and environmental benefits in developing countries.

1.35 The Budget also reports on the Government's strategy for tackling other environmental challenges including:

- an increase from 1 April 2008 in the standard rate of the landfill tax by £8 per tonne per year, until at least 2010-11; and an increase in the lower rate of the landfill tax from £2 per tonne to £2.50 per tonne from 1 April 2008; and

- an increase in the aggregates levy rate to £1.95 per tonne from 1 April 2008.

BUDGET MEASURES AND THEIR IMPACT ON HOUSEHOLDS

1.36 The measures introduced in this and previous Budgets support the Government's objectives of promoting enterprise, skills and science, creating employment opportunity, tackling child and pensioner poverty, and protecting the environment. Consistent with the requirements of the *Code for fiscal stability*, the updated public finance projections in Budget 2007 take into account the fiscal effects of all firm decisions announced in the Budget. The fiscal impact of Budget policy decisions is set out in Table 1.2. Full details are provided in Chapter A of the FSBR.

1.37 As a result of personal tax and benefit measures announced in Budget 2007, by April 2009, in real terms:

- families with children will be, on average, £200 a year better off, while those in the poorest fifth of the population will be, on average, £350 a year better off;

- a single earner couple with 2 children, on median earnings – £27,000 per year – will be around £500 a year better off, and the same family on male mean earnings – £35,900 – will be around £320 a year better off; and

- a lone parent with 2 children, working 16 hours a week at the National Minimum Wage, will be at least £320 per year better off.[3]

1.38 As a result of personal tax and benefit measures introduced since 1997, by April 2009, in real terms:

- households will be, on average, £1,150 a year better off;

- families with children will be, on average, £1,800 a year better off;

- families with children in the poorest fifth of the population will be, on average, £4,000 a year better off.

1.39 As a result of personal tax and benefit measures introduced since 1997, in 2007-08:

- pensioner households will be £1,500 a year better off in real terms; and

- the poorest third of pensioner households will have gained £2,200 a year in real terms.

---

[3] The National Minimum Wage will be £5.52 for adults from October 2007.

Table 1.2: Budget 2007 policy decisions

		(+ve is an Exchequer yield)		£ million
	2007-08 indexed	**2008-09 indexed**	**2009-10 indexed**	**2007-08 non-indexed**
Corporate tax reform				
1 Main rate of Corporation Tax reduced to 28%	−140	−1,385	−2,230	−140
2 General plant and machinery capital allowances at 20%	0	+1,490	+2,270	0
3 Long-life plant and machinery capital allowances at 10%	0	−210	−380	0
4 Integral fixtures capital allowance at 10%	0	+70	+200	0
5 Industrial Buildings Allowance: phased abolition	0	+75	+225	0
6 Small Companies Rate of Corporation Tax phased to 22%	+10	+370	+820	+10
7 One-year extension of 50% First Year Allowances for small enterprises	−35	−250	+80	−35
8 New Annual Investment Allowance at £50,000	0	−30	−920	0
9 R&D tax credit increase to 130%	0	−40	−90	0
10 SME R&D tax credit increase to 175%	0	−30	−60	0
11 Payable Enhanced Capital Allowances	0	−20	−40	0
12 Reform of Venture Capital Schemes	0	+30	+30	0
13 VAT: revalorisation of registration and deregistration thresholds	0	0	0	−5
Personal tax reform				
14 Income Tax: indexation of starting and basic rate limits	0	0	0	−870
15 Remove starting rate of Income Tax on non-savings income	0	+7,320	+8,630	0
16 Increase Age Allowances by £1,180 and raise for 75s and over to £10,000	0	−810	−950	0
17 Increase Child Tax Credit by £150 above indexation	0	−880	−1,020	0
18 Raise the threshold of the Working Tax Credit by £1,200	0	−1,310	−1,310	0
19 Increasing the Tax Credit withdrawal rate by 2 per cent	0	+600	+620	0
20 Income Tax and NICs: phased alignment of higher thresholds	0	+1,110	+1,490	0
21 Income Tax and NICs: raising the higher rate threshold and upper earnings limit	0	0	−250	0
22 Basic rate of Income Tax reduced to 20 pence	0	−8,090	−9,640	0
23 Working Tax Credit continued for 4 weeks after leaving work	−10	−15	−20	−10
Supporting families and communities				
24 Raising the ISA cash limit by £600 and the overall limit by £200	0	−15	−50	0
25 Benefit simplification	0	−5	*	0
26 VAT: reduced rates on products for the elderly	−5	−10	-10	−5
Modernising the tax system				
27 Extension of the dividend tax credit	0	−5	−15	0
28 VAT: reduced rate for smoking cessation products	−10	*	0	−10
29 Energy Products Directive: expiry of derogation	0	+10	+30	0
30 Abolition of Small Consignments' Relief for excise duties	+5	+5	+5	+5
31 Gift aid: increase in benefits	0	−5	−5	0
32 Sale and repurchase agreements: tax treatment	+40	+60	+60	+40
33 VAT: non-business use of assets	+10	+15	+20	+15
34 General insurers' reserves: transitional relief	0	−70	−20	0
Protecting tax revenues				
35 Life insurance companies: financing arrangements	+120	+165	+165	+120
36 Loss-buying	+30	+45	+50	+30
37 VAT: countering missing trader fraud	+50	+45	+35	+50
38 Strengthening the disclosure regime	+15	+30	+30	+15

Table 1.2: Budget 2007 policy decisions

	(+ve is an Exchequer yield)			£ million
	2007-08 indexed	2008-09 indexed	2009-10 indexed	2007-08 non-indexed
Duties changes				
39 Alcohol duties: revalorise beer, wine and sparkling wine, freeze spirits	−20	−15	−10	+210
40 Tobacco duties: revalorise	0	0	0	+40
41 Gaming duties: changes to duty bands and rates	+30	+35	+35	+35
Property				
42 Rationalisation of empty property relief	0	+950	+900	0
Protecting the environment				
43 Expansion of Enhanced Capital Allowances for water-efficient technologies	*	*	−5	*
Supporting a clean and efficient transport system				
44 VED: enhancing environmental incentives	+125	+220	+280	+230
45 Road fuel duties: increases from 1 October 2007	−380	+490	+660	+480
46 Rebated oils duties: increases from 1 October 2007	+50	+125	+135	+65
47 Biofuels: extension of differential to 2009-10	0	0	+10	0
48 Road fuel gas: continuation of differentials to 2009-10	0	0	+5	0
49 Renewal of reduced pollution certificate scheme for lorries	0	0	−5	0
Protecting the UK's natural resources				
50 Aggregates levy: encouraging the sustainable use of resources	−10	+40	+45	0
Improving waste management				
51 Landfill tax: supporting recycling	0	+175	+325	0
Other policy decisions				
52 Special reserve	−400	0	0	−400
TOTAL POLICY DECISIONS	**−525**	**+280**	**+125**	**−130**
* Negligible				
MEMO ITEM				
Resetting of the AME margin	−1,000			

GOVERNMENT SPENDING AND REVENUE

1.40   Chart 1.1 presents public spending by main function. Total managed expenditure (TME) is expected to be around £587 billion in 2007-08. TME is divided into Departmental Expenditure Limits (DEL), shown in Table C13 of the FSBR, and Annually Managed Expenditure (AME), shown in Table C11 of the FSBR.

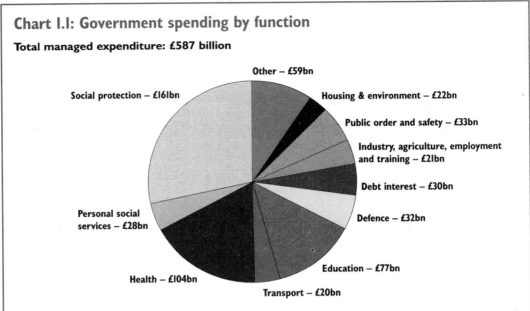

Chart 1.1: Government spending by function

Total managed expenditure: £587 billion

Other – £59bn

Housing & environment – £22bn

Public order and safety – £33bn

Social protection – £161bn

Industry, agriculture, employment and training – £21bn

Debt interest – £30bn

Defence – £32bn

Personal social services – £28bn

Education – £77bn

Health – £104bn

Transport – £20bn

Source: HM Treasury, 2007-08 near-cash projections. Spending re-classified to functions compared to previous presentations and is now using methods specified in international standards. Other expenditure includes spending on general public services; recreation, culture, media and sport; international cooperation and development; public service pensions; plus spending yet to be allocated and some accounting adjustments. Social protection includes tax credit payments in excess of an individual's tax liability, which are now counted in AME, in line with OECD guidelines. Figures may not sum to total due to rounding.

1.41   Chart 1.2 shows the different sources of government revenue. Public sector current receipts are expected to be around £553 billion in 2007-08. Table C8 of the FSBR provides a more detailed breakdown of receipts consistent with this chart.

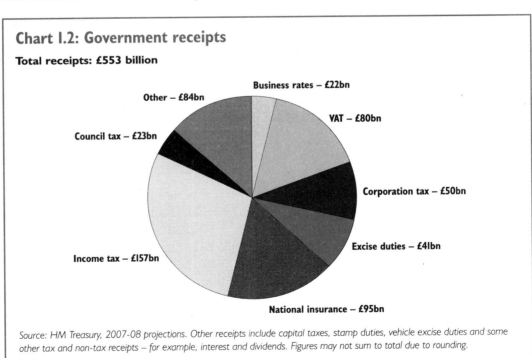

Chart 1.2: Government receipts

Total receipts: £553 billion

Business rates – £22bn

Other – £84bn

VAT – £80bn

Council tax – £23bn

Corporation tax – £50bn

Excise duties – £41bn

Income tax – £157bn

National insurance – £95bn

Source: HM Treasury, 2007-08 projections. Other receipts include capital taxes, stamp duties, vehicle excise duties and some other tax and non-tax receipts – for example, interest and dividends. Figures may not sum to total due to rounding.

MAINTAINING MACROECONOMIC STABILITY

The UK economy is currently experiencing its longest unbroken expansion on record, with GDP now having grown for 58 consecutive quarters. Over the past ten years, the Government's macroeconomic framework has delivered more stability in terms of GDP growth and inflation rates than in any decade since the war. This historically low volatility puts the UK in a strong position to respond to the global economic challenges of the next decade.

Overall economic developments are as forecast at the Pre-Budget Report. The UK economy grew by 2¾ per cent in 2006, as forecast in the Pre-Budget Report. The rebalancing of domestic demand gathered pace during 2006, with business investment ending the year growing at the fastest rate for eight years. Following five consecutive quarters of above-trend growth, the UK economy is estimated to have ended 2006 operating close to its trend level, although there remains evidence of some slack in the labour market. The Budget 2007 economic forecast is little changed from that of the Pre-Budget Report. GDP is forecast to grow by 2¾ to 3¼ per cent in 2007. With the economy expected to have returned to trend early in 2007, growth is expected to remain close to trend levels of 2½ to 3 per cent. CPI inflation is expected to return to target in the second half of 2007.

The Budget 2007 projections for the public finances show that the Government is meeting its strict fiscal rules:

- the current budget shows an average surplus as a percentage of GDP over the current economic cycle ensuring the Government is meeting the golden rule. Beyond the end of the current cycle, the current budget moves clearly into surplus; and
- public sector net debt is projected to remain low and stable over the forecast period, stabilising below 39 per cent, below the 40 per cent ceiling set in the sustainable investment rule.

THE MACROECONOMIC FRAMEWORK

2.1   The UK economy is currently experiencing its longest unbroken expansion since quarterly National Accounts data began, with GDP now having grown for 58 consecutive quarters. With volatility in the UK economy at historically low levels and now the lowest in the G7, the domestic stability delivered by the Government's macroeconomic framework puts the UK in a strong position to respond to the challenges of the next decade.

2.2   The Government's macroeconomic framework is designed to maintain long-term economic stability. Large fluctuations in output, employment and inflation add to uncertainty for firms, consumers and the public sector, and can reduce the economy's long-term growth potential. Stability allows businesses, individuals and the Government to plan more effectively for the long term, improving the quality and quantity of investment in physical and human capital and helping to raise productivity.

2.3   The macroeconomic framework is based on the principles of transparency, responsibility and accountability.[1] The monetary policy framework seeks to ensure low and stable inflation, while fiscal policy is underpinned by clear objectives and two strict rules that ensure sound public finances over the medium term while allowing fiscal policy to support monetary policy over the economic cycle. The fiscal rules are the foundation of the

---

[1] Further details can be found in *Reforming Britain's economic and financial policy*, Balls and O'Donnell (eds.), 2002.

Government's public spending framework, which facilitates long-term planning and provides departments with the flexibility and incentives they need to increase the quality of public services and deliver specified outcomes. These policies work together in a coherent and integrated way.

Monetary policy framework   **2.4**   Since its introduction just under a decade ago, the monetary policy framework has successfully delivered low and stable inflation, and has kept inflation expectations firmly anchored to the Government's target. The framework is based on four key principles:

- clear and precise objectives. The primary objective of monetary policy is to deliver price stability. The adoption of a single, symmetrical inflation target ensures that outcomes below target are treated as seriously as those above, so that monetary policy also supports the Government's objective of high and stable levels of growth and employment;

- full operational independence for the Monetary Policy Committee (MPC) in setting interest rates to meet the Government's target. **The Government reaffirms in Budget 2007 the target of 2 per cent for the 12-month increase in the Consumer Prices Index (CPI), which applies at all times;**

- openness, transparency and accountability, which are enhanced through the publication of MPC members' voting records, prompt publication of the minutes of monthly MPC meetings, and publication of the Bank of England's quarterly Inflation Report; and

- credibility and flexibility. The MPC has discretion to decide how and when to react to events, within the constraints of the inflation target and the open letter system. If inflation deviates by more than one percentage point above or below target, the Governor of the Bank of England must explain in an open letter to the Chancellor the reasons for the deviation, the action the MPC proposes to take, the expected duration of the deviation and how the proposed action meets the remit of the MPC.

2.5   These arrangements have removed the risk that short-term political factors can influence monetary policy and ensured that interest rates are set in a forward-looking manner to meet the Government's symmetrical inflation target.

Fiscal policy framework   **2.6**   The Government's fiscal policy framework is based on the five key principles set out in the *Code for fiscal stability*[2] – transparency, stability, responsibility, fairness and efficiency. The Code requires the Government to state both its objectives and the rules through which fiscal policy will be operated. The Government's fiscal policy objectives are:

- over the medium term, to ensure sound public finances and that spending and taxation impact fairly within and between generations; and

- over the short term, to support monetary policy and, in particular, to allow the automatic stabilisers to help smooth the path of the economy.

2.7   These objectives are implemented through two strict fiscal rules, against which the performance of fiscal policy can be judged. The fiscal rules are:

- the golden rule: over the economic cycle, the Government will borrow only to invest and not to fund current spending; and

- the sustainable investment rule: public sector net debt as a proportion of GDP will be held over the economic cycle at a stable and prudent level. Other things being equal, net debt will be maintained below 40 per cent of GDP over the economic cycle.

---

[2] *Code for fiscal stability*, HM Treasury, 1998.

2.8   The fiscal rules ensure sound public finances in the medium term while allowing flexibility in two key respects:

- the rules are set over the economic cycle. This allows the fiscal balances to vary between years in line with the cyclical position of the economy, permitting the automatic stabilisers to operate freely to help smooth the path of the economy in the face of variations in demand; and

- the rules work together to promote capital investment while ensuring sustainable public finances in the long term. The golden rule requires the current budget to be in balance or surplus over the cycle, allowing the Government to borrow only to fund capital spending. The sustainable investment rule ensures that borrowing is maintained at a prudent level. To meet the sustainable investment rule with confidence, net debt will be maintained below 40 per cent of GDP in each and every year of the current economic cycle.

Public spending   **2.9**   The fiscal rules underpin the Government's public spending framework. The golden
framework   rule states that, over the economic cycle, the Government will only borrow to invest. Departments are therefore given separate resource and capital allocations, which increases the efficiency of public spending as public investment is not crowded out by short-term current spending pressures. Departments are now given separate allocations for resource and capital spending to help ensure adherence to the rule. The sustainable investment rule sets the context for the Government's public investment targets and ensures that borrowing for investment is conducted in a responsible way.

Financial stability   **2.10**   The framework for co-operation on financial stability between the Bank of England,
framework   the Financial Services Authority (FSA) and HM Treasury is set out in the 2006 Memorandum of Understanding.[3] The Memorandum of Understanding between the three authorities defines the roles and responsibilities of each in maintaining financial stability, in responding to operational disruptions to the financial sector, and for financial crisis management.

2.11   The Standing Committee on Financial Stability, comprising the Chancellor, the Governor of the Bank of England and the Chairman of the FSA, meets monthly (at Deputies level) to discuss individual cases and developments relevant to financial stability, focusing on risks to the financial system. The Committee regularly reviews the key systemic risks to the UK's financial intermediaries and infrastructure and coordinates the three authorities' response and contingency plans. In the event of a crisis, it would meet at short notice and is the principal forum for agreeing policy, and, where appropriate, coordinating and agreeing action between the three authorities.

---

[3] The 2006 Memorandum updates the version published in 1997 and the full text is available at www.hm-treasury.gov.uk.

PERFORMANCE OF THE FRAMEWORK

2.12   The frameworks for monetary policy, fiscal policy and public spending provide a coherent strategy for maintaining high and stable levels of growth and employment, and for minimising the adverse impact of external events.

2.13   The UK's macroeconomic policy framework continues to deliver unprecedented growth and stability. GDP in the UK has now expanded for 58 consecutive quarters, the longest unbroken expansion since quarterly National Accounts began more than half a century ago. Over the past 10 years, the UK has enjoyed more stability in terms of GDP growth and inflation than in any decade since the war. Despite recent energy and food-related price rises, discussed below, inflation, on the RPI measure, has remained within a range of $^3/_4$ to $4^3/_4$ per cent over the past 10 years, compared with a range of 1 to 11 per cent in the 1990s, $2^1/_2$ to 22 per cent in the 1980s and 5 to 27 per cent in the 1970s.

2.14   The success of the framework in delivering low inflation has been widely recognised. As the IMF recently emphasised, "macroeconomic policies have contributed to growth and stability". The IMF also added that, as a result of these foundations, "growth of real GDP per capita was higher and less volatile than in any other G7 country".

Monetary policy **2.15**   The monetary policy framework has improved the credibility of policy making and continues to deliver clear benefits, as discussed in Box 2.1.

2.16   The monetary policy framework has given the MPC the flexibility to respond decisively to unexpected economic events over recent years. Consistent with its forward-looking approach, the MPC has increased interest rates three times since August 2006. This pre-emptive action has helped to ensure that inflation is forecast to return to around target in the second half of 2007.

2.17   Low inflation expectations and a period of entrenched macroeconomic stability have helped long-term interest rates remain at historically low levels. Low long-term interest rates reduce the Government's debt interest payments, free up resources for public services and help promote investment. Over the current economic cycle, long-term spot interest rates have averaged 5 per cent compared with an average of just over 9 per cent in the previous cycle.

2.18   Ten-year forward rates, which abstract from cyclical influences, are around 0.7 percentage points lower than those in the United States and very slightly above those in the euro area.[4] Ten-year forward rates in February 2007, at 4.2 per cent, are at the same level as at Budget 2006. This compares with a rate of 8 per cent in April 1997 before the introduction of the new macroeconomic framework.

---

[4] Ten-year forward rates are market expectations, formed today, of short rates in ten years' time. They are less affected by short-term factors, such as the current cyclical position of the economy, than spot rates and are therefore a better basis for making international comparisons when cyclical conditions differ.

Box 2.1: The monetary policy framework ten years on

The Government's monetary policy framework will mark its first decade in May 2007, and has ensured that interest rates are set in a forward-looking manner to meet the Government's symmetrical inflation target.

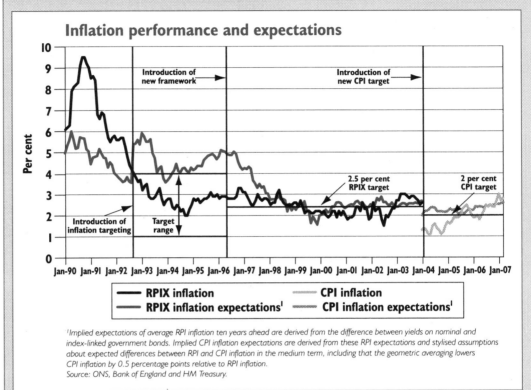

Inflation performance and expectations

¹Implied expectations of average RPI inflation ten years ahead are derived from the difference between yields on nominal and index-linked government bonds. Implied CPI inflation expectations are derived from these RPI expectations and stylised assumptions about expected differences between RPI and CPI inflation in the medium term, including that the geometric averaging lowers CPI inflation by 0.5 percentage points relative to RPI inflation.
Source: ONS, Bank of England and HM Treasury.

Since the new framework was introduced:

- the annual increase in inflation up to December 2003, when RPIX was used as the inflation target measure, remained close to the target value of 2¹/₂ per cent, the longest period of sustained low inflation for the past 30 years; and

- inflation expectations have remained close to target following the switch to a 2 per cent CPI target. CPI inflation has been within 1 percentage point of its target at all times since its inception in December 2003.

In the past decade, only Japan, which suffered a prolonged period of deflation, has had lower average inflation than the UK among the G7 economies. This contrasts sharply with the decade preceding 1997, when the UK had the highest inflation rate in the G7, bar Italy.

While previously low inflation in the UK has only been achieved through high interest rates, the entrenched credibility of the macroeconomic framework has allowed low interest rates to coincide with low inflation; both UK interest rates and inflation since 1997 have averaged less than half that recorded over the previous two decades. Low and stable interest rates have also given the MPC the flexibility to deal with shocks, helping to ensure low inflation has also been accompanied by strong and stable growth throughout the past decade.

2.19   Alongside the UK's macroeconomic stability in recent years, the effective exchange rate has also been relatively stable, as seen in Chart 2.1. The sterling effective exchange rate remains close to levels at Budget 2004. Since the introduction of the euro in 1999, the volatility of sterling's effective exchange rate has been under half that of the euro and around a quarter of that of the US dollar.

Chart 2.1: Movements in leading effective exchange rate indices since 1999

Index, 4 January 1999 = 100

Source: Bank of England.

Fiscal policy   **2.20**   The Government has taken tough decisions on taxation and spending to restore the public finances to a sustainable position. Public sector net debt was reduced from just under 44 per cent of GDP in 1996-97 to 35 per cent in 2004-05. Public sector net borrowing was reduced sharply from 1997-98 on, with surpluses over 1998-99 to 2000-01 when the economy was above trend. As the economy moved below trend in 2001, net borrowing increased, reaching 3.3 per cent of GDP in 2004-05, allowing fiscal policy to support monetary policy. This is in contrast to the position in the previous cycle when borrowing peaked at 7.8 per cent of GDP. As Chart 2.2 shows, since 1997 the UK's public finances compare favourably with other countries.

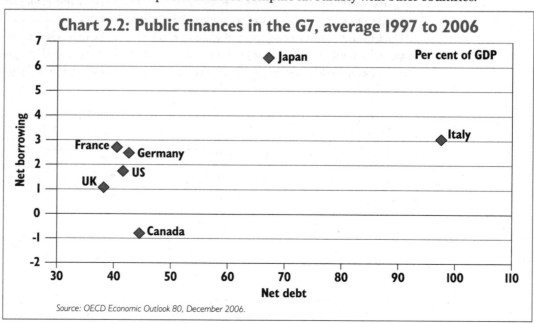

Chart 2.2: Public finances in the G7, average 1997 to 2006

Per cent of GDP

Net borrowing

Net debt

Source: OECD Economic Outlook 80, December 2006.

Box 2.2: Achievements of fiscal policy

The Government's fiscal policy framework is based on the five key principles set out in the *Code for fiscal stability* – transparency, stability, responsibility, fairness and efficiency.

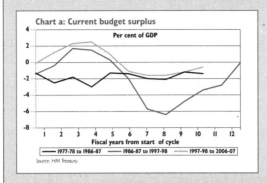

Chart a: Current budget surplus

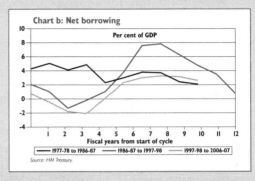

Chart b: Net borrowing

In the last decade, the introduction of strict fiscal rules and clear objectives for fiscal policy have put the public finances on a more sound and sustainable footing than in previous economic cycles. The golden rule is being met in this cycle with a surplus of 0.1 per cent of GDP, in contrast to the last cycle's average deficit of 2.0 per cent of GDP, and the 1977-78 to 1986-87 cycle's average deficit of 1.8 per cent of GDP. Debt has remained at low and sustainable levels, while at the same time public sector net investment is now over three times higher as a share of the economy than it was in 1997-98. Public sector net borrowing has remained low and stable over the current cycle, averaging 1.1 per cent of GDP, compared with an average of 3.1 per cent of GDP over the cycle from 1986-87 to 1997-98 and 3.6 per cent from 1977-78 to 1986-87.

Responsible management of public finances, in line with the Government's objectives, has enabled fiscal policy to effectively support monetary policy over the current cycle. The IMF noted in March this year, that in the UK "shocks, such as the global downturn of 2000-03 and the increase in oil prices during 2004-06, were managed with good policy responses", and noted "the shallowness of the UK growth slowdown during the last global downturn".[a]

The credibility of the framework has been established not only by the performance of the key fiscal aggregates, but also by the enhanced transparency introduced by the *Code for fiscal stability*. This includes the publication of illustrative long-term projections and the requirement for the Government to invite the National Audit Office (NAO) to audit the key assumptions underpinning the fiscal projections. These have been developed further with the annual publication of the *Long-term public finance report*, the *End of year fiscal report*, providing backward-looking analysis of the Treasury's fiscal projections, and the extension of NAO audits to 12 key assumptions from five at the first audit.

2004 Spending Review 2.21 The 2004 Spending Review set spending plans for the years 2005-06 to 2007-08, locking in the increased investment of previous spending reviews while providing for further investment in the most crucial areas of the public services. These plans provide for:

- current spending to increase by an annual average of 3.3 per cent in real terms between 2004-05 and 2007-08;

- public sector net investment rising to 2 per cent of GDP by 2007-08, compared with $\frac{1}{2}$ per cent of GDP in 1997-98, to continue to address historic under-investment in the UK's infrastructure while meeting the sustainable investment rule; and

- agreed efficiency targets for all departments, delivering over £21 billion of efficiency gains a year by 2007-08 to be recycled to front-line public services.

Comprehensive Spending Review   **2.22**   The overall spending limits set in Budget 2004 and confirmed in the 2004 Spending Review remain sustainable and fully consistent with the fiscal rules. Building on these firm foundations, the 2007 Comprehensive Spending Review (CSR) provides the opportunity for a fundamental and long-term review of the Government's priorities and expenditure, ensuring the UK is equipped to meet the challenges of the decade ahead. This Budget confirms the firm overall spending limits for the CSR years, 2008-09, 2009-10 and 2010-11, which ensure that the Government meets its strict fiscal rules while allowing it to increase total public spending by an average of 2 per cent per year in real terms with:

- current spending increasing by an average of 1.9 per cent per year in real terms; and

- net investment rising to $2\frac{1}{4}$ per cent of GDP compared with $\frac{1}{2}$ per cent of GDP in 1997-98, locking in the step change in investment over the past decade.

2.23   The 2007 CSR will report later this year, setting a full set of departmental spending plans for 2008-09, 2009-10 and 2010-11. Chapter 6 provides further details of the programme of analytical work the Government is conducting in preparation for the 2007 CSR.

RECENT ECONOMIC DEVELOPMENTS AND PROSPECTS

2.24   As forecast at the time of the Pre-Budget Report, the UK economy grew by $2\frac{3}{4}$ per cent in 2006. Having expanded at a rate of 0.7 per cent for four consecutive quarters, GDP growth picked up slightly to 0.8 per cent in the fourth quarter of 2006.

Recent economic developments   **2.25**   The world economy grew at a faster rate in 2006 than at any time since 1990, with GDP growth of 5 per cent, reflecting a pick-up in G7 activity and continued strength in emerging markets. Global growth is expected to slow slightly in 2007, though to remain high by historical standards at $4\frac{3}{4}$ per cent. World trade growth has recovered strongly over the past five years, rising from zero growth in 2001 to $9\frac{3}{4}$ per cent in 2006. A modest slowdown in world trade growth is expected in 2007.

Table 2.1: Summary of world forecast

| | Percentage change on a year earlier, unless otherwise stated | | | |
| | | Forecasts | | |
	2006	2007	2008	2009
World GDP	5	$4\frac{3}{4}$	$4\frac{3}{4}$	$4\frac{1}{2}$
Major 7 countries[1]:				
Real GDP	$2\frac{3}{4}$	$2\frac{1}{2}$	$2\frac{1}{2}$	$2\frac{1}{2}$
Consumer price inflation[2]	$1\frac{1}{2}$	2	2	2
Euro area GDP	$2\frac{3}{4}$	$2\frac{1}{4}$	$2\frac{1}{4}$	$2\frac{1}{4}$
World trade in goods and services	$9\frac{3}{4}$	$7\frac{3}{4}$	$7\frac{1}{2}$	7
UK export markets[3]	$8\frac{1}{2}$	7	$6\frac{1}{2}$	$6\frac{1}{4}$

[1] G7: US, Japan, Germany, France, UK, Italy and Canada.

[2] Per cent, Q4.

[3] Other countries' imports of goods and services weighted according to the importance of imports from the UK in those countries' total imports.

Economic prospects

2.26   The latest estimates of GDP and non-oil GVA growth to the fourth quarter of 2006 are consistent with the 2006 Pre-Budget Report forecast. The Budget 2007 GDP growth forecast is unchanged from the Pre-Budget Report: the small negative output gap is expected to have closed early in 2007 and growth is forecast to continue at close-to-trend rates throughout the forecast horizon. This implies GDP growth of $2\frac{3}{4}$ to $3\frac{1}{4}$ per cent in 2007, and $2\frac{1}{2}$ to 3 per cent a year thereafter.

2.27   The rebalancing of domestic demand already evident during 2006 is expected to continue to a somewhat greater degree than was envisaged in the 2006 Pre-Budget Report forecast. Latest estimates of business investment in the second half of 2006 show particularly strong growth, which surprised on the upside, and some of that momentum is expected to carry through into 2007. Private consumption growth is expected to moderate as recent increases in interest rates feed through to disposable income growth and households' desire to save. The contribution of net trade to GDP growth is expected to remain slightly negative in 2007, but to be neutral thereafter.

2.28   The pick-up in headline inflation over the past year has mainly been attributable to energy and food prices, rather than domestic cyclical pressures, factors that are expected to unwind during 2007. By far the largest contributor to the rise in inflation during 2006 was energy prices, particularly domestic gas and electricity prices. At the time of the 2006 Pre-Budget Report, developments in wholesale gas prices pointed to energy prices stabilising, with their contribution to inflation falling during 2007. Since the Pre-Budget Report, a number of major energy providers have announced significant cuts in utility tariffs that imply the contribution of energy prices to inflation is likely to turn negative by the middle of 2007. Unless harvests prove worse during 2007 than in 2006, when the unusually hot summer pushed food prices higher, the contribution of food prices to overall inflation should also fall.

2.29   As a result of these expected energy and food-related price developments, CPI inflation is likely to fall quite sharply from its current level, returning to around target in the second half of 2007.

2.30   Inflation expectations remain anchored to the inflation target and earnings growth has remained subdued, suggesting there have been no second-round effects from the recent above-target rates of inflation, although this risk has not yet subsided.

2.31 Leading forecasters expect the UK's record of strong and stable growth to be maintained going forward, with the credibility of the monetary policy framework keeping inflation expectations firmly anchored. For example, the IMF has recently revised up its forecast for UK GDP growth in 2007 to 2.9 per cent, fully consistent with the Budget 2007 forecast.[5]

Table 2.2: Summary of UK forecast[1]

	Estimate	Forecasts		
	2006	2007	2008	2009
GDP growth (per cent)	$2^3/_4$	$2^3/_4$ to $3^1/_4$	$2^1/_2$ to 3	$2^1/_2$ to 3
CPI inflation (per cent, Q4)	$2^3/_4$	2	2	2

[1] See footnote to Table B9 for explanation of forecast ranges.

Risks **2.32** Risks to the Budget 2007 economic forecast appear balanced, given broadly offsetting developments since the 2006 Pre-Budget Report.

2.33 A key risk to the UK economic forecast remains the uncertainties over labour market data, and the possibility that if growth in the working-age population has been greater than officially recorded, there may be a greater degree of slack in the economy and thus more scope for growth.

2.34 In terms of the components of demand, despite strong growth in consumption at the end of 2006, forecast quarterly consumption growth rates in 2007 have been revised down from the 2006 Pre-Budget Report to reflect developments in interest rates and saving intentions. Risks to the forecast are therefore balanced between the upside risk from recent momentum and the downside risk that developments in households' finances will have a larger than expected impact on consumer spending. Business investment ended 2006 with even more momentum than was expected at the time of the Pre-Budget Report. To the extent that internal and external financing conditions remain supportive, and firms' margins recover as input cost pressures ease, there is again scope for investment growth to exceed expectations.

2.35 With inflation expected to remain above target during the first half of 2007, the risk remains that higher rates of actual inflation could feed through to inflation expectations and earnings growth. However, the evidence so far suggests that monetary policy has kept inflation expectations anchored to the inflation target and, while wage settlements growth has picked up a little, there has been no discernable impact on earnings growth.

2.36 Growth in the final quarter of 2006 was strong in most of the world's major economies, including the UK, suggesting there is more momentum in these economies, particularly in the euro area, than was apparent at the time of the Pre-Budget Report. Additionally, the strength of growth in Asia, particularly China and India, surprised forecasters once more in 2006, and could do so again in 2007.

2.37 Episodes of financial market volatility, such as that experienced in late February and early March this year, represent a further global risk to the outlook. Large and rapid fluctuations in the value of financial assets, possibly reflecting investors' changing attitudes to risk, can have an impact on global growth. These risks may be mitigated to some extent by the development of deeper and more diversified capital markets, and improvements in macroeconomic policy frameworks. In recent years, emerging markets, which tend to be particularly sensitive to developments in global financial markets, have generally improved macroeconomic fundamentals and significantly increased holdings of foreign currency reserves.

---

[5] *United Kingdom: Staff Report for the 2006 Article IV Consultation*, IMF, March 2007.

Box 2.3: Inflation and pay

Since the introduction of the new monetary policy framework in 1997, the UK has experienced the longest period of sustained low inflation since the late 1960s. Over the recent past, inflation has been subjected to temporary, unforeseen shocks: increases in energy prices, driven by developments in the oil and wholesale gas markets, have fed through to higher utility prices; and increases in food prices, resulting from exceptionally hot summer weather and global factors. Against this background, CPI inflation rose through 2006, reaching 3 per cent in December, but was lower at 2.8 per cent in February 2007.

But in contrast to previous decades, the credibility of the UK's monetary policy framework has kept inflation expectations anchored and earnings growth has remained subdued. Once temporary, volatile factors have been stripped out, 'core' inflation has been at or below 2 per cent. Measures of core inflation exclude items with volatile price effects, including energy prices and seasonal food prices. These measures of underlying inflation in the economy are a better reflection of the balance of pressures of demand and supply and thus more relevant for the horizon over which pay settlements are determined. The chart below shows that, while headline inflation has risen in tandem with oil prices over the past year, core inflation has remained much more subdued, at rates close to its average over the past five years. Moreover, wholesale energy prices have already fallen and the effect of food price rises is expected to unwind in 2007. As energy price induced pressures recede, inflation is expected to return to target within the year. The latest average of independent forecasts suggests CPI inflation is expected to return to around its 2 per cent target in the second half of 2007, consistent with the Budget forecast.

As inflation returns to around target in the second half of 2007 it is important that the Government continues to be vigilant and disciplined in the fight against inflation. An important part of this means ensuring pay settlements continue to be consistent with the Government's inflation target of 2 per cent, as set out in Chapter 6. Demonstrating this commitment to combining discipline with fairness in pay the Chancellor announced in Parliament on 1 March 2007 that the overall headline settlements for public sector workforces covered by Pay Review Bodies are to be less than the 2 per cent inflation target, averaging 1.9 per cent, in 2007-08. The overall package of settlements provides a sustainable, affordable set of pay awards that helps contribute to low inflation and economic stability.

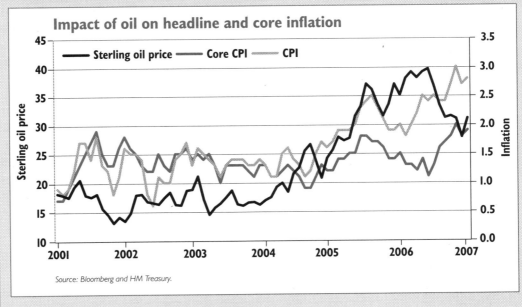

Impact of oil on headline and core inflation

Source: Bloomberg and HM Treasury.

The economic cycle **2.38** As announced in July 2005, the Treasury's judgement is that the current economic cycle began in the first half of 1997.[6] The Comptroller and Auditor General audited this judgement alongside the 2005 Pre-Budget Report and concluded that, though there were uncertainties, there are reasonable grounds to date the end date of the previous economic cycle to 1997 and that this would not reduce the extent of caution in making the fiscal projections. The economy is expected to have returned to trend early in 2007.

Caution and the public finances **2.39** The Comptroller and Auditor General reviewed the yield from the Budget 2004 compliance package for direct tax and national insurance contributions and found that the estimated yield from the package was greater than the Treasury's revised forecasts of yield, and that on this basis the forecasts were therefore cautious.

2.40 The Comptroller and Auditor General has also audited the assumptions for forecasting VAT revenues. He concluded that the use of the VAT gap assumption had resulted in forecasts that were cautious in three of the four years of the rolling review period since Budget 2003, and cautious over the period as a whole. The Comptroller and Auditor General was not able to draw a conclusion on the reasonableness of the allowance made in VAT forecasts for the impact of the 2002 VAT compliance strategy because of difficulties in identifying the separate contributions of the underlying trend in the VAT gap, the compliance strategy and the impact of legislative measures on VAT receipts.

2.41 As explained in Chapter C, a new NAO-audited assumption has been used in Budget 2007 for the purposes of projecting VAT receipts. This revised assumption is set out in Box C1. The Comptroller and Auditor General has audited the revised assumption and concluded that it is a reasonable one for the purposes of forecasting future VAT revenues and that it will be cautious to the extent that historical trends in the VAT gap are a good indicator of future trends.

2.42 Under the rolling review, for Budget 2007 the Comptroller and Auditor General has audited the assumptions relating to debt financing and factor income shares. The review concluded that the calculations of debt interest payments were consistent with forecasts of the government's net financing requirement and with its debt financing policy. For factor income shares the assumptions were reasonable and continue to be so for the future.

2.43 The assumption for forecasting revenue from duty on tobacco, that the illicit market share is set at least at the latest published outturn level, has been audited by the Comptroller and Auditor General under the rolling review process for the period since Budget 2003. However, due to the absence of firm data for the illicit market share for 2005-06 and 2006-07, it is not possible to reach a conclusion for the rolling review period as a whole. The Comptroller and Auditor General has therefore reviewed the evidence for 2003-04 and 2004-05, concluding that the assumption proved cautious in those years.

2.44 As explained in Chapter C, because of the difficulties involved in making estimates of the illicit market share, a new NAO-audited assumption has been used for the purposes of forecasting tobacco revenues in Budget 2007. This revised assumption is set out in Box C1. The Comptroller and Auditor General has audited the revised assumption and concluded that it is a reasonable one and, though there are a number of uncertainties as to how cautious the assumption will be in practice, it introduces an element of caution into the forecasts.

---

[6] *Evidence on the UK economic cycle*, HM Treasury, July 2005.

Box 2.4: The UK's international and European objectives

In both a global and a European context, there is a need to address the challenges of structural economic reform, resist protectionist pressures and promote free trade. The UK is working closely with the G7/8, the EU, International Financial Institutions and other international partnerships, including emerging market economies, to promote global prosperity and economic stability, tackle unfairness and deliver social justice, and promote environmental stewardship, by:

- promoting external openness and a freer and fairer international trading system, in the face of rising protectionism – using the last window of opportunity to deliver an ambitious and pro-development outcome to the Doha Development Round, which increases market access in agriculture, industrial goods and services, ends export subsidies and substantially reduces all trade-distorting domestic support. The UK Government continues to work hard with partners in the EU and in the WTO to build on the resumption of full-scale negotiations of the Doha Development Agenda. The Government is also pressing for concrete and credible Aid for Trade financing to help poor countries build their capacity to trade;

- building a global consensus, in line with the conclusions of the Stern Review, on the need to stabilise greenhouse gas concentrations and fostering an international response to the threat of climate change by effectively pricing carbon through a global carbon market; promoting investment in low-carbon technologies worldwide; promoting European and international energy efficiency standards; and assisting developing countries to adapt to climate change;

- pushing for progress on the commitments made in 2005 by donors to provide an extra $50 billion in aid each year to help achieve the Millennium Development Goals; promoting debt relief for a wider group of countries than the heavily indebted poor countries who have received 100 per cent multilateral debt relief; establishing a $4 billion vaccination programme through the International Finance Facility for Immunisation and catalysing the development of new vaccines through the recently-launched pilot Advanced Market Commitment scheme;

- strengthening the ability of EU and global institutions to respond to global challenges to economic stability, including increasing the IMF's focus on credible and independent surveillance, reforming the IMF's governance and supporting reform of the UN's institutional operations;

- promoting structural reform in the EU through the further development of a competitive Single Market equipped for the changing global environment; reform of the EU budget through the fundamental review and improved financial management; radical Common Agricultural Policy reform; measurable reductions in EU administrative burdens, and greater use of a risk-based approach to regulation; and monitoring progress on Lisbon agenda reforms; and

- ensuring sustainable, reliable and affordable energy sources by promoting transparent and open international energy markets, building on the 2005 Hampton Court summit agenda with EU partners and continuing work on extending the principles of the G7 oil initiative to gas.

RECENT FISCAL TRENDS AND OUTLOOK

2.45   Budget 2007 presents the Government's annual fiscal forecast and updates the 2006 Pre-Budget Report interim projections.[7]

2.46   In making its fiscal projections, the Government distinguishes between non-discretionary factors which affect the public finances, such as changing consumption patterns affecting receipts and changes to the economic forecast, for example to GDP growth, and discretionary Budget measures. This chapter first outlines the non-discretionary changes which form the fiscal context for the Budget decisions.

Non-discretionary changes in receipts   **2.47**   The lower forecast for North Sea revenues throughout the projection period more than explains the increase in net borrowing from 2007-08 onwards. North Sea revenue forecasts have been reduced as a result of sterling's appreciation against the dollar, lower oil prices, lower production and higher investment in the North Sea since the Pre-Budget Report. The forecast for total current receipts excluding North Sea revenues has increased since the Pre-Budget Report, driven by higher income tax and national insurance contributions, increased growth in VAT receipts, higher stamp and capital taxes. Some of this improvement over the projection period is offset by lower than expected corporation tax receipts.

Non-discretionary changes in spending   **2.48**   The forecast for expenditure before discretionary measures is slightly above the forecast in the Pre-Budget Report. Spending is slightly higher as a result of resetting the AME margin, as well as the impact of inflation on the costs of servicing government debt.

2.49   Overall, when compared with the 2006 Pre-Budget Report interim projections, the Budget 2007 projections show slightly higher forecasts for net borrowing, more than accounted for by revisions to the forecast for North Sea oil revenues. The overall impact of changes to other receipts and expenditure is to reduce net borrowing over the projection period. The estimate for borrowing in 2006-07 is revised down from the Pre-Budget Report, as in this year the reduction in borrowing from other tax and expenditure changes outweighs the increase in borrowing from North Sea revenue changes.

Table 2.3: Public sector net borrowing compared with the 2006 Pre-Budget Report

	Outturn		Estimate	Projections				
	2004-05	2005-06	2006-07	2007-08	2008-09	2009-10	2010-11	2011-12
2006 Pre-Budget Report (£ billion)	39.2	37.5	36.8	31	27	26	24	22
Changes since the 2006 PBR								
North Sea revenues	0	0	1.3	$2\frac{1}{2}$	$2\frac{1}{2}$	$2\frac{1}{2}$	2	$1\frac{1}{2}$
Other tax and expenditure changes	−0.1	0.3	−3.1	−1	0	0	$-\frac{1}{2}$	$\frac{1}{2}$
Total before discretionary measures	39.1	37.8	35.0	33	30	28	26	24
Discretionary measures	0	0	0.0	$\frac{1}{2}$	$-\frac{1}{2}$	0	$-\frac{1}{2}$	$-\frac{1}{2}$
Budget 2007	39.1	37.8	35.0	34	30	28	26	24

Note: Figures may not sum due to rounding.

---

[7] The Budget 2007 fiscal projections take account of the February outturns for receipts, spending and borrowing.

Estimate for   **2.50**   Net taxes and national insurance contributions are estimated to have grown by 6.3
2006-07   per cent from the previous year. Excluding North Sea revenues, total current receipts growth
is estimated to have been above that in the Pre-Budget Report forecast. Income tax and
national insurance contributions are growing strongly, boosted by financial sector bonuses
and the impact of anti-avoidance measures. VAT receipts have strengthened considerably,
underpinned by the success of measures to reduce fraud and by the increase in consumption
growth compared with 2005. Capital and stamp duties are also higher than expected. Stronger
than expected revenues in these areas are offset by changes to corporation tax receipts and
North Sea revenues.

2.51   The estimated outturn for the public sector current budget is a deficit of £9.5 billion
compared with projected deficits of £7.9 billion and £7.1 billion in 2006 Pre-Budget Report
and Budget 2006 respectively. The current budget moves into surplus in 2008-09, in line with
the projections in the 2006 Pre-Budget Report. For public sector net borrowing the estimated
2006-07 outturn is £35.0 billion, lower than the estimates of £36.8 billion projected in the 2006
Pre-Budget Report and £35.8 billion projected in Budget 2006.

2.52   The cyclically-adjusted deficit on the current surplus fell by approximately $\frac{1}{2}$ per cent
of GDP from 2005-06 to 2006-07. Cyclically-adjusted net borrowing fell by less, around $\frac{1}{4}$ per
cent of GDP, reflecting increased spending on public investment. The estimate of cyclically-
adjusted net borrowing for 2006-07 is slightly lower, at 2.5 per cent of GDP, than at the Pre-
Budget Report, while the cyclically-adjusted deficit on the current balance is slightly higher.
On the basis of cautious, audited assumptions, the Government is meeting its strict fiscal
rules over the economic cycle.

BUDGET DECISIONS

2.53   The Budget is the definitive statement of the Government's desired fiscal policy
settings. In making its Budget decisions the Government has considered:

- the need to ensure that, over the economic cycle, the Government will
continue to meet its strict fiscal rules;

- its fiscal policy objectives, including the need to ensure sound public finances
and that spending and taxation impact fairly both within and between
generations; and

- how fiscal policy can best support monetary policy over the economic cycle.

2.54   Against this backdrop, and building on steps already taken, Budget 2007 announces:

- reforms to simplify the tax system, to provide help for pensioners, support for
families and make work pay, including:

  - removing the 10 pence starting rate of tax and cutting the basic rate of
  income tax from 22 pence to 20 pence from April 2008;

  - increasing the upper earnings limit for national insurance and fully
  aligning it with the point at which taxpayers start to pay the higher rate
  of income tax, raising the aligned upper earnings limit and basic rate
  limit by £800 a year above indexation in April 2009:

  - increasing further the child element of the Child Tax Credit by £150 per
  year above earnings indexation in April 2008; and

- increasing the threshold for Working Tax Credit by £1,200 to £6,420; raising the withdrawal rate on tax credits by 2 per cent to 39 per cent and increasing the weekly rate of Child Benefit for the eldest child to £20 in April 2010.

- a major package of reforms to the corporate tax system, including reducing the headline corporate tax rate from 30 per cent to 28 per cent from April 2008, simplifying capital allowances, further enhancing research and development tax credits, and increasing the small companies rate to tackle individuals incorporating to minimise tax;

- restricting tax relief available on empty commercial properties, to encourage the supply of office, retail and industrial premises;

- further reforms to modernise the tax system, and a number of measures to tackle tax fraud and avoidance;

- taking further steps to tackle the global challenge of climate change including an increase in fuel duty rates from 1 October 2007, reforms to Vehicle Excise Duty and measures to improve the energy efficiency of homes.

2.55   Table 1.2 lists the key Budget policy decisions and their impact on the public finances, including resetting the AME margin. Further details are set out in Chapter A of the *Financial Statement and Budget Report*.

MEDIUM-TERM FISCAL PROJECTIONS

2.56   Table 2.4 compares the projections for the current balance, net borrowing and net debt with those published in Budget 2006 and in the 2006 Pre-Budget Report. It includes the impact of all Budget decisions in accordance with the *Code for fiscal stability*. Further detail is provided in Chapter C of the *Financial Statement and Budget Report*.

2.57   The revised outturn for 2005-06 shows the deficit on the current budget to be £0.1 billion lower than in the 2006 Pre-Budget Report, and £3.6 billion higher compared with Budget 2006. The outturn for net borrowing in 2005-06 is £0.2 billion higher than in the Pre-Budget Report, accounted for by the increase of £0.3 billion in net investment. Net borrowing for 2005-06 is £0.7 billion higher than the estimate in Budget 2006.

Table 2.4: Fiscal balances compared with Budget 2006 and the 2006 Pre-Budget Report

	Outturn[1]	Estimate[2]	Projections				
	2005-06	2006-07	2007-08	2008-09	2009-10	2010-11	2011-12
Surplus on current budget (£ billion)							
Budget 2006	−11.4	−7.1	1	7	10	12	−
Effect of forecasting changes	−3.7	−1.0	−5	−5¹/₂	−5	−4	−
Effect of discretionary changes	0.0	0.2	2	2¹/₂	2	2	−
PBR 2006	−15.1	−7.9	−1	4	7	10	14
Effect of forecasting changes	0.1	−1.6	−2¹/₂	−1¹/₂	−1¹/₂	−1¹/₂	−2
Effect of policy decisions since PBR 2006	0.0	0.0	−¹/₂	¹/₂	0	¹/₂	¹/₂
Budget 2007	−15.0	−9.5	−4	3	6	9	13
Net borrowing (£ billion)							
Budget 2006	37.1	35.8	30	25	24	23	−
Changes to current budget	3.7	0.8	3	3	3	1¹/₂	−
Changes to net investment	−3.3	0.1	−1	−¹/₂	−1	−1	−
PBR 2006	37.5	36.8	31	27	26	24	22
Changes to current budget	−0.1	1.6	3	1¹/₂	1¹/₂	1	1¹/₂
Changes to net investment	0.3	−3.4	−¹/₂	1	1	0	0
Budget 2007	37.8	35.0	34	30	28	26	24
Cyclically-adjusted surplus on current budget (per cent of GDP)							
Budget 2006	−0.3	0.4	0.7	0.7	0.7	0.8	−
PBR 2006	−1.0	−0.4	−0.1	0.3	0.5	0.6	0.8
Budget 2007	−1.0	−0.5	−0.3	0.2	0.4	0.6	0.8
Cyclically-adjusted net borrowing (per cent of GDP)							
Budget 2006	2.4	1.9	1.6	1.6	1.6	1.5	−
PBR 2006	2.8	2.6	2.2	1.9	1.7	1.5	1.3
Budget 2007	2.8	2.5	2.4	2.0	1.8	1.6	1.4
Net debt (per cent of GDP)							
Budget 2006	36.4	37.5	38.1	38.3	38.4	38.4	−
PBR 2006	36.4	37.5	38.2	38.6	38.7	38.7	38.5
Budget 2007	36.5	37.2	38.2	38.5	38.8	38.8	38.6

Note: Totals may not sum due to rounding.
[1] *The 2005-06 figures were estimates in Budget 2006.*
[2] *The 2006-07 figures were projections in Budget 2006.*

2.58 The estimated surplus on the current budget in 2006-07 is lower than expected at the 2006 Pre-Budget Report. The current surplus remains slightly below that forecast at the 2006 Pre-Budget Report, driven by lower than expected North Sea revenues, but by 2010-11, the difference narrows, so that as a percentage of GDP, the current surplus is unchanged compared with the Pre-Budget Report. The estimate for net borrowing in 2006-07 is lower by £1.8 billion, and in future years the projections for borrowing are slightly higher than expected at the Pre-Budget Report.

2.59 Table 2.4 also sets out the underlying structural position of the fiscal balances, adjusted for the impact of the economic cycle on the public finances.[8] Cyclically-adjusted net borrowing is lower in 2006-07 than estimated in the Pre-Budget Report, and then slightly higher out to the end of the projection period. The cyclically-adjusted current budget deficit is slightly higher in 2006-07, but by 2010-11 is back in line with the projections made at the 2006 Pre-Budget Report.

---

[8] Details of the Treasury's approach to cyclical adjustment can be found in Annex A of the 2003 *End of year fiscal report*, HM Treasury, December 2003.

ADHERING TO PRINCIPLES

2.60   Table 2.5 presents the key fiscal aggregates based on the five themes of fairness and prudence, long-term sustainability, economic impact, financing and European commitments. The table indicates that, after allowing for non-discretionary changes to receipts and spending and taking into account the Budget decisions, the Government is meeting both of its strict fiscal rules.

Table 2.5: Summary of public sector finances

| | Outturn | Estimate | Per cent of GDP | | | | |
| | | | Projections | | | | |
	2005-06	2006-07	2007-08	2008-09	2009-10	2010-11	2011-12
Fairness and prudence							
Surplus on current budget	−1.2	−0.7	−0.3	0.2	0.4	0.6	0.8
Average surplus since 1997-98	0.2	0.1	0.0	0.1	0.1	0.1	0.2
Cyclically-adjusted surplus on current budget	−1.0	−0.5	−0.3	0.2	0.4	0.6	0.8
Long-term sustainability							
Public sector net debt[1]	36.5	37.2	38.2	38.5	38.8	38.8	38.6
Core debt[1]	35.8	36.4	37.4	37.7	38.0	38.1	38.0
Net worth[2]	27.0	25.7	24.9	24.9	24.5	24.4	24.4
Primary balance	−1.4	−1.0	−0.8	−0.5	−0.3	0.0	0.2
Economic impact							
Net investment	1.8	2.0	2.1	2.2	2.2	2.2	2.2
Public sector net borrowing (PSNB)	3.0	2.7	2.4	2.0	1.8	1.6	1.4
Cyclically-adjusted PSNB	2.8	2.5	2.4	2.0	1.8	1.6	1.4
Financing							
Central government net cash requirement	3.3	2.8	2.7	2.0	2.2	1.8	1.8
Public sector net cash requirement	3.2	2.6	2.6	1.9	2.1	1.6	1.7
European commitments							
Treaty deficit[3]	2.9	2.8	2.5	2.1	1.9	1.7	1.5
Cyclically-adjusted Treaty deficit[3]	2.7	2.6	2.5	2.1	1.9	1.7	1.5
Treaty debt ratio[4]	42.7	43.5	44.3	44.4	44.5	44.4	44.1
Memo: Output gap	−0.5	−0.2	0.0	0.0	0.0	0.0	0.0

[1] *Debt at end March; GDP centred on end March.*
[2] *Estimate at end December; GDP centred on end December.*
[3] *General government net borrowing on a Maastricht basis.*
[4] *General government gross debt on a Maastricht basis.*

Golden rule   **2.61**   The current budget balance represents the difference between current receipts and current expenditure, including depreciation. It measures the degree to which current taxpayers meet the cost of paying for the public services they use and it is therefore an important indicator of intergenerational fairness. The current budget strengthens through the projection period, returning to surplus in 2008-09 and showing a surplus of 0.8 per cent of GDP by 2011-12, as expected at the Pre-Budget Report.

2.62   The golden rule is set over the economic cycle to allow fiscal policy to support monetary policy in maintaining stability through the operation of the automatic stabilisers. Progress against the rule is measured by the average annual surplus on the current budget as a percentage of GDP since the cycle began.

2.63   The average surplus on the current budget since the start of the current cycle in 1997-98 is in balance or surplus in every year of the projection period. The economy is expected to have returned to trend early in 2007. On this basis, and based on cautious assumptions, the Government is meeting the golden rule and there is a margin against the golden rule of £11 billion in this cycle, higher than at the 2006 Pre-Budget Report.

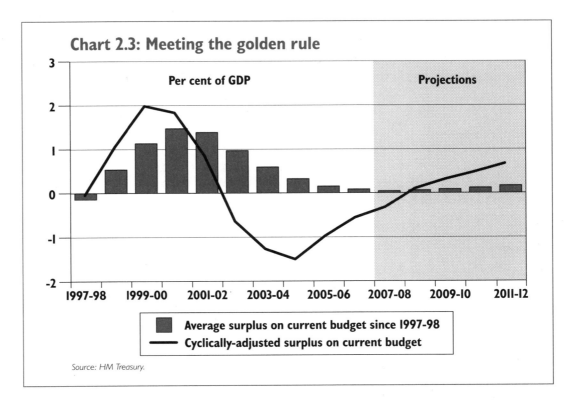

Chart 2.3: Meeting the golden rule

2.64   With the economy expected to have returned to trend early in 2007, Budget projections show that the current budget moves into surplus in 2008-09, with the surplus rising to 0.8 per cent of GDP by 2011-12. At this early stage and based on cautious assumptions, the Government is therefore on course to meet the golden rule after the end of this economic cycle.

Box 2.5: Borrowing for investment

The fiscal framework is designed to remove the bias against capital spending by making a distinction between capital and current spending. Historically, it has been extremely rare for public investment to grow during periods of fiscal consolidation, and prior to the introduction of the macroeconomic framework, it had not happened for 40 years. The effectiveness of the golden rule in eliminating this historic bias against capital spending is illustrated by the break in the relationship between borrowing for current spending and borrowing for investment illustrated in the chart. As the chart shows, this pattern of reducing borrowing while maintaining net investment will continue in the coming years.

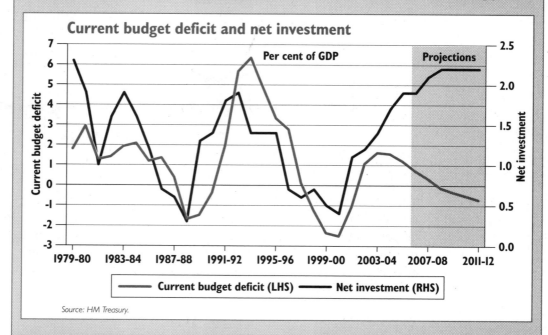

Current budget deficit and net investment

Source: HM Treasury.

Public sector net investment is now over three times higher as a share of the economy than it was in 1997-98, having risen from less than ¾ per cent to 2 per cent of GDP this year. As a result of this sustained increase, public investment in priority areas has grown significantly: annual average real growth in capital budgets from 2000-01 to 2007-08 will be 23 per cent in the NHS, 14 per cent in education and 19 per cent in transport. The Government's strategy for public investment is discussed in more detail in Chapter 6.

Sustainable investment rule **2.65**   The Government's primary objective for fiscal policy is to ensure sound public finances in the medium term. This means maintaining public sector net debt at a low and sustainable level. To meet the sustainable investment rule with confidence, net debt will be maintained below 40 per cent of GDP in each and every year of the current economic cycle.

2.66   Chart 2.4 shows that despite output being generally below trend since 2001, net debt remains below 39 per cent of GDP, and starts to decline at the end of the projection period, reaching 38.6 per cent in 2011-12. Therefore the Government meets its sustainable investment rule while continuing to borrow to fund increased long-term capital investment in public services. Chart 2.4 also illustrates projections for core debt, which excludes the estimated impact of the economic cycle on public sector net debt.

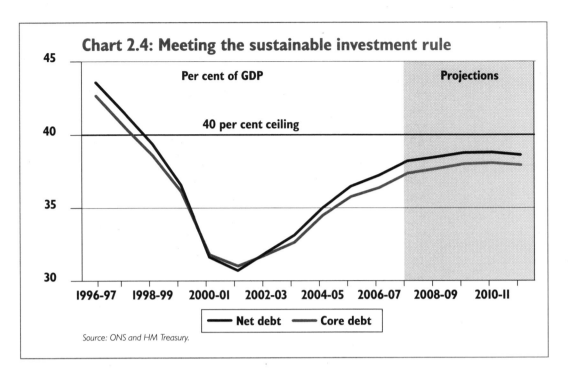

Chart 2.4: Meeting the sustainable investment rule

Source: ONS and HM Treasury.

Economic 2.67 While the primary objective of fiscal policy is to ensure sound public finances, fiscal
impact policy also affects the economy and plays a role in supporting monetary policy over the cycle.
The overall impact of fiscal policy on the economy can be assessed by examining changes in
public sector net borrowing (PSNB). These can be broken down into changes due to the
effects of the automatic stabilisers and those due to the change in the fiscal stance, as
illustrated in Chart 2.5.

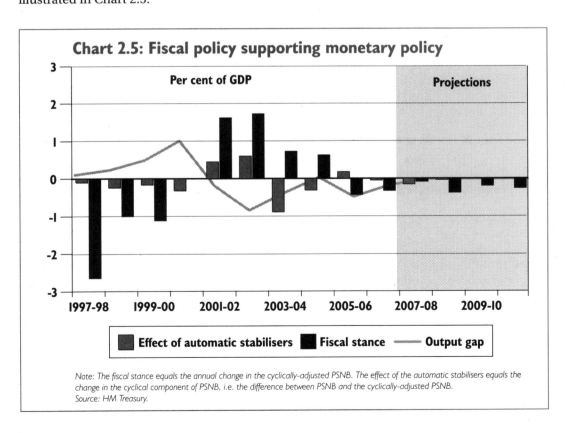

Chart 2.5: Fiscal policy supporting monetary policy

Note: The fiscal stance equals the annual change in the cyclically-adjusted PSNB. The effect of the automatic stabilisers equals the
change in the cyclical component of PSNB, i.e. the difference between PSNB and the cyclically-adjusted PSNB.
Source: HM Treasury.

2.68   As shown in Chart 2.5, during the late 1990s, the fiscal stance and the automatic stabilisers tightened at a time when the economy was above trend. As the economy moved below trend in 2001, the automatic stabilisers and the fiscal stance supported the economy, with the degree of support moderating as the economy moved back towards trend in early 2004. With the economy approaching trend levels in 2006-07, borrowing is lower compared with 2005-06, so that fiscal policy is slightly tighter.

2.69   The overall impact of fiscal policy on the economy is made up of changes in:

- the fiscal stance – that part of the change in PSNB resulting from changes in cyclically-adjusted PSNB; and

- the automatic stabilisers – that part of the change in PSNB resulting from cyclical movements in the economy.

2.70   Between Budgets and Pre-Budget Reports, the fiscal stance can change as a result of a discretionary measure to:

- achieve a desired change in the fiscal stance; or

- accommodate or offset the impact of non-discretionary factors (non-cyclical or structural changes to tax receipts or public spending).

2.71   Table 2.6 explains how these concepts relate to the projections in the Budget. It shows the changes in both the fiscal stance and the overall fiscal impact between the 2006 Pre-Budget Report and Budget 2007. In Budget 2007 discretionary changes are broadly neutral across the projection period. With borrowing lower in 2006-07 than expected in the Pre-Budget Report, there is a tightening in the fiscal stance in 2006-07 compared with the Pre-Budget Report. As discussed above, non-discretionary changes, driven by North Sea revenues, account for the relative fiscal loosening over the projection period compared with the 2006 Pre-Budget Report.

Table 2.6: The overall fiscal impact[1]

	Outturn[2]	Estimate[3]	Per cent of GDP Projections				
	2005-06	2006-07	2007-08	2008-09	2009-10	2010-11	2011-12
Change from 2006 PBR to Budget 2007							
Budget measures	0.0	0.0	0.0	0.0	0.0	0.0	0.0
+							
non-discretionary factors	0.0	–0.1	0.1	0.2	0.2	0.1	0.1
=							
CHANGE IN FISCAL STANCE	0.0	–0.1	0.2	0.2	0.2	0.1	0.1
+							
automatic stabilisers	0.0	0.0	0.0	0.0	0.0	0.0	0.0
=							
OVERALL FISCAL IMPACT	0.0	–0.1	0.2	0.2	0.2	0.1	0.1

[1] All the numbers represent the impact of changes on public sector net borrowing. A negative number represents a fiscal tightening.
[2] The 2005-06 figures were estimates in Budget 2006.
[3] The 2006-07 figures were projections in Budget 2006.

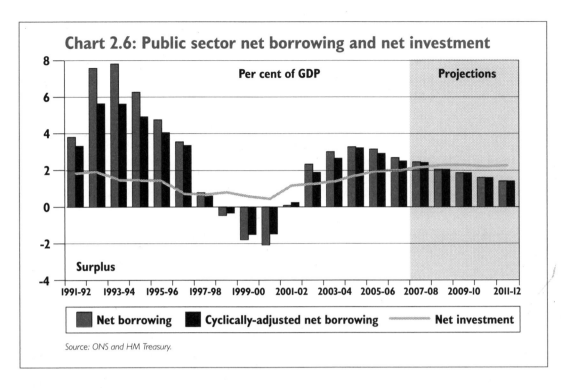

Chart 2.6: Public sector net borrowing and net investment

Source: ONS and HM Treasury.

2.72 On average since 1997-98 public sector net investment has exceeded net borrowing, reflecting the average surplus on the current budget. This is projected to continue as the Government borrows to invest in public services while continuing to meet its strict fiscal rules. Chart 2.6 shows net borrowing falling to 1.4 per cent of GDP by the end of the projection period.

Financing **2.73** The forecast for the central government net cash requirement (CGNCR) for 2006-07 is £37.0 billion, a decrease of £4.2 billion from the 2006 Pre-Budget Report forecast of £41.2 billion.

2.74 The forecast for the CGNCR for 2007-08 is £37.6 billion. Gross gilt redemptions are £29.2 billion and National Savings and Investments' net contribution to financing is estimated to be £2.8 billion. The net financing requirement for 2007-08 is forecast to be £59.8 billion. The net financing requirement will be met by:

- gross gilt issuance of £58.4 billion; and

- an increase in the Treasury bill stock to £17.0 billion.

2.75 Full details and a revised financing table can be found in Chapter C. Box 2.6 considers the factors underlying low gilt yields and the Government's weighting of its gilt issuance programme towards longer maturities in the last few years. In 2007-08, approximately two-thirds of total issuance is forecast to be in long maturity and index-linked gilts. Further details can be found in the *Debt and reserves management report 2007-08* which is published alongside the Budget.

European commitments

2.76 The Government supports a prudent interpretation of the Stability and Growth Pact, as described in Box B1 and as reflected in reforms to the Pact agreed in March 2005. This takes into account the economic cycle, the long-term sustainability of the public finances and the important role of public investment. The public finance projections set out in Budget 2007, which show the Government is meeting its fiscal rules over the cycle, maintaining low debt and sustainable public finances, combined with sustainable increases in public investment, are fully consistent with a prudent interpretation of the Pact.

Dealing with uncertainty

2.77 Forecasts for the public finances are subject to a considerable degree of uncertainty, in particular the fiscal balances, which represent the difference between two large aggregates. The use of cautious assumptions audited by the NAO builds a safety margin into the public finance projections to guard against unexpected events. The degree of caution in the assumptions underpinning the public finance projections increases over the projection period. The Government bases its public finance projections on a trend growth assumption that is a $\frac{1}{4}$ percentage point lower than its neutral view, to accommodate potential errors arising from misjudgements about the trend rate of growth of the economy in the medium term. This implies that the level of GDP used in the public finance forecast is $1\frac{1}{4}$ per cent below the neutral view by 2011-12.

2.78 A second important source of potential error results from misjudging the position of the economy in relation to trend output. To minimise this risk, the robustness of the projections is tested against an alternative scenario in which the level of trend output is assumed to be one percentage point lower than in the central case. Chart 2.7 illustrates the projections for this cautious case.

2.79 The Government is, on the basis of cautious, independently-audited assumptions, meeting the golden rule in the central case. In the cautious case, Chart 2.7 shows that the cyclically-adjusted balance will be in surplus at the end of the projection period.

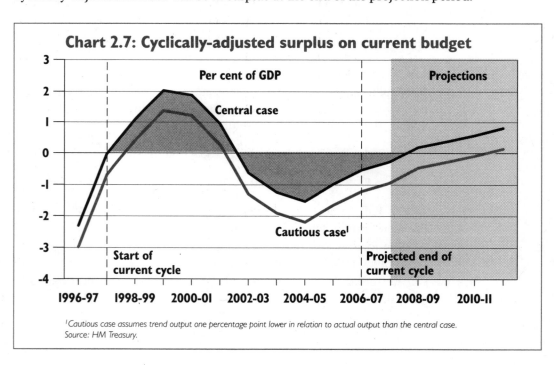

Chart 2.7: Cyclically-adjusted surplus on current budget

[1] *Cautious case assumes trend output one percentage point lower in relation to actual output than the central case.*
Source: HM Treasury.

Box 2.6: Low yields and the government bond market

Following the drop in interest rates at long maturities to very low levels in January last year, yields have risen but remain at close to historic lows (Chart a). This reflects, in part, a global phenomenon associated with the success of central banks around the world in maintaining low inflation, but also reflects trends in global saving and investment. However, unlike the yield curve in the United States and the euro-area, the UK yield curve has been inverted for most of the past decade, suggesting a sustained UK-specific influence on long conventional and real gilt yields over and above that exerted by global influences (Chart b).

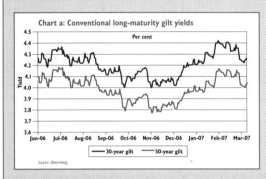

Chart a: Conventional long-maturity gilt yields

Source: Bloomberg

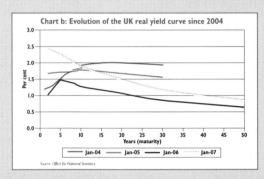

Chart b: Evolution of the UK real yield curve since 2004

Source: Office for National Statistics

One possible reason for the inversion of the yield curve is the rising demand from defined-benefit pension schemes for long-dated bonds.[1] Over the past decade, pension schemes have gradually shifted the composition of their portfolios from equities to bonds and fixed-income assets. Underlying the increased attractiveness of long-dated and index-linked bonds for pension funds' portfolios are a number of factors including:

- the growing maturity of pension schemes both due to ageing of schemes' members and in some cases to the closure of defined benefit schemes to new entrants and/or restrictions on the acquisition of new rights for existing members;

- the cumulative effect of regulation over a long period of time, designed to provide more protection to scheme members which made pension fund liabilities a more explicit liability;

- a better understanding of risks (including their measurement) and a decrease in the risk tolerance of both trustees and corporate sponsors; and

- the implementation of new accounting standards which highlighted risks that were not apparent in the previous system and encouraged pension funds to invest in liability-matching assets, such as bonds, in order to offset balance sheet volatility.

These factors are likely to underpin sustained demand for long conventional and index-linked gilts from defined-benefit pension schemes in the medium term. The Government's debt management objective is to minimise cost subject to risk. In line with this objective, the Government has weighted its gilt issuance programme increasingly towards longer maturities over the past few years (from 28 per cent of total issuance in 2003-04 to 59 per cent in 2006-07) and has extended the yield curve to 50 years. Further details of the Government's financing programme for 2007-08 can be found in the *Debt and reserves management report 2007-08*, which is published alongside the Budget and is available on the Treasury's website at: www.hm-treasury.gov.uk.

[1] Although there are also important non-pension related sources of demand for long-dated and index-linked gilts.

Box 2.7: Independence for statistics

Following the commitment made by the Chancellor in November 2005, and a full public consultation, the Government has introduced to Parliament this session legislation for the reform of the UK statistical system. This will build on earlier reforms, helping to reinforce the quality and integrity of statistics produced in government, supporting the Government's agenda for better public services, and contributing to long-term stability in the UK economy.

Following its introduction on 21 November 2006 and its passage through the House of Commons, the Bill entered the House of Lords on 14 March 2007. The Bill will establish an independent Statistics Board, reporting directly to Parliament, responsible for promoting and safeguarding the quality and comprehensiveness of all official statistics, wherever produced in government. The Board will have a statutory duty to set professional standards in a Code of Practice, and to assess independently all National Statistics against this Code. The Board will also replace Ministers as the top layer of governance for the Office for National Statistics.

As the Financial Secretary to the Treasury announced during the Bill's Second Reading in the Commons on 8 January 2007, the Government intends that the new system will be up and running by Spring 2008, and is therefore working to ensure a smooth transition to the new system. A key part of this will be the early appointment of a Chair of the Board, to enable preparatory work to begin on the transition to the new system, including on how the Board's statutory functions might operate in practice.

Also, in order to assist planning and provide funding certainty, the Government has announced a budget of £1.2 billion for the next five years for the new Statistics Board, which will allow the Board to be established and to deliver on its new functions, together with a high quality Census in 2011.

Further details of the Government's proposals, including the Bill and associated documentation, can be found on the HM Treasury website at http://www.hm-treasury.gov.uk.

LONG-TERM FISCAL SUSTAINABILITY

2.80   While a key objective of fiscal policy is to ensure sound public finances over the short and medium term, the Government must also ensure that fiscal policy decisions are sustainable in the long term. Failure to do so would see financial burdens shifted to future generations, with detrimental effects on long-term growth. It would also be inconsistent with the principles of fiscal management set out in the *Code for fiscal stability*.

2.81   An analysis of long-term fiscal sustainability is presented in Annex A. The analysis shows that given assumptions regarding tax revenues and the projected profile for transfers, current public consumption can grow at around assumed GDP growth after the medium term while meeting the Government's golden rule. Public sector net investment can also grow broadly in line with the economy without jeopardising the sustainable investment rule.

2.82   These illustrative long-term fiscal projections yield similar conclusions to those presented in the Government's 2006 *Long-term public finance report*. Using a range of sustainability indicators, and based on current policies and reasonable assumptions, the report shows that the public finances are sustainable in the longer term.

3 MEETING THE PRODUCTIVITY CHALLENGE

> Globalisation and the continuing pace of technological change are driving rapid shifts in the competitive environment and creating new opportunities and challenges. Raising productivity in the UK is critical for sustained economic growth and continued prosperity. Reforms introduced since 1997 have built on the foundations of macroeconomic stability, flexibility and openness to competition to strengthen UK productivity growth. Maintaining this flexibility, supported by key long-term investments in infrastructure, skills and science, is essential to increase productivity and seize new global opportunities. Budget 2007 sets out how the Government will build on the progress over the last decade through:
>
> - **a major package of reforms to the corporate tax system** to promote growth by enhancing international competitiveness, encouraging investment and promoting innovation:
>   - a reduction in the headline corporate tax rate from 30 per cent to 28 per cent from April 2008, making it the most competitive rate in the G7 and other major economies;
>   - modernising and simplifying the capital allowance system;
>   - further enhancements to the SME and large company R&D tax credit schemes;
>   - increasing the small companies' rate to reduce the advantage of extracting labour income by way of dividends;
>   - the introduction of a new Annual Investment Allowance (AIA) of £50,000 for all businesses who invest to grow;
> - **driving forward the risk-based approach to regulation** by implementing the Hampton Review's risk-based approach, consulting on applying it to employment tribunals and encouraging regulatory reform in Europe based on risk;
> - **maintaining the Government's ambition that private and public sector R&D investment reach 2.5 per cent of GDP**, with the announcement of early CSR settlements for the Department for Trade and Industry's science budget and the Department for Education and Skills, which together will ensure that total investment in the public science base will rise by 2.5 per cent in real terms over the CSR period; and
> - **reforming empty property relief in business rates** alongside a wider package of land and property incentives to increase competitiveness, encourage investment and deliver sustainable increases in housing supply.

Globalisation and productivity
3.1   The world is changing rapidly, and the global economy is becoming more integrated and competitive. Improving productivity and developing a dynamic economy is increasingly important for sustaining growth, prosperity and opportunities for all. The UK is well placed to meet the long-term challenges presented by a changing global economic environment, but continued progress on fostering productivity growth depends critically on building a flexible, open economy, with a highly skilled workforce, and well-developed infrastructure. Reforms introduced since 1997 have made significant progress in supporting productivity, by investing in infrastructure and skills to support the shift to a globalised, knowledge-based economy, and improving the UK as a place for businesses to start up, invest and grow.

The five driver framework
3.2   The Government's strategy for increasing the UK's productivity is based on two fundamental pillars: providing macroeconomic stability to enable firms and individuals to plan for the future, and implementing microeconomic reforms to the business and policy environment to remove the barriers that prevent markets from functioning efficiently.

3.3 This Budget sets out the next steps to improve the UK's productivity performance through five key drivers of productivity:

- improving competition to create the right incentives for firms to innovate, adopt new technologies and improve business efficiency;

- supporting science and innovation to spur new ideas and translate them into innovative goods and services for the UK's long-run economic success;

- raising skills levels to create a more flexible and productive workforce that can rapidly take advantage of new technologies and organisational structures;

- promoting enterprise to build a more flexible business environment, capable of adjusting to the opportunities and challenges in a more globalised economy; and

- encouraging investment to increase the quantity and quality of physical capital used in the production process.

Box 3.1: UK productivity performance

Productivity and employment growth are key to achieving high and stable rates of economic growth and higher standards of living. The latest international comparisons of productivity estimates show the UK is making real progress towards narrowing the productivity gap with its main industrialised competitors. Chart a illustrates the narrowing of the output per worker gap since 1995. The UK has halved the output per worker gap with France, closed the output per worker gap with Germany and, despite some recent cyclical widening, is the only G7 country to have kept pace with the US's impressive productivity performance since the mid 1990s. Similar progress has been made on an output per hour worked basis; the UK has narrowed the output per hour worked gap with France by 11 percentage points, narrowed the output per hour worked gap with Germany by 10 percentage points and while the gap with the US has not closed significantly since 1995, the UK is once again the only G7 country to have kept pace with the US's impressive performance.

There are also encouraging signs that the UK is on track to raise its productivity performance over the current economic cycle, compared with previous cycles. Trend productivity growth over the first half of the economic cycle (1997H1 – 2001Q3) was 2.60 per cent per year compared with 1.92 per cent in the previous economic cycle.

These latest achievements in productivity are particularly significant, as they have occurred during a period of unprecedented employment growth. Over 2.5 million more people are in jobs since 1997 and the UK has the highest employment rate in the G7. Traditionally, strong employment growth tends to lower productivity growth, as new workers are less productive while they learn job-specific skills. The UK is now experiencing the longest period of combined productivity and employment growth since current records began, as illustrated in Chart b.

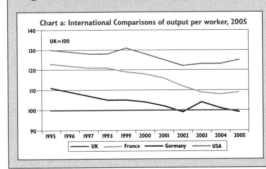

Chart a: International Comparisons of output per worker, 2005

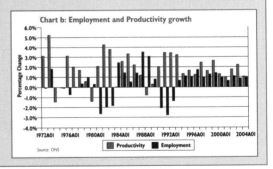

Chart b: Employment and Productivity growth

Product and capital market flexibility

3.4 Flexible product and capital markets enable a more efficient allocation of resources and clearer price signals, promoting competition and encouraging growth. Flexibility enables firms to respond rapidly to changing market conditions in an increasingly integrated global economy. This chapter reports on progress in enhancing the UK's product and capital market flexibility. In addition, the UK is working with international partners to respond to the impacts of globalisation, as discussed in Box 2.4.

European economic reform

3.5 Twenty years of the Single Market has delivered real and sustained benefits for the UK economy, but further structural reform in the EU is still needed to create more competitive, open and flexible economies. To this end, the government has argued for a European target to reduce administrative burdens arising from EU legislation by 25 per cent, which was agreed at the Spring European Council. To ensure that the EU's regulatory framework is appropriate and encourages growth and job creation, the Government is promoting a risk-based approach to the design and enforcement of regulation and to the decision as to whether or not to regulate at all. The Government continues to support the Lisbon Strategy for Jobs and Growth, and reports annually on progress towards the Lisbon goals in the UK National Reform Programme.

Productivity in the regions

3.6 An essential element of raising the rate of productivity growth in the UK is to improve the economic performance of every part of the UK. The Government has a target to make sustainable improvements in the economic performance of all English regions by 2008, and over the long-term to reduce the persistent gap in growth rates between the best and worst performing regions.[1] The Government reported progress to date in meeting its regional economic performance target alongside the 2006 Pre Budget Report.[2]

Regional Development Agencies

3.7 The Government's approach to regional economic performance builds on the national approach of a stable macroeconomic framework and microeconomic reforms by seeking to devolve significant resources and responsibilities to Regional Development Agencies (RDAs). Building on their role as strategic leaders of economic growth in each region, the RDAs have contributed to the development of regional policy in Budget 2007 in three key areas: the role of the private sector in promoting regional economic growth, regional competitiveness in a global context and improving evaluation of RDA spend. The Government welcomes this advice and has responded in full. Following Christopher Allsopp's review of statistics for economic policy making, the Office for National Statistics, working in partnership with the RDAs, is establishing a full regional statistical presence this month.

Sub-national economic development and regeneration

3.8 The Government is undertaking a review of sub-national economic development and regeneration in England. It aims to build on the work of RDAs and local authorities in England and consider how to further improve the efficiency and effectiveness of existing sub-national structures in England so as to strengthen economic performance in regions, cities and localities throughout the country. It looks at mechanisms to drive sub-regional collaboration, such as city-regions.

3.9 The review includes an assessment of the impact, effectiveness and accountability of sub-national delivery agencies, including the outcomes of RDA spending and opportunities for efficiency savings. It also considers the long-term challenges that face the RDAs and other sub-national agencies to help ensure a robust prioritisation of activities in support of economic growth in each region and locality.

---

[1] The Devolved Administrations in Scotland, Wales and Northern Ireland work in partnership with the UK Government to promote economic development in their territories.

[2] *Regional Economic Performance: Progress to date*, HM Treasury, DTI, DCLG, December 2006 available at http://www.hm-treasury.gov.uk.

3.10   The review has benefited from extensive consultation with a wide variety of stakeholders across the public and private sectors, including Local Authorities, Regional Assemblies, RDAs, neighbourhood organisations and business groups in every English region, as well as inputs from national-level organisations. Box 3.2 below sets out the issues identified as part of this consultation and the potential areas for reform going forward. The review will help inform the 2007 Comprehensive Spending Review.

Box 3.2: Review of sub-national economic development and regeneration

Government reforms to improve sub-national economic development and regeneration have delivered improved economic performance in many areas. In order to further improve the prosperity of regions, cities and localities, the review has identified a range of issues which include: addressing problems of complexity, increasing local and regional flexibility, clarifying responsibilities, strengthening accountability frameworks and incentives to strengthen capacity and ensure coordinated and focused action at sub-national levels, and securing business engagement in all areas. In many areas the analysis supports further decentralisation and devolution, while in others, such as business support, the need is to improve consistency and coordination across the country. In response to this, the review is focusing on the following areas for potential reforms:

- strengthening local authority incentives and decision making powers to improve economic outcomes and tackle concentrations of deprivation, following the analysis in the Lyons Inquiry;

- developing mechanisms to drive sub-regional collaboration across functional economic areas, including city regions, building on the Local Government White Paper, and considering the case for devolving individual powers and functions;

- improving the economic planning and decision-making processes at the regional level, including through better alignment of regional strategies, enhancing the strategic role of RDAs, improving RDA capacity, efficiency and effectiveness and increasing regional accountability;

- ensuring clearer objectives for regeneration and renewal at national, regional, local and neighbourhood levels, with sharper incentives for improving performance, clearer accountability and more effective coordination, and a stronger link to wider economic strategies; and

- strengthening the interface between the public and private sectors to maximise the effectiveness of investment. The review will take account of the recommendations of the *Leitch Review of Skills and Employment*.

BUSINESS TAX REFORM

3.11   Since 1997, the UK economy has enjoyed an unprecedented period of stability, allowing businesses to plan and invest more effectively for the long term.

Taking advantage of economic stability   3.12   Macroeconomic stability provides the foundation for businesses to take efficient investment decisions. The UK has halved its output per worker gap with France and closed the gap with Germany, but more can be done to support business investment and promote productivity growth. It is important that the tax system provides the right incentives for businesses to meet the challenges presented by globalisation.

3.13   Since 1997, the UK has led the way among G7 countries, reducing the corporate tax rate from 33 per cent to 30 per cent. The Government has also continued to modernise the business tax system to ensure that it remains fit for purpose, in line with its twin principles for reform: business competitiveness and fairness.[3] However, globalisation and new patterns of business activity have created fresh pressures for reform to ensure the UK remains internationally competitive.

3.14   The Government today announces further reforms to the business tax system to allow businesses to exploit fully the advantages of macroeconomic stability and to meet the challenges of the modern business environment, while ensuring that businesses pay a fair share towards the public services they consume.

Objectives of reform

3.15   The package of reforms announced in Budget 2007 are designed to achieve three key objectives, while maintaining sound public finances:

- enhancing the international competitiveness of UK based business;

- encouraging growth through investment and innovation; and

- ensuring fairness across the tax system.

International competitiveness **3.16**   Growing international competition increases the importance of having an efficient business tax system. To ensure that business decisions are based on commercial, rather than tax, considerations:

- a low tax rate helps keep any economic distortions to a minimum for any given level of revenue; and

- a broad base helps to ensure that there are fewer boundaries where differences in tax treatment can distort commercial decisions.

3.17   The main rate of Corporation Tax (CT) is one of a range of factors that influence the competitiveness of UK businesses. A lower rate of CT can boost the competitiveness of UK companies in the global economy and attract greater levels of foreign direct investment. Alongside factors such as skilled labour, infrastructure and easy access to customers, it is important that the main CT rate is set at a level that helps to maintain and improve competitiveness and the UK's already impressive record in attracting and retaining FDI.

3.18   The measures announced in Budget 2007 will complement the improvements to business tax administration that HMRC has committed to deliver following the Varney Review and the forthcoming consultation document on the taxation of foreign profits. This chapter and Chapter 5 contain more detail on the Review and the consultation document.

Growth through investment **3.19**   The main rate of CT is one of the factors that can affect the level of large firm investment;[4] capital allowances, which provide prescribed rates of tax relief for the depreciation of capital assets, can also have an impact. The rates and qualifying rules for capital allowances have remained substantially unchanged for over 20 years, with some originating in the immediate post-war period. Many of the incentives they seek to provide were based on the need to support particular industries and sectors and they no longer reflect the needs of a modern economy.

Growth through innovation **3.20**   As one of the key drivers of productivity growth, the Government has ensured the tax system acts as a positive incentive for business innovation. There is a strong body of

---

[3] For example, see HM Treasury/Inland Revenue (2001) *Large Business Taxation: The Government's strategy and corporate tax reforms*.

[4] For a survey of the empirical literature see Hassett and Hubbard (2002), "*Tax Policy and Business Investment*," in A. Auerbach and M. Feldstein, eds., Handbook of Public Economics 3.

economic evidence to demonstrate that the private returns to business research and development (R&D) are exceeded by the wider spillover benefits to society, causing an undersupply of R&D. Worldwide evidence[5] on the success of tax incentives in addressing this market failure led to the introduction of the R&D tax credit in 2000. As innovation becomes increasingly important in maintaining the UK's globally competitive position, R&D tax credits play an even greater role in the UK's response to globalisation.

Fairness   **3.21**   The Government's discussion paper: *Small Companies, the self-employed and the tax system*[6] set out a framework for discussion on the incentives for small business investment in the current tax system.

3.22   Successive Governments have tried to encourage greater investment through low rates of tax for small companies with the Small Companies' Rate (SCR). However:

- it has become apparent that the SCR can be taken advantage of by people incorporating with the main aim of reducing their personal tax and national insurance liability by extracting labour income as dividends. This results in an unfair difference between the overall tax and NICs paid by the incorporated and the unincorporated, even where they are engaged in the same economic activity. This tax-motivated incorporation, if left unaddressed, would pose a growing risk to the Exchequer; and

- the SCR is not well targeted. As companies qualify according to their taxable profits, not their size, around one third of tax paying large companies benefit from the SCR.

Budget 2007 reforms

3.23   Budget 2007 announces a major package of reforms to enhance international competitiveness, encourage investment, promote innovation and ensure fairness across the tax system in line with the key principles that have underpinned business tax policy since 1997. Full detail on these Budget announcements is continued in Box 3.3.

- a reduction in the main rate of Corporation Tax from 30 per cent to 28 per cent;

- first-year capital allowances will be replaced by an Annual Investment Allowance (AIA) of £50,000 for all firms. This will target support on all businesses that are investing for growth. The AIA will be particularly beneficial to small and medium-sized businesses;

- an extensive set of reforms to the capital allowances regime to increase the efficiency of the system, and remove outdated incentives, some of which date from the immediate post-war period and a new payable enhanced capital allowance for environmentally beneficial investments;

- an increase in the SME and large company R&D tax credits to build on the success of the current incentives; and

- a staged increase in the small companies rate of CT from 19 per cent to 20 per cent from April 2007, 21 per cent from April 2008 and 22 per cent from April 2009, to reduce the differential between incorporated and unincorporated businesses and refocus investment incentives for small businesses.

3.24   The Government is committed to open consultation with business on major reforms to the tax system. Over the following year, the Government will publish draft legislation and

---

[5] Hall and Van Reenen (1999), *How Effective are Fiscal Incentives for R&D? A Review of the Evidence*, NBER Working paper No. 7098.

[6] *Small companies, the self-employed and the tax system: a discussion paper.* HM Treasury December 2004.

will consult with business on the implementation of the new AIA, changes to the treatment of integral fixtures and payable enhanced capital allowances.

Meeting the objectives

Increasing international competitiveness

3.25 The reduction in the main rate of CT will build on the established principle that low tax rates reduce economic inefficiencies in the tax system. The reduction firmly establishes the UK's CT rate as the lowest among the G7 and other major economies and also below the EU15 average (Chart 3.1).

3.26 The Government's goal is, and will continue to be, to maintain the most competitive CT rate of the major economies. The Government will continue to assess the case for further reductions in the CT rate, consistent with its objective to maintain sound public finances.

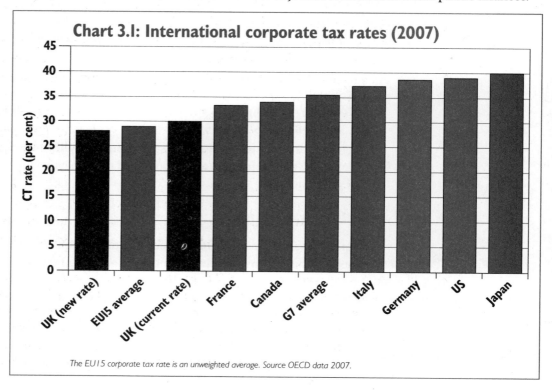

Chart 3.1: International corporate tax rates (2007)

The EU15 corporate tax rate is an unweighted average. Source OECD data 2007.

Encouraging growth through investment

3.27 A lower CT rate will both stimulate both large company domestic investment and make the UK a more attractive location for FDI. By reducing the difference between pre- and post-tax returns, the lower rate will reduce the extent to which commercial decisions are influenced by tax considerations.

3.28 While reducing the main rate of CT will promote higher investment, the reforms to capital allowances will promote more efficient and more long-term investment by bringing the value of allowances more closely into line with economic depreciation. Elements of the current regime are outdated and distortive. The current Industrial Buildings Allowance (IBA), for example, was introduced in 1945 to encourage post-war reconstruction. It is poorly focused, applying to a disparate range of assets that includes foreign plantations and hotels, but not commercial offices or science parks. IBAs have been a long-standing and unjustified distortion in commercial property investment. This Budget also announces a simplified structure for capital allowances, ensuring all depreciating assets receive allowances at two clear rates: 20 per cent and 10 per cent. Assets that appreciate, such as land and buildings, will not receive depreciation allowances.

3.28 Budget 2007 announces a major package of reforms to the UK business tax system. Box 3.3 sets out details of the key reforms.

Box 3.3: Detail of the Budget announcement

The following reforms are announced in Budget 2007:

Cutting the rate of corporation tax

- a reduction in the main rate of CT from 30 per cent to 28 per cent, effective from April 2008;

A simpler two-rate system of capital allowances

- a reduction in the rate of capital allowances on the general pool of plant and machinery from 25 per cent to 20 per cent, effective April 2008, bringing it closer into line with economic depreciation;

- an increase in the rate of capital allowances on the pool of long-life assets, which applies to assets with expected lives of more than 25 years, from 6 per cent to 10 per cent, effective April 2008;

- fixtures that are integral to a building will be separately classified and will be included in the 10 per cent capital allowances pool, effective April 2008;

- the phased removal of the Industrial Buildings Allowances (IBA) and Agricultural Building Allowance (ABA) with the effective rate of allowance falling to 3 per cent from April 2008, 2 per cent from April 2009, 1 per cent from April 2010 and full abolition taking effect from April 2011. As part of this phased withdrawal, balancing adjustments will be withdrawn from today (21 March);

Re-focusing the incentives for small companies

- a phased increase in the small companies' rate from 19 per cent to 20 per cent from April 2007, 21 per cent from April 2008 and 22 per cent from April 2009 to reduce the differential between incorporated and unincorporated businesses;

- the 50 per cent first year allowance for small enterprises will continue to April 2008;

- the introduction of an Annual Investment Allowance (AIA) available to all businesses regardless of size and regardless of their legal form. This new allowance will mean that 100 per cent of expenditure up to £50,000 on general plant and machinery (other than cars) can be offset against taxable profits. The AIA will be effective from April 2008 and will target support on all businesses that are investing for growth. It will be particularly beneficial to small and medium sized businesses;

Promoting innovation

- an increase in the large company R&D tax credit from 125 per cent to 130 per cent from April 2008; and

- an increase in the enhanced deduction element of the SME and mid-sized R&D tax credit from 150 per cent to 175 per cent from April 2008 subject to state aid clearance.

The Government will consult over the coming year on the detail of draft legislation to implement the AIA, changes to the treatment of integral fixtures and payable Enhanced Capital Allowances. Further details on payable ECAs are described in Chapter A.

Encouraging growth through innovation **3.30** Developed through consultation with business, the R&D tax credit lies at the heart of the Government's strategy to raise levels of business R&D and encourage business innovation. Take-up of the R&D tax credit has been strong, more than 6,000 claims were received in 2004-05 alone amounting to nearly £600 million of Government support for business R&D. In total, more than £1.8 billion of support has been given to business R&D through R&D tax credits since their introduction in 2000.

3.31 Building on the Government's commitment to ensure high levels of innovation and growth, **Budget 2007 announces additional major enhancements to the R&D tax credit.** The Government will increase the value of both the SME and the large company R&D tax credits.

Ensuring fairness across the tax system **3.32** Through a staged increase in the small companies' rate to 22 per cent by 2010, and a more valuable incentive for investment, the tax system can be refocused to better meet the Government's objective of fairness between the self-employed and incorporated. The measures in this Budget focus incentives directly on those small businesses that invest, regardless of whether they are operating in the corporate or non-corporate form.

3.33 Chapter 5 sets out how the Government will continue to monitor small business investment patterns and the level and extent to which labour income is extracted in dividends.

Business and the environment **3.34** The Budget announces that the landfill tax escalator will rise by £8 per tonne per year from 2008 until at least 2010-11. In line with previous commitments to make the landfill tax escalator revenue neutral to business as a whole, revenue from this measure will be recycled back to business through the package of business tax cuts. The landfill tax reforms are therefore consistent with the Government's statement of intent to shifting the burden of tax from 'goods' to 'bads' such as pollution. Chapter 7 sets out more detail on the environment.

3.35 The Government is committed to supporting renewable electricity generation and will work with this industry over the coming year to understand the impacts of Budget reforms on the sector, and to ensure that its support for renewable electricity generation is maintained.

Simplifying the tax structure **3.36** The reforms announced in Budget 2007 represent a simplification of the underlying tax structure. Together with the £300 million reduction in administrative burdens referred to later in this chapter and the improvements in tax administration delivered by *Sir David Varney's Review of Links with Large Business*,[7] these reforms will help deliver significant improvements to the way that the tax system is administered, building a relationship based on greater trust.

North Sea tax regime **3.37** The Government recognises that the North Sea presents unique challenges and opportunities for both industry and government. In recognition of these challenges, this Government has introduced a unique capital allowance regime that encourages investment by providing full relief on cashflow outflow as it arises. This minimises the impact of the fiscal regime on investment decisions. In light of this, and of the need for stability and certainty, and given continuing high levels of profitability and investment, the reforms to business tax announced in Budget 2007 will not therefore apply to activity within the North Sea fiscal regime, which will retain its existing capital allowances regime and rate of tax.

3.38 In the 2005 Pre-Budget report, the Government announced that it would hold discussions with the North Sea oil and gas industry on wider structural issues that have implications for the stability of the North Sea fiscal regime. A paper has been published alongside the Budget summarising these discussions, setting out the Government's initial conclusions and confirming that discussions on these issues will continue over the following months.

Taxation of foreign profits **3.39** The Government has held a productive dialogue with business on the taxation of foreign profits in the context of maintaining the overall competitiveness of the UK. The Government will issue a consultation document later in the spring, which will consider in particular the taxation of foreign dividends received by UK companies and the Controlled

---

[7] HMRC 2006 Review of Links with Large Business.

Foreign Companies (CFC) rules. This is an area where business has expressed a preference for reform and where options that will be considered include European-style exemption for foreign dividends and income-based CFC rules. The document will also consider the implications of any such reform for other aspects of the UK tax regime, such as interest relief.

COMPETITION

3.40 Competition is a fundamental aspect of the business and policy environment. It rewards efficiency, flexibility and innovation in business, driving productivity. Competitive and open markets at home increase the global competitiveness of UK firms, raising economic growth and standards of living in the UK and benefiting consumers by ensuring lower prices and a greater variety of goods and services.

Promoting competition in UK markets

A world class competition regime **3.41** Through recent reforms the Government has been able to secure a world-class competition regime, ranked among the top three globally.[8] The Enterprise Act 2002 made UK competition authorities independent – the Office of Fair Trading (OFT) and the Competition Commission (CC) – by removing ministerial involvement from almost all cases. It introduced criminal penalties for cartel activity as well as an improved framework for investigating and remedying mergers or markets raising potential competition concerns.

Public enforcement **3.42** The 2006 Pre-Budget Report outlined the achievements to date, with the competition authorities launching investigations into 800 mergers and 150 potential abuse of dominance or cartel cases, generating consumer savings of at least £750 million between 2000 and 2005.

3.43 Since the start of this year the OFT has obtained £31.2m in fines from cartelists and finalised its investigations into at least 12 mergers. The OFT is currently finalising its decision on whether or not to refer the UK airport services market, which served over 200 million passengers in 2005,[9] to the CC for further investigation and possible remedy and the CC is currently studying the groceries market, a sector with an annual sales of around £120 billion.[10] However, the Government recognises the need to continue to monitor the operation of the competition regime and consider possible enhancements to its speed, efficiency, and effectiveness.

3.44 As part of the 2007 Comprehensive Spending Review (CSR) settlement agreed with HM Treasury, as set out in more detail in chapter 6, the OFT have committed to continue to increase the impact of their work for consumers through increased prioritisation and efficiency savings. The OFT have agreed to new performance targets, which include delivering benefits to consumers worth more than five times the organisation's spending on competition enforcement and three and a half times its spending on consumer activities.

Private actions **3.45** Private actions are an important aspect of a well-functioning competition regime. An effective regime would allow those affected by anti-competitive behaviour to receive redress for harm suffered and broaden the scope of cases that can be investigated, promoting a greater awareness of competition law and reinforcing deterrence, without encouraging ill-founded litigation.

3.46 The Enterprise Act 2002 enhanced the framework for private actions. It ensured that decisions on infringements of competition law by the UK Competition Authorities or European Commission are binding on the courts and allowed designated consumer groups

---

[8] *Peer Review of Competition Policy*, KPMG and the Department of Trade and Industry (2007). Publication pending.

[9] *Summary of activity at UK airports*, CCA, 2005. Available at www.caa.co.uk/

[10] *Groceries Market: Statement of Issues*, CC (2006) Available at www.competition-commission.org.uk/

to bring representative actions, following such decisions, to the Competition Appeals Tribunal (CAT). However, to date very few private action cases have been heard by courts in the UK.

3.47   In April 2007, the OFT will consult on a discussion paper identifying barriers to private actions, including the complexity, uncertainty and cost required in bringing claims. The paper will also discuss options for addressing these, such as widening the scope for representative bodies to bring representative actions and allowing such bodies to bring cases not previously investigated by the Competition Authorities.

3.48   The Government welcomes the progress the OFT has made on this issue and will continue to work with the OFT to identify the key barriers to private actions. Over the coming year the Government intends to identify and consult on measures needed to overcome the barriers to redress without encouraging ill-founded claims, in particular examining the arrangements for representative actions.

Premium rate   **3.49**   OFCOM has agreed to conduct a review of whether the existing regulatory model for
servcies   premium rate telephone services is fully effective and proportionate and whether the code for regulating these services needs strengthening, particularly in relation to broadcasting.

European competition policy

3.50   In recent years the European Commission has made significant progress in adopting a more proactive approach to exercising its competition powers. The modernisation of EU competition policy[11] has allowed the Commission to focus attention on more important mergers and anti-competitive cartel cases with clear Single Market impacts. Faced with a number of challenges over the past 12 months the Commission has led a robust defence of Single Market rules, taking tough action where they have been breached. The first two sector inquiries into the energy and financial services sectors have been an important step towards a better understanding of the functioning of those markets.

Strengthening   **3.51**   The Government believes that the Commission must continue to take a robust stance
the EU   in pushing forward a pro-active competition policy to improve the Single Market. The UK's
competition   recently published vision for the Single Market is summarised in Box 3.4.[12] In addition, the
regime   Government believes that the central role of competition policy should be strengthened by promoting:

- greater use of market investigations. As part of its fundamental review of the Single Market the Commission should commit to embedding sector inquiries into the EU competition regime and to undertaking further inquiries into priority sectors, where competition is lacking. Sector inquiries should be followed up with strong action;

- a greater role for private actions against anti-competitive behaviour. The Government recognises that some of the barriers to private actions might be best solved at the European level and it will continue to support the Commission in the follow-up to its 2005 Green Paper; and

- an "economic approach" to tackling state aid. The UK believes that further reform to state aid rules and their enforcement should be pursued within an overall framework in which aid which has a minimal impact on competition can be swiftly agreed, whilst tough action is taken against subsidies that seriously harm competition.

[11] Council Regulation 1/2003 of 14 December 2002 on the implementation of the rules on competition laid down in Articles 81 and 82 of the Treaty.

[12] *The Single Market: A vision for the 21st Century*, HMT and DTI, January 2007. Available at www.hm-treasury.gov.uk

---

Box 3.4: The Single Market: a vision for the 21st century

The Government welcomes the European Commission's Review of the Single Market, due to report this year, which provides an opportunity to look again at how the Single Market can equip Europe to compete in the 21st century global economy. The Government has set out a strategy for a modern Single Market that delivers for Europe's citizens, businesses and consumers through a pro-competition, flexible and outward-looking approach. It believes that Single Market policy should be based on the following key principles:

- focusing policy on outcomes of promoting jobs, growth and prosperity;
- prioritising actions in areas where economic impacts are greatest;
- emphasising cooperation and the principle of subsidiarity; and
- using a wider range of policy tools.

In putting these principles into action, the Government would like to see action to:

- strengthen the role of pro-active competition policy and market based monitoring to identify sectors where competition is lacking and priorities for future market investigations, building on the work carried out by the Commission in the recent sector inquiries into energy and financial services;
- embed better regulation principles across the Single Market, with proper consideration of the alternatives to legislation in every case, such as information and guidance or codes of practice. The Government would like to see greater use of flexible regulatory mechanisms, such as the Lamfalussy arrangements in financial services, and strengthening of the mutual recognition principle;
- improve implementation and strengthen enforcement of existing EU rules. The Government would like to see a new system for prioritising investigations into breaches of EU law, and improved redress mechanisms for businesses and consumers, both informal problem solving techniques and improved access to courts; and
- match community level policy with renewed commitment of Member States to undertake structural reforms and pursue modern social policies, and commitment to external openness to trade, with conclusion of full negotiations in the Doha round of trade talks.

New economic research published alongside the paper argues for the prioritisation of further reforms in key sectors, notably in Europe's network industries, such as energy, communications and post, that impact on the wider economy. Further market opening in the network industries could increase Europe's GDP by 1.7 per cent and create up to 360,000 additional jobs.

ENTERPRISE

3.52   In an increasingly open and competitive global economy, a vibrant and thriving business and policy environment for firms and enterprise is critical in ensuring that the UK can respond flexibly to new challenges, and to increase productivity and living standards for all.

3.53   It is not the case that most businesses, if unregulated, will act irresponsibly. Well-informed consumers, responsible companies, unions and pressure and interest groups have all encouraged businesses to take measures to reduce risks to society. Regulatory regimes need to adapt to this changing world, delivering what is intended while minimising unnecessary regulatory burdens, and retaining public confidence. To this end, the Government is delivering better regulation by implementing the Hampton review's risk-based approach to enforcement, ensuring that regulatory costs are proportionate to the risks posed, and encouraging risk-based regulatory reform in Europe.

Delivering better regulation

Implementing Hampton 3.54 The Better Regulation Executive (BRE) and National Audit Office (NAO) have been working with regulators, business groups, local authorities and consumer groups to develop a framework for external review of national regulators' adherence to the Hampton principles.[13] The framework will be published in May. The Health and Safety Executive has volunteered to work with the BRE and the NAO on the first of the reviews, with the Food Standards Agency, the Environment Agency, the Office of Fair Trading and Financial Services Authority to follow in 2007.

3.55 At the 2006 Pre-Budget Report, the BRE was tasked with setting up the Local Better Regulation Office (LBRO) to encourage the implementation of a consistent and coordinated risk-based approach to enforcement and inspection at local authority level. The recruitment process for the independent Chair, Chief Executive and Board is underway, with the appointment of the Chair due to be announced in the next month, followed by the Chief Executive and Board appointments.

Employment law 3.56 Disputes in the workplace are costly for employers, stressful for individuals and harmful to productivity. In December, the Secretary of State for Trade and Industry asked Michael Gibbons, a former Director at Powergen and current member of the independent Better Regulation Commission, to undertake a review of government support for resolving disputes in the workplace. His review has looked at the current legal requirements, how employment tribunals work and the scope for new initiatives to help resolve disputes at an earlier stage.

Box 3.5: Gibbons Review of dispute resolution

The review proposes a package of measures to promote early resolution of disputes and reduce the number of tribunal claims.

It recommends repealing the current statutory dispute resolution procedures and replacing them with non-prescriptive guidelines on grievances, discipline and dismissal. This would reduce administrative burdens and enable employers and employees to use the most appropriate way of resolving disputes.

The review also recommends that additional free ACAS conciliation should be offered to employers and employees in dispute in the period before a tribunal claim is made. To encourage use of this and other dispute resolution mechanisms, the review recommends improving government advice to employers and employees on resolving disputes, and integrating the improved advice service into the tribunal application process.

The review also recommends:

- engaging employer and employee bodies in promoting early dispute resolution in the workplace;
- directing simple monetary claims to a new fast-track resolution process; and
- simplifying employment tribunal processes and paperwork.

3.57 The Government welcomes the recommendations of the Gibbons Review of employment dispute resolution published today. A consultation on these proposals is published alongside the review. The Government is committed to piloting any new approach to dispute settlement that results from this consultation.

Rogers Review 3.58 In order to ensure that local authorities focus their enforcement on high-risk policy areas, the Government asked Peter Rogers, Chief Executive of Westminster City Council, to

---

[13] Box 2.2 *Reducing administrative burdens: effective inspection and enforcement*, Philip Hampton, March 2005.

examine approximately 60 policy areas that local authorities enforce. The Rogers Review, published today, recommends that the Government should specify that the five enforcement priorities for trading standards and environmental health services in England are air quality, alcohol licensing, hygiene of businesses, improving health in the workplace and fair trading. The Rogers Review also recommends that animal and public health should be a further, time-limited enforcement priority.[14] The LBRO should refresh these enforcement priorities on a regular basis, and recommend them to Government.

3.59 **The Government welcomes the Rogers Review and accepts the recommendations in full.** These national priorities for local authority trading standards and environmental health services will ensure that they can plan their resources and prioritise their activities to ensure that the most critical of central government regulatory objectives are achieved. This will result in a substantially rationalised burden around regulatory services. Businesses will benefit from improved consistency of enforcement and sharper regulatory focus.

Data sharing **3.60** One of the key Hampton principles is that business should not have to give unnecessary information, nor give the same piece of information twice. Data sharing is a key route through which Government and regulators can reduce the burden on business. Two recent examples include:

- the Department for Environment, Food and Rural Affairs (Defra), the Environment Agency and the Food Standards Agency are identifying opportunities for sharing information on the performance of businesses in managing risk. This will provide valuable input to the development of any shared business confidence assessment methodologies and regulator data sharing protocols; and

- the Environment Agency and the Health and Safety Executive are undertaking a scoping study to identify if there is a significant benefit to business from the streamlining of existing systems by sharing data on asbestos notification between the two regulatory bodies.

3.61 Chapter 6 sets out in more detail the Government's approach to decreasing the cost to frontline service deliverers of central data requests.

Small firms **3.62** The Small Firms Impact Test (SFIT) is a key part of the Government's commitment to
impact test 'think small first' when developing policy, and is integrated into the process of Impact Assessment. In 2006, the Government consulted publicly on changes to Impact Assessment and is currently preparing a response to the consultation. As part of this work, the Government plans to update the SFIT, so that increased consideration is given to the needs of small firms in policy design, including giving fuller consideration to exemptions, either complete or partial, for small firms where possible.

Planning **3.63** The final report of *Kate Barker's Review of Land Use Planning*, published in December
regulations 2006, makes clear that planning is a valued and necessary activity but that there is further scope for reducing the burdens that the system imposes on applicants. The Government will set out its plans in a forthcoming planning reform White Paper. These will include measures to deliver a substantial reduction in the bureaucracy associated with making planning applications, including a reduction in paperwork. More details of the Government's response to the Barker Review are set out later in Chapter 3.

Regulation of **3.64** In the 2005 Pre-Budget Report, the Government set out a ten-point action plan aimed
financial services at reforming wholesale and retail financial markets. These issues drew on the two-year review of the Financial Services and Markets Act 2000 (FSMA) and represent the greatest concerns of

---

[14] The roles and responsibilities of local authorities and other bodies involved in regulatory and enforcement activities for animal health and welfare have been subject to a review by David Eves CB. The Government intends to consult on this.

business in relation to the burden of financial services regulation. Further progress has been made against this action plan including reform of the controller's regime through an EU Directive and progress with the financial services authorities reviews into its conduct of business rules covering mortgages and general insurance.

European regulatory reform

3.65 The UK continues to drive regulatory reform in Europe and helped to ensure that all 27 Member States and the Commission agreed to a target to reduce administrative burdens arising from EU legislation by 25 per cent by 2012. This complements the UK's own target for administrative burden reduction and will boost the competitiveness of business, especially SMEs, which suffer most from over-burdensome regulation.

3.66 The UK is pressing for rapid results and has worked successfully with the Commission in putting together a concrete programme of action. The programme has started with Commission proposals for immediate action to cut 10 specific burdens in the areas of company law, agriculture, statistics, transport and food hygiene. The Commission estimates that these proposed changes would save business in the EU £1.3 billion. This programme will be backed by actions to address the greatest burdens in identified priority areas and the establishment of an Impact Assessment Board to scrutinise and challenge Impact Assessments and improve their quality.

3.67 The principles that will be used to guide burden reduction include the use of a risk-based approach for information obligations and the consideration of exemptions from providing information for SMEs. The UK recognises that more can be done and will continue to promote the use of a risk-based approach to improve the rationale, design and enforcement of regulation.

Davidson Review **3.68** Lord Davidson published his final report on the implementation of European legislation in the UK in November 2006.[15] The Government accepted his recommendations in full. The BRE will publish revised guidance on transposing EU law for policy makers and lawyers in the spring. Departments are also taking forward his recommendations, for example:

- the Department for Transport (DfT) will consult later in spring on options for reforming the MOT regime; and

- the Treasury published a consultation document on removing the insurance activities of freight forwarders from Financial Services Authority regulation on 21 December 2006.

Modernising tax administration

Simplification **3.69** At Budget 2006, the Chancellor announced targets for HMRC to reduce the administrative burdens imposed on business by the tax system, focusing on forms and returns, and on audits and inspections. By April 2007, HMRC will have reduced these significant burdens by an estimated £170m per annum, and will have also reduced wider administrative burdens on business by £130m. The major reforms delivering all of these savings include:

- a simplified pensions tax regime, welcomed by the industry, which from April 2006 has reduced much of the complexity caused by the previous rules;

---

[15] *Davidson Review of the Implementation of EU Legislation*, November 2006.

- the revised P46, introduced in April 2006, which reduced enquiries to employers from employees who are unable to provide their latest pay and tax details;

- exempting, since April 2006, ninety per cent of new companies from the requirements of Form 42, benefiting around 300,000 companies every year;

- the redesigned VAT 1 form, launched in December 2006, improving the process for the 280,000 businesses registering for VAT each year; and

- the reformed construction industry scheme, effective from April 2007, which provides an electronic alternative to paper processes, replaces individual vouchers with a contractor's monthly return, and removes the need for the contractor's end of year return.

3.70   Although HMRC is making significant progress, these reforms are only a first step towards making noticeable improvements to businesses' experience of the tax system. HMRC will continue to work closely with the Administrative Burden Advisory Board[16] and with the business community to identify new areas for action that tackle the burdens of most concern to business. HMRC has today published further details of this work.[17]

3.71   These changes compliment a range of policy reforms outlined in this chapter that will also impact on the administrative burden placed on business. Overall, these will be deregulatory for business. For example, Box 3.3 outlines how capital allowances will be reformed; further detail of its impact on business will be published once implementation plans have been finalised.

HMRC Review of Links with Large Business   **3.72**   The 2006 Review of Links with Large Business, published in November 2006, made proposals aimed at delivering a modern, responsive tax administration to foster an environment in which business can flourish and to improve the competitiveness of the UK. HMRC today publishes a detailed delivery plan setting out the implementation plans and timeframes for delivering the Review's proposals in consultation with business, including how HMRC will develop a framework of advance agreements to give both UK business and significant inward investors certainty on the tax treatment of their transactions. Chapter 5 provides further information on the delivery plan.

Supporting growing businesses

Better business support   **3.73**   Budget 2006 announced plans to reduce the number of business support services offered from over 3,000 to 100 or fewer by 2010. As part of this process, the programme is taking a fresh look at the kinds of business support – the products and services – it is most appropriate for Government to provide. A consultation document will be published before the Summer Recess, seeking views from businesses and other stakeholders on the proposals for the design of the new portfolio of government business support. This programme will also inform the sub-national review of economic development and regeneration and will be reflected in the 2007 CSR.

3.74   Building on the progress announced at the 2006 Pre-Budget Report, further rationalisation can now be announced, including closure of UK Trade and Investment's "New Products from Britain" service and DTI's "Grant for Investigating an Innovative Idea" – allowing

---

[16] The Administrative Burden Advisory Board, independently chaired by Teresa Graham, was appointed at Budget 2006.

[17] *Delivering a new relationship with business: Progress towards reducing the administrative burdens on business*, HMRC, March 2007. This is available at http://www.hmrc.gov.uk

the re-direction of funds to higher performing support products – and rationalisation of all the South East England Development Agency's existing investment funds into one.

3.75   The Business Link brand will be strengthened as the channel for all publicly-funded business information, support and advice. Progress is already being made, by bringing into Business Link:

- Defra's business advice to farmers; and

- The East Midlands Development Agency and the East of England Development Agency's support to start-ups.

VAT registration threshold

3.76   **From 1 April 2007 the Government will increase the VAT registration threshold in line with inflation from £61,000 to £64,000, maintaining the highest threshold in Europe and keeping up to a further 6,000 small businesses out of the VAT system.**

Tax based venture capital schemes

3.77   Following the publication of the new State Aid for Risk Capital Guidelines[18] by the European Commission, the Government is required to introduce changes to the Enterprise Investment Scheme (EIS), Venture Capital Trusts (VCTs) and the Corporate Venturing Scheme (CVS). Although the Government believes that the changes risk reducing the effectiveness of the schemes in addressing the equity gap faced by smaller companies with high growth potential, it is imperative that these changes are made to giver greater certainty to investors and the companies they invest in, and to secure the future of the schemes. The Government will introduce, effective 6 April 2007 for VCTs and from Royal Assent for EIS and CVS:

- an annual investment limit across the three schemes of £2 million per target company; and

- for target companies, at the time of investment, a limit equivalent to fewer than 50 full-time employees.

3.78   The Government continues to believe in the importance of a strong and effective state aids regime that prevents aid that threatens to undermine competition and efficiency of the Single Market. However, it also believes that there is a clear role for well-targeted interventions to promote structural reform and tackle market failures in support of the goals of the Lisbon agenda. The Government has therefore written to the European Commission calling on it to review the way in which it applies the state aids guidelines to ensure that proper account is taken of the economic arguments for government intervention.

3.79   Savings from these changes will be wholly recycled to fund enhancements to R&D tax credits, as described earlier in this chapter, to promote innovation and productivity in the UK.

3.80   In response to feedback from users, the Government is also introducing a number of changes to improve the commercial, effectiveness, usability and consistency of the schemes.

Local Authority Business Growth Incentive scheme

3.81   The Government introduced the Local Authority Business Growth Incentive (LABGI) scheme in April 2005 to create a direct financial incentive for local authorities to promote local business growth. LABGI delivers financial rewards directly to local authorities that promote the greatest levels of continued economic growth in their local areas by allowing them to retain increases in revenue derived from business rates. The money is genuinely additional and the scheme encourages local authorities to build partnerships with local business and promote long-term economic sustainability in their areas. Last year 278 authorities received £126 million in LABGI. In 2006-07, the second year of the scheme, 328 local authorities received grants totalling £316 million. The Government expects to see up to

---

[18] Community Guidelines on State Aid to Promote Risk Capital Investments in Small and Medium-sized enterprises, Official Journal of the European Union, August 2006

£1 billion allocated to local authorities by 2007-08. Following the publication of the Lyons Inquiry report today (see Chapter 6) the Government will bring forward proposals to reform the LABGI Scheme before the summer to continue to provide strong incentives for local authorities to act to increase economic prosperity.

Enterprise in disadvantaged areas

Community Development Finance Institutions
3.82   Many enterprises in disadvantaged communities currently face problems in obtaining access to suitable support, advice, and finance from mainstream commercial providers. To address this problem, Government introduced support to the Community Development Finance (CDF) sector in 2000 to grow the CDF sector in a sustainable way and to assist enterprises in disadvantaged areas access finance. To ensure sustainability of the CDF model, the Government will liase with the banking sector, including the European Investment Bank and Community Development Finance Institutions, to explore how the framework could be developed further.

Community Investment Tax Relief
3.83   As part of its ongoing review of the operation and delivery of the Community Investment Tax Relief (CITR) scheme, the Government will improve the flexibility of the scheme by changing the onward investment requirements after the third anniversary of accreditation from 75 per cent at all times to an average of 75 per cent over the course of the year. The scheme's accreditation and reporting procedures will also be updated, to reflect the forthcoming change to the status of the Small Business Service.

Creating an enterprise culture

Enterprise education
3.84   Attitudes towards entreprenership are improving with the proportion of young people aged 16-24 considering going into business having risen from 14 per cent in 2003 to 18 per cent in 2005[19]. There have been increases in the number of people who encourage friends to start their own business, 66 per cent in 2005, up to 2 percentage points from 2003, and a reduced averse attitude to starting businesses, 56 per cent were averse in 2005, compared with 60 per cent in 2003. The Government is committed to strengthening further the UK's enterprise culture and is working to promote even greater enterprise capability among young people in education. To maintain the momentum of implementing the recommendations of the Davies Review,[20] the Government will continue the funding of enterprise education at £60 million per year over the 2007 CSR period, as part of Department for Education and Skills' (DfES) 2007 CSR settlement. The Government aims to build on the achievements to date, developing a strategy to encompass all tiers of education and is working to foster closer links between financial capability and enterprise education in the curriculum. In particular it is encouraging all secondary schools to participate fully in enterprise education, including by working in partnership with primary schools, colleges and higher education institutes.

3.85   To raise awareness of the benefits of enterprise learning and to showcase particular examples of the most enterprising schools, DfES will be publishing *Enterprising Heads, Enterprising Schools*, in late spring 2007.

3.86   To facilitate greater support from employers to teachers, in the 2006 Pre-Budget Report the Government announced the launch of 50 Young Chambers of Commerce. In March 2007, participating schools and Chambers were allocated nearly £2 million to set these up. Government also welcomes the further development of a quality assurance scheme for the members of the National Education Business Partnership Network, that help schools to work with over 200,000 businesses in England. This scheme aims to further incorporate other

---

[19] *Household Survey of Entrepreneurship 2005*, DTI.

[20] *A review of enterprise and the economy in Education* 2002.

Education Business Links to drive self improvement by the organisations that help businesses and schools to work together for young people's economic wellbeing.

3.87 As part of the wider enterprise education strategy and to build on the progress made to date in raising the awareness of entrepreneurship amongst graduates, **the National Council for Graduate Entrepreneurship will work with the Government and other stakeholders to assess the feasibility and viability of an enterprise foundation** intended to develop further programmes to raise awareness of graduate entrepreneurship and to facilitate key research.

SCIENCE AND INNOVATION

3.88 In a global economy, innovation is increasingly important to UK competitiveness, productivity and long-term growth. The Government is committed to providing the right environment for innovation and creativity to flourish, in both maturing industries and in new emerging sectors.

Building an innovation system

3.89 *The Science and Innovation Investment Framework 2004-2014*[20] set out the Government's intention to increase investment in the public science base at least in line with the trend growth rate of the economy over the ten-year period, contributing toward the Government's long-term ambition for public and private investment in R&D to reach 2.5 per cent of GDP. The last spending period saw an unprecedented increase in public funding for the research base, and by 2007-08, total UK science spending will be £5.4 billion. This has been critical in establishing the long-term sustainability of the science base. To assess the effectiveness of the Government's science and innovation policies, the Government asked Lord Sainsbury to carry out a review taking a forward look at what more needs to be done to ensure the UK's continued success.

3.90 **Budget 2007 announces early 2007 CSR settlements for the Department of Trade and Industry's ring-fenced science budget and the Department for Education and Skills, which together deliver average annual growth of 2.5 per cent in real terms over the CSR period.** These early settlements provide long-term certainty for the research community, and will deliver resources to meet a range of priorities, including further investment to support excellent research; increasing the economic impact of the science base; and implementing the recommendations of the Sainsbury and Cooksey Reviews.

Technology Strategy Board
3.91 The UK is second only to the US in global scientific excellence, but in order to meet the challenges of globalisation, it is essential that excellent research is translated more effectively into innovative products and services. *The Science and Innovation Investment Framework 2004-2014* announced increased support for the Technology Strategy Board (TSB) to support collaborative R&D with businesses, with funding of at least £178 million by 2007-08. Due to its success in supporting innovation, the TSB will now take on a wider remit to stimulate business innovation in those areas that offer the greatest scope for boosting growth and productivity. This covers all areas of the economy, from the manufacturing industries to the arts and creative industries.

3.92 In order to give the TSB greater independence in delivering a national, business-focused innovation strategy, the Secretary of State for Trade & Industry announced in November that the TSB would have the status of an executive Non Departmental Public Body (NDPB). This will enable the TSB to operate at arm's length from central government, with a business-led Board taking a strategic overview of innovation priorities across all sectors of the UK economy, creating closer links between the science base and industry and advising the

---

[20] *Science & innovation investment framework 2004-2014*, July 2004. Available at www.hm-treasury.gov.uk

Government on the allocation of resources to priority technology areas. This new structure will become fully operational by July 2007. To support the TSB's enhanced leadership role as an independent body, the Government is today announcing a number of initiatives to strengthen the impact of the TSB, building on the early conclusions of the Sainsbury Review.

Box 3.6: The Technology Strategy Board

The UK Research Councils are actively working to strengthen their economic impact and increase the amount of collaborative research they conduct with business. To date, Research Councils have invested £25 million in TSB programmes to support collaborative R&D projects. Building on the success of this model, **the Director-General of Science and Innovation will agree specific targets with each Research Council to increase the amount of collaborative R&D they conduct in partnership with the TSB over the Comprehensive Spending Review period.** This planned Research Council business collaboration funding will be allocated in a joint process by the Research Councils and the TSB, and will form a clear basis for investment for the Research Councils over the CSR. It will maximise the capacity of investment from the science base to attract matching funding from other sources.

Today, **the TSB will allocate £100 million for Collaborative R&D,** bringing business and the research community together to work on user driven R&D from which new products, processes and services emerge. Over 600 R&D projects have been approved for funding so far and this new call will include substantial funding directed to larger projects that provide maximum economic impact.

The TSB will explore three new Innovation Platforms, bringing the Government and business together to generate innovative solutions to policy challenges, and engage different stakeholders through procurement opportunities. Two Innovation Platforms have been piloted in Intelligent Transport Systems and Services and Network Security. The three new Platforms will focus on assisted living and health care technologies, low environmental impact buildings, and environmentally friendly vehicles.

A key challenge for the new Board is to develop an appropriate strategy and support for the Creative Industries recognising the different nature of the sector. In addition to the existing 22 networks (such as sensors, micro and nano technology), **the TSB is announcing support for two new Knowledge Transfer Networks (KTNs) in the areas of Creative & Media Industries and Digital Communications,** bringing business and academia together to identify opportunities for collaboration.

The new Board plans to learn from the US Defence Advanced Research Projects Agency (DARPA) and recruit secondees directly from industry. The TSB will also complement its portfolio of support by taking over responsibility for leading the Knowledge Transfer Partnerships (KTPs) that provide support to companies who need to bring skills or knowledge from the research base into the business.

3.93   The Sainsbury Review is looking at what more can be done to ensure the UK's success in the face of the opportunities and challenges of globalisation. At both regional and national levels, the review is identifying areas in which effective government intervention can continue to support the UK's world-class science base and better enable wealth-creation, reporting by summer 2007.

Box 3.7: Sainsbury Review Emerging Conclusions

Building on the Government's existing policy agenda, the Review will set out a range of policies to enable the UK to respond to the opportunities and challenges of globalisation:

Providing leadership: the Government is today taking forward early recommendations from the Sainsbury Review regarding changes to the Technology Strategy Board (see Box 3.6).

Delivering skills: to further raise the standards of STEM skill delivery, the Review is considering ways to improve: the qualifications of school science teachers and support for their professional development; measures to recruit and retain teachers; and careers services. It is also considering the impact of the introduction of the second maths GCSE in 2010.

Furthering Knowledge transfer: the Review is considering how the effectiveness of the Higher Education Innovation Fund (HEIF) could be improved to support knowledge exchange and promote economic growth involving the full spectrum of Higher Education Institutions. The conclusions of the Review will inform decisions by the Office of Science and Innovation, the Department for Education and Skills, and the Higher Education Funding Council for England on the method of allocation for future rounds of HEIF. The Review is also considering a shorter more flexible Knowledge Transfer Partnership scheme targeted at SMEs.

Improving effectiveness of government departments: the Review is exploring how Innovation Platforms can be used to enhance departmental procurement through more strategic supplier engagement. It is also looking at how departments' R&D strategies can be used to stimulate innovation in industry, and how they can be better coordinated to address the Government's long-term challenges.

Supporting entrepreneurship: the Review believes an improved Small Business Research Initiative could provide support to early-stage high-technology companies, encouraging innovation.

Enabling the regions: in consultation with the Sub-National Review and the RDAs, the review will explore options for a new strategic framework for the regions for allocating resources to key science and innovation objectives. It will also explore ways in which RDAs can make best use of their science and innovation expenditure to drive regional economic growth.

Encouraging international collaboration: the Review is looking at how to deliver the collaborative scientific research a globalised economy demands. It is considering: Research Council representation abroad; the Science Bridges programme; and a Royal Society scheme to encourage internationally recognised researchers to come to the UK. In association with the Sub-National Review, the Review is also looking at ways to optimise UK representation abroad.

Business Research and Development

R&D tax credits 3.94   As part of the wider package of reforms to the corporate tax system, the Government is introducing further improvements to R&D tax credits, increasing the enhanced deduction of the SME R&D tax credit to 175 per cent and the large company R&D tax credit to 130 per cent from April 2008. Details on the R&D tax credit reforms are set out earlier in this chapter. A more generous R&D tax credit will ensure the tax system supports the Government's desire to enable UK businesses to compete in an increasingly globalised, knowledge-based economy. The UK's current R&D tax credit already compares very favourably in international comparisons. Increases in the rate of relief available for R&D will further cement the UK's position as a prime location for R&D investment.

3.95 Recognising the importance of fully supporting the growth of the UK's mid-sized innovators, Budget 2006 announced an expansion to R&D tax credits to further enhance support for this vital segment of the economy. Legislation will be included in Finance Bill 2007 to extend the current SME R&D tax credit to companies with fewer than 500 employees. The extension will provide firms with between 250 and 500 employees with 150 per cent tax relief and a payable cash credit for loss-making companies. The legislation will be activated upon receipt of state aid clearance.

Energy Technologies Institute   **3.96** Budget 2006 announced that the Government, after discussions with some of the world's biggest energy companies, agreed to work in partnership with business to create a new energy and environmental research institute. The Energy Technologies Institute (ETI) will be fully operational in 2008 as a 50:50 Public: Private Partnership. The aspiration is to raise £100 million per year for UK-based energy research, design, demonstration and development: a total of £1 billion over a ten-year period. BP, Shell, E.ON UK, EDF, Rolls Royce and Scottish and Southern Energy have already committed to support the Institute, and **this Budget announces that in addition Caterpillar has committed £5 million a year over the 10 year period, bringing the total private sector commitment up to £312.5 million.**

Intellectual Property Rights   **3.97** The *Gowers Review of intellectual property*, which reported to the Government in December 2006, suggested a number of reforms to ensure the UK's Intellectual Property (IP) system is fit for the digital age. In the 2006 Pre-Budget Report, the Government announced its intention to take forward those recommendations for which it is responsible, and significant progress has been made since then.

3.98 The Gowers Review highlighted the importance of supporting the creative industries through tackling IP Crime. IP crime has already been recognised as an area for Police action in the updated National Community Safety Plan. Trading Standards Officers will be able to enforce copyright offences from this April, and £5 million will be made available to local government to fund this function in the first year.

3.99 The Government will also provide greater support to UK business to help recognise, protect and maximise the value of their intellectual property, and will implement a pilot scheme offering IP health checks to small businesses. The pilot is part of the Patent Office's Innovation Support Strategy, and will start in March 2007. Implementation of Gowers' recommendations is scheduled to be completed by the end of 2008. A number of consultations exploring options for implementation of the recommendations on UK copyright exceptions, Patent Office fees, fast-track services for the grant of patents and registration of trade marks, civil damages and fast track litigation are planned, most of which will be launched in spring 2007.

3.100 The UK and Japanese Patent Offices will trial a new initiative, the Patent Prosecution Highway, which will allow accelerated examination of a patent application where examination has already taken place in the other country. In addition to speeding up the patenting process for UK businesses in Japan, the initiative will help promote work sharing between patent offices around the world, thereby reducing costly duplication of effort.

Northern Ireland Innovation Fund   **3.101** Subject to the St. Andrew's Agreement being implemented and devolution restored on 26 March, a Northern Ireland Innovation Fund will be established to promote R&D and the science base, reinforcing the Northern Ireland peace process. The fund will be established in April 2007 building on the substantial existing levels of funding to promote private sector investment and collaborative research, including with the Republic of Ireland, subject to detailed decisions being made by the incoming devolved administrations.

Excellent research

Cooksey Review   **3.102**   The *Cooksey Review of UK Health Research Funding* recommended new institutional arrangements for a new single health research fund to improve the coordination of health R&D and facilitate the translation of this research into health and economic benefits to the UK. The Government has established the Office for Strategic Coordination of Health Research (OSCHR) to implement these recommendations. In order to maximise impact while maintaining the 'light touch' recommended in the Review, OSCHR will work through two Boards – the Translational Medicine Board (TMB) and the Public Health Research Board (PHRB) – as well as beginning to realise the research benefit of NHS IT systems through a separate E-Health funding stream.

3.103   Today's early settlement of the Department of Trade and Industry's ring-fenced science budget ensures that the recommendations of the Cooksey Review will be implemented. The budget for OSCHR will be confirmed at the end of the 2007 CSR process.

3.104   The main role of the TMB and PHRB will be to develop and oversee a single, integrated strategy for translational research and public health research, realising the vision for innovation and commercialisation of the outcomes of research funded by the Medical Research Council and the National Institute of Health Research, and ensuring sustainable culture change and cross-working between agencies.

Stem cells   **3.105**   In the 2005 Pre-Budget Report, the UK Stem Cell Initiative reported back to Government on a strategy for the next decade of stem cell research in the UK. The first recommendation was for the Government to establish a Public-Private Partnership (PPP) using stem cells to enhance pre-competitive aspects of drug development. The Government continues to work in partnership with industry to establish this consortium and will begin work with a series of pilot projects in 2007. Work is also progressing on the establishment of a not-for-profit company, with board membership from both the public and private sectors. The company should become operational during 2007.

SKILLS

3.106   The skills of the workforce are increasingly important in determining the UK's ability to respond to the emerging challenges presented by globalisation: demographic, socio-economic and technological change. Improving the UK's skills profile has benefits for individuals, companies and the economy. Individuals can increase their productivity and mobility and gain more opportunities for sustainable employment and progression in the labour market. Companies with a highly skilled workforce are better able to innovate and compete on the basis of higher value added products and services. For the economy as a whole, improving skills can deliver clear benefits in terms of improved productivity, social justice and mobility. In the last ten years, the UK has seen improvements in its skills profile at all levels. However, to become comparable with countries possessing a world-class skills profile, more needs to be done, in particular to tackle low skills.

Leitch Review of   **3.107**   The Leitch Review of Skills, *Prosperity for all in the global economy – world-class skills*, **Skills**   was published on 5 December 2006, setting out an ambitious and stretching vision for skills in the UK in 2020. It set out a series of objectives for improving skills at all levels, with the aim of creating a world-class skills base comparable to other advanced industrial economies. In the 2006 Pre-Budget Report, the Government accepted both the ambition of the Leitch Review, and the underpinning delivery principles of its approach.

3.108   In the context of the significant increases in resources for education for the 2007 CSR period outlined in Chapter 6, the Government will publish a full implementation plan for the Leitch Review in the summer. It will set out in detail how the Government is taking forward the recommendations made by the Review and the timetable for implementation.

Public Service Agreements   **3.109**   There are a number of areas where progress is already being made to ensure the UK is able to respond to the challenges set out by the Leitch Review. The Government recently achieved the interim milestones for both the Basic Skills and Level 2 targets within the adult skills Public Service Agreement (PSA). Over 1.6 million adults have improved their basic skills and achieved qualifications in literacy, language and numeracy since the Skills for Life strategy was introduced in 2001. 1.2 million adults have achieved a first Level 2 qualification since 2002, reducing the stock of adults who lack the basic platform of skills needed for sustainable employment in the modern workplace. Achieving these targets will create a strong foundation, necessary to meet the ambitious vision for skills in the UK set out in the Leitch Review.

Demand-led skills   **3.110**   Ensuring that the training delivered through the Further Education sector is tailored to the needs of employers is central to ensuring that vocational qualifications are economically valuable and deliver real returns both to individuals and to businesses. The Government is continuing to expand the availability of the Train to Gain service, which provides firms with free, flexibly delivered training in the workplace for their low-skilled employees. So far, over 25,000 employers have engaged with the service and almost 90,000 low-skilled individuals have already started training. This is in addition to the 30,000 employers and 260,000 employees who participated in the pilot scheme. A recent evaluation of the Train to Gain skills broker network highlighted continuing high levels of employer satisfaction with the service.[21] In particular, employers value the knowledge and expertise of the brokers and their ability to identify appropriate training.

3.111   Building on the 2006 Further Education White Paper[22] and the recently published Leitch Review, the Government is exploring the steps required to channel a greater proportion of funding available for adult skills through demand-led routes, such as Train to Gain. In January 2007, the Learning and Skills Council launched a formal and detailed consultation seeking views from the Further Education sector,[23] including providers and learners, to create a more demand led system.

Commission for Employment and Skills   **3.112**   The Government recognises that employers should play a central role in ensuring that the employment and skills systems work together to meet the needs of employers and support individuals in progressing in the labour market. A Commission for Employment and Skills will be created, following the vision set out in the Leitch Review, which will be responsible for providing a strong employer voice and leadership of the employment and skills system. It will increase employer engagement and investment in skills and ensure that an integrated employment and skills service meets the needs of individuals, including those on benefits, by focusing on sustaining employment and progression as an outcome. A Chair for the Commission is currently being recruited. Once in post, the Chair will work closely with the Government to appoint the members of the Commission and to establish the new body by the end of 2007.

---

[21] *Evaluation of Employer Satisfaction with the National Employer Training Programme/Train to Gain*, BMG Research, December 2006.

[22] *Further Education: Raising Skills, Improving Life Chances*, DfES, March 2006.

[23] *Delivering World-class Skills in a Demand-led System*, Learning and Skills Council, January 2007.

Government Envoy for Skills

3.113   The Government Envoy for Skills, Sir Digby Jones, is working with employers from key sectors of the economy to build a consensus on improving skills of their workforce. Sir Digby Jones is calling upon employers to sign up to a Skills Pledge to ensure that all their employees reach a skills level equivalent to five good GCSEs. The Skills Pledge was recommended by Lord Leitch as one way to help drive up the UK's skills. It seeks to share responsibility between the State, employer and employees and will be open to all employers irrespective of size, status or sector. It is designed to stimulate demand for training services and support a new culture where gaining skills is taken as a matter of course.

Skills for young people

3.114   Achieving world-class skills in the UK will require improving the skills of young people flowing into employment. Improving the number of young people continuing in education and training after the end of the compulsory school age will provide the foundation to improve the skills of young people and ensure the UK has a strong, flexible labour market in the future. The Government has introduced a number of measures to encourage young people to continue to participate in education and training until the age of 18, including reforms to the financial support system and the advice, guidance and support structures.

3.115   The *14-19 Education and Skills White Paper*, published in February 2005, set out the next steps the Government is taking to engage young people in education and training until the age of 18. Tailored support for young people at risk of disengagement and reform of the 14-19 curriculum will provide young people with the opportunity to learn in ways which motivate and engage them, providing the skills valued by further and higher education and employers.

3.116   Since April 2006, the Government has been piloting new learning agreements. These are aimed at 16 and 17 year olds who are in work but not receiving accredited training, to ensure they undertake appropriate learning. Building on the existing statutory right to paid time off to train or study for this group, the pilot is testing the effectiveness of formal learning agreements, financial incentives and wage compensation for young people and their employers when engaging in training. **Budget 2007 announces an extension of the Learning Agreement pilot into the 2007 CSR period.** As outlined in chapter 5, the Government will also extend Activity Agreement pilots to re-engage young people not in education, employment and training.

3.117   The Government has made progress in recent years in increasing the number of young people continuing in education and training until the age of 18. Despite this, further progress is required. The Government believes that raising the age of compulsory participation in education from 16 to 18 is the best way to lay the foundations to improve skills of all young people, and equip them to succeed in life. To this end, a Green Paper on raising the age of compulsory participation in education and training[24] to 18 will be published on 22 March 2007. Young people will be required to participate either at school, in college, in work-based learning, or in accredited training provided by an employer.

3.118   The Green Paper will consider how individuals, the Government, and employers can work together to ensure that young people have the skills they need for the future. The Government will consult with business on ways in which this objective can be achieved while meeting the principles of better regulation. Under the Green Paper proposals:

---

[24] *The Raising the Participation Age Green Paper*, DfES, March 2007.

- the Government will continue to pay for accredited training, and support employers to get their training accredited where it meets requirements;

- the Government will support employers to find training opportunities for their employees through Train to Gain; and

- employers who do not want to provide or arrange training for their employees would be required to release young people from work to undertake training (equivalent to around a day a week).

INVESTMENT

3.119   The accumulation of physical capital through investment is an important determinant of an economy's productivity performance. Physical capital stock is closely correlated with productivity performance, as it directly influences how much a unit of labour can produce. Investments in physical capital are complementary to other forms of investment such as skills and innovation. The Government's macroeconomic reforms have provided an environment of low and stable interest rates and a flexible labour market. These reforms help to provide a certain and rewarding environment for businesses to invest for the future.

3.120   This supportive environment for investment has meant business investment has now expanded for eight consecutive quarters, the longest continuous expansion in nine years. However, this impressive performance is from historically low levels, compared with comparator countries. Investment in housing has been low, relative to comparable economies over long periods of the UK's post-war history. Furthermore, investments in infrastructure have become increasingly important in a globalised world: a good transport infrastructure improves productivity by facilitating the movement of goods and services influencing the location decisions of business.

Investing in housing and property

Investing in housing supply   **3.121**   A responsive and flexible housing market is essential to secure the UK's future economic prosperity. Published alongside the 2005 Pre-Budget Report, *The Government's Response to Kate Barker's Review of Housing Supply* sets out a range of measures to increase housing supply and improve affordability.[25] This included a target to raise the number of new houses being built to at least 200,000 net additions a year by 2016. Substantial progress towards this target is being made with over 180,000 net additions in the year to March 2006. However, an ageing and growing population indicates that further rises in new housing supply will be required over the coming decade.

3.122   To support Local Authorities in meeting their housing targets, the Government has recently consulted on, and now plans to introduce, a new Housing and Planning Delivery Grant.[26] A new independent National Housing and Planning Advice Unit is also being established to provide expert advice to regional planning bodies, helping them to better understand the relationship between housing supply and affordability.

---

[25] *The Government's Response to Kate Barker's Review of Housing Supply,* HM Treasury and ODPM, December 2005

[26] *Housing and Planning Delivery Grant: Consultation Paper,* DCLG, July 2006

Housing infrastructure

3.123 To ensure that its ambitious plan for a step-change in housing supply is supported by the necessary investment in infrastructure, the Government's response to Kate Barker's Review of Housing Supply announced a *Policy Review into Supporting Housing Growth* to determine the social, transport and environmental infrastructure implications of housing growth, establish a framework for sustainable and cost-effective patterns of growth, and ensure that departmental resources across government are targeted appropriately to support growth (see Box 3.8).

Box 3.8: Policy Review into Supporting Housing Growth

Flourishing communities are not created by new housing alone. New housing comes with the need to provide public services, such as schools, health centres, waste disposal, public transport, green space and policing. There may also be a need for additional flood defence and transport infrastructure.

The 2007 CSR Policy Review into Supporting Housing Growth has been developing the Government's approach to address this infrastructure challenge and has been actively engaging with key stakeholders to understand the barriers to delivery and develop possible solutions.

For central government, the Review is proposing using the CSR performance management framework to ensure that housing growth is given appropriate prioritisation by key infrastructure departments, with subsequent changes to allocation systems, alongside strong ministerial governance and greater incentives for local authorities to increase housing growth. At the local and regional level, the Review is proposing changes to infrastructure planning and delivery (discussed in the Planning Gain Supplement section below), and is committed to working with stakeholders to develop suitable mechanisms for 'front funding' infrastructure at an early stage of development. Further announcements on the Review will be made as part of the 2007 CSR.

Building sustainable homes

3.124 At the 2006 Pre-Budget Report, the Government set out its ambitions for ensuring that new homes contribute to tackling climate change and are constructed to high standards of sustainability: the consultation document *Building a Greener Future* set out the Government's proposals for moving towards zero carbon in new housing.[27] This included the proposition to progressively incorporate energy efficiency standards set out in *the Code for Sustainable Homes* into future building regulations, thereby ensuring that, within a decade, all new homes will be zero carbon.[28] **Supporting this aim, today's Budget announces further details of a stamp duty exemption for zero-carbon homes.** See Chapter 7 for details.

Surplus Public Sector Land

3.125 A taskforce on Surplus Public Sector Land was established at the 2005 Pre-Budget Report as part of the Government response to the Barker Review of Housing Supply. At the 2006 Pre-Budget Report, the Chancellor raised the Government's ambition for housing delivery on surplus public land to 130,000 new homes from existing and new sites over the next decade. Delivery of this ambition will involve a strengthened commitment across central government, Local Authorities and the wider public sector.

---

[27] *Building a Greener Future – Consultation Document*, DCLG, December 2006.

[28] *Code for Sustainable Homes*, DCLG, December 2006.

Promoting Shared Equity and Shared Ownership

3.126 The Shared Equity Taskforce reported in the 2006 Pre-Budget Report that the Government now expects over 160,000 households to access home-ownership through private or public shared equity products by 2010, double the original plans.[29] One element of the Government's response to this report is to extend the reach of the Open Market HomeBuy scheme to households on lower incomes. **The Government is today launching the first stage of a new competition, inviting market providers to work with the Housing Corporation in developing affordable shared equity products for first time buyers.**

3.127 The Task Force also recognised the important role charitable Registered Social Landlords (RSLs) play in helping to deliver the Government's affordable housing agenda through shared ownership. The Government will work with charitable RSLs in ensuring that corporation tax is not a barrier to investment in affordable housing and will, if necessary and feasible, introduce legislation aimed at clarifying the tax position. Further details will be made available at Pre-Budget Report 2007.

3.128 One structure currently used to provide affordable housing is the 'shared ownership lease'. Shared ownership leases give the benefits of ownership to people who cannot afford to buy a property outright, even with the mortgage finance available to them. The Commonhold and Leasehold Reform Act 2002 introduced commonhold as a new type of property ownership. However, shared ownership leases are not feasible for commonhold. To provide the same treatment for commonhold shared ownership as is currently available to leasehold, Budget 2007 announces that the Government will legislate in this year's Finance Bill to replicate the stamp duty and land tax arrangement that is currently in place for shared ownership leases for shared ownership trusts.

Sinking funds

3.129 The Finance Act 2006 provided relief from the 40 per cent trust rate of tax on income arising from service charges and sinking funds in the social housing sector. Sinking funds are an efficient way to save money for the upkeep and repair of properties. To place the private housing sector on the same footing as the social housing sector, the Government announces that it will extend this relief to the income on service charges and sinking funds held by private sector landlords on trust.

Planning Reform and major infrastructure

3.130 The Government is committed to ensuring that the planning system delivers the housing and economic development the UK needs in a way which is sustainable and consistent with the Government's wider objectives including on climate change, the environment, energy security and improving UK competitiveness. The Chancellor and the Deputy Prime Minister asked Kate Barker at the 2005 Pre-Budget Report to conduct a review to consider how planning policy and procedures can better deliver economic growth and prosperity alongside other sustainable development goals. The final report of *Kate Barker's Review of Land Use Planning*, published in December 2006, makes clear that planning is a valued and necessary activity that can deliver positive economic outcomes, alongside important social and environmental objectives. However, it concluded that the context for the planning system is becoming ever more challenging and therefore recommends further wide-ranging reform, building on recent changes and the plan-led approach, to ensure that the planning system addresses long-term challenges, supporting sustainable economic growth in a global economy and contributing to climate change mitigation. The Government welcomed Kate Barker's report and agrees with her overall analysis.

3.131 Sir Rod Eddington's Study, published on 1 December last year, reaffirmed the importance of well-targeted investment in transport to the continued success of the UK economy in the global marketplace. The Government has endorsed Rod Eddington's strategic analysis. It is actively pursuing the major reforms to the planning, funding and delivery of transport interventions his report outlined.

---

[29] *Report of the Shared Equity Taskforce*, HM Treasury and DCLG, December 2006.

3.132   These reforms are wide-ranging. They cover strategy, processes and delivery. On strategy, this will include as an output of the 2007 CSR a policy and decision-making framework over the medium term, incorporating Eddington's strategic recommendations across the DfT objectives. On processes, it will cover appraisal, planning and resource allocation. On delivery, it will include consideration of proposals to reform planning for transport infrastructure, and taking forward Eddington's analysis of sub-national governance in the 2007 CSR.

3.133   This review is a key part of the delivery of sustained economic growth. The Government is determined to pursue its implementation quickly, and the Department for Transport has reformed its board structure to align better with Eddington's conclusions. It will report on progress in taking forward the measures, and its further consideration of the new evidence and analysis presented by the Eddington Study, in the course of this year.

3.134   Later this spring, the Government will set out in a White Paper its proposals in response to Kate Barker's recommendations for improving the speed, responsiveness and efficiency in land use planning, and for taking forward Kate Barker's and Rod Eddington's proposals for reform of major infrastructure planning.

3.135   Kate Barker's analysis shows that the planning system does not always fully consider the benefits that economic development can bring in terms of increasing employment and prosperity or ensuring transparent, certain and efficient decision making on infrastructure of national economic importance. Therefore, the White Paper will include measures, as part of a wider package of proposals to ensure that, by reflecting properly the economic, social and environmental costs and benefits, planning takes a positive approach to sustainable economic development by:

- setting out a new single system of planning for major infrastructure, with clear national policy statements which balance economic, social and environmental objectives, effective public consultation, and decisions taken by an Independent Planning Commission;

- a significant streamlining of national planning policy, including a new framework for positive planning for economic development, and a more explicit role for market signals to inform plans and planning decisions; and

- a substantial improvement in the process for obtaining planning permission for all users with clearer and simpler processes and quicker handling of appeals cases, backed by a more efficient plan-making process.

Business aspects   **3.136**   The report of Sir Michael Lyons' Inquiry into Local Government Finance is published
of the Lyons   alongside this Budget. The Inquiry's recommendations on personal taxes and broader local
Inquiry   government finance are discussed in Chapter 6. However, Sir Michael argues that the role of local government should not just be defined in relation to public services, but also local economic prosperity and investment.

3.137   The Inquiry considered the structure and incentives in the local system of business rates, and concludes that the current link between the Retail Price Index and yield from business rates should be retained. The Inquiry also considered the case for returning business rates to local control. Its analysis is that this would not be appropriate at this time. The Government agrees that the current structure of business rates provides certainty for business and therefore promotes investment, and so is not proposing changes to the RPI cap and the national system of business rates.

3.138 In order to promote the role of Local Authorities in boosting economic growth and to create communities with sustainable environments for business growth, the Inquiry proposes local supplements on business rates. The Government believes that a local supplement has the potential to support local economic development, but would need to be subject to credible accountability to rate payers and real protection for any businesses – particularly SMEs – that might be disproportionately affected. The Government will give consideration to what the best options may be, working closely with business, local government and other stakeholders.

3.139 The Inquiry also examined options for development of specific taxes or charges on tourism as a means of financing investment in local communities with significant visitor populations. It concluded that a robust evidence base has not been developed to support the introduction of such taxes. The Government therefore does not intend to introduce a tourist tax.

Modernising empty property relief **3.140** The system of business rates includes a number of reliefs and exemptions. The Inquiry recommends that some of these should be reformed. In response to these recommendations and those of the Barker Review of Land Use Planning, as described above, **the Government today announces its intention to modernise empty property relief from business rates.** These reforms will reduce the duration of the existing empty property relief to three months for all properties and six months for industrial and warehouse properties. These reforms will reduce the current distinction between different types of property. The duration of empty property relief (EPR) will be limited to three months for all property when they first fall empty with a further three months for industrial and warehouse properties only. Complete exemptions from rates will be awarded to empty properties held by charities.

3.141 This will enhance the supply of commercial property, reducing rents and improving access for new and existing firms. Downward pressure on rents will have significant benefits for UK business and wider UK competitiveness with particular benefits for new starters, and companies investing in additional property, in addition to all companies – especially SMEs – who rent their premises. The Government will consult on the various additional exemptions that are currently offered. This measure will also enhance the supply of brownfield sites for redevelopment, helping to meet the Government's commitment to use brownfield land for new housing and commercial property developments wherever possible.

3.142 The Inquiry recommends that the other relief and exemptions in business rates be subject to review. The Government accepts this recommendation, with the exception of the relief for charities, which will remain in its current form. The Department for Communities and Local Government will consider the merits of extending rates to include derelict and vacant previously developed land, and assess other reliefs and exemptions in business rates.

Land remediation relief reform **3.143** This Budget launches a consultation on brownfield land tax incentives. The Government is considering reform of land remediation relief and the landfill tax exemption for waste from contaminated land. The consultation seeks to improve the efficiency of land remediation relief and proposes extending it to long-term derelict land, allowing expenditure on Japanese Knotweed to qualify, and improving its development focus. It also invites comments on timing issues and asks whether relief for cleaning up contaminated land is more efficiently given through land remediation relief than the landfill tax exemption for waste from contaminated land.

3.144   The Government aims to respond to the consultation by the end of 2007. Any changes in legislation will take place no earlier than 2008. The Government intends that overall support for remediation of hard to remediate sites through the tax system should not be less after reform than it is at present. The reformed reliefs will support the Government's wider objectives for redeveloping vacant and derelict previously developed land on which a separate consultation will be conducted.

Onerous leases   **3.145**   To further encourage efficient use of commercial land and property, the Government will also consult during the course of the year on the tax treatment of onerous leases.

Business   **3.146**   Budget 2007 announces that the Business Premises Renovation Allowance will be
premises   introduced for expenditure incurred on the renovation of businesses premises on or after 11
renovation   April 2007. The original proposals will be modified by secondary legislation to meet EU state
allowance   aid rules, and will apply in Assisted Areas, excluding certain sensitive industries. It will provide 100 per cent capital allowances for the capital costs of bringing empty business properties back into use in Assisted Areas. The Government will consider whether it may be possible to reduce restrictions in the scheme in a manner compatible with EU law.

Progress on the Planning-gain Supplement

Planning gain   **3.147**   The Planning-gain Supplement (PGS) is a proposed levy on the value uplift accruing
Supplement   to land granted planning permission. Kate Barker originally recommended the introduction of PGS, alongside a scaled-back system of planning obligations, in her 2004 Review of Housing Supply as a means of generating resources to finance local infrastructure.[30] The Government has discussed these proposals widely with stakeholders across the UK and twice consulted formally, including detailed consultations on valuations, the payment process, and changes to planning obligations which closed on 28 February 2007. The Government is now considering the responses to these consultations carefully, alongside levels of the need for infrastructure investment and the range of mechanisms for delivering this. If after further consideration it continues to be deemed workable and effective, PGS would be introduced no earlier than 2009.

3.148   Alongside planning reforms and other tax measures described in this chapter, PGS aims to support growth and the efficient supply of land. PGS would be levied at a modest rate to ensure that incentives to develop land are preserved. Budget 2007 makes further proposals on the allocation of PGS revenues in England as part of a package of reforms aimed at improving the planning and delivery of infrastructure to support growth.

Local revenue   **3.149**   At the 2006 Pre-Budget Report, the Government committed to returning at least 70
allocation   per cent of PGS revenues to the local authority area from where the revenues derived, to ensure that developers see local benefit from the PGS contribution they have made. The Government now proposes that, to lock in this local benefit, the local share of PGS would be paid directly to the Local Planning Authority (LPA) that granted the planning permission to which the PGS liability is attached. Payments would be made on a regular basis to ensure that Local Authorities could deploy PGS receipts in a timely way to support infrastructure delivery. The Government will consider whether special arrangements should be made where there exists a special purpose vehicle with planning powers (such as an Urban Development Corporation) and for consents granted by county authorities.

3.150   The Government proposes that the LPA would manage the local share of PGS revenues. Working with local businesses, communities and other public sector bodies, they would be expected to use PGS resources, in combination with other funding streams, to

---

[30] *Review of Housing Supply: Delivery Stability: Securing our Future Housing Needs*, HM Treasury, March 2004.

secure delivery of infrastructure in pursuit of the objectives identified in their statutory Local Development Framework (LDF). Through their participation in local housing market partnerships, and through consultation on the LDF, developers and other local businesses will have a voice in infrastructure planning in their areas. The Government will also explore ways of ensuring robust joined working in two-tier areas and pooling of PGS revenues across local boundaries.

Regional revenue allocation 3.151   The remaining share of all PGS revenues raised in a region would be returned to that region. Regions would have access to a fund for spending in support of regional infrastructure priorities in pursuit of the objectives identified in Regional Spatial Strategies (RSSs). This would enable regional PGS revenues to be spent on infrastructure projects or areas of the region where additional resources, particularly transport, are most needed. *The Eddington Transport Study* and the work of the 2007 CSR Review into Supporting Housing Growth (see Box 3.8) have both identified the central importance of transport for growth.[31] The expectation is therefore that transport will be the focus of regional PGS spending in the short term.

London 3.152   The Government proposes that either the Mayor of London, or one of his functional bodies, would directly receive the regional share of PGS revenues for infrastructure to deliver the objectives identified in the London Plan. As in other regions, the expectation is that transport will be the focus of spending in the short term.

Planning and delivering infrastructure 3.153   The Government's commitments on PGS revenue allocation form part of a wider package of investment and reform being taken forward as part of the 2007 CSR Policy Review into Supporting Housing Growth (see Box 3.8). To build on existing good practice and to promote a more systematic approach to infrastructure planning and delivery, the Review proposes that:

- LPAs should be required to undertake sound infrastructure planning as part of the formation and review of their LDFs, maximising the use of existing infrastructure and deploying demand management options before setting out plans for new infrastructure. The Government will encourage local areas to use Annual Monitoring Reports to review plans and manage infrastructure delivery;

- key stakeholders, such as local developers, public sector infrastructure providers, utility companies, Local Strategic Partnerships (LSPs) and local communities should be involved in the infrastructure planning process; and

- in deciding whether to approve LDFs, the Planning Inspectorate should consider the soundness of infrastructure planning, taking into account the resources likely to be available to implement the plan (which should include PGS revenues were PGS to be introduced).

3.154   Once areas have developed robust infrastructure plans, strong governance needs to be in place to ensure effective delivery of the plans. As such, the Review proposes that:

- LPAs (and where appropriate Local Delivery Vehicles) should have lead responsibility for coordinating and driving forward infrastructure delivery, working in partnership with LSPs, local developers and key infrastructure providers;

---

[31] *The Eddington Transport Study*, HM Treasury, December 2006.

- where unlocking housing growth is reflected as an improvement priority outcome in the Local Area Agreement (LAA), the effective and timely provision of infrastructure to support housing growth should be assessed as part of the LAA performance management system; and

- the Government seeks to develop guidance setting out the components of good infrastructure planning, working in consultation with stakeholders.

Planning obligations 3.155   Alongside the introduction of PGS, the Government has proposed to scale back the current planning obligations regime in England to matters relevant to the environment of the development-site itself and affordable housing. In its recent consultation, *Changes to Planning Obligations*, the Government consulted further on its approach, including proposals for a criteria-based test to reduce the scope of matters subject to planning obligations.[32] In considering options for reform of the planning obligations regime, the Government is examining carefully the views of respondents to the consultation, including on how best to achieve clarity in the criteria-based approach.

Protecting the haulage industry

Protecting the haulage industry 3.156   Following the successful co-operation with the haulage industry through the Haulage Industry Task Group, the 2006 Pre-Budget-Report announced that Government would undertake a feasibility study into options for delivering a database of foreign vehicles, including through a "vignette". The Department for Transport will engage with the haulage industry, enforcement agencies and ferry operators through a stakeholder-working group. The feasibility study is expected to report final conclusions in time for the 2007 Pre-Budget Report.

3.157   It is important to protect the competitiveness of legitimate hauliers by maximising the likelihood that non-compliant vehicles are identified and stopped. **The Government is therefore announcing today that it will triple the amount that is currently spent on the South East International Traffic pilot in order to improve further the targetted enforcement achieved by rolling out the combined use of intelligence and technology to target those who compete unfairly and threaten the safety of other road users.** At least 50,000 such targeted checks of vehicles on international journeys are planned for 2007-08. The Government welcomes the contributions the haulage industry has made to enhance the enforcement and will continue to discuss developments with the representative industry bodies.

The UK as a competitive centre for global investment

UK Trade and Investment 3.158   The strategy for marketing the UK economy internationally, as set out in *Globalisation and the UK: strength and opportunity to meet the economic challenge*, published on 2 December 2005 and *Prosperity in a Changing World* published in July 2006, forms an important part of the UK's response to Globalisation. The strategy outline the steps that the Government will take to achieve a step change in its efforts to attract high quality inward investment and promote UK businesses.

UKTI skills response 3.159   UK Trade and Investment (UKTI) are responsible for coordinating and driving the strategy. A key theme of the strategy is being responsive to potential investors needs. Many investment decisions are dependent on the availability of skilled labour in the host country. That is why, as part of their services, UKTI will now deliver a rapid response framework for skills to ensure the UK has the skills profile it needs to attract foreign investment and new jobs.

---

[32] *Changes to Planning Obligations: a Planning-gain Supplement Consultation*, Communities and Local Government, December 2006.

3.160   To help harness existing talent in the UK and fill specific short-term skills gaps, UKTI will broker links between investors, RDAs and universities to set up courses to deliver targeted, high level skills, as well as assisting firms to access recent graduates. To complement this new approach, UKTI will also assist firms to supplement the UK skills mix with expertise from abroad. Where skills are not immediately available in the UK, and while UK talent is being trained through training placements and new training programmes, UKTI will assist firms to navigate the current points-based migration system and provide advice for employees and their families. This will enable firms to bring essential highly skilled employees to fill the short-term need without which the investment would not take place.

UKTI Services for **3.161**   UKTI also provides a range of more general services, on issues wider than skills
companies availability. Each investor's needs are different, so within this broad package of services UKTI
locating in UK will tailor its approach to the individual case. This Budget announces the general prospectus of services UKTI will provide to companies locating in the UK: UKTI will provide a single dedicated client manager and team for targeted firms who will oversee UKTI's relationship with a potential investor from initial approach to aftercare once they have located in the UK. UKTI will also provide basic information to firms in all areas necessary to setting up a business in the UK.

3.162   In order that both Government policy and UKTI's services keep pace with the changing global business climate, UKTI will submit an annual "State of Investment" report to DTI and HMT. It will be based on detailed surveying of all the firms they approach. UKTI will also benchmark themselves against leading competitors to drive up their standard of service.

UKTI sectors **3.163**   UKTI are making progress on a number of other fronts including leading the
strategy development and implementation of five international marketing strategies for sectors vital to the UK's future global competitive position. The Financial Services strategy, agreed by the Chancellor and the high-level industry group in October 2006, is now being delivered. A similar approach is being taken for four other sectors: Creative Industries, Life Sciences, Information & Communication Technologies, and Energy strategies will be produced during 2007 that bring together industry, stakeholders and relevant government departments to identify core UK strengths, prioritise overseas opportunities, coordinate activity and target resources. These will be built on solid propositions to market the UK as the springboard for global growth – both for overseas companies to invest in the UK, and for UK companies to penetrate overseas markets.

UKTI R&D **3.164**   Over the coming months UKTI will be working with other government departments
strategy to implement a new R&D programme to attract and support high value-added R&D investment into the UK. The programme will target the world's leading high-tech companies and is an important part of the wider UKTI-led strategy on marketing the UK more effectively abroad, launched last year.

International **3.165**   In March 2006, the Chancellor established the International Business Advisory
Business Council (IBAC). The role of the IBAC is to advise the Government on how the UK can rise to
Advisory Council the challenge of globalisation, promote itself as one of the key locations of choice for international business investment in high value-added activity, and work with international partners to pursue a less protectionist world. Its inaugural meeting took place on 17 November 2006. The Government also hosted a Business Advisory Summit in November 2006 with over seventy Chairs and CEOs from many leading UK companies. The Government strongly welcomes this engagement with business on the challenges of globalisation, particularly in the areas of trade, economic flexibility and education. Looking forward, the IBAC is expected to meet formally once a year to discuss the challenges that the UK faces in a globalised economy

Financial services   **3.166**   Supporting and promoting London, and the UK, as a centre for financial and business services remains a priority for the Government. London is the world's most competitive financial centre and is in a strong position to benefit from opportunities presented by continuing global economic growth and integration.

3.167   In March 2006 the Chancellor established the High-Level Group, bringing together senior representatives from across the financial services sector, to develop a strategy to enhance the UK and the City of London's international competitiveness. The High Level Group, chaired by the Chancellor of the Exchequer, had its inaugural meeting in October 2006 and will next meet in May. The Government is taking forward substantive proposals in a number of key areas, as set out in Box 3.9.

Box 3.9: High-Level Group on the City of London's international competitiveness

Following the first meeting of the High-Level Group on 18 October 2006 the Government agreed to take forward proposals to:

- maintain cutting edge, principle based regulation – the Government is examining, with the Financial Services Authority, whether the regulatory regime might be lightened for those services with lower consumer detriment or systemic risk. In order to help protect our risk-based regulatory system the Government introduced the Investment Exchanges and Clearing Houses Act 2006. This legislation will help protect the well-regulated but proportionate environment for listing and trading securities in the UK;

- modernise the wholesale insurance market – a review group, led by Lord Levene, has been considering the modernisation of London's wholesale insurance and reinsurance markets. The Group's initial report is expected shortly. The Treasury is, in parallel, conducting an analysis of the business environment for wholesale insurance;

- boost professional financial skills. Lord Currie is chairing a working group to develop the proposal for an international centre for financial regulation in the UK. The Government will make a financial contribution towards the start-up costs for the centre for three financial years. The Working Group is scheduled to report on the detailed framework for the centre in May. In addition to this the Financial Services Skills Council will also publish their assessment of the skills needed to maintain future competitiveness of the sector; and

- promote, in a co-ordinated strategy led by UKTI, the UK based financial sector in high growth overseas markets. This work includes developing country specific strategies for China and India that will be finalised by May. As part of this ongoing work, the Chancellor and the Secretary of State for Industry visited India earlier this year.

On 20 February 2007 the Economic Secretary to the Treasury chaired an informal meeting of the High-Level Group, with EU Commissioners McCreevy and Kroes in attendance, to discuss the future policy direction for financial services in Europe. A further informal meeting, chaired by the Economic Secretary to the Treasury, will take place on 19 April with the focus on principle-based regulation.

In addition to this, work continues on a number of broader issues affecting the financial and business services sector, including migration and infrastructure. The Chancellor is scheduled to chair the next meeting of the full High-Level Group on 9 May, where progress on these issues will be reviewed and the Secretary of State for Scotland will lead a discussion on the contribution of the Scottish Financial Services Sector.

3.168   Ensuring that the tax system continues to support business competitiveness is vital to support the further development of an innovative and fast moving financial sector. With this in mind, the Government keeps the corporate tax system and other taxes related to financial services under review. For example the Government is continuing to work in partnership with the Investment Management Association to consider issues raised by the recent KPMG report on *Taxation and the Competitiveness of UK Funds*. The Economic Secretary is due to report the findings of this working group to the next meeting of the High Level Group in May.

3.169   In Budget 2007, London's current pre-eminence as a leading financial centre will be further strengthened by measures announced to reduce the main rate of corporation tax from 30 per cent to 28 per cent in 2008-09, a rate that compares favourably internationally, and particularly with other G7 countries. Chapter 5 provides more information on tax measures.

4 INCREASING EMPLOYMENT OPPORTUNITY FOR ALL

> The Government's long-term goal is employment opportunity for all - the modern definition of full employment. Delivering this requires that everyone should be provided with the support they need to find, retain and progress in work, and adapt to and benefit from a global labour market. This chapter describes the principles which underpin the Government's welfare reform agenda, and the further steps it is taking towards its aim of employment opportunity for all, including:
>
> - **to provide further help to lone parents to stay in employment, by continuing to make In-Work Credit available to eligible lone parents in the current pilot areas until June 2008, benefiting over 250,000 lone parents, and offering a higher rate of £60 across the whole of London;**
>
> - **introducing a four-week run-on in entitlement to Working Tax Credit** from the day that a previously eligible claimant ceases to work 16 hours;
>
> - **testing reforms to the education and training offered to participants on New Deal for young people,** and testing a seamless link from New Deal to in-work training delivered through Train to Gain;
>
> - **announcing local employment partnerships with large retail employers working in partnership with Jobcentre Plus** at a local level, to help the long-term unemployed and economically inactive back to work;
>
> - **trialling short, work-focused approaches for English as a second or other language (ESOL)** courses in the London Cities Strategy pathfinders for parents on benefits or tax credits;
>
> - **further improve the administration of Housing Benefit, and setting out an intention to reform Housing Benefit subsidy for temporary accommodation;**
>
> - **introducing a package of measures to align further and simplify the benefits system; and**
>
> - following the Low Pay Commission recommendations, **raising the adult rate of the National Minimum Wage to £5.52 per hour,** the youth rate, for workers aged between 18 to 21, to £4.60 and the development rate, for 16 and 17- year olds to £3.40; all from October 2007.

4.1 The Government's long-term goal is employment opportunity for all – the modern definition of full employment. The strong labour market performance of recent years has helped deliver this, with many of the previously most disadvantaged groups and regions demonstrating the most significant improvements.

Labour market performance **4.2** Employment in the UK reached 29 million in 2006 for the first time; the highest figure since comparable records began in 1971. As Chart 4.1 shows, the working age employment rate is now 74.4 per cent, up from 72.7 per cent in 1997. The International Labour Organisation (ILO) unemployment rate, meanwhile, is 5.5 per cent, down from 7.2 per cent in 1997. The temporary rise in the unemployment rate during 2006 has abated, with the broader ILO measure falling in the final quarter of the year. The UK unemployment rate remains significantly below the EU average of 7.5 per cent.

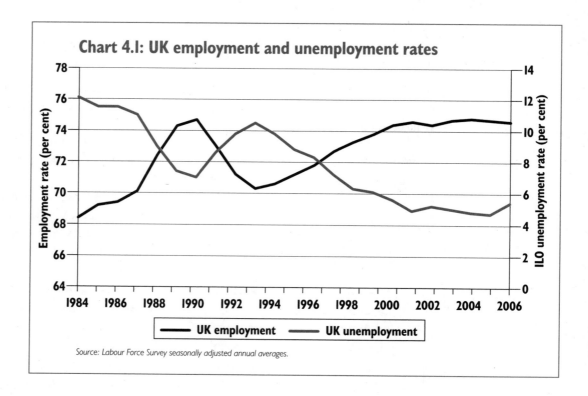

Chart 4.I: UK employment and unemployment rates

Source: Labour Force Survey seasonally adjusted annual averages.

4.3   The improvements in labour market performance have been of particular benefit to groups traditionally disadvantaged in the labour market. Since 1997, the employment rate of lone parents has risen by 11.8 percentage points;[1] of working age people aged over 50, by 6.4 percentage points; and of people with a health condition or disability, by 9.8 percentage points.[2] Since 2001, the employment rate of ethnic minority groups has also risen by 2.5 percentage points and is now over 60 per cent.

Inactivity   **4.4**   Labour supply growth in 2006 was the strongest in over 20 years due to strong working age population growth and declining inactivity, especially among people with a health condition or disability. The working age inactivity rate decreased by 0.3 percentage points over the year to January 2007, with 71,000 people moving out of inactivity and into the labour market.

Working age   **4.5**   For the majority of jobseekers, unemployment is a short-term state of transition;
benefits   around 80 per cent move off benefit within 6 months. Jobseeker's Allowance (JSA) is designed to provide financial support in a way that encourages a quick return to work through independent jobsearch. The intervention regime supports, monitors and enforces independent jobsearch for short-term claimants, and provides more intensive support for the minority who fail to find work quickly. The regime has directly contributed to a fall in the claimant count from 1,662,600 in 1997 to 922,200 in February 2007. As Chart 4.2 shows, the rise in the claimant count through 2006 has begun to reverse, and the total has held under 1 million for 73 consecutive months – the longest period below this level since the 1970s.

---

[1] Under Eurostat regulations the Labour Force Survey has changed from being based on seasonal quarters to calendar quarters. Some figures have therefore changed from those published in Pre-Budget Report 2006 (see Chart 4.5 for details).
[2] Change is since 1998 for figures for people with a health condition or disability, as the figures for 1997 are not comparable due to changes in definitions.

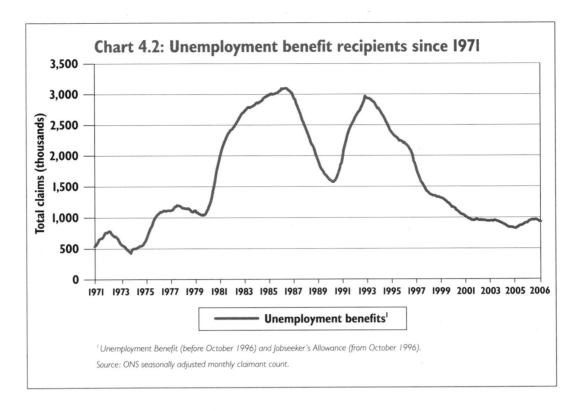

Chart 4.2: Unemployment benefit recipients since 1971

[1] *Unemployment Benefit (before October 1996) and Jobseeker's Allowance (from October 1996).*

Source: ONS seasonally adjusted monthly claimant count.

DELIVERING EMPLOYMENT OPPORTUNITIES FOR ALL

The challenge for the next decade

Key principles of welfare reform **4.6**   The challenge now is to build on the successes of the past decade with further steps to deliver employment opportunity for all. The integration of benefits and employment support through Jobcentre Plus has transformed the delivery of welfare to work. This now needs to be complemented by an integrated employment and skills agenda and even more effective active labour market programmes, ensuring that everyone has the opportunity to find and progress in work.

4.7   The Government's approach to ongoing welfare reform is based on five key principles. Informed by the development of active labour market policy over the past decade, these principles will underpin further reforms over the coming years, and are described in more detail in Box 4.1.

Box 4.1 Principles of welfare reform

In taking forward its welfare reform agenda, the Government has set itself two ambitious and inter-related goals:

- to ensure **employment opportunity for all**, giving everyone the opportunity to fulfil their individual, social and economic potential. Achieving this requires effective labour market policies set against a background of macroeconomic stability; and

- to foster a **world class skills base**, equipping everyone with the means to find, retain and progress in work, and the ability to adapt to and benefit from a globalising labour market. Integrating the employment and skills agendas is central to achieving this.

While substantial progress has already been made in the direction of these goals, much more remains to be done. Informed by the successful active labour market policies of the past decade, the Government's approach to labour market reform over the coming years will be underpinned by five key principles:

- **rights and responsibilities** underpin the welfare reform agenda. Everyone should have the opportunity to work; and for this to be effective, it needs to be supported by access to appropriate training, information and advice, by action to prevent or remedy discrimination, and by measures to make work pay, including a minimum wage. These responsibilities on the part of the Government are matched by the responsibility of individuals, where possible, to prepare for, look for and engage in work;

- employment support should be focused not just on **job entry, but also on retention and progression**. Helping people into work is clearly central to the welfare reform agenda. This does not, however, preclude a focus also on helping people – particularly those at a disadvantage in the labour market – remain and advance in work, through advice, incentives and training opportunities;

- the system should be sufficiently flexible as to allow, where appropriate, a **personalised and responsive** approach. The New Deals have achieved considerable success by tailoring policy to particular groups. Where possible, policy should be tailored to individual needs and integrated with skills, health and financial support;

- delivery should be **joined up**, making best use of expertise across the public, private and third sectors. The resources of each should be focused on where they can add the greatest value, in the context of a clear strategy and set of required outcomes; and

- regions, cities and localities can play an important role in identifying strategic priorities and delivering solutions, and this should be recognised, where appropriate, through **devolution and local empowerment**.

Integrating benefits and employment support

Jobcentre Plus: transforming customer service   4.8   The delivery of employment support and benefits services has, over the past five years, been transformed by the operations of Jobcentre Plus, the introduction of which marked a key stage in transforming a previously too often passive welfare state into a pro-active, personalised and work-focused service. Jobcentre Plus was launched in April 2002, bringing together the Employment Service and those parts of the Benefits Agency that delivered services to people of working age; a very visible manifestation of the integrated rights and responsibilities agenda that underpins the Government's approach to welfare reform. By facilitating more effective delivery and improved customer service, Jobcentre Plus has made a substantial contribution to tackling poverty, reducing worklessness, and promoting growth and opportunity.

4.9   The roll out of the new Jobcentre Plus network is now almost complete with over 850 of 865 sites rolled out. The process of modernising Jobcentre Plus processes and operations is, however, continuing. The Agency's organisation has been redesigned to focus resources on customer facing services. Jobcentre Plus is also boosting the capacity of its contact centres and investing in a new network of Benefit Delivery Centres to streamline the delivery of its services.

Integrating the employment and skills agenda

Implementing the Leitch agenda

4.10   In a global economy, skills become increasingly important in enabling people to adapt to and benefit from change, providing individuals with the flexibility that delivers genuine economic security. As the Leitch Review of Skills, *Prosperity for all in the global economy – world class skills,* published on 5 December 2006, recommended, support should not necessarily be confined to helping someone into work, but should also, where appropriate, extend to helping that person stay in and progress in work.

4.11   This requires both Jobcentre Plus and the Learning and Skills Council to work together on longer term support and retention and advancement – delivering a seamless service that enables low-skilled individuals to get the skills they need to build a career. The Government will consider the incentives given to both organisations to ensure that there is a sufficient focus on retention and progression. The Government will also take steps to improve the vertical and horizontal coordination across government and between government, business and the private and third sector to help the low-skilled enter, remain in and advance in the labour market, including the establishment of the Commission for Employment and Skills. (Chapter 3 sets out the plans for the Government's response to the Leitch Review's recommendations).

Building on the success of the New Deal

Strengthening the New Deal

4.12   The New Deal has been fundamental to the success of the Government's labour market policies. It provides support from Personal Advisers, followed by – for JSA claimants – mandatory full time training or subsidised employment to ensure that no claimant remains indefinitely and passively on benefit. Over the last decade, the New Deal has found 1.9 million jobs for participants, including 858,000 for young people and 298,000 for unemployed adults. This success has contributed to a nearly two-thirds reduction in the long-term claimant count since 1997, as Chart 4.3 illustrates.

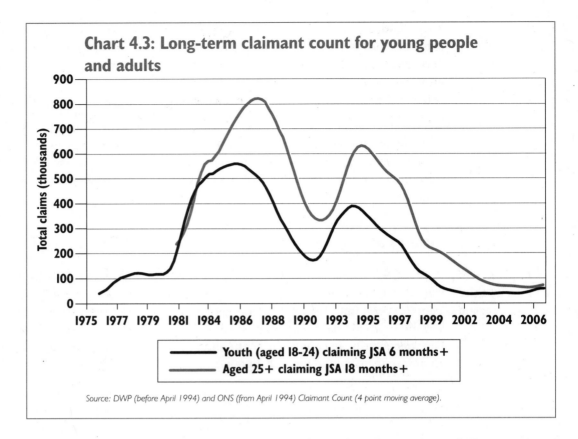

Chart 4.3: Long-term claimant count for young people and adults

Source: DWP (before April 1994) and ONS (from April 1994) Claimant Count (4 point moving average).

4.13   Independent evaluations have repeatedly highlighted the New Deal's success and cost effectiveness. The National Institute of Economic and Social Research (NIESR) concluded in 2000[3] that the level of long-term unemployment would have been twice as high without the New Deal for young people (NDYP), and that the economy as a whole was richer by £500 million as a result of NDYP. More recent studies show that: NDYP has significantly increased exit rates from unemployment in all regions;[4] overall youth unemployment has been reduced by between 30,000 and 40,000;[5] young men are now 20 per cent more likely to find work as a result of NDYP;[6,7] and the social benefits of NDYP outweigh the costs.[8]

4.14   As the labour market evolves over the next decade, with globalisation, and the increasing use of technology shifting labour demand further towards the higher skilled, the New Deal will also need to evolve to respond to the changing needs of the unemployed. The challenge for the New Deal is to ensure that those without the basic level of skills needed to compete in the labour market, can access the training they need. Any young person who fails to find work in the early stages of the New Deal 'Gateway'[9] should have the opportunity to build up his or her skills in a workplace environment. This should be done in a way that both increases the number of people moving into employment, and improves their prospects of staying and progressing in work.

---

[3] *The New Deal for Young People: implication for employment and the public finances*, NIESR, December 2000.

[4] *How well has the New Deal for Young People worked in the UK?* McVicar and Podivinsky, Northern Ireland Economic Research Centre, April 2003.

[5] *New Deal for young people: evaluation of unemployment flows*. D.Wilkinson, Policy Studies Institute, 2003

[6] *Evaluating the employment impact of a mandatory search program*, R. Blundell, M. Costa Dias, C. Meghir, J. Van Reenan, in Journal of the European Economic Association, June 2004.

[7] Active labour market policies and the British New Deal for unemployed youth in context, J.Van Reenan, in *Seeking a premier league economy*, R. Blundell, D.Card, R. Freeman, (eds) University of Chicago Press, June 2004.

[8] ibid

[9] The first stage of the New Deal for young people.

4.15   One way of improving the New Deal's performance is to examine and focus on its most successful elements. 'Subsidised Employment' is by far the most successful New Deal option. Participation in this option has, however, been declining over recent years, while that of a less effective option – Full Time Education and Training (FTET) – has been rising. The Government will therefore test changes to NDYP that will improve performance of the education and training offered through the New Deal, and increase the proportion taking up more successful options. The Government will therefore test the impact of:

- restricting the choice of options for those who already have the basic level of skills needed to compete in the labour market; and

- enabling low-skilled NDYP participants to return to mainstream education and training leading towards a first level 2 qualification, ending the separate FTET provision procured by Jobcentre Plus.

4.16   Running alongside these changes to New Deal itself, it is important to make sure that New Deal participants are able to access appropriate support once they move into work. The ease with which New Deal participants can enter Train to Gain is a key element in ensuring that the New Deal is not simply a gateway into a job, but a gateway into both work and training. The Government will therefore develop and test measures to ensure that New Deal advisors and Train to Gain brokers together provide a seamless link from New Deal to in-work training.

Working in partnership

Local employment partnerships   **4.17**   Effective design and operation of the New Deal needs real engagement from employers, to ensure that the support delivered provides the long-term unemployed and the economically inactive with the preparation and training that enables them to meet employers' expectations and requirements. Partnership working between Jobcentre Plus and employers at a local level is critical to making this happen.

4.18   A number of large retail employers have agreed to work in partnership with Jobcentre Plus at a local level, to help the long-term unemployed and economically inactive back to work. The signatory employers will encourage their managers to enter into a Local Employment Partnership with Jobcentre Plus. This Partnership agreement incorporates steps which employers will take to help Jobcentre Plus in supporting benefit claimants into work. These measures will include one or more of:

- offering two to four week work trials to a number of local benefit claimants;

- increasing the number of subsidised employment places available to New Deal participants;

- helping Jobcentre Plus and partners design pre-employment training programmes that meet employers' needs, and agreeing in turn to guarantee interviews or jobs to local benefit claimants who complete this training;

- encouraging their employees to volunteer to provide mentoring for long-term benefit claimants, to help prepare them for work; and

- review their application processes to ensure that local benefit claimants are not inadvertently excluded by, for example, requirements for qualifications or overly complicated procedures.

Benefiting from private and third sector expertise

4.19   Private sector and third sector organisations can bring a distinctive approach to service delivery based on their specialist knowledge, experience and skills. Jobcentre Plus already contracts out a significant proportion of its labour market provision, both in delivering mainstream programmes and in testing out different models of delivery; around a third of Jobcentre Plus expenditure is directed towards contracted-out provision.

4.20   Since 2000, the Government has been systematically testing the impact of opening up the design and delivery of labour market support to competition. Thirteen Employment Zones have been providing support to unemployed adults, to young people who have already been through the New Deal, and to lone parents. These sectors have also made a key contribution to the delivery of the New Deal for disabled people, Action Teams and Working Neighbourhood pilots.

4.21   Broadening the role of the private and third sectors in the provision of employment support opens up new opportunities, allowing Jobcentre Plus to target its own resources where these have the highest value added. For example, David Freud's report[9] to the Department for Work and Pensions (DWP) proposed greater private and third sector involvement in service delivery, using outcome-based contracts.

Flexibility and regional performance

4.22   Delivery of welfare to work support through Jobcentre Plus needs to combine a standard and appropriate level of service for everyone, with sufficient flexibility to enable local managers and front line staff to direct support where it is most needed. Effective delivery needs also to take account of the different needs and opportunities in local and regional labour markets, including making best use of local delivery partners' resources in delivering the more holistic, intensive support necessary to help the most disadvantaged claimants into work.

Labour market flexibility

4.23   Flexibility describes the capacity of individuals, firms and markets to respond to economic change efficiently and quickly. Labour market flexibility is central to the performance of the UK economy; a more flexible and efficient labour market has the ability to adapt more rapidly, allowing shocks to be accommodated and their costs in terms of lost output and jobs, minimised. The Government's labour market policies ensure that flexibility goes hand in hand with fairness, providing security and support so that people can cope with change. The progress the Government has made in promoting labour market flexibility and helping achieve economic stability is outlined throughout this chapter.

Regional performance and London

4.24   The benefits of improved labour market performance have been spread widely across the country. In every region, as Chart 4.4 shows, employment rates today are higher than in 1997. As Chart 4.4 also demonstrates, the employment rate in London is below that of all other UK regions and has shown the least improvement since 1997. The reasons for this are considered in *Employment opportunity for all: tackling worklessness in London,* published today and summarised in Box 4.2 below.

---

[9] *Reducing dependency, increasing opportunity; options for the future of welfare to work. An independent report to the Department for Work and Pensions, David Freud. 5 March 2007.*

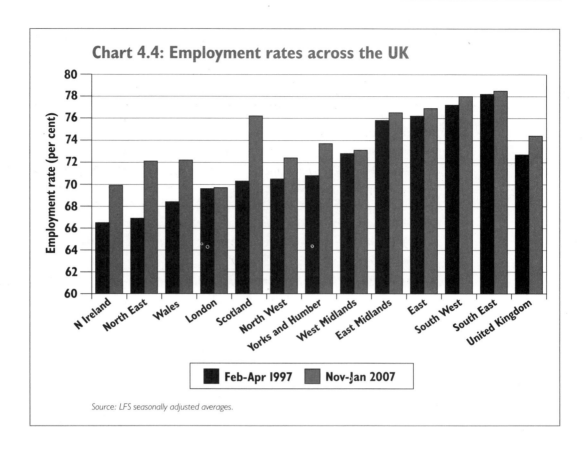

Chart 4.4: Employment rates across the UK

Source: LFS seasonally adjusted averages.

Box 4.2 Employment opportunity for all: tackling worklessness in London

There has been strong growth in the number of jobs and in the level of employment in London since 1997. However, at just under 70 per cent, London's employment rate is lower than both the national rate and that of every other UK country and region, and child poverty rates are higher than other regions (on an after housing costs measure). Many Londoners are not sharing the gains generated by the capital's economic strength.

Economic growth provides the essential foundation to address poverty and worklessness. The challenge for government at all levels – national, city and local, working with relevant partners – is to combine this economic strength with greater economic inclusiveness. To this end, *Employment opportunity for all: tackling worklessness in London,* published today sets out to inform the analysis of the issues and help in developing a consensus around the necessary steps towards meeting it.

The issues identified by the report are that a relatively large share of London's population is disadvantaged in the labour market by their individual circumstances; that there is strong competition for lower-skilled jobs in London's labour market, which reduces employment chances both for low skilled people in general, but also for young people and mothers; and that parental employment rates in London are low underpinning relatively high rates of child poverty in the capital.

The document makes recommendations as to the areas where future policy should be directed to meet these challenges:

- first, the **labour market**: there should be an explicit focus on policies to relieve the congestion in London's low-skilled labour market that reduces the employment chances of many Londoners.

- second, **employment programmes**: a more strategic London-wide approach to identifying the most appropriate solutions to the capital's problems is required, alongside sufficient operational flexibility at the appropriate levels to implement these approaches effectively but systematically; and

- third, **parents**: in line with the findings of the Harker Report,[a] policies should have a clearer focus on the employment needs of parents in London, including efforts to improve further the functioning of the childcare market.

Local autonomy is important to allow the flexibility to address area specific problems. A strategic London-wide approach, bringing together all levels of government and other partners, is important to coordinate policy in line with the recommendations in the document. The institutional arrangements that would be best suited to implementing these changes should now be considered.

---

[a] *Delivering on Child Poverty: What would it take?* Lisa Harker, November 2006.

Cities Strategy   **4.25**   As *Employment opportunity for all: tackling worklessness in London* shows, many cities have lower employment rates than their surrounding regions. Addressing the localised pockets of worklessness found in many cities requires strategic coordination and joined up working across a range of agencies and employers. Under DWP's Cities Strategy, local partners (including local authorities, private businesses, third sector organisations, Jobcentre Plus, and the Learning and Skills Council) have formed consortia in 15 cities or city regions. These consortia are pooling funding streams and rationalising and joining up services, and together control over £42m with which to commission services tailored to meet local needs. They are working with Jobcentre Plus to ensure best use is made of the flexibilities available to Personal Advisers to provide tailored support to individuals.

4.26   Cities Strategy consortia will focus on disadvantaged groups such as lone parents and incapacity benefit claimants. For those with the greatest barriers to work, such as people with drug or alcohol dependency, closer working between the key partners can be even more important, and the experience of the Cities Strategy will provide important information on how this can be achieved.

4.27   Individuals should be able to receive a personalised service that meets their specific needs, but which operates to high quality standards and is joined up across the public sector. Where appropriate, this may entail pooled funding streams to deliver services that cross traditional organisational boundaries, such as employment, skills and health, and the scope for this will be explored as part of the Comprehensive Spending Review process.

EXTENDING EMPLOYMENT OPPORTUNITY TO ALL

Lone parents

Lone parent employment   **4.28**   The Government is committed to the eradication of child poverty by 2020, a key cause of which is adult worklessness. Although there are now 440,000 fewer children in workless households than in 1997, there are still 1.7 million children living in households where no one works. Of those children living in a workless households, 68 per cent live in a lone parent household. A move into employment is the best route out of poverty for individuals and their children, and the best means of improving an individual's life chances.

4.29   The Government's support for lone parents focuses on ensuring that work pays, that barriers to employment are addressed and that lone parents are made aware – in particular, through Work-Focused Interviews (WFIs) with skilled Personal Advisers – of the employment opportunities available to them. The New Deal for lone parents (NDLP) has so far helped over 480,000 lone parents into work, with independent evaluation suggesting that participating in NDLP doubles an individual's chances of finding employment.[10]

4.30   There are now over 1 million lone parents in work – over 310,000 more than in 1997; and, as Chart 4.5 shows, the lone parent employment rate has increased by 11.8 percentage points to 56.5 per cent. Since spring 1997, the gap in the employment rates of lone parents and partnered mothers has narrowed from 23.6 to 14.9 percentage points.[11]

---

[10] *New Deal for lone parents: Second synthesis report of the national evaluation*, Department for Work and Pensions, June 2003.

[11] Under Eurostat regulations the Labour Force Survey has changed from being based on seasonal quarters to calendar quarters. Some figures have therefore changed from those published in Pre-Budget Report 2006 (See Chart 4.5 for details).

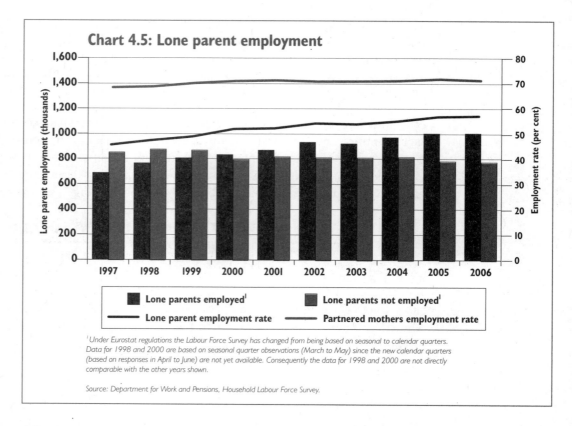

Chart 4.5: Lone parent employment

[Under Eurostat regulations the Labour Force Survey has changed from being based on seasonal to calendar quarters. Data for 1998 and 2000 are based on seasonal quarter observations (March to May) since the new calendar quarters (based on responses in April to June) are not yet available. Consequently the data for 1998 and 2000 are not directly comparable with the other years shown.

Source: Department for Work and Pensions, Household Labour Force Survey.

New Deal Plus for lone parents

4.31   The New Deal Plus for lone parents (NDLP+) pilots are testing the impact of a wide-ranging, coherent package of support to lone parents including enhanced adviser support, financial incentives, initiatives such as childcare 'tasters' that aim to reassure parents of the benefits of formal childcare provision, and events to build personal confidence. Introduced in 2005, the NDLP+ pilots were extended to two further Jobcentre Plus districts in Scotland and Wales[12] from October 2006; and in their existing five locations[13] for a further two years to 2008.

Skills and retention

4.32   While the probability of lone parents leaving work has fallen from 14 per cent in 1992 to around 10 per cent in 2003,[14] lone parents are still more likely to leave their job than are non-lone parents and single childless women.

4.33   Since April 2004, the Government has piloted the In-Work Credit (IWC); a £40 per week payment for lone parents who have been on income support for more than 12 months, for their first 12 months back in work. The IWC provides a clear financial benefit from a move into employment and is helping lone parents move away from benefit dependency. **To provide further help to lone parents to stay in employment, this Budget announces that the IWC will continue to be available to eligible lone parents in the current pilot areas until June 2008, benefiting over 250,000 lone parents. This Budget also announces that, to address the higher costs of living in London and the consequently reduced returns to work, the IWC will be offered in London at a higher rate of £60.**

4.34   In five areas, lone parents receive support through Employment Zones rather than NDLP.[15] Employment Zone providers are incentivised to help both unemployed and lone parent clients into work within a specific time period. While, for most lone parents, help to find work as soon as possible is the most appropriate approach, some may be further from

[12] Edinburgh, Lothian and Borders, and the former Cardiff and Vale sites within the new SE Wales district.

[13] Leicestershire, Bradford, London South East, North London, Dudley and Sandwell.

[14] *Lone parents cycling between work and benefits,* DWP research report 217, September 2004.

[15] Tower Hamlets and Newham, Brent and Haringey, Southwark.

the labour market and need longer periods of training in order to develop the skills and confidence to move back into work. The Government will explore ways of encouraging Employment Zone providers to improve lone parent skills.

4.35 The Government recently announced[16] steps to meet commitments made in response to the Women and Work Commission recommendations,[17] including: a £500,000 programme to increase the availability of quality, part-time work; an exemplar employer initiative in which employers give a commitment to reduce the gender pay gap; and £10 million for the Women and Work Sector Pathways initiative to support innovative ways of helping women advance in their careers. Progress will be published in a report to mark the first anniversary of the Women and Work Commission's findings.

Rights and responsibilities **4.36** The Government has significantly improved support for lone parents since 1997, and continues to develop employee rights in the workplace. Flexible working practices are increasingly being adopted, and maternity pay and child benefits have been increased. From April 2005, the Government introduced new reforms to encourage employer supported childcare. These reforms, and the ten-year strategy for childcare[18] which aims to provide high-quality, affordable childcare for all parents who need it, provide the opportunity better to balance work and family life.

4.37 Childcare Partnership Managers act as a focal point in each Jobcentre Plus district for the resolution of childcare issues and provide Personal Advisers with information about local childcare and Sure Start programmes. Links with Children's Centres are continuing to be developed, and the Childcare Act 2006 introduced a new duty for local authorities to work with childcare providers to secure sufficient childcare supply in their area. To ensure that lone parents are fully informed of the help and support available to them, the Government is increasing the frequency of compulsory WFIs for those who have been on Income Support for at least a year to a minimum of once every 6 months, from April 2007.[19]

Couple parents

4.38 Partners of benefit claimants have, since 2004, been able to access a similar level of support to that provided to lone parents through a targeted WFI regime and the relaunched New Deal for partners (NDP). This programme provides support and encouragement to partners of benefit claimants to acquire the skills and confidence they need to move into work. Since April 2004, over 4,300 job entries have been recorded for partners who have either attended a WFI or joined NDP. The Government is reviewing the system of work-focused support available to partners of benefit claimants and couple parents.

4.39 The ability to speak English can be an important step towards finding work; for parents, not being able to speak English increases the chances their children will be in poverty. Around a fifth of Londoners do not speak English as a first language, and 40 per cent of London's workless parents have English as a second language.[20] **This Budget announces that the Government will trial short, work-focused approaches to provide training in English as a second or other language (ESOL) in the London Cities Strategy pathfinders for parents on benefits or tax credits.**

---

[16] *Government Action Plan: Implementing the Women and Work Commission recommendations*, September 2006.

[17] *Shaping a Fairer Future*, February 2006, Women and Work Commission.

[18] Published alongside the 2004 Pre-Budget Report.

[19] As announced in Budget 2006.

[20] *A Profile of Londoners by Language: An analysis of Labour Force Survey data on first language*, L. Spence, Data Management and Analysis Group 2006/26, Greater London Authority, September 2006.

People with a health condition or disability

4.40 Of the nearly 5.6 million people of working age with a disability, only around half are in employment. Ensuring that many more are able to take up the opportunity to work is central to extending employment opportunity to all.

Growth in incapacity benefit claims
4.41 During the 1980s and early 1990s, the welfare system did little to support people with a health condition or disability back to work. As a result, many drifted into long-term benefit receipt, despite the fact that as many as 90 per cent of people expect to return to work when they start a claim for incapacity benefits. As a consequence, the number of incapacity benefits claimants[21] in the UK more than trebled between the early 1980s and mid 1990s, despite improvements in general health and life expectancy.

Support for a return to work
4.42 For many incapacity benefits claimants, a return to work is possible with appropriate help and support. Reforms to the system of support mean that incapacity benefits claimants now receive active encouragement and support to plan their return to work, through, for example:

- access to early and ongoing work–focused advice from Jobcentre Plus;

- help with identifying and moving into employment. By August 2006, the New Deal for Disabled People (NDDP) had found over 152,000 jobs for people with a health condition or disability;

- steps to tackle discrimination through the Disability Discrimination Act 2005, and improved opportunities to participate in society, as discussed in Chapter 5; and

- measures to ensure that work pays through the Working Tax Credit and National Minimum Wage.

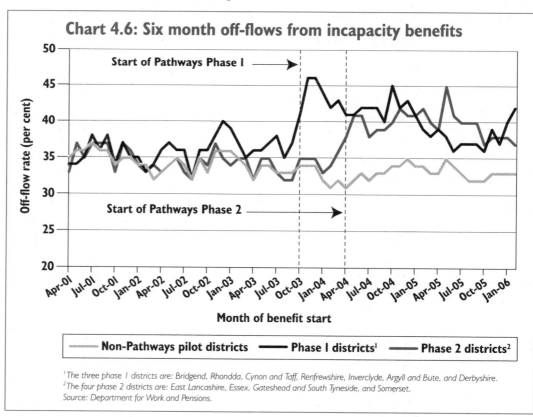

Chart 4.6: Six month off-flows from incapacity benefits

Start of Pathways Phase I ——→

Start of Pathways Phase 2 ——→

Off-flow rate (per cent)

Month of benefit start

········· Non-Pathways pilot districts ——— Phase I districts[1] ——— Phase 2 districts[2]

[1] The three phase 1 districts are: Bridgend, Rhondda, Cynon and Taff, Renfrewshire, Inverclyde, Argyll and Bute, and Derbyshire.
[2] The four phase 2 districts are: East Lancashire, Essex, Gateshead and South Tyneside, and Somerset.
Source: Department for Work and Pensions.

---

[21] The current system of incapacity benefits includes: Incapacity Benefit, Income Support on the grounds of incapacity, and Severe Disablement Allowance.

Pathways 4.43   The Government's Pathways to Work pilots are testing a new framework that combines ongoing mandatory contact with highly skilled Personal Advisers at Jobcentre Plus, and high quality employment, health and financial support. The Organisation for Economic Co-operation and Development has described Pathways to Work as a "considerable success",[22] and this is demonstrated by:

- a significant increase in flows off incapacity benefits after six months of a claim (Chart 4.6).[23] Independent evaluation by the Institute for Fiscal Studies[24] found, ten and a half months after an initial enquiry to claim benefits, an eight percentage points increase in people leaving benefits in Pathways areas compared to matched non-Pathways areas;

- over 26,500 job entries through the Pathways to Work pilots by June 2006;

- around 21 per cent of claimants taking up elements of the Choices package[25] following their initial WFI, with over 12,500 referrals to the new Condition Management Programmes; and

- one in fifteen participants being longer-term claimants who are not required to participate in the programme, but wish to do so. In February 2005, the Government extended a mandatory WFI regime to some existing claimants, alongside a new Job Preparation Premium of £20 per week to encourage steps towards finding work.

4.44   These reforms have started to change attitudes and expectations. The longstanding rising trend in the number of claimants has stopped and the caseload is now beginning to fall. Annual inflows to the benefits have fallen by a third since the mid 1990s; and at 2.68 million, the total number of incapacity benefits claimants in August 2006 was over 40,000 lower than the previous year. The incapacity benefits claimant rate is falling fastest in the regions where it was highest during the 1980s and 1990s, and the total number of claimants in Wales, the North East, the North West and Scotland has fallen by almost 100,000 in the last five years. Within a declining total, however, the average duration of claims has increased, and the composition changed (with a growing proportion of claimants citing a mental health condition as the primary cause of their incapacity). Notwithstanding recent and considerable success, there is more to be done to ensure that everyone receives the appropriate support.

Welfare 4.45   The success of the Pathways to Work pilots has demonstrated that, with the right help
Reform Bill and support, many people on incapacity benefits can move back into work. Building on this, the Welfare Reform Bill, presented to Parliament in July 2006, makes provision for a new integrated and simplified Employment and Support Allowance (ESA) to replace the current system of incapacity benefits for new claimants from 2008.

---

[22] *Economic Survey of the United Kingdom*, OECD, 2005.

[23] The off-flow rates presented are produced from the Working Age Statistical Database (WASD). WASD does not include a proportion of short-term incapacity benefit claims, therefore the off-flows presented will be lower than actual rates.

[24] *Early quantitative evidence on the impact of Pathways to Work pilots*, Institute of Fiscal Studies, on behalf of the Department for Work and Pensions, June 2006.

[25] The Choices package is a range of provision aimed at improving labour market readiness and opportunities. This includes NDDP and the Condition Management Programmes.

4.46   The new ESA will have a clearer balance of rights and responsibilities than the current system. For most people, full receipt of the new benefit will require: attendance at WFIs; an agreed action plan; and, as resources allow, engagement in work related activity. People with the most severe health conditions and disabilities will be supported by ESA at a higher level with no requirement for work related activity, although they will still be able to take up programme support on a voluntary basis. The Personal Capability Assessment (the eligibility test conducted at the start of an Incapacity Benefit claim) will be reformed to focus on what a person can, rather than cannot, do.

Mental health and employment   **4.47**   As Chart 4.7 shows, the number of incapacity benefits claimants citing mental health conditions as the primary cause of their incapacity has increased significantly over the last 10 years, from 645,000 in 1996 to over one million in 2006. To inform the 2007 Comprehensive Spending Review, Budget 2006 announced a review' of the policies needed to improve mental health and employment outcomes. The review's consultations have identified the need for a holistic approach, set out in Box 4.3 below.

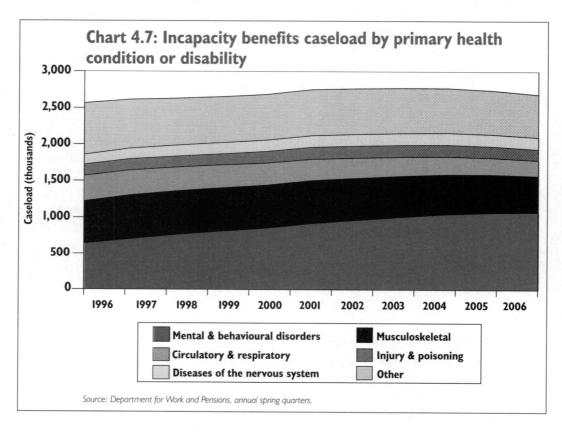

Chart 4.7: Incapacity benefits caseload by primary health condition or disability

Source: Department for Work and Pensions, annual spring quarters.

Box 4.3 Review of Mental Health and Employment Outcomes

Common mental health conditions, such as depression and anxiety, affect around 1 in 6 adults at any one time. As well as causing distress and reducing people's quality of life, such conditions can also adversely affect economic outcomes. While many people with common mental health conditions are employed, individuals in this group are in general, more likely to be unemployed or economically inactive than are those with good mental health; and unemployment, in turn, has been shown to be bad for mental health. Over 40 per cent of all incapacity benefits claimants report a mental health condition as their main health concern. Supporting people to manage their health condition and remain in, or move back into, work, is therefore key for health outcomes, and crucial to reducing the numbers on incapacity benefits. Budget 2006 announced a Review of the policies needed to improve mental health and employment outcomes.

The Review is considering options for the way that people with a mental health condition are supported and treated. The consultations have identified the need for a holistic approach that changes the way common mental health concerns are addressed across the spectrum. To best achieve this, the Review has found four key groups that are important in helping those with mental health conditions realise their full potential in the labour market:

- **employers** currently employ 4 million people with a common mental health condition, and many employers have strong programmes that help people to manage their condition and stay in work, such as addressing stress and encouraging flexible working;

- **GPs** are trusted by people with mental health conditions and are often a first point for those seeking help and advice. Many GPs recognise that employment is an effective part of the rehabilitation process;

- many **individuals** do not even seek treatment, and of those that do, not all receive the most modern effective treatments; and

- the role of **employment programmes and the benefit system**; prolonged periods out of work can worsen mental health. Pathways to Work and the Condition Management Programme are showing promising signs of improving employment outcomes for those on incapacity benefits; however there may be even more that we can do for long term or repeat benefit claimants with common mental health conditions.

The Review will report as part of the 2007 Comprehensive Spending Review.

Older workers

4.48   The Government is committed to ensuring that everyone who wishes to extend his or her working life should have the opportunity to do so. Not only is this important to the Government's long-term aspiration of an employment rate equivalent to 80 per cent of the working age population, but evidence also suggests that remaining in work can increase social inclusion and improve health. In line with the European Employment Directive, the Government introduced legislation in October 2006 to outlaw age discrimination in employment and vocational training. The financial incentive to work, meanwhile, has been enhanced through the Working Tax Credit, which includes additional support for people aged over 50.

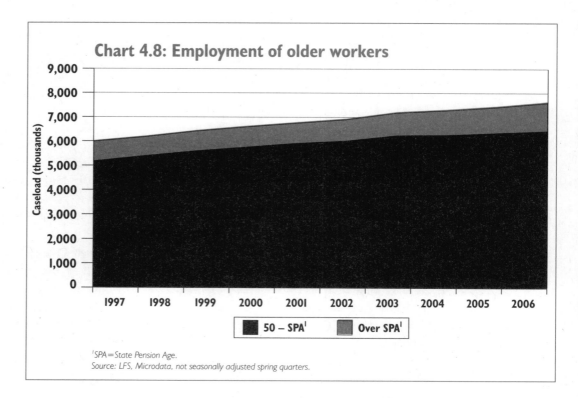

Chart 4.8: Employment of older workers

Caseload (thousands)

Legend: 50 – SPA¹ · Over SPA¹

¹SPA = State Pension Age.
Source: LFS, Microdata, not seasonally adjusted spring quarters.

4.49 These measures have, in a strong and stable economy, delivered impressive results. Since 1997, the employment rate of people aged between 50 and State Pension Age has risen from below 65 per cent to over 70 per cent. Furthermore, there are now more than 1.2 million people over state pension age in employment. The increase in the UK female state pension age from 60 years to 65 years between 2010 and 2020 is expected to lead to significant growth in female labour market participation rates.

Ethnic Minority Groups

4.50 The employment rate for people from ethnic minority groups rose to over 60 per cent in October-December 2006 and, as Chart 4.9 illustrates, the gap between it and the overall national employment rate has narrowed. The chart also shows, however, the diversity of labour market outcomes across different ethnic minority groups. The employment rate for women of Pakistani origin is, for example, 26.2 per cent, and for women of Bangladeshi origin, 26.0 per cent. This compares with an average employment rate for women from other ethnic minority groups of 52.1 per cent, and a national female employment rate of 70.1 per cent.

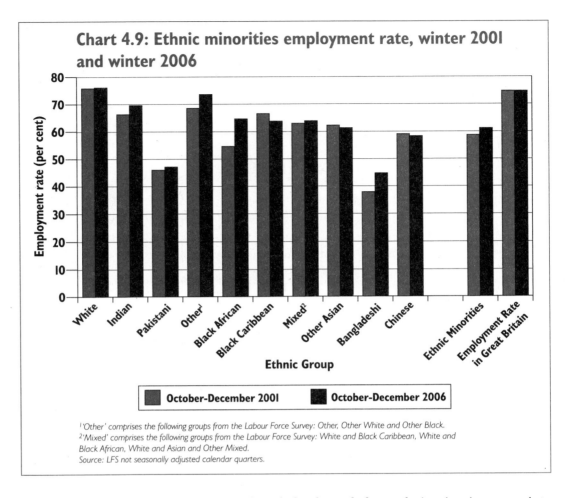

Chart 4.9: Ethnic minorities employment rate, winter 2001 and winter 2006

1 'Other' comprises the following groups from the Labour Force Survey: Other, Other White and Other Black.
2 'Mixed' comprises the following groups from the Labour Force Survey: White and Black Caribbean, White and Black African, White and Asian and Other Mixed.
Source: LFS not seasonally adjusted calendar quarters.

Partners Outreach

4.51   DWP employment programmes have helped people from ethnic minority groups into over 245,000 jobs. In the 2005 Pre-Budget Report the Government announced new private and third sector led employment outreach services to help partners of people on low income, who were neither working nor on benefit. Partners Outreach provision is located in deprived areas with high ethnic minority group populations in Birmingham, Bradford, Leicester, Leeds, London and Manchester.

Business Commission

4.52   In the 2005 Pre-Budget Report, the Chancellor announced that he would ask a group of private sector leaders to advise on policies and practical measures to increase the recruitment, retention and progression of ethnic minorities in the private sector. The National Employment Panel's Business Commission on Race Equality in the Workplace, chaired by Gordon Pell, will publish its final report in the summer.

Young People Not in Education, Training or Employment

4.53   Around 850,000 18-24 year olds are not in education, employment or training (NEETs). For many, this is a short-lived experience; some 25 per cent of NEETs move into education or employment within three months. Others (around 100,000) are living with their partner and looking after young children. Of the remainder, the large majority are claiming benefits, and receive work-focused support through Jobcentre Plus.

4.54   There are, however, a small number of people who are not receiving support through Jobcentre Plus and who have been NEET for over six months, and have no visible means of support. These individuals are at risk of long-term detachment from the labour market. Voluntary activity, supported through organisations such as the youth volunteering charity V, can provide an important stepping-stone from inactivity to employment. The London Development Agency, through its Pre-Volunteering Programme for the 2012 London Games, will also be taking steps to help these disadvantaged young people participate. Chapter 5 announces Activity Agreements for 16-17 year old NEETs in receipt of JSA (severe hardship).

BENEFIT REFORM

Reforming Housing Benefit

Housing Benefit reform **4.55** Over four million low income tenants receive help with their rent costs from Housing Benefit (HB). It is important that HB claims are dealt with quickly and accurately, as this influences the mobility and employment choices of claimants. The Government is therefore continuing to reform HB through administrative improvements, structural reform, and steps to streamline and aligning benefits.

Administrative improvements **4.56** Government investment in local authorities' IT has led to considerable improvements in processing times. In the first quarter of 2002-03, local authorities took an average of 57 days to process a new HB claim. By the third quarter of 2006-07 this had been reduced to an average of 34 days, with the 60 worst performing local authorities reducing processing time by an average of 44 days.

4.57 The Government is keen to ensure both that tenants continue to receive appropriate levels of HB, and that fraud and error in the administration of the benefit is reduced. Building on the considerable investment already made in this area, **the Government is investing in further IT development to: improve information gathering processes in Jobcentre Plus and The Pension Service; develop enhanced data links between DWP and local authorities; and extend the collection of fraud and error data.**

Structural reform **4.58** The Government is taking forward structural reform of HB through the flat-rate Local Housing Allowance (LHA). LHA was first piloted in nine local authorities from November 2003 and in a further nine from April 2005, and is a simpler and more transparent way of administering HB. LHA rates are based on household size and area, and are published monthly. This makes it easier for tenants to find out in advance how much rent can be covered by HB, allowing them to make more informed housing choices. LHA is normally paid direct to tenants, thereby increasing financial inclusion and helping develop budgeting skills as a step towards employment.

4.59 **The Government intends to work closely with local authorities on future structural changes to HB arrangements for temporary accommodation.** Identifying and separating out reasonable costs for the rent and management of temporary accommodation will improve transparency and value for money. It will also contribute both to improved work incentives for tenants, and to the Government's 2010 target to reduce the number of households in temporary accommodation.

Benefit simplification

Improving benefit delivery and accuracy **4.58** Although the vast majority of benefits (just under 98 per cent) are paid correctly, the Government continues to explore ways of further simplifying the system and thereby reducing error further. **This Budget announces a package of alignment measures, which will streamline rules on: benefit payment periods; the backdating period for Disability Living Allowance and Attendance Allowance forms; the treatment of rental income; and termination payments.**

MAKING WORK PAY

4.61 The Government believes that work is the best route out of poverty, and is committed to making work pay by improving incentives to participate and progress in the labour market. Through the Working Tax Credit (WTC) and the National Minimum Wage, the Government has boosted in-work incomes, thereby improving financial incentives to work and tackling poverty among working people.

The National **4.62** The National Minimum Wage guarantees a fair minimum income from work. The **Minimum Wage** Government has accepted the Low Pay Commission's recommendations to increase the adult rate to £5.52 per hour from October 2007. The youth rate, for workers aged between 18 to 21, will rise to £4.60, and the development rate for 16 and 17 year olds, to £3.40.

4.63 In the 2006 Pre-Budget Report, the Government announced that the resources devoted to National Minimum Wage enforcement would be increased by 50 per cent in order to raise standards of enforcement. This will come into force from April 2007.

The Working **4.64** The WTC provides financial support on top of earnings for households with low **Tax Credit** incomes. In December 2006, over 2.25 million families with children and over 323,000 households without children were benefiting from the WTC. Some 103,000 families benefited from the disabled workers element of WTC; over double the number who received support through its predecessor, the Disabled Person's Tax Credit.

4.65 The 2006 Pre-Budget Report announced, that in order to ensure that people claiming HB or Council Tax Benefit would gain from the increases in the rates of WTC, the earnings disregard in HB and Council Tax Benefit would be raised in line with inflation to £15.45. This will come into effect in April 2007.

Four-week **4.66** From April 2007, HM Revenue & Customs will introduce a four-week run-on in **run-on in WTC** entitlement to WTC from the day a claimant ceases to work over 16 hours. This will reduce the number and value of overpayments – occurring when people are late in reporting that they are no longer entitled to WTC. It also reflects the fact that, from this April, claimants are subject to a four-week mandatory reporting period when they cease work or have other changes of circumstances.

Increasing WTC **4.67** From April 2008 the income threshold below which WTC is received in full will **threshold from** increase by £1,200, to £6,420 per annum. This will be introduced alongside a wider package of **April 2008** reforms to the personal tax and tax credit system announced in Chapter 5, and will increase the gain to work for many low-income households.

Tackling the **4.68** The unemployment trap occurs when those without work find the difference between **unemployment** in-work and out-of-work incomes too small to provide an incentive to move into work. Table **trap** 4.1 shows that, since the introduction of the National Minimum Wage in April 1999, the Government has increased the minimum income that people can expect on moving into work, thereby reducing this problem.

Table 4.1: Weekly Minimum Income Guarantees (MIGs)

	April 1999	October 2007	April 2008[2]
Family[1] with one child, full-time work	£182	£276	£290
Family[1] with one child, part-time work	£136	£217	£225
Single person, 25 or over, full-time work	£113	£180	£186
Couple, no children, 25 or over, full-time work	£117	£212	£220
Single disabled person in full-time work	£139	£224	£228
Single disabled person in part-time work	£109	£165	£168

Assumes the prevailing rate of NMW and that the family is eligible for Family Credit/Disability Working Allowance and Working Tax Credit/Child Tax Credit. Full-time work is assumed to be 35 hours. Part-time work is assumed to be 16 hours.
[1] Applies to lone parent families and couples with children alike.
[2] Projections are based on RPI and AEI growth taken from HM Treasury's economic forecast.

Tackling the poverty trap

4.69   The poverty trap occurs when those in work have little incentive to move up the earnings ladder because of only limited net gains. Marginal deduction rates (MDRs) measure the extent of the poverty trap by showing how much of each additional pound of gross earnings is lost through higher taxes and withdrawn benefits or tax credits.

4.70   The Government's reforms are ensuring that workers have improved incentives to progress in work. Table 4.2 shows that, as a result of these reforms, about half a million fewer low income households face MDRs in excess of 70 per cent now than in April 1997. The increase in the number of households facing MDRs of between 60 and 70 per cent is due primarily to the introduction of tax credits, which have extended financial support so that a larger number of families benefit, including low income working people without children.

4.71   It is important to note, however, that these figures do not take account of any likely behavioural changes caused by a rise in income (changes in, for example, labour market participation or hours worked). They also do not include the effect of the £25,000 disregard in tax credits, which allows income to rise between one year and the next by up to this amount before tax credits begin to be withdrawn. This means that the actual marginal deduction rates for many families will in practice be significantly lower, at least in the first year.

Table 4.2: The effect of the Government's reforms on high marginal deduction rates

Marginal deduction rate[1]	Before Budget 1998	2007-08 system of tax and benefits
Over 100 percent	5,000	0
Over 90 percent	130,000	50,000
Over 80 percent	300,000	170,000
Over 70 percent	740,000	210,000
Over 60 percent	760,000	1,680,000

[1] Marginal deduction rates are for working heads of households in receipt of income-related benefits or tax credits where at least one person works 16 hours or more a week, and the head of the household is not claiming the disabled worker element of WTC.
Note: Figures are cumulative. Before Budget 1998 figures based on 1997-98 estimated caseload and take-up rates; estimates for the 2007-08 system of tax and benefits are based on caseload and take-up rates in 2004-05.

Box 4.4: The effect of Government reforms on marginal dedication rates.

Chart (a) shows marginal deduction rates (MDRs) by gross income for a lone parent with two children under the 2007-08 and indexed 1997-98 tax and benefit systems, assuming the National Minimum Wage rate. Consistent with Table 4.2, this shows a reduced MDR at low income levels, reflecting the lower withdrawal rate of in-work support under tax credits, but with withdrawal of support now extending further up the income scale, due to now more generous support overall. This pattern is typical for single earner families with children.

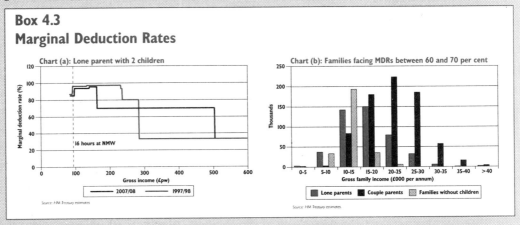

Box 4.3
Marginal Deduction Rates

Chart (a): Lone parent with 2 children

Chart (b): Families facing MDRs between 60 and 70 per cent

Source: HM Treasury estimates

Chart (b) shows the distribution of those families likely to be facing MDRs of 60 to 70 per cent in 2007-08, by gross income and family type. Most of these families face an MDR of around 70 per cent, reflecting basic rate income tax and employee NICs combined with the withdrawal rate for tax credits. The characteristics of this group are typical of tax credit claimants: over 80 per cent have children, and three quarters have gross incomes between £10,000 and £25,000. The changes to income tax and tax credits announced in this Budget do not materially affect these conclusions.

MDRs suffer a number of limitations that make interpretation difficult. They ignore some key features of the tax and benefit system, such as the effect of the £25,000 disregard in tax credits, which allows people to increase their income without having their tax credits withdrawn. They also look at very small changes in income; in reality, changes in income are larger and can move people off the tax credit taper or bring them into eligibility for additional support (through, for example, the 30 hours element). This means that it may be more useful to look at empirical studies.

A number of published studies have assessed the labour market impacts of the Government's tax and benefit reforms.[a] These studies suggest that the reforms have increased the lone parent employment rate by around 5 percentage points. They provide no evidence of any reduction in hours worked for working parents. In fact, average hours are estimated to have risen for lone mothers, perhaps reflecting enhanced incentives to cross 16 and 30 hour tax credit thresholds.

Evidence on incentives to acquire skills or move into better paid jobs is less comprehensive, but one study[b] argues that the impacts are not clear-cut. To the extent that workers pay for general training through lower wages, higher MDRs also mitigate such costs. This study finds an increase in short-term wage growth for those groups facing increased MDRs under tax credits.

[a] An overview of these studies is provided in Brewer, M. and Browne, J. (2006), The effect of the Working Families' Tax Credit on labour market participation, IFS Briefing Note No. 69.
[b] Lydon, R. and Walker, I. (2005), Welfare-to-work, wages and wage growth, Fiscal Studies, Vol. 26, No. 3.

FUNDING FOR WELFARE FOR WORK

4.72   The welfare to work programme is delivered by DWP. Originally funded by the Windfall Tax on the excess profits of the privatised utilities, the programme has since 2003-04 been funded from resources allocated to DWP through the spending review process as the Windfall Tax receipts have been exhausted. Table 4.3 sets out that element of the welfare to work programme, and other programmes, funded from the Windfall Tax. Further detail of expenditure on welfare to work programmes can be found in the DWP Departmental Report.

Table 4.3: Allocation of the Windfall Tax

£ million	1997-98	1998-99	1999-00	2000-01	2001-02	2002-03	2003-04[2]	2004-05	2005-06	TOTAL
Spending by programme[1]										
New Deal for young people[3]	50	200	310	300	240	260	170	0	0	1,530
New Deal for 25 plus	0	10	90	110	200	210	150	0	0	770
New Deal for over 50s	0	0	5	20	10	10	10	0	0	60
New Deal for lone parents	0	20	40	40	40	80	60	0	0	280
New Deal for disabled people[4]	0	5	20	10	10	30	30	0	0	100
New Deal for partners	0	0	5	10	10	10	10	0	0	40
Childcare[5]	0	20	10	5	0	0	0	0	0	35
University for Industry[6]	0	5	0	0	0	0	0	0	0	5
Workforce development[7]	0	0	0	0	0	40	50	150	80	320
ONE pilots[8]	0	0	0	5	5	0	0	0	0	10
Action Teams	0	0	0	10	40	50	50	0	0	150
Enterprise development	0	0	0	10	20	10	0	0	0	40
Modernising the Employment Service	0	0	0	40	0	0	0	0	0	40
Total Resource Expenditure	50	260	480	560	570	700	530	150	80	3,380
Capital Expenditure[9]	90	270	260	750	450	0	0	0	0	1,820
Windfall Tax receipts	2,600	2,600								5,200

[1] In year figures rounded to the nearest £10 million, (except where expenditure is less than £5 million). Constituent elements may not sum to totals because of rounding.

[2] Windfall tax expenditure on welfare to work programmes is reduced from 2003-04 onwards as windfall tax resources are exhausted. Remaining in-year expenditure will be topped up with general Government revenues.

[3] Includes funding for the Innovation Fund.

[4] Includes £10 million in 1999-2000, an element of the November 1998 announcements on welfare reform.

[5] Includes £30 million for out-of-school childcare. The costs of the 1997 Budget improvements in childcare through Family Credit are included from April 1998 to October 1999, after which the measure was incorporated within the Working Families' Tax Credit.

[6] Start up and development costs. Other costs of the University for Industry are funded from within Departmental Expenditure Limits.

[7] Includes £219 million funding for Employer Training Pilots.

[8] Funding for repeat interviews. Other funding is from the Invest to Save budget.

[9] Includes capital spending on renewal of school infrastructure, to help raise standards.

5 BUILDING A FAIRER SOCIETY

The Government is committed to promoting fairness alongside flexibility and enterprise to ensure that everyone can take advantage of opportunities to fulfil their potential. Since 1997, the Government has undertaken a comprehensive programme of reform to the tax and benefit system with the aims of simplifying the system, eradicating child poverty, supporting families, promoting saving, and ensuring security for all in old age. The Government is also committed to a modern and fair tax system that ensures that everyone pays their fair share of tax. This Budget announces the next stage in modernising the tax and benefit system, offering more support for work, families and pensioners:

- **removing the starting rate and cutting the basic rate of income tax from 22 pence to 20 pence in April 2008,** creating a simpler structure of two rates: a 20 pence basic rate and a 40 pence higher rate;

- **increasing the upper earnings limit for national insurance by £75 a week above indexation in April 2008 and, from April 2009, fully aligning it with the higher rate threshold** – the point at which taxpayers start to pay the higher rate of income tax, further simplifying the system;

- **raising the aligned higher rate threshold and upper earnings limit by £800 a year above indexation in April 2009;**

- **increasing the higher personal allowances for those aged 65 or over by £1,180 above indexation in April 2008,** removing 580,000 pensioners from paying tax. **By April 2011, no pensioner aged 75 or over will pay any tax until their income reaches £10,000;**

- **increasing the child element of the Child Tax Credit by £150 a year above earnings indexation in April 2008,** raising the child element to £2,080 a year;

- **increasing the threshold for Working Tax Credit by £1,200 to £6,420 in April 2008,** further strengthening the incentives to work for families with children and low-income working households;

- **raising the withdrawal rate on tax credits by 2 per cent to 39 per cent,** helping to retain the current focus of tax credits; and

- **increasing the weekly rate of Child Benefit for the eldest child to £20 in April 2010,** providing support to all families in line with the principle of progressive universalism.

This Budget also announces:

- **an increase in the annual Individual Savings Accounts investment limit from April 2008 to £7,200, with an increase in the cash limit to £3,600,** in order to encourage saving further;

- **an increase in the inheritance tax allowance to £350,000 in 2010–11,** to continue to provide a fair and targeted system;

- measures to support the third sector, **including £80 million in small grants for community organisations, a campaign to drive up giving through gift aid, and gift aid changes to facilitate relationship building with donors;** and

- **further reforms to modernise the tax system and protect tax revenues, including measures to tackle avoidance.**

5.1   The Government's aim is to promote a fair and inclusive society in which everyone shares in rising national prosperity and no one is held back from achieving their potential by disadvantage or lack of opportunity. The Government is committed to advancing fairness and flexibility together, so that all people, at all stages of life, can benefit from the UK's modern and dynamic economy.

NEXT STEPS IN MODERNISING BRITAIN'S TAX AND BENEFIT SYSTEM

5.2   During the 1980s and early 1990s, while incomes rose on average, standards of living fell for many families with children and for pensioners, leading to significant rises in child and pensioner poverty. As set out in *The Modernisation of Britain's Tax and Benefit System 11*,[1] the tax and benefit system did not do enough to support families to find and progress in work, and the complex interactions of the income tax and national insurance systems created an excessive tax burden on low-income workers, and discouraged job creation at the lower end of the earnings distribution.

5.3   Since 1997, the Government has undertaken a comprehensive programme of reform to the tax and benefit system. These reforms have aimed to simplify the system, to tackle child and pensioner poverty, and to make work pay. Budget 2007 announces the next stage in these reforms, offering more support for work, families and pensioners.

Modernising the personal tax system

5.4   The Government has already introduced a number of reforms to simplify the tax and national insurance system and reduce the burden on those with low incomes, including aligning the starting point for paying both employees' and employers' national insurance contributions (NICs) with the income tax personal allowance and removing the NICs entry fee. As the next stage of reform, the Government will simplify the system further by creating two income bands covering both income tax and NICs, with additional support for low-income families delivered through tax credits.

Two rates of income tax   **5.5**   The Government will simplify the tax system by removing the starting rate and cutting the basic rate of income tax from 22 pence to 20 pence from April 2008, creating a simpler structure of two rates:[2] a 20 pence basic rate and a 40 pence higher rate. This is the lowest basic or standard rate of income tax for over 75 years. To continue to reward saving, the Government will maintain the existing ten pence rate of tax for savings income, which is identified separately in the income tax system.

Aligning NICs and income tax thresholds   **5.6**   In April 2001, the Government aligned the starting point for employee NICs with the personal allowance for income tax. As part of the next stage of reform, the Government will align the upper earnings limit (UEL) and upper profits limit (UPL) for NICs with the higher rate threshold - the point at which taxpayers start to pay the higher rate of income tax. **In April 2008, the Government will increase the UEL for national insurance by £75 per week above indexation and, from April 2009, fully align it with the higher rate threshold.** These reforms will mean that there are only two main rates of income tax, and that income tax and NICs rates will apply to the same bands of income.

Raising the higher rate threshold   **5.7**   In April 2009, the Government will increase the higher rate threshold for income tax by £800 a year above indexation.

---

[1] *Tax credits: reforming financial support for families*, HM Treasury, 2005.

[2] For all income other than savings and dividend income.

Increasing age-related allowances   **5.8**   Alongside tackling pensioner poverty, the Government is committed to supporting those pensioners who pay tax. Increases in the age-related income tax allowances will mean that in 2007-08 no one aged 65 or over will pay tax on an income of up to £145 a week, and around half of pensioners will pay no tax whatsoever on their income. As part of the modernisation of the tax system, **Budget 2007 announces that the age-related income tax allowances for those aged 65 or over and 75 or over will rise by £1,180 above indexation in April 2008, thereby removing a further 580,000 pensioners from paying tax. Furthermore, by April 2011 no pensioner aged 75 or over will pay any tax until their income reaches £10,000 a year.**

5.9   As announced in the 2006 Pre-Budget Report, all income tax personal allowances and the NICs thresholds and limits will increase in line with statutory indexation for 2007-08. There are no changes to the income tax rates for 2007-08 and the starting and basic rate limits for that year will also be increased in line with statutory indexation.

Eradicating child poverty

Progress to date   **5.10**   Child poverty more than doubled in the 1980s and early 1990s. The Government's first challenge was to address this underlying increase, and then make progress to eradicating child poverty by 2020. Reforms to financial support for families, combined with employment opportunity for parents, have ensured that the Government has decisively reversed the upwards trend in child poverty.

5.11   Between 1998-99 and 2004-05 (the latest data available), relative poverty fell by 700,000, the equivalent of 17 per cent (after housing costs) or 23 per cent (before housing costs). Over the same period, absolute poverty has fallen by 2 million (after housing costs), or 1.5 million (before housing costs). This was less than the Government's ambition, and the Government remains committed to doing more in order to halve child poverty between 1998-99 and 2010-11, on the path to eradication by 2020.

5.12   The Pre-Budget Report announced that, **from April 2007, the child element of Child Tax Credit will increase by £80 to £1,845 a year,** in line with the Budget 2006 commitment to raise the child element at least in line with earnings until the end of this Parliament. This represents a total increase of £400 since its introduction in April 2003. In 2007-08, a family with two young children and a full-time earner on £16,500 (half male mean earnings) will receive over £110 per week in Child Tax Credit and Child Benefit, more than double the equivalent support in 1997-98.

5.13   As part of the personal tax and benefit reforms announced in this Budget, **in April 2008 the Government will increase the child element by a further £150 a year above earnings indexation, raising it to £2,080 a year.** This will do more to support work and families and, combined with other measures announced in Budget 2007, will lift around 200,000 children out of poverty. By April 2009:

- households with children will be, on average, £250 per year better off as a result of personal tax and benefit measures announced in this Budget, and £1,800 better off as a result of all such measures since 1997; and

- households with children in the poorest fifth of the population will be, on average, £425 per year better off as a result of personal tax and benefit measures announced in this Budget, and £4,000 better off as a result of all such measures since 1997.

5.14   Table 5.1 shows the levels of support that Child Tax Credit and Child Benefit will provide for families from April 2008.

Table 5.1: Minimum annual levels of support for families from April 2008[A]

Annual family income	up to £15,525	up to £50,000	all families
Per cent of families	30	79	100
1 child	£3,595	£1,515	£970
2 children	£6,325	£2,165	£1,620
3 children	£9,055	£2,815	£2,270

Source: HM Treasury
A On current projections for indexation

Supporting working families

5.15   Chapter 4 sets out the progress the Government has made in tackling the unemployment trap and the poverty trap, so that individuals see a financial gain from moving into, and then progressing in, work. As part of the personal tax and benefit changes announced in this Budget, from April 2008 the income threshold at which Working Tax Credit is received in full will increase by £1,200, to £6,420 a year. This will support work as the best route out of poverty by increasing the gain to work for many low-income households, and reducing the net tax burden for working families. To help ensure that this and other increases in tax credits retain their current focus, from April 2008 the Government will also increase the rate at which tax credit awards are withdrawn by 2 per cent to 39 per cent. As a result of these measures, by April 2009:

- a single-earner family with two children on male mean earnings (£35,900) will be £320 a year better off, with the direct tax burden on the family falling to 20.1 per cent, lower than any year of the 1980s and 1990s;

- a single-earner family with two children on median earnings (£27,000) will be around £500 a year better off; and

- a single-earner couple without children on half median earnings (£13,500) and receiving the Working Tax Credit will be £175 a year better off.

5.16   Chart 5.1 shows the effect by April 2009 of all personal tax and benefit measures since 1997, as a proportion of income for each income decile. Box 5.1 sets out a summary of the changes from April 2008 to Britain's tax and benefit system.

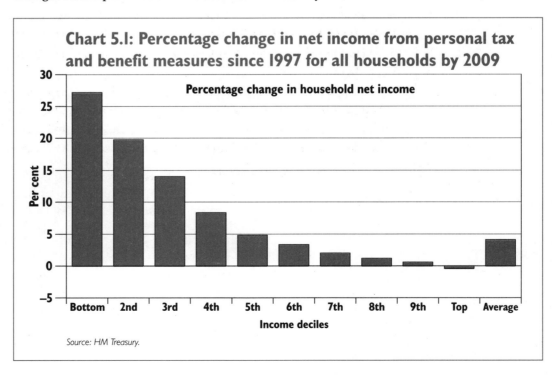

Chart 5.1: Percentage change in net income from personal tax and benefit measures since 1997 for all households by 2009

Source: HM Treasury.

Box 5.1: Modernising Britain's tax and benefit system – summary of changes

The reforms announced in this Budget represent the next stage in the Government's programme of reform to the tax and benefit system. The Government will:

- remove the starting rate and cut the basic rate of income tax from 22 pence to 20 pence, creating a simpler structure of two rates:[a] a 20 pence basic rate and a 40 pence higher rate from April 2008;

- increase the upper earnings limit for national insurance by £75 a week above indexation in April 2008, and then from April 2009 fully align it with the higher rate threshold – the point at which taxpayers start to pay the higher rate of income tax, further simplifying the system;

- raise the aligned higher rate threshold and upper earnings limit by £800 a year above indexation from April 2009;

- increase the higher personal allowances for those aged 65 or over by £1,180 above indexation from April 2008;

- raise the child element of the Child Tax Credit by £150 a year above earnings indexation in April 2008, making further progress in helping families and tackling child poverty, and raising the child element to £2,080 a year;

- increase the threshold for Working Tax Credit by £1,200 to £6,420 a year in April 2008, further increasing the incentives to work for families with children and low-income working households; and

- raise the withdrawal rate on tax credits by 2 per cent to 39 per cent in April 2008, helping to retain their current focus.

Once fully implemented, these reforms to the direct tax system mean that by April 2009:

- a single-earner family with two children on male mean earnings (£35,900) will be £320 a year better off, with the direct tax burden on the family falling to 20.1 per cent, lower than any year of the 1980s and 1990s;

- a single-earner family with two children on median earnings (£27,000), will be around £500 a year better off;

- a single-earner couple without children on half median earnings (£13,500) and receiving the Working Tax Credit will be £175 a year better off;

- the numbers of children in relative poverty will be around 200,000 lower as a result of these changes;

- around 580,000 fewer pensioners will pay income tax than would otherwise be the case, so that in total only 43 per cent of pensioners will be taxpayers; and

- the tax burden on small unincorporated businesses will be reduced by £50 million in 2009-10, as the self-employed pay income tax and NICs on their business profits.

[a] For all income other than savings and dividend income.

Tax credits

5.17   A key element of tax and benefit reform has been the introduction of tax credits. The Child and Working Tax Credits were introduced in 2003 to help make work pay, tackle child poverty, and give support to most families with children. Tax credits have a number of advantages over other ways of achieving these objectives, which have been set out in previous government documents on tax and benefit modernisation.[3] Higher tax allowances on their own benefit the richest most, and cannot reduce tax liability below zero. Putting all the money into universal Child Benefit would fail to target support at people who need it most. Tax credits can tailor support to family circumstances, including number of children, childcare costs or disability.

5.18   In the 2005 Pre-Budget Report, the Government announced a series of reforms to improve the tax credit system by increasing certainty for claimants. End-of-year adjustments leading to an overpayment fell by a fifth between 2003-04 and 2004-05. Once the measures announced in 2005 come fully into effect, this is expected to fall by a further third. As set out in Chapter 4, from April 2007, HM Revenue and Customs (HMRC) will introduce a four-week run-on in entitlement to Working Tax Credit from the day a claimant ceases to work over 16 hours. This will reduce the number and value of overpayments occurring when people are late in reporting that they are no longer entitled to Working Tax Credit.

5.19   In addition to these policy measures, HMRC has improved its service and communications to claimants, and its accuracy in processing awards. After the success in the implementation of the shortened five months renewal period in 2006, as announced in the 2006 Pre-Budget Report, the renewal period will be shortened again to four months in 2007. This further reduces the time when claimants are paid on potentially out-of-date information.

---

[3] *Tax credits: reforming financial support for families*, HM Treasury, 2005.

> **Box 5.2: Take-up of tax credits**
>
> Take-up in the first year of the new system was higher than any previous system of income-related financial support for families in work. Data published in March 2007 showed that it has risen further since then, and that it is highest among those who need it most.
>
> The latest figures show that:
>
> * in 2004-05 take-up of the Child Tax Credit rose from 79 per cent to 82 per cent, with over 90 per cent of the money available being claimed; and
>
> * take-up amongst those of incomes of less than £10,000 is now 97 per cent, up from 93 per cent in the first year of tax credits; and take-up amongst lone parents is now 93 per cent, up from 91 per cent in the first year of tax credits.
>
> This compares to take-up of 50 per cent in the early years of Family Income Supplement, 57 per cent for Family Credit, and 62-65 per cent for Working Families Tax Credit.
>
> HMRC has in place a programme of activity to improve take-up. For example, it puts information about tax credits in packs of information which are given to all new mothers, and advertising in parenting magazines to ensure new mothers are aware of their entitlement. HMRC are also working closely with the voluntary and community sector to encourage applications for tax credits.
>
> In response to evidence that there are some groups with lower rates of take-up, including some ethnic minority groups and people without children, HMRC is testing more effective ways of reaching these people to encourage greater take-up.

SUPPORT FOR FAMILIES AND YOUNG PEOPLE

Child benefit **5.20** To provide support for all families in line with the principle of progressive universalism, this Budget announces that the weekly rate of Child Benefit for the eldest child will rise to £20 in April 2010.

5.21 In addition, the Government recognises the importance of a healthy diet in the final weeks of pregnancy and the additional costs faced by parents when their children are born. Low-income families may already claim the Sure Start Maternity Grant, worth £500 per child, to help with these additional costs. Additional support for all families was announced at the 2006 Pre-Budget Report: from April 2009, every mother-to-be will become eligible for Child Benefit from week 29 of their pregnancy, so that women will be up to £200 better off by the birth of their first child, and up to £130 better off at the birth of subsequent children.

Financial support for young people

5.22 Globalisation and rapid technological change are presenting new challenges for the UK, with the labour market requiring highly skilled individuals to meet these challenges. Achieving world-class skills in the UK will require improving the skills of young people flowing into employment. Improving the number of young people continuing in education and training after the end of the compulsory school age will provide the foundation to improve the skills of young people. In support of this, the Government is committed to a vision of a single, coherent system of financial support for 16-19 year olds, which ensures that all young people have the support and incentives they need to participate and achieve in education and training.

Engaging the **5.23**   Evidence suggests that where young people spend prolonged periods unemployed or
most inactive, it has a negative impact on their employment prospects and life chances. Since April
disadvantaged 2006, the Government has been piloting Activity Agreements and Allowances targeted on the
young people most disadvantaged 16-17 year olds. These schemes have extended conditional financial
support to this group, setting a clear expectation that young people progress into learning, and
offering them the financial support and opportunity to do so. **Budget 2007 announces an
extension of the pilot into the 2007 CSR period. This Budget also announces Activity
Agreements for 16 and 17 year olds not in education, employment or training and in receipt
of Jobseekers' Allowance (severe hardship), to help them to re-engage, and take up their
statutory right to an appropriate place in education or training, or find a job with training.**
The Green Paper, *Raising the participation age*, to be published on 22 March 2007, will consult
on raising the compulsory age for participation in education and training to 18.

Support for children and young people

Review of **5.24**   Budget 2006 launched a joint HM Treasury and Department for Education and Skills
children and (DfES) policy review on how to secure further improvement in outcomes for children and
young people young people. The analysis of this policy review has played an important part in informing
the key announcements that the Government is making on education and children in this
Budget. The final report of the review will be published later in the spring. Further details on
the review are set out in Chapter 6.

Children in **5.25**   The state has special responsibility for children in care, and yet outcomes for this
care group are extremely poor, both in absolute terms and relative to their peers. For this reason,
these young people sit at the heart of the Government's wider programme to tackle the poor
outcomes and social exclusion of the most vulnerable groups in society. Fulfilling the
commitment in the Schools White Paper[4] to consult on a wide-ranging set of proposals to
transform outcomes for children in care, the Government published the Green Paper, *Care
matters: Transforming the lives of children and young people in care,* for consultation in
October 2006.

Budget- **5.26**   *Support for parents: the best start for children*[5] set out an ambition to promote greater
holding lead personalisation of services. It announced a series of single account-holder pathfinders to test
professionals whether better service packages for children, young people and families can be delivered by
giving lead professionals a budget with which to procure goods and commission services
directly from providers. £10 million in additional funding over two years has been made
available to support the pilots. Since June 2006, 15 pilots have been established in 16 Local
Authorities,[6] to run until April 2008.

Parent Support **5.27**   *Support for parents* also announced £20 million to support the piloting of a new
Advisers school-based outreach role, Parent Support Advisers, in over 600 primary and secondary
schools in the most deprived areas. This new, preventative role is intended to support
children and families where there are early signs that they could benefit from additional help.
A total of 20 local areas have been selected to run the pilots and 615 schools now have Parent
Support Advisers in place. It is anticipated that as many as 900 schools will have Parent
Support Advisers provision during 2007.

Listening **5.28**   The National Society for the Prevention of Cruelty to Children (NSPCC) runs listening
services services to provide support and advice for children and young people. **This Budget provides
additional resources to help support an expansion of these services.**

---

[4] *Higher Standards: better schools for all,* Department for Education and Skills, October 2005.

[5] *Support for parents: the best start for children,* HM Treasury and Department for Education and Skills, December 2005.

[6] Blackpool, Bournemouth, Poole, Brighton & Hove, Derbyshire, Devon, Gateshead, Gloucestershire, Hertfordshire,
Knowsley, Leeds, Redbridge, Telford & Wrekin, Tower Hamlets, Trafford and West Sussex.

Childcare and work-life balance

Delivering the ten year strategy 5.29   Flexible, affordable and high-quality childcare provision is an important element of the Government's strategy to provide support to families and eradicate child poverty. *Choice for parents, the best start for children: a ten year strategy for childcare,*[7] published alongside the 2004 Pre-Budget Report, set out the Government's long-term vision for childcare and early years services.

5.30   The Government is committed to ensuring that parents have greater choice and flexibility in balancing work and family life. From this April, paid maternity leave will be extended from six to nine months, and the Government has a goal of 12 months of paid maternity leave by the end of the Parliament. The right to request flexible working is currently available to parents of children under six, and will be extended to carers from April. The Government will also continue to examine the case for extending the right to request flexible working to parents of older children in the future.

5.31   As set out in Chapter 6, this Budget announces the overall resource plans for the DfES for the 2007 CSR period. In order to achieve and build on the commitments made in the ten-year strategy for childcare, this Budget announces significant additional funding for Sure Start, childcare and early years of at least £340 million by 2010-11 compared with 2007-08 - over £1.6 billion by 2010-11. Final allocations will announced in due course.

5.32   There are currently over 1,150 Sure Start Children's Centres across the country, reaching over 925,000 children and offering integrated childcare, health, parenting and family support. The additional resources announced in this Budget will deliver a nationwide network of 3,500 centres as planned by 2010 – one in every community of the country – as well as additional parenting support for fathers and those parents who need it most.

Affordability for parents 5.33   The Government wants families to be able to afford flexible, high-quality childcare that is appropriate to their needs, and continues to believe that the childcare element of the Working Tax Credit is the most effective way of delivering support for low-to-moderate income families. This offers parents support with up to 80 per cent of costs, up to a limit of £300 per week (£175 for one child). Alongside this, the £55 per week income tax and NICs exemption for employer-supported childcare is improving childcare affordability for parents. From this April, a wide range of childcare providers will be able to register on the voluntary part of the Ofsted Childcare Register giving many, such as providers of activity-based childcare, their first opportunity to demonstrate to parents that essential standards are being met. Parents will be able to claim the childcare element of the Working Tax Credit and income tax and NICs exemptions on employer-supported childcare in respect of costs relating to providers on the register, increasing access and affordability further. In addition, this Budget offers free childcare places for up to 50,000 workless parents undertaking training, to enable more parents to move back into work.

FAIRNESS FOR DISABLED PEOPLE

5.34   The Government is committed to improving opportunities for disabled people, as well as improving their rights and outcomes. The proposals set out in the Welfare Reform Green Paper (see Chapter 4 for further detail), including the reforms to incapacity benefits contained within the Welfare Reform Bill, will develop opportunities for disabled people to participate fully in society. This will entail putting in place extensive support to help individuals re-engage with the labour market and gain employment, while providing

---

[7] *Choice for parents, the best start for children: a ten year strategy for childcare,* HM Treasury, Department for Education and Skills, Department for Work and Pensions, Department of Trade and Industry, December 2004.

adequate support to those who are not able to work. The additional provisions of the Disability Discrimination Act 2005 came into force from December 2006. The new Disability Equality Duty means that all public sector organisations now have a statutory requirement to promote equality of opportunity for disabled people, eliminate unlawful harassment and publish a Disability Equality Plan.

Improving the life chances of disabled people **5.35** The Office for Disability Issues (ODI), set up in December 2005, has a strategic role across government, and is taking forward the recommendations of the 2005 Strategy Unit report. A new advisory non-departmental public body, *Equality 2025: the United Kingdom Advisory Network on Disability Equality*, was launched in December 2006 to ensure that the views of disabled people are heard. The ODI is currently consulting on possible indicators to measure equality for disabled people by 2025.

Independent living **5.36** The Government is committed to ensuring disabled people have choice and control over the support they need to live their everyday lives. Individual budget pilots, running in 13 Local Authorities, are examining the effectiveness of giving individuals a choice of their budget in the form of cash, services, or a combination of the two. One of the three strands of the *Children and Young People's Review* (see Chapter 6 for further detail) focuses on support for disabled children, empowering them and their families to influence their own provision, and encouraging earlier intervention and best practice support. The *Mental Health and Employment Review* (see Chapter 4 for further detail) is examining ways of helping those with mental health conditions into work. These reviews are being taken forward as part of the 2007 CSR.

PROMOTING SAVING, ASSET OWNERSHIP AND INCLUSION

5.37 The Government seeks to support saving and asset ownership for all across the lifecycle – from childhood, through working life and into retirement. Since 1997, the Government's savings strategy has focused on improving the environment for saving, developing a range of savings opportunities suitable for each life stage, providing adequate incentives for saving through the tax and benefit system, and empowering individuals with the capability to make the right saving choices. In addition, the Government aims to promote financial capability and financial inclusion – to ensure that people have the knowledge, skills and confidence to manage their finances, and that they have access to appropriate financial products and services.

Promoting saving and asset ownership for all

Child Trust Fund **5.38** The Child Trust Fund (CTF) was introduced in April 2005 to promote saving and financial education and ensure that in future all children have a financial asset at age 18. Under the scheme, all newborn children receive £250 to be invested in a long-term savings and investment account, and children from lower-income families receive £500. Budget 2006 announced further payments at age seven, of £250 for all children, with children from lower-income families receiving £500.

5.39 Around 2.5 million CTF accounts are now open. In the first year of operation, over three quarters of parents opened their child's account and over a third of children received an extra payment from the Government.[8] To raise awareness and participation among parents, the Government ran a successful CTF Week in January 2007, which received wide coverage.

5.40 The Government recognises that children in care are a particularly vulnerable group. In view of this, the Government announced in October 2006 that it would provide an extra £100 per year to every child who spends the year in care, in order that their CTF provides a more significant asset for them to access on entering adult life. Following consultation, the scheme will come into effect for children in care from 1 April 2007.

---

[8] *Child Trust Fund: Statistical Report 2006*, HM Revenue & Customs, September 2006.

5.41   Budget 2006 announced that the Government was exploring the use of a 'Schools Money Week' as a focus for financial education. The Government is continuing to work with financial education bodies in developing tailored CTF resources to support this initiative.

Individual **5.42**   Individual Savings Accounts (ISAs) were introduced in 1999 as a replacement for Tax-
Savings Exempt Special Savings Accounts (TESSAs) and Personal Equity Plans (PEPs). The objective
Accounts has been to develop and extend the savings habit and to ensure that tax relief on savings is more fairly distributed. The evidence shows that ISAs have been successful in meeting these objectives: for example, over 17 million people now have an ISA, with over £220 billion subscribed since their launch. ISA and PEP savings are supported by an estimated £2.1 billion each year in tax relief.

5.43   In order to build on this success, the Government announced in the Pre-Budget Report that, following its review of ISAs, it will simplify the ISA regime, make it more flexible for savers and providers, and further promote saving by introducing the following package of reforms:[9] to make ISAs permanent beyond 2010; bring PEPs within the ISA wrapper; remove the Mini/Maxi distinction within ISAs; allow transfers from the cash into the stocks & shares component of ISAs; and allow CTF accounts to roll over into ISAs on maturity.

5.44   Building on this package of reforms, and in order to encourage further saving in ISAs, **the Government will raise the annual ISA investment limit from April 2008 to £7,200, with an increase in the cash limit to £3,600.** This will benefit around 5 million individuals who are currently making full use of either their cash or overall investment limits. In response to stakeholder views, the Government will also extend the reform to allow transfers from cash into stocks & shares to include all cash held in ISAs, not just that subscribed in previous tax years. The Government will implement the package of ISA reforms from April 2008. Draft implementing legislation is being published alongside the Budget.

Saving **5.45**   Through the Saving Gateway, the Government is exploring the use of matching (a
Gateway Government contribution for each pound saved) to encourage saving among lower-income households and to promote engagement with mainstream financial services. Evidence from an initial pilot showed that matching could encourage genuinely new savers and new saving.[10]

5.46   A second pilot is now drawing to a close. Early evidence suggests that the scheme has brought some individuals into contact with a bank for the first time, and that savers have found the experience useful in familiarising themselves with the mechanics of saving. A full evaluation of the second pilot is due to be published in the spring and the Government will make an announcement on the next steps in summer 2007.

Promoting financial capability

5.47   The Government published its long-term approach for financial capability in January of this year.[11] Its aim is to ensure that consumers have the knowledge, skills and motivation to manage their finances – with the potential for securing lasting benefits for individuals, the financial services industry and the wider UK economy. The Government's long-term aspirations are to ensure that:

- all adults have access to high quality generic financial advice to help them engage with their financial affairs;

---

[9] *Individual Savings Accounts: proposed reforms,* HM Treasury, December 2006.

[10] *Incentives to save: Encouraging saving among low-income households,* University of Bristol, Personal Finance Research Centre, March 2005.

[11] *Financial Capability: the Government's long-term approach,* HM Treasury, January 2007.

- all children and young people have access to a planned and coherent programme of personal finance education, so they leave school with the skills and confidence to manage their money well; and

- a range of Government programmes is focused on improving financial capability, particularly to help those who are most vulnerable to the consequences of poor financial decisions.

5.48   The Government believes that there is currently a lack of access to generic financial advice, i.e. personalised but unregulated advice that helps consumers to understand their financial needs and take appropriate action. To address this, the Government has launched an independent feasibility study, led by Otto Thoresen, Chief Executive of AEGON UK, to research and design a national approach to generic financial advice. The study will report around the end of the year. The Government has also established a ministerial group, chaired by the Economic Secretary to the Treasury, to develop and coordinate the Government's work in this area. Building on consultation, the work of the ministerial group, and the recommendations of the Thoresen study, the Government will publish a financial capability action plan around the end of the year.

Promoting financial inclusion

5.49   The Government is committed to ensuring that everyone has access to appropriate financial products and services. On 14 March 2007, the Government announced a new policy framework for the spending period from 2008-2011. This includes:

- a new Financial Inclusion Fund to maintain financial inclusion activity at the current level of intensity;

- the continuation of the Financial Inclusion Taskforce to monitor progress against existing initiatives and advise the Government on new priorities and directions for policy; and

- a new cross-governmental ministerial working group that will develop a financial inclusion action plan for implementation after 2007 CSR.

5.50   Building on this policy framework, the Government will shortly publish a new financial inclusion strategy. This will be followed by a detailed action plan later in the year, drawing on emerging findings on the success of existing initiatives, and taking into account the work of the Financial Inclusion Taskforce. In the longer term, work on financial inclusion will be mainstreamed into departmental budgets.

Access to   **5.51**   Lack of access to banking services imposes costs on those who can least afford them.
banking   In December 2004, the banks and the Government agreed to work together towards a goal of halving the number of adults in households without a bank account, and making significant progress within two years. The Financial Inclusion Taskforce has reported that steady progress is being made towards the shared goal and definitive evidence will be available shortly.

5.52   In December 2006 a working group on Automatic Teller Machines (ATMs), chaired by the Rt Hon John McFall MP, reported that, while most low-income areas are relatively well-served by free ATMs, a small but significant number of areas are currently without convenient access to free machines. The working group concluded that around 600 new free ATMs would meet access gaps in such areas. As of 1 March 2007, banks and independent ATM operators have made progress to install nearly 400 of the required new free ATMs.

Access to affordable credit   **5.53**   Many low-income households rely on credit products with interest rates of over 100 per cent. The Financial Inclusion Fund has been used to establish a Growth Fund of £36 million to support third sector lenders in providing affordable and appropriate credit. Over 100 credit unions and community development finance institutions have received funding, and over 12,000 affordable loans have been made to financially excluded people. In December 2006 the Government announced further funding for the training requirements of staff and volunteers working in third sector lenders. A training needs analysis for the sector is being conducted.

5.54   In order to reduce some of the increased risk and cost associated with lending to vulnerable groups, the Government has implemented a scheme where, under certain circumstances, third sector lenders can apply for repayment by deduction from benefits, where normal repayment arrangements have broken down. The scheme came into force in December 2006.

5.55   The Government also recognises the damage inflicted on individuals and neighbourhoods by illegal lending, and has announced that projects to tackle illegal lending and provide support for victims will be rolled out to every region of the country. The Department of Trade and Industry (DTI) and HM Treasury are now working with Local Authorities and representative bodies to identify suitable regional locations for the operation of the projects, and to bring them into operation as soon as possible.

Access to money advice   **5.56**   Credit is a useful tool for managing expenditure for most people, but some have difficulty managing their borrowing and become over-indebted. The Government has committed £47.5 million of the Financial Inclusion Fund to increase the supply of free face-to-face money advice. There are now 385 full-time equivalent advisers in post, rising to more than 500 by the end of April 2007, and over 18,000 clients have been advised. The Government has also awarded £6 million to organisations across England and Wales to pilot debt advice outreach. Recent data shows that over 8,000 clients have been helped, more than 90 per cent of them financially excluded.

Now let's talk money campaign   **5.57**   To assist financially excluded people to access mainstream banking and credit products, the Government has launched the *Now let's talk money* campaign. The £5.4 million campaign, being delivered through the Department for Work and Pensions (DWP), will work with trusted intermediaries in day-to-day contact with the financially excluded to achieve an increase in the awareness and take-up of mainstream financial services across England, Wales and Scotland.

Pomeroy Review   **5.58**   In November 2006, the Government asked Brian Pomeroy, the Chairman of the Financial Inclusion Taskforce, to investigate the Christmas savings market to look at the reasons why people opt to use hamper schemes and similar vehicles instead of mainstream financial services products and, in the light of this, to consider how the savings needs of this group of consumers might be better met. The review is expected to report shortly. Separately the DTI has been working closely with the hamper companies to develop an industry-led scheme to ensure consumers' interests are fully protected through the establishment of secure, ring-fenced accounts.

FAIRNESS FOR PENSIONERS

5.59 One of the most significant demographic trends projected to occur over the next ten years is the ageing of the population. For example, by 2017 the number of those aged over 85 will increase by over a third.[12] To respond to the needs of today's older people and the challenges posed by demographic change, the Government has developed its Opportunity Age[13] strategy, which promotes independence and well-being in later life and aims to ensure that the Government adapts to, and benefits from, an ageing society. A comprehensive programme of reforms seeks to ensure that pensioners can share in rising national prosperity, and that older people are able to play a full and active role in society.

5.60 The Government is committed to tackling pensioner poverty, rewarding saving, and helping extend working lives to enable people to meet their retirement income aspirations. Its strategy for pensioners is based on the principle of progressive universalism, providing support for all and more for those who need it most, through both financial support, access to services, and action to tackle age discrimination, improve public services, and encourage and support healthy active ageing.

Fairness for today's pensioners

Security for the poorest pensioners   **5.61** The Pension Credit, launched in 2003, is the foundation through which the Government provides security for the poorest. It is made up of the standard minimum guarantee (Guarantee Credit), which ensures a minimum income for those aged over 60, and the Savings Credit, which rewards those who have built up small savings for retirement. 2.7 million pensioner households currently receive Pension Credit: 2.1 million receive the Guarantee Credit, a take-up level achieved a year ahead of target, and 1.9 million receive the Savings Credit.

5.62 In 2004, the Government committed to uprating the Guarantee Credit in line with earnings until 2008. Accordingly, from April 2007, it will rise to £119.05 for single pensioners and £181.70 for couples. From April 2007, the Savings Credit will also rise to a maximum of £19.05 a week for single pensioners and £25.26 for couples. The Pensions White Paper[14] announced that the Guarantee Credit will be uprated in line with earnings over the long term in order to ensure that the gains made against pensioner poverty are secure into the future.

5.63 Concentrating resources on the poorest pensioners has contributed significantly to reductions in pensioner poverty. Between 1996-97 and 2004-05, over 1 million pensioner households were lifted out of relative poverty and 2 million pensioner households were lifted out of absolute poverty. Half a million pensioner households have been lifted out of relative low-income poverty since the introduction of Pension Credit. The risk of a pensioner household being poor has fallen to 17 per cent, and a pensioner is now no more likely to be poor than the population as a whole.

Support for all pensioners   **5.64** The Government has continued to build on the foundations of support for retirement incomes provided by the basic and additional state pensions. Steps that have already been, or are being, taken to provide support for all pensioners include:

- guaranteeing that the April increase in the basic state pension will be in line with the Retail Prices Index for the previous September, or 2.5 per cent, whichever is higher. From April 2007, the basic state pension will rise to £87.30. As described later in this chapter, the Government has also committed to uprating the basic state pension by average earnings in the longer term;

[12] *Long-term opportunities and challenges for the UK: analysis for the 2007 Comprehensive Spending Review*, HM Treasury, November 2006.

[13] *Opportunity Age: Meeting the challenges of ageing in the 21st century*, Department for Work and Pensions, March 2005.

[14] *Security in retirement: towards a new pensions system*, Department for Work and Pensions, May 2006.

- supporting pensioners who pay income tax, by increasing the higher personal allowances for those aged 65 or over by £1,180 above indexation in April 2008, thereby removing 580,000 pensioners from paying tax and ensuring 43 per cent of pensioners overall pay no tax. By April 2011, no pensioner aged 75 or over will pay any tax until their income reaches £10,000;

- the introduction and extension of Winter Fuel Payments of £200 for households with someone aged 60 or over, rising to £300 for households with someone aged 80 or over, for the duration of this Parliament;

- free television licences for those aged over 75, and free prescriptions and eye tests for those aged 60 and over;

- ensuring that those entering hospital receive their full entitlement to the basic state pension and some other benefits for the duration of their stay;

- introducing free off-peak local area bus travel, and committing to extend this to off-peak nationwide bus travel from April 2008, for those aged over 60 and all disabled people in England; and

- to support the needs of elderly people within their own homes, the Government will reduce the rate of VAT for certain home adaptations to 5 per cent – the lowest rate available under EU VAT agreements. This 5 per cent rate will operate alongside the existing zero rate for certain goods and services provided for disabled people.

Financial Assistance Scheme **5.65**   The Financial Assistance Scheme was established in 2004 to assist those who lost significant amounts when their pension schemes started winding up between 1 January 1997 and 5 April 2005 as a result of the sponsoring employer becoming insolvent. Budget 2007 announces that the Government will now **extend the Financial Assistance Scheme further so that all members of affected pension schemes receive assistance of 80 per cent of the core pension rights accrued in their schme. The cap on maximum assistance will be increased to £26,000 and the *de minimis* rule that excludes those whose FAS payment would be £10 or less a week will be removed.** This includes an additional 85,000, ensuring all 125,000 who lost their pensions will benefit, bringing total long-term expenditure to £8 billion. **The Secretary of State for Work and Pensions will set up a review to look at making best use of assets within these schemes, which will report later this year.**

Helping vulnerable households heat their homes **5.66**   The Government is committed to ensuring that the most vulnerable households can afford to heat their homes to an adequate standard. The Pre-Budget Report announced a new investment of £7.5 million to fund projects using an area-based approach to identify households in fuel poverty and give them the right coordinated help. This will target 300,000 of the most vulnerable households to give them the assistance they need. This adds to the 1.1 million households who have already been helped by Warm Front, which aims to help low-income households, including the poorest pensioners, heat their homes to an adequate standard of warmth by providing heating, energy efficiency measures, and benefit entitlement checks.

Effects of measures to support pensioners **5.67**   As a result of measures implemented since 1997, the Government is spending around £11.5 billion a year more in real terms on pensioners, focusing support on those who need it most. From April 2007, the poorest third of households will be on average £2,200 a year, or around £42 a week, better off. Overall, pensioner households will be on average £1,500 per year, or around £29 a week better off. Women pensioners have also particularly benefited from the Government's support for older people. 3.2 million women have gained an average of £32 a week, while 1.1 million men are £30 per week better off. Chart 5.2 shows the distributional impact of the Government's measures to support pensioners.

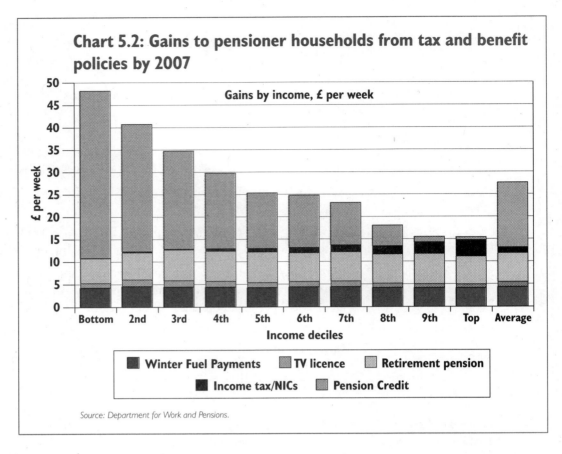

Chart 5.2: Gains to pensioner households from tax and benefit policies by 2007

Source: Department for Work and Pensions.

Fairness for tomorrow's pensioners

5.68 Since 1997 the macroeconomic environment has been characterised by low inflation and high employment, both key to economic stability. This has provided the platform on which individuals can now confidently plan for retirement, with more people having the ability and opportunities to save. Building upon these achievements, the Government is committed to providing a clear retirement framework, enabling individuals to take personal responsibility for their decisions around how much to save and when to retire.

Pension **5.69** Following the recommendations of the Pension Commission, the Government
reform published a White Paper[15] outlining proposed reforms to the state and private pensions systems. The Pensions Bill currently before Parliament introduces reforms to state pensions, including:

- re-linking the basic state pension to average earnings. The Government's objective, subject to affordability and the fiscal position, is to do this in 2012 but, in any event, by the end of the next Parliament at the latest;

- streamlining the contribution conditions to the basic state pension by reducing the number of years needed to qualify to 30; and

- gradually raising the state pension age in line with life expectancy.

5.70 DWP is taking forward reforms to the private pension system, including, as outlined in the December 2006 White Paper[16], proposals for personal accounts. These would:

---

[15] *Security in retirement: towards a new pensions system*, Department for Work and Pensions, May 2006.

- for the first time, give eligible employees the right to a workplace pension with a minimum level of employer contribution, either in an existing scheme or in personal accounts;

- utilise the National Pension Savings Scheme approach to delivering personal accounts. Individuals will not have a choice of pension administrator, but they will have a choice of investments;

- utilise private sector expertise to design and implement personal accounts through a delivery authority; and

- be designed to minimise the administrative burden on all employers, especially small employers.

5.71   The consultation period for the Personal Accounts White Paper ended on 20 March 2007. DWP will respond to this consultation later this year.

Pensions tax **5.72**   Successive governments have provided generous tax relief to encourage pension **relief** saving. A radical simplification of the pensions tax rules came into effect on 6 April 2006 (A-day). To provide greater clarity, the Government has restated the principles that underpin this tax regime[17] – these are set out at Box 5.3. The Government will continue to base any further reforms on these principles. In addition, the Government will implement a package of technical improvements to the regime announced at the Pre-Budget Report and simplify some of the rules around payments of non-cash benefits.

---

[16] *Personal Accounts: a new way to save*, Department for Work and Pensions, December 2006.

[17] Speech by the Economic Secretary to the Treasury, Ed Balls MP, to the NAPF Investment Conference, Edinburgh, 15 March 2007.

Box 5.3: Tax relief for pension saving - principles

A principled and transparent pensions tax regime is crucial to providing the right environment and incentives to encourage long-term saving. Tax relief on pensions products, currently worth £14 billion per year, is a long-standing part of the UK pensions landscape. It is a valuable tool that raises incentives to save in a pension relative to other products, encourages employer engagement, and sits alongside the Government's role in tackling pensioner poverty.

Following many years of change and reform at the margins, the pensions tax rules had become too complex. In response to this, and following extensive consultation, the Government introduced a new regime that radically simplified the pensions tax rules from 6 April 2006. In making these changes, the Government's ambition has been to maintain stability, fairness and encourage long-term saving, providing a transparent and flexible regime, and enabling individuals to make informed choices about pension saving. The following key principles have guided, and continue to underpin, the Government's approach to pensions tax relief:

- generous tax relief is provided to support pension saving to produce an income in retirement. Pension saving is not, however, provided to support pre-retirement income, asset accumulation or inheritance;

- pensions are provided with more favourable tax treatment, compared to other forms of saving, in recognition that they are less flexible than other savings, and are locked away until retirement;

- incentives for employer contributions are provided as it is more efficient for pensions to be provided on a collective basis through the employer; and

- the cost of pensions tax incentives must be affordable and fall within current fiscal projections.

The Government recognises the importance of a stable environment that allows the pensions industry to plan ahead and minimise disruption to the regimes already in place that are working well. At the same time, the Government will need to respond to circumstances that move away from the above principles, or where the market seeks to identify loopholes in legislation that permit behaviours clearly outside the original intention of the legislation. In making these principles transparent, Government is seeking to provide greater clarity for the industry.

Alternatively Secured Pensions

5.73 In line with the principle that pensions tax relief is provided to produce an income in retirement, the Government will bring forward legislation to make changes to the rules governing Alternatively Secured Pensions (ASPs). This will introduce a new requirement to withdraw a minimum level of income each year from an ASP fund. The facility to transfer funds on death as a lump sum to pension funds of other members of the scheme will be removed from the authorised payments rules, with these payments attracting an unauthorised payments charge. Following consultation with industry, there will be special rules for those scheme members who cannot be traced at age 75 and the level of the minimum income will be set at 55 per cent of the level of the annual amount of a comparable annuity for a 75 year old. Rules will be introduced to deal with the interaction of inheritance tax and the unauthorised payments charge. The Government will consult on further measures to prevent the inheritance of tax-relieved pension savings.

Tax-relieved **5.74**   As set out in Box 5.3, pensions tax relief is provided to support pension saving to
term assurance produce an income in retirement. In the 2006 Pre-Budget Report, the Government set out its
policies concerns over a new and fast-growing trend: life insurance policies providing lump-sum
death benefits alone being offered as personal pension arrangements eligible for pensions tax
relief. The Government announced that it would work with the industry to address this issue
and explore how the principles for pensions tax relief should be applied to pensions term
assurance contracts. Following detailed consultation, it has become clear that providing a
meaningful link between term assurance contracts and pension saving is not practical or
commercially viable, due to the additional administrative burdens this would impose. This
conclusion is consistent with the experience pre-A-day, where rules for members of personal
pension schemes requiring term assurance premiums to be no more than 10 per cent of
pension contributions made the products not commercially viable. Therefore, in line with the
principle that pensions tax relief is provided to produce an income in retirement, and to
provide certainty going forward, **the Government confirms that it will no longer provide tax
relief on individuals' contributions that are used to fund personal term assurance policies.**
For contributions under occupational pension schemes, this will apply where the insurer
received the application for the policy on or after 29 March 2007. For contributions under
other registered pension schemes, this will apply where the insurer received the application
for the policy on or after 14 December 2006. There is no change for employers, so death-in-
service benefits and other death benefits funded by the employer will not be affected by this
measure.

Information **5.75**   Personal accounts are to be delivered without the need for regulated financial advice,
and advice ensuring that the costs of pension provision are minimised. The combination of the employer
contribution, tax relief, and lower charges, combined with a reformed state pension system,
will mean that the large majority can expect to benefit from saving in personal accounts,
subject to factors such as growth in the stock market. The Government is currently consulting
on what sort of information should support personal accounts, and the responsibilities of
different organisations in communicating this information, and will develop an evidence-
based information strategy for both pensions and personal accounts over the next year. This
will complement the Government's Financial Capability Strategy and the work to develop
generic advice.

SUPPORTING CHARITIES AND THE THIRD SECTOR

5.76   A vibrant third sector is a key component of a fair and enterprising society, and the
Government is continuing to support the third sector to build communities, empower
marginalised groups of people, and contribute to the design and delivery of key public
services. The Government is also working to support a philanthropic culture of volunteering
and giving, which plays a pivotal role in enabling the third sector to flourish and benefit from
connections to the corporate sector and the general public.

Working to support the third sector

Third Sector **5.77**   Budget 2006 announced that the largest ever consultation with the third sector would
Review shape the outcomes of a review into the future role of the third sector in social and economic
regeneration, to feed into the 2007 CSR. The Government listened to all parts of the sector and
the interim report[18] of the first stage of this consultation, published alongside the 2006 Pre-
Budget Report, set out the most consistent messages from across the 93 consultation events
and over 250 written submissions received. The interim report also announced measures to

---

[18] *The future role of the third sector in social and economic regeneration: interim report,* HM Treasury/Cabinet Office,
December 2006.

boost communities, through a Community Assets Fund, and additional funding for the Safer and Stronger Communities block of local area agreements. **This Budget announces additional support to promote community action and voice with £80 million to be made available to provide core funding to grass-roots community organisations.** The funding will be run by the Office of the Third Sector, and channelled through third sector partners at a local level [such as Community Foundations].

5.78   Following the interim report, a second stage of analysis and engagement with the third sector is taking place and the final recommendations of the third sector review will be published later in the year under the five key themes of the review: enabling voice and campaigning; strengthening communities; transforming public services; encouraging social enterprise; and supporting the environment for a healthy third sector.

Futurebuilders **5.79**   The interim report also acknowledged the role that many third sector organisations play in delivering public services, designing services, and giving voice and advocating on behalf of service users. The Government supports this role with capacity building investment through the Futurebuilders fund, **which will be open to all third sector organisations from spring 2008.** This will particularly help organisations working on environmental activities and those involved in community leisure and sports, many of which are social enterprises.

Social **5.80**   Social enterprises are a key component of the third sector, but also make up a part of
enterprises the mainstream business landscape. Encouraging social enterprises also remains a key theme of the third sector review. In November 2006, the Government published an action plan detailing measures to support and promote a dynamic and sustainable social enterprise sector.[19] Chapter 3 contains both important business tax reforms, with relevance for social enterprises, and progress on the operational review of the Community Investment Tax Relief (CITR) scheme, which encourages private investment in small and medium-sized enterprises, including social enterprises, in disadvantaged communities.

5.81   There is evidence to suggest that levels of equity investment in social enterprises are significantly lower than in other enterprises. The Office of the Third Sector will consider the evidence for whether this is due to market imperfections in the supply of equity investment, or whether social entrepreneurs feel that traditional forms of equity do not meet their needs. If the evidence supports the case for further government intervention in the supply of equity, the Government will examine whether, subject to state aids approval, the CITR model might be enhanced to encourage this form of investment, for example by increasing the limit for Community Development Finance Institutions making equity investments in social enterprises.

Invest to Save **5.82**   The Government also wants to promote partnership-working with the third sector at
Budget all levels. Budget 2006 announced a ninth Invest to Save Budget (ISB) allocation round with a focus on promoting partnerships between third sector organisations and Local Authorities. **This Budget announces that £11 million from the ISB fund will go to 24 new projects supporting innovative approaches to the delivery of local services by third sector organisations.** This funding round has allocated the remaining funding in the ISB pot, which since 1998 has allocated over £100 million to the third sector.

---

[19] *Social enterprise action plan: scaling new heights,* Cabinet Office, November 2006.

Volunteering and giving

Volunteering 5.83   The Government has invested significantly in increasing the number and quality of volunteering opportunities available, and increasing awareness and understanding of the benefits of volunteering to a diverse range of groups. This includes investment in v[20] to create a framework to support youth volunteering, which has so far generated 100,000 volunteering opportunities. Government investment of up to £100 million in v includes a fund available to match contributions from business, and v have raised over £20 million from 63 private companies. Building on this support, at the 2006 Pre-Budget Report, the Government signalled its intent to examine incentives to further encourage volunteering, including by creating a new pathway to university where students receive a discount on their tuition fees in return for volunteering. Following initial consultation with the third sector, v will now conduct a consultation with young people on the design of a potential scheme.

Supporting giving 5.84   **There is much greater scope for charities to claim additional funds through gift aid. The Government will consult with the charitable sector on measures to increase take-up of gift aid and conduct an awareness-raising campaign. The Government will also work with the sector on payroll giving, and publish guidance on tax efficient giving for individuals.** In addition, the Government recognises the need for charities to build ongoing relationships with their major donors, giving them the opportunity to thank their donors and to demonstrate how effectively donations are used, as well as to encourage continued giving. To facilitate the ability of charities to build relationships with donors, **this Budget announces an increase in the value of benefits that donors may receive, in consequence of a donation made within the gift aid regime, to 5 per cent of the donation for those donating £1,000 or more, with the upper limit on benefits received increased to £500.**

Increasing donations to universities 5.85   The Government is aware of the appetite in the higher education sector, in particular to increase voluntary donations. However, the sector may not be exploiting existing incentives for giving, particularly gift aid, to their full capacity. The Government will therefore seek to engage with universities, as part of the wider campaign on gift aid, to increase awareness and application of gift aid, and other incentives for giving to help drive up donations to this sector.

Guidance for giving by businesses 5.86   To support the corporate sector in its work with the third sector, and in response to questions raised during the third sector review consultation regarding tax incentives for employers who want to give to charity or encourage employees to volunteer, **the Government will soon publish updated details that illustrate the incentives for giving and seconding of employees by businesses.**

Unclaimed assets 5.87   Following the announcement in the 2006 Pre-Budget Report that the Government intends to bring forward legislative proposals to enable the banking industry to set up an unclaimed assets scheme, HM Treasury published a consultation document on 20 March detailing the proposed scheme. The Government welcomes the ongoing commitment of the bank and building society sector to a scheme to allow unclaimed assets to be reinvested in society, with a focus on youth services responsive to the needs of young people, and on financial capability and inclusion. The Government plans to release a second consultation document on the distribution mechanism later in the spring.

DELIVERING A MODERN AND FAIR TAX SYSTEM

5.88   A fair and modern tax system encourages work and saving, responds to business developments and globalisation, and supports the provision of world-class public services. To ensure this, the Government will continue to develop a fair and effective tax system that provides a level playing field for all taxpayers.

---

[20] The new charity launched in May 2006 to take forward the recommendations of the Russell Commission report on youth action and engagement.

Modernising tax administration

5.89 The Government continues to work on simplifying tax administration to provide better support for compliant taxpayers, and on transforming HMRC's relationship with business. This work proceeds alongside simplification policies whose progress is described in Chapter 3.

HMRC Review of Links with Large Business **5.90** The Government's 2006 *Review of Links with Large Business*, published in November 2006, made proposals aimed at delivering a modern, responsive business tax administration to foster an environment in which business can flourish, and to improve the UK's competitiveness. **HMRC today publishes a detailed plan[21] for delivering these proposals in consultation with business.**

5.91 The delivery plan also outlines:

- a risk-based approach to enquiries: HMRC will seek to deal with issues in real time, and reduce interventions with low-risk businesses;

- a commitment to incorporating the business perspective whenever significant changes to operational policy, legislation or administrative processes are planned;

- the statutory clearance procedures and rulings available to business, including the relevant circumstances and the necessary contact details; and

- a timetable for consultation in summer 2007 on introducing an advance rulings process and on extending existing clearance procedures to give business earlier certainty.

Treaty financing applications **5.92** The Government has agreed that HMRC can expedite its procedures for agreeing relief from UK tax on loan interests paid to non-residents, and extend the circumstances in which UK residents can enter into thin capitalisation agreements. A detailed announcement will be made later this spring.

Review of HMRC powers, deterrents and safeguards **5.93** HMRC's review of powers, deterrents and safeguards seeks to provide modern tools for the department, and corresponding safeguards for taxpayers. The next stage of consultation will focus on taxpayer safeguards, making it easier to pay, tackling late payment, and compliance assurance checks. The Government has decided not to proceed with proposals for a New Management Act at this time. Some elements of that work will be taken forward by the review of powers. Once substantive changes have been made, further simplification of tax administration will be considered.

HMRC's criminal investigation powers **5.94** Following consultation, **the Government has today announced changes to HMRC's criminal investigation powers.** Under the new approach, HMRC's investigation powers in England, Wales and Northern Ireland will be based on the Police and Criminal Evidence Act (PACE). Comparable provisions will be introduced for Scotland, where PACE does not apply.

Penalties for incorrect tax returns **5.95** In addition, **the Government has today announced a new approach to penalties for incorrect tax returns.** This will make a clear distinction between those who make a genuine mistake, who will not incur a penalty, and those who deliberately under-state their tax liability. These reforms will improve the match between taxpayer behaviour and HMRC's response. The new approach will apply to income tax, corporation tax, capital gains tax, PAYE, NICs and VAT, providing consistency of approach across these taxes.

---

[21] *Making a difference: delivering the review of links with large business*, http://www.hmrc.gov.uk

HMRC on-line services **5.96** Following Lord Carter's *Review of On-line Services* last year, HMRC continues to invest in its on-line infrastructure. Over 35 per cent, 2.9 million in total, of self-assessment returns were submitted on-line by 31 January deadline. To encourage greater on-line filing, the deadline for filing paper returns will be brought forward to 31 October from 2008, as recommended by Lord Carter. HMRC is aiming for universal electronic delivery of business tax returns, starting with large and medium-sized employers. Following representations, the Government today announces a more gradual introduction of requirements to file on-line to give business greater time to prepare. Requirements for PAYE are to be introduced from 2009, VAT is now expected from 2010, and company tax returns in 2011. And, to remove the current disincentive to make payments electronically, the Government intends to change the date on which cheque payments are treated as made for corporation tax and VAT.

Modernising the tax system

5.97 The Government believes that the tax system should ensure fairness between all taxpayers and support the Government's wider economic and social objectives. Budget 2007 announces changes to the tax system to ensure that it remains modern and relevant in a changing world.

Business tax **5.98** An efficient and fair tax system is integral to fostering economic growth. The Government is today bringing forward a package of major reforms to the corporate tax system to promote growth by enhancing international competitiveness, encouraging investment and promoting innovation. Chapter 3 sets out full details of this package, which includes a reduction in the main corporation tax rate from 30 per cent to 28 per cent from April 2008, with accompanying reforms to the capital allowance system, R&D tax credit schemes and the small companies rate.

Capital allowances for cars **5.99** In response to business representations, the Government is publishing a consultation update document, *Modernising tax relief for business expenditure on cars,* outlining more detail on proposals for reforming the current system of capital allowances for cars. These proposals are aligned with the wider reform to the capital allowance system, announced today and set out in Chapter 3.

Film tax **5.100** Finance Act 2006 introduced new rules, which came into effect from 1 January 2007, for the taxation of film production companies, and in particular an additional incentive for the production of British cinema films. From Budget 2007, companies that do not want to take advantage of this incentive may elect out of the new films rules, and would then not have to comply with the administrative requirements for these rules. Such an election can apply to films starting principal photography from 1 January 2007 onwards. An election once made applies to all films produced by the company and is irrevocable.

Financial services **5.101** A competitive tax system is also vital in supporting and promoting UK financial services, in particular ensuring the ongoing pre-eminence of London as an international financial and business services centre. Chapter 3 provides more details of recent progress through the Chancellor's High-Level Group on the international competitiveness of the City of London, and of ongoing work with the fund management industry to consider the recent KPMG report, *Taxation and the competitiveness of UK funds.* Budget 2007 provides support for this strategic work through the reduction of the main rate of corporation tax from 30 per cent to 28 per cent from April 2008. In addition, the steps outlined in the following paragraphs will help to modernise, simplify and clarify taxation of financial services, and so better foster innovative development of the sector.

Modernising tax legislation to reflect MiFID
5.102   On 20 February 2007, the Government announced action to remove obstacles to competition and expand choice in trading and reporting financial instruments, in line with the forthcoming liberalisation of financial markets through the Markets in Financial Instruments Directive (MiFID). As well as changes to enable a wider group of intermediaries to benefit from stamp duty relief, the Government is modernising the definition of recognised stock exchange[22] to allow listed shares traded on markets regulated under MiFID to benefit from the tax arrangements that currently apply only to the London Stock Exchange.

Change to the offshore funds tax regime
5.103   As announced in the 2006 Pre-Budget Report, the Government will introduce legislation in Finance Bill 2007 to remove a restriction in the offshore funds tax regime on the structure of multi-tiered funds. The Government is continuing to consult with industry on wider reform to the regime to address other tax barriers currently impacting on the development of offshore funds of funds. Subject to the outcome of consultation, the Government intends to legislate for a modernised offshore funds tax regime in Finance Bill 2008.

Property Authorised Investment Funds
5.104   Alongside the introduction of UK-REITs (Real Estate Investment Trusts) on 1 January 2007, the Government has been continuing to consider the taxation position for Authorised Investment Funds investing in property. Following constructive discussions with industry, the Government is today announcing a framework for taking this issue forward, so that investors in Property Authorised Investment Funds face broadly the same tax treatment as they would have, had they owned real property or UK-REIT shares directly. Further details are available on the HM Treasury website.

Investment Manager Exemption
5.105   Budget 2007 announces an extension of the Investment Manager Exemption (IME) to include certain instruments for carbon trading. The Government intends this extension to be effective from mid-April 2007. The Government is also considering responses to the recent consultation exercise on proposed changes to the Statement of Practice underpinning the IME, and will report on this at the end of March. Beyond this, the Government will continue to engage with the industry and its representatives to ensure the IME continues to attract investment management business to London.

Islamic finance
5.106   The Government announces today a new tax regime that enables alternatives to conventional securitisations, such as sukuk, to be issued, held and traded within the UK on the same basis as conventional securities. In addition, HMRC is publishing guidance today on how HMRC will view alternative finance products. This includes the treatment of diminishing shared ownership arrangements, such as diminishing musharaka, for capital gains and capital allowances purposes, and how alternatives to conventional insurance, such as takaful, will fall within insurance rules. Finally, the Government encourages funders and market participants to examine ways in which Islamic finance structures can be utilised in UK-REITs and the development of Private Finance Initiative (PFI) projects.

Taxation of insurance
5.107   The taxation of insurance remains a key issue raised during the Government's consultation with the industry through the High-Level Group and elsewhere. The policy measures, announced today and detailed below, aim to modernise the tax rules to reduce complexity and increase clarity, and have been discussed in detail with insurance industry bodies.

General insurance
5.108   The 2006 Pre-Budget Report announced that the existing complex tax rules dealing with the reserves of general insurance companies and Lloyd's would be repealed, subject to a transitional rule, and replaced. **The detail of the transitional rules and basis for replacement accounts-based rules are now announced.** The new rules will have effect for periods of account ending on or after Royal Assent.

5.109   Representations have been made to the Government that the repeal of the tax rules

---

[22] As defined from today, in Section 1005 of the Income Tax Act 2007.

dealing with general insurance reserves will impact unfairly on the sector's ability to use losses. **The Government will consult with industry on the impact of repeal of those rules.**

Lloyd's modernisation **5.110** Following the meeting of the Chancellor's High Level Group on 18 October, a review is underway to look at modernising Lloyd's market practice. To support this process, **the Government will consult with Lloyd's on whether existing tax rules dealing with equalisation reserves should be extended to its members.**

Life insurance **5.111** In 2006, the Government published a consultation on certain aspects of the taxation of life insurance companies and measures were announced in PBR as an initial response. The Government welcomes the continuing dialogue that it has had with industry and, as a further response, will introduce legislation to clarify the definition and tax treatment of structural assets. In addition, it will announce minor miscellaneous amendments to clarify and simplify the tax treatment of life companies and friendly societies. Following further consultation, the Government will bring forward legislation to replace the Crown option with new rules.

Insurance premium tax **5.112** The Government is committed to ensuring business does not face undue regulatory and compliance burdens. **It today announces that it will publish a consultation document reviewing tax representative provisions of insurance premium tax.**

Tax-motivated incorporation **5.113** The Government remains concerned that the corporation tax system is being used to achieve a reduction of personal tax and national insurance liabilities, through the extraction of labour income as dividends. The Government considers that this has eroded the balance between providing low rates of corporation tax to encourage business investment and maintaining a tax system that is fair for all. It has therefore decided to refocus the way in which the tax system supports investment by small businesses, to provide better incentives for those businesses that reinvest their profits for growth. **Budget 2007 announces the introduction of an Annual Investment Allowance** that will provide a major cash-flow benefit to those small businesses that invest to grow their business. The Government will be increasing the Small Companies Rate to reduce the advantage of incorporation and extraction of labour income by way of dividends, providing a fairer outcome for all (further details are set out in Chapter 3).

5.114 The Government will continue to monitor the level and extent to which labour income is extracted in dividends.

Managed Service Companies **5.115** In the 2006 Pre-Budget Report, the Government announced action to tackle Managed Service Company (MSC) schemes used to avoid paying employed levels of tax and NICs, and published a document consulting on the draft legislation. The consultation has shown widespread support for action on MSCs and the Government will be introducing legislation as planned. However, the Government is amending its approach in response to some key concerns raised in the consultation, as explained in *Tackling Managed Service Companies: summary of responses,* published today. The definition of an MSC will be strengthened to give greater clarity and certainty; the scope of the transfer of debt legislation will be clarified; and the Government will delay the application of the debt transfer legislation to third parties (other than MSC scheme providers, and directors, office holders or associates of the MSC) until 6 January 2008.

Personal tax **5.116** As well as fostering economic growth, an efficient and fair tax system provides fairness and transparency for individuals. The Government is today also announcing important reforms to personal taxation. These are detailed earlier on in this chapter and include: **changes to the starting and basic rates of income tax, increases in the higher rate threshold for income tax and in age-related income tax allowances, and aligning the UEL and UPL for NICs.**

Review of alignment of income tax and NICs 5.117   As announced at Budget 2006, the Government is also conducting a review of the case for further alignment of the income tax and national insurance systems.

Dividend tax credit: non-UK dividends 5.118   To simplify the tax system for UK individuals with foreign shares, the Government will, from April 2008, extend the non-payable dividend tax credit to dividends from non-UK companies, subject to certain conditions. A person will qualify for the non-payable dividend tax credit if they own less than a 10 per cent shareholding in a foreign company and receive less than £5,000 of non-UK dividends a year. The Government will also consider whether it is possible, without creating scope for abuse, to extend the non-payable dividend tax credit to people who do not satisfy these conditions.

Homes abroad 5.119   The Government today announced its intention to publish draft legislation later this year which will ensure that individuals owning or planning to buy a home abroad will not face a benefit-in-kind tax charge for private use, if it is owned through a company. The Government will discuss the draft legislation with interested parties to ensure that it achieves these aims.

Residence and domicile 5.120   The review of the residence and domicile rules as they affect the taxation of individuals is ongoing.

Inheritance tax 5.121   As announced at Budgets 2005 and 2006, the inheritance tax allowance will increase to £300,000 in 2007-08, £312,000 in 2008-09 and £325,000 in 2009-10. To continue to provide a fair and targeted system, the Government can now announce that the inheritance tax allowance will increase to £350,000 in 2010-11.

5.122   Budget 2007 also introduces a change to the pre-owned assets rules to ensure that, in certain situations, people can elect back into the IHT regime after the normal self-assessment deadline, rather than incurring the pre-owned assets charge.

Stamp duty and stamp duty land tax 5.123   Budget 2007 announces that provision will be made in this year's Finance Bill to provide that exchanges of property between connected persons are no longer treated as linked transactions, and to make other simplifications to stamp duty and stamp duty land tax (SDLT).

Alcohol duty 5.124   Budget 2007 announces that spirits duties are again frozen, for the tenth successive Budget, meaning the total tax on a standard bottle of spirits will be £1.77 lower than if duty had risen in line with inflation since 1997; duties on beer, wine, sparkling wine and cider will increase in line with inflation, adding 1 penny to a pint of beer, 5 pence to a standard 75 centilitre bottle of wine, 7 pence to a 75 centilitre bottle of sparkling wine and 1 penny to a litre of cider.

5.125   It is also important that businesses are treated fairly. Currently, inconsistencies and omissions in the excise duty regimes mean that businesses may not always have the appropriate rights of review or appeal against decisions made by HMRC. The Government will consult over the summer to identify areas where the review and appeal process for excise duties can be improved.

Tobacco duty 5.126   Smoking remains the greatest cause of preventable illness and premature death in the UK. Maintaining high levels of tax helps to reduce overall tobacco consumption. Budget 2007 therefore announces that, from 6pm on Budget day, tobacco duties will increase in line with inflation, adding 11 pence to the price of a packet of cigarettes.

Smoking cessation products 5.127 Alongside the ban on smoking in public places from 1 July, and consistent with broader NHS measures to support people wishing to quit smoking, from 1 July 2007 the rate of VAT chargeable on smoking cessation products will be reduced to 5 per cent for one year.

Gambling duty 5.128 Following consultation with affected businesses, Finance Bill 2007 will introduce a new duty of excise known as Remote Gaming Duty on the net receipts from remote gaming of all operators licensed by the Gambling Commission. The rate of Remote Gaming Duty will be set at 15 per cent, in line with the rate of General Betting Duty.

5.129 The Government today announces changes to Gaming Duty bands and rates. These changes increase the effective rate of duty on the majority of casinos to 15 per cent, in line with the rate applied to other parts of betting and gaming, and introduce a new top rate of 50 per cent to ensure that this vibrant and expanding sector continues to make a fair contribution to tax receipts.

5.130 In October 2006, the Department for Culture, Media and Sport (DCMS) announced changes to the stakes and prizes of certain gaming machines. In particular, machines available in pubs and clubs saw their maximum stake rise from 30 pence to 50 pence and the maximum prize available increase from £25 to £35. Budget 2007 announces changes to align Amusement Machine Licence Duty categories with the DCMS Order, which will take effect from today.

VAT: housing alterations for the elderly 5.131 The Government will, from 1 July 2007, reduce the rate of VAT for certain home adaptations that support the needs of elderly people to 5 per cent – the lowest rate available under EU VAT agreements. This 5 per cent rate will operate alongside the existing zero rate for certain goods and services provided for disabled people.

VAT: changes to non-business charges 5.132 The Government has decided to reduce to ten years the period over which businesses must account for VAT on non-business use of land and buildings. This change, which will take effect from 1 September 2007, brings this period into line with the Capital Goods Scheme period, following the ruling by the European Court of Justice (ECJ), and reduces the scope for revenue loss through artificial avoidance schemes.

VAT: non-alcoholic drinks 5.133 The Government is committed to maintaining the VAT zero rate for food and drink, which saves consumers £10.5 billion every year. Consistent with this commitment and in view of developments in the non-alcoholic drinks market, the Government will explore the case for modernising and clarifying the VAT legislation, as currently applied.

Rebated oils 5.134 The Government's recent policy has been to maintain the differential between rebated oils and main road fuel duty rates in support of the oils fraud strategy. While the Government recognises the impact that increases can have on heavy users of rebated oils, it is also aware that the duty on rebated oils does not currently recognise the environmental costs of the fuel. In the light of these considerations, the Government will maintain the differential between rebated oils and main road fuels for 2007-08, and in the subsequent two years will increase rebated oils rates by the same proportions as main road fuels in those years. Details on incentives to encourage the use of biofuels among users of rebated gas oil are set out in Chapter 7.

Energy Products Directive 5.135 A number of derogations to the Energy Products Directive, which allowed the Government to charge a reduced rate of duty on fuels used in private pleasure boats and planes, and on waste oils, expired on 31 December 2006. The European Commission has to date declined to renew the majority of derogations for all member states, including the UK's derogations for private boats and planes. It has yet to respond on waste oils. The Government will implement the changes required on 1 November 2008, after further consultation with industry about the best way to minimise the longer-term compliance burden on the sectors concerned.

Protecting Tax revenues

5.136 The vast majority of business and individual taxpayers in the UK comply with their tax obligations and it is the Government's responsibility to ensure that they are not disadvantaged by the actions of the minority who seek to avoid paying their fair share. The Government will continue to support those who seek to be compliant while responding to non-compliance, avoidance and tax fraud with timely and targeted action. The Government will also continue to defend the tax system robustly against legal challenges under EU law.

Tackling tax avoidance **5.137** The Government will continue to tackle avoidance using legislation and litigation, while ensuring that the competitiveness of the UK is maintained. The disclosure regime, introduced at Budget 2004, allows the Government to respond to avoidance swiftly and in a targeted fashion. Following a Pre-Budget Report announcement and subsequent consultation, **the Government will introduce new powers to allow HMRC to investigate a scheme where there are reasonable grounds to believe that a promoter has failed to comply with statutory disclosure obligations.**

5.138 The Government will introduce further measures that will:

- **counter the avoidance of tax-using schemes involving life insurance policies and commission arrangements;**
- **amend the insurance premium tax definition of premium to prevent exploitation of a potential loophole;**
- **amend one of the targeted anti-avoidance rules on buying corporate capital gains and losses to ensure that it operates as intended;**
- **counter employers sidestepping provisions introduced in Finance Act 2003, in response to misuse of Employee Benefit Trusts, in order to obtain a deduction from taxable profits; and**
- **make permanent the measures introduced at the 2006 Pre-Budget Report to close known SDLT avoidance schemes.**

Life insurance companies **5.139** With effect from periods commencing on or after 1 January 2007, **the Government will simplify and strengthen the tax law relating to certain financing arrangements used by life insurance companies.**

Corporate finance **5.140** A new accounts-based regime for taxing sale and repurchase (repo) agreements for companies will be introduced to replace the current mechanical rules. The Government will consult further with business and representative bodies on the detail of the new regime. In addition, as announced on 8 March 2007, the Government will review the current rules that apply to the use of shareholder debt, that has features of equity but is treated as debt for tax purposes, in the light of market developments to ensure that existing rules are working as intended.

Loss-buying **5.141** **The Government will legislate to prevent companies buying the trading losses of corporate members of Lloyd's who are leaving the market and with whom they have no previous economic connection.**

VAT low-value consignment relief **5.142** The Government has monitored closely exploitation of the relief by companies making VAT-free supplies from outside the EU, particularly from the Channel Islands. It notes the action already taken by the authorities there to counter such exploitation. It welcomes the commitment made by the Jersey authorities, in discussions with the Government, to limit the activities of companies continuing to operate on the island, with the associated revenue loss to the Exchequer. The Government remains in discussion with the Guernsey authorities on this issue. It hopes that they will shortly be in a position to make a similar commitment. The Government will continue to keep the situation under close review.

Excise small gift relief **5.143** In light of the ECJ judgment in the Joustra case, which ruled that reliefs from duty for small, non-commercial consignments of excise goods have no basis in EC law, the Government intends to repeal the Excise Duties (Small Non-Commercial Consignments) Relief Regulations 1986.

Tackling tobacco smuggling **5.144** Following a period of consultation, the Government has reached agreement with tobacco manufacturers on the introduction of state-of-the-art pack markings that will enable HMRC and other enforcement agencies to detect counterfeit tobacco products simply and effectively. Manufacturers have agreed to introduce the new pack markings voluntarily during 2007.

Tackling alcohol fraud **5.145** In light of an increased threat from the manufacture of counterfeit alcoholic drinks in the UK and elsewhere in the EU, the Government is announcing a package of measures to tighten up controls on the distribution of alcohol intended for industrial and other non-drinks uses. Following consultation in 2006, in response to an increased risk of excise repayment fraud, the Government is clarifying its guidance to tighten up the verification of claims for drawback of excise duty.

Tackling MTIC fraud **5.146** Missing Trader Intra-Community (MTIC) fraud is an organised criminal attack on the EU VAT system. As announced in the 2006 Pre-Budget Report, HMRC's strengthened operational strategy has successfully reduced attempted fraud levels in the UK during 2006-07. The Government is determined to sustain that impact and maintain downwards pressure on the fraud. It announced this week the introduction, with effect from 1 June 2007, of a change of VAT accounting procedure (the reverse charge) on domestic business-to-business supplies of mobile phones and computer chips. This removes the mechanism by which fraudsters can steal VAT using those goods.

5.147 The Government today announces that, from 1 May 2007, it will also extend the scope of the joint and several liability provisions, which were introduced in 2003 and currently cover a narrow range of goods most commonly used by the fraudsters. These changes will allow the provisions to be applied to a wider range of specified goods. The Government will also include legislation in this year's Finance Bill to allow further changes to the joint and several liability provisions to be made by Treasury Order in the future. These changes will limit the scope for, and allow a more flexible response to any future changes in the nature of the fraud.

TACKLING GLOBAL POVERTY

5.148 Tackling global poverty remains a key priority for the Government. The Government is dedicated to ensuring that the international community delivers on the commitments it made in 2005. The UK is leading action in a number of areas to keep these promises and deliver assistance to developing country governments and their citizens. The UK is also responding to new challenges and working in innovative ways, responding to the growing environmental challenges that impact upon human development, and working with partners to launch Advance Market Commitments (AMCs) to stimulate the development of vaccines for diseases afflicting developing countries. The Government remains focused upon meeting the Millennium Development Goals (MDGs), and will continue to work with all of its partners to pursue these goals.

Delivering aid commitments **5.149** The Government's 2004 Spending Review announced that the Department for International Development's (DfID) budget would grow from £3.8 billion in 2004-05 to £5.3 billion in 2007-08. UK aid to developing countries is helping to reduce permanently the number of people living in poverty by an estimated 2 million each year. The Government is committed to a timetable of reaching Official Development Assistance of 0.7 per cent of Gross National Income by 2013. The 2007 CSR will set out the resources to 2010-11 to help meet this goal.

Debt relief **5.150**   The experience of the last ten years of the Heavily Indebted Poor Countries (HIPC) Initiative has shown that debt relief can be an extremely effective tool in support of poverty reduction. Under the HIPC initiative, the debt burden of the world's poorest countries is being reduced over time by some $100 billion, allowing the savings from debt relief to fund country-owned strategies for poverty reduction. In addition, debt relief worth $38 billion is already being delivered under the Multilateral Debt Relief Initiative (MDRI), to the 21 countries that have completed the HIPC Initiative as a result of the cancellation of debts owed to the International Monetary Fund (IMF) and the concessional lending arms of the World Bank and the African Development Bank. Further countries will qualify on completion of HIPC. The UK is working closely with its international partners to secure the financing of Liberia's arrears to the international financial institutions, including by committing new donor resources. This will allow Liberia to benefit from debt relief through the HIPC initiative.

5.151   The UK attaches great importance to extending multilateral debt relief to all of the poorest countries, not just those countries deemed eligible under the HIPC Initiative. The UK will therefore continue to pay its share of the debt service owed to the World Bank and African Development Bank by other low-income countries that meet criteria for ensuring that the debt service savings are used for poverty reduction. The UK urges other donor countries to agree to debt relief for all low-income countries.

Education for all **5.152**   Education is one of the most cost-effective investments that a country can make to support long-term development, enhancing economic growth and improving health outcomes. Every day, almost 80 million primary school-aged children are denied an education, and almost 60 per cent are girls. Many of those children who do not go to school live in fragile states and states affected by conflict. Education in the midst of conflict and in fragile states can provide an important mechanism for the registration of young children and protection against abuse, and can help states to recover from conflict.

5.153   Developing countries in Asia and Africa are preparing ambitious long-term plans to meet the education MDGs. In May 2006, 22 African countries committed to preparing ten-year plans aimed at ensuring universal primary education by 2015. 15 of these countries have now completed their plans, with five more in development. Many countries in Asia are also developing long-term plans to get all their children into school.

5.154   Long-term planning needs to go hand-in-hand with long-term predictable financing, to enable investment in schools and teaching materials, and to train teachers to deliver quality education. It is estimated that between $7 billion and $10 billion extra will be required each year by 2010, which corresponds to only $10 a year, or two pence a day, for each person in the rich countries. The UK announced in 2006 that it will spend at least £8.5 billion ($15 billion) on aid for education over the following ten years and that, for the first time, it will enter into ten-year agreements to help countries finance their education plans. The UK has already entered into ten-year agreements with the Government of Ghana to provide £105 million, and with the Government of Mozambique to provide £150 million, in support of their ten-year education plans. The UK is providing £200 million to support India's plan to achieve universal primary education by 2010.

5.155   The UK is providing £200 million to support India's plan to achieve universal primary education by 2010. In the run-up to a major international conference on education, which the European Commission will host in Brussels on 2 May, the UK will continue to call on donors to deliver on their promises and provide long-term predictable financing to support countries' education plans. The UK will work with donor partners, developing countries and international agencies to strengthen the delivery of education to children living in fragile states, and to children affected by conflict, as part of a coordinated humanitarian response.

Health   5.156   Alongside education, access to basic health services is essential for developing countries to break out of the cycle of poverty and achieve economic development. Significant financing is needed to strengthen health systems and improve access to basic health services. Many of the major causes of ill health and mortality can be prevented and treated with known and affordable technologies. Stronger basic health services, supported where appropriate by innovative financing mechanisms, can transform our approach to the health MDGs.

Health systems and services   5.157   Many developing countries face significant challenges in providing the basic health services that are essential to delivering the health-related MDGs, such as reducing child and maternal mortality. Severe under-funding, a global shortage of 4.3 million health workers and barriers to increased take-up of services, such as user fees, limit poor people's access. The UK is committed to increasing spending on basic services, such as health, within its bilateral aid programme. The UK strongly supports the priority Germany has placed in its G8 Presidency on strengthening health systems and combating HIV/AIDS. The Government will work closely with its international partners to develop these proposals. As with education, more long-term, predictable support is needed, alongside improved coordination of existing support, to help strengthen basic health services and help partner governments abolish user fees for basic health services.

International Finance Facility for Immunisation   5.158   Worldwide, nearly 30,000 children under the age of five die every day: one child every three seconds. Around a quarter of these deaths – 2-3 million – are caused by diseases for which we have, or soon will have, a vaccine. The International Finance Facility for Immunisation (IFFIm) will dramatically expand the resources available now for immunisation by using the capital markets to convert long-term legally binding commitments from donors into upfront resources. Already $1 billion has been raised in this way, and is helping to support a variety of programmes, including the polio eradication effort. **As part of the new investment made possible by IFFIm, the GAVI Alliance (formerly the Global Alliance for Vaccines and Immunisation) have committed to provide $500 million over five years to finance the strengthening of basic health systems in developing countries. Ultimately, IFFIm will provide an additional $4 billion to immunise an extra 500 million children and save 10 million lives.**

Advance Market Commitments for vaccines   5.159   As access to existing vaccines is expanded, so too must the development of new vaccines be accelerated. 7 million children die every year from diseases like malaria, tuberculosis and AIDS where there is no effective vaccine. Yet only 10 per cent of global research and development funding is spent on such diseases. The UK will double development research funding by 2010. The Government also believes that Advance Market Commitments (AMCs) can complement this direct funding, helping to catalyse private sector investment into research and development for vaccines in developing countries. That is why the UK, along with Italy and Canada, led international efforts to establish a $1.5 billion Advance Market Commitment for a vaccine against pneumococcal disease – the leading cause of pneumonia – which kills 1 million children every year. This pilot AMC was launched in February (see Box 5.4). The UK believes that AMCs have the potential to accelerate the discovery of vaccines against other killer diseases like malaria and AIDS.

HIV/AIDS   5.160   The AIDS pandemic risks undermining progress towards the MDGs. The UK is strongly committed to achieving the goal – set at the 2005 G7 Finance Ministers and Gleneagles G8 Summit and confirmed by the UN in June 2006 – of universal access to comprehensive HIV prevention, treatment and care by 2010, and has pledged £1.5 billion to AIDS programmes in the two years up to 2008. Strengthening basic health systems, improving access to prevention and affordable medicines, and improving education, particularly for girls, are critical to success. The UK also supports the long-term replenishment of the Global Fund for AIDS, TB and malaria (GFATM). We are working closely with Germany, as G8 Presidency, to ensure that international action on AIDS in 2007 makes a significant contribution to the goal of universal access by 2010.

> ### Box 5.4: Launch of Advance Market Commitment pilot
>
> On 9 February 2007, at a ceremony in Rome attended by the Chancellor of the Exchequer Gordon Brown, Her Majesty Queen Rania Al-Abdullah of Jordan, President Wolfowitz of the World Bank, and Ministers from Canada, Italy, Malawi, Norway and Russia, the first Advance Market Commitment was launched.
>
> The AMC is an innovative, market-based mechanism with the potential to save millions of lives by accelerating the development and production of vaccines for the world's poorest countries, vaccines that would not otherwise be available for many years. The first AMC will target pneumococcal disease, bringing potentially life-saving vaccines more quickly to 100 million children and preventing over 5 million deaths by 2030.
>
> The AMC for pneumococcal disease will provide $1.5 billion in future financial commitments to the poorest countries, giving them the purchasing power to buy a suitable vaccine at discounted prices when one becomes available. By creating a market for vaccines in the poorest countries, the AMC creates incentives for the pharmaceutical companies to invest in research, development and production capacity for new vaccines that serve the poor.
>
> Canada, Italy, Norway, Russia, the UK, and the Gates Foundation made commitments to the pneumococcal AMC.

Poverty reduction through environmental protection

5.161 As the Stern Review highlights, all countries will be affected by climate change, but it is the poorest countries that will suffer earliest and most, since they are most vulnerable. Climate change is a serious long-term threat to continued growth and poverty reduction in developing countries and to reaching the MDGs. It will affect agriculture, water supplies and infrastructure, potentially resulting in reduced food security, poorer health and the increased risk of natural disasters. Alongside international action to reduce greenhouse gas emissions, support is needed to help the poorest countries adapt to climate risks, so that the changing climate does not undermine poverty reduction.

5.162 In the 2007 CSR, the Government will create a new international window of the Environmental Transformation Fund (ETF) with £800 million of official development assistance (ODA) to support development and poverty reduction through environmental protection, and help developing countries respond to climate change. This fund will be used through bilateral projects in developing countries as well as multilateral facilities such as the World and Regional Development Banks' Clean Energy Investment Frameworks. It will support adaptation and provide access to clean energy, and help tackle unsustainable deforestation.

5.163 The world's forests have extraordinary environmental, economic and cultural value, and are an essential resource for poor people: 1.2 billion people in developing countries obtain food from trees, and over 2 billion people use mainly wood for cooking and heating. Protecting these resources is a pressing development challenge. At the same time, the Stern Review highlighted that deforestation is responsible for around 18 per cent of world greenhouse gas emissions, and prompt action to tackle deforestation is a critical part of the global response to climate change. There is work underway internationally, including through the German G8 Presidency, to build long-term mechanisms to mobilise donors, countries and the carbon market in order to prevent deforestation, and the UK strongly supports the development of global partnerships on deforestation. But this is an urgent challenge, and there is a strong case for taking early action.

> **Box 5.5: Conservation of the Congo Forest**
>
> **The Secretary of State for International Development will allocate £50 million from the international window of the UK's Environmental Transformation Fund to support proposals that have been made by ten Congo Forest countries to help them protect the Congo Basin's forests and people.** The Congo Basin Forest is an essential resource providing food, shelter, and livelihoods for over 50 million people. It is the second largest tropical forest in the world and one of our most important wildernesses; but it is under increasing pressure from the unsustainable extraction of timber and other resources and from population growth. Some 1.5 million hectares of forest are lost each year and deforestation is expected to accelerate if action is not taken; a catastrophe for the 50 million people who depend on the forest, as well as for climate change and biodiversity. The UK will establish a fund that will slow the rate of deforestation by developing the capacity of people and institutions in the Congo Basin countries to manage their forests and by helping local communities find livelihoods that are consistent with the conservation of forests. The new fund will strengthen the work of the aid donors who are already active in the region, including Belgium, Canada, France, Germany, and the US, and it will open a channel for new donors to add their support.
>
> Professor Wangari Maathai, distinguished former winner of the Nobel Peace Prize and tireless campaigner for integrating the issues of development, climate change and transparency, will lead this work. She and the UK have asked the Rt. Hon. Paul Martin; Canada's former Prime Minister and a long-standing advocate for debt relief and for African leadership in development, to help establish the fund as Goodwill Ambassador alongside Prof Maathai. They will advise on the Fund's governance and how the work is implemented, helping to develop a clear governance framework designed to ensure that it has strong African ownership and supports the needs of the Congo Basin's countries, that it protects the livelihoods and rights of forest people, and that it is spent effectively, with good financial management free from corruption.

5.164   The UK is providing assistance to the World Bank and the Regional Development Banks to develop a Clean Energy Investment Framework to accelerate public and private investment in low carbon energy in developing countries. To promote adaptation, the UK is already providing £5 million towards the expected total cost of £36 million for the ClimDev Africa Program, previously known as the Global Climate Observing System, to improve climate data for development in Africa. To increase climate change research the UK has initiated a £30 million programme (in collaboration with the Canadian International Development Research Centre) to build and maintain the capacity and knowledge of African researchers. The UK is committed to mainstreaming climate risk reduction and is working with the World Bank to put measures in place for screening development assistance by 2008. The UK is committed to giving a higher priority to disaster risk reduction, through allocating 10 per cent of the funding provided in response to each natural disaster to prepare for and mitigate the impact of future disasters.

Trade 5.165   Trade can, under the right circumstances, be a driver of economic growth, development and poverty reduction, benefiting developed and developing countries alike, provided they have the economic infrastructure and capacity to trade competitively. In the face of a current rise in protectionist sentiment, urgent reform of the global trading system is needed. The UK is delighted that, following the suspension of negotiations in the Doha Round of world trade talks last July, full negotiations have now resumed. The UK continues to do all it can to achieve a conclusion to the negotiations at the earliest opportunity. For the talks to conclude successfully, all key World Trade Organisation (WTO) players will need to play their part and deliver increased market access in agriculture, industrial goods and services; end export subsidies; substantially reduce all trade-distorting domestic support; and provide effective special and differential treatment to enable developing countries to capture the gains from trade. Developing countries must also have the flexibility to design, plan and sequence trade reforms in line with their country-owned development and poverty reduction strategies.

Aid for trade **5.166**   Efforts to increase market access and phase out subsidies will only generate a limited supply-side response from poorer countries unless they are complemented by the necessary investments to boost their capacity to trade, and to help them participate effectively and fairly in the global trading system. This is also critical in building support for open markets. Before the WTO ministerial in Hong Kong in December 2005, developed countries made 'aid for trade' pledges and agreed to prioritise investments in infrastructure. At the annual meetings of the IMF and the World Bank in Singapore in September 2006, the UK announced that its support for 'aid for trade', which includes training trade specialists and building trade institutions, as well as support for infrastructure – such as roads, ports, and telecommunications – is expected to increase by 50 per cent by 2010-11. This will equate to $750 million a year in 2010.

5.167   Together, European countries and the European Commission will increase assistance to a total of €2 billion a year by 2010. Japan has also promised $10 billion over three years and the US a total of $2.7 billion a year by 2010. The UK calls for all countries to turn their commitments into concrete and credible financing, starting by making the enhanced Integrated Framework operational as soon as possible.

6 DELIVERING HIGH QUALITY PUBLIC SERVICES

The Government's aim is to deliver world-class public services through sustained investment matched by far-reaching reform. A decade on from the first Comprehensive Spending Review (CSR), the Government has been conducting a second CSR, reporting in 2007, which will identify what further investments and reforms are needed to equip the UK to respond to the challenges and opportunities of the decade ahead.

A central element of preparations for the 2007 CSR is a comprehensive value for money programme which will embed efficiency into departmental planning and release the resources needed to meet new priorities. This Budget announces further details of that programme, including:

- having established the baseline savings ambition for the 2007 CSR period of 3 per cent per year across central and local government, **this Budget confirms that all of these savings will be net and cash-releasing, thereby maximising the resources available to improve frontline services and fund new priorities; and**

- **an early CSR07 settlement for the Attorney General's Departments, which sees their budgets fall by 3.5 per cent per year in real terms** and provides the early certainty needed to take forward an ambitious programme of reform and improvement across the criminal justice system.

Budget 2007 also confirms the firm overall spending limits for the CSR07 years 2008-09, 2009-10 and 2010-11, which ensure that the Government meets its strict fiscal rules while allowing it to increase total public spending by an average of 2 per cent per year in real terms with:

- **current spending increasing by an average of 1.9 per cent per year in real terms;** and

- **net investment rising to 2¼ per cent of GDP compared with ½ per cent of GDP in 1997-98, locking in the step change in investment over the past decade.**

This increase in overall resources, together with savings released by the CSR07 value for money programme, will enable the Government to sustain the pace of improvement in frontline services and focus additional investment on key priorities within a framework that entrenches the macroeconomic stability secured over the past decade.

To ensure that the UK has the skills and science base it needs to prosper in an increasingly competitive global economy, alongside **the early CSR07 settlement for the science budget** announced in Chapter 3, Budget 2007 announces:

- **an early CSR07 settlement for the Department for Education and Skills which sees education spending in England rise by 2.5 per cent a year in real terms (5.3 per cent a year in nominal terms) on average over the period,** increasing UK education spending from 4.7 per cent of GDP in 1996-97 to 5.6 per cent by 2010-11; and

- **substantial additional resources to support the Government's vision for personalised education,** including funding for one-to-one teacher-led tuition for over 300,000 under-attaining pupils a year in English by 2010-11 and 300,000 in Maths.

To accelerate the ongoing development of counter-terrorism capabilities, **Budget 2007 announces a further £86.4 million for the Security and Intelligence Agencies.**

6.1   The Government's aim is to deliver world-class public services through sustained investment matched by far-reaching reform. High quality education and training, a modern and reliable transport network, an effective criminal justice system, and a modern health service provide the essential foundations for a flexible economy and a fair society, ensuring the UK can seize the opportunities and meet the challenges of the decade ahead.

Investing in   **6.2**   In June 1997 the incoming Government launched the first Comprehensive Spending
priorities   Review (CSR), laying the foundations for a modernised public spending and performance management framework which supports prudent and efficient planning of expenditure over the medium to long term.

6.3   The 1998 CSR involved the most fundamental and in-depth examination of public spending ever attempted, enabling resources to be re-focused on the incoming Government's priorities in health, education and transport. Subsequent spending reviews in 2000, 2002 and 2004 delivered further increases in resources for these areas, made possible by stable and sustainable economic growth with falling debt interest payments and low unemployment, as illustrated in Chart 6.1.

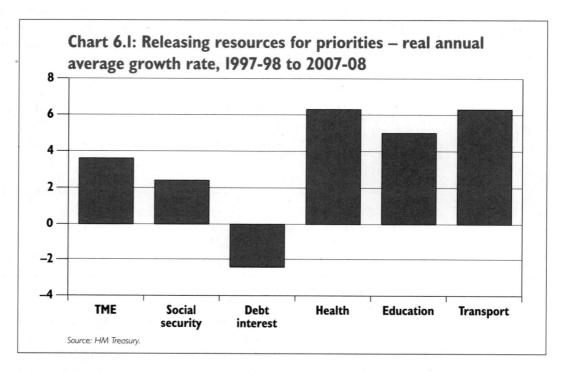

Chart 6.1: Releasing resources for priorities – real annual average growth rate, 1997-98 to 2007-08

Source: HM Treasury.

6.4   By matching this growth in spending with an ambitious reform programme to support the efficiency, delivery and accountability of public services, the Government has been able to achieve major improvements in outcomes across front-line services. By 2007-08, compared with 1997-98:

- UK health spending will be 85 per cent higher in real terms helping to substantially reduce waiting times so that today almost no one waits for over six months, compared to a quarter of a million in 1997;

- total spending on education will have more than doubled, with over 58 per cent of pupils now achieving five or more good GCSEs, up from 45 per cent in 1997, with some of the biggest improvements seen in disadvantaged areas with a history of low achievement;

- spending on the police will have increased by 39 per cent in real terms to over £11 billion, and overall spending on crime, justice and security in the Home

Office will be 75 per cent higher in real terms, delivering 14,000 more police officers and 10,000 more Police Community Support Officers; and

- public expenditure on transport is planned to increase by over 60 per cent in real terms, with investment currently over £250 million a week, ensuring 85 per cent of trains arrive on time, six months ahead of the Government's scheduled target.

THE 2007 COMPREHENSIVE SPENDING REVIEW

Preparing for the decade ahead **6.5** In July 2005, the Chief Secretary to the Treasury announced the launch of a second Comprehensive Spending Review reporting in 2007. The 2007 CSR will set departmental spending plans and priorities for the years 2008-09, 2009-10 and 2010-11. In a rapidly changing world, the 2007 CSR will deliver the investments and reforms needed to equip the UK to prosper in the decade ahead, through:

- a robust response to the long-term challenges and opportunities that will transform both the environment in which public services operate and the UK's role in the world. A detailed understanding of future trends together with innovative cross-departmental policy responses are being developed through a series of policy reviews;

- an ambitious and far-reaching value for money programme to release the resources needed to address these challenges, which combines further development of the SR04 efficiency programme with a set of zero-based reviews of departments' baseline expenditure. Alongside departmental value for money preparations, the Government is taking forward a government-wide service transformation programme based on the recommendations of Sir David Varney to better join up service delivery, making public services more efficient and responsive to the needs of users;

- a more strategic approach to asset management and investment decisions to ensure the UK is equipped with the infrastructure needed to support both public service delivery and the productivity and flexibility of the wider economy; and

- transforming the delivery of public services by developing the performance management framework to continue driving outcome focused improvements and target resources on the Government's priorities. These reforms combine a focused and cross-cutting set of Public Service Agreements with greater emphasis on local communities' voice in the design of public services and empowering users to play an active role in service delivery and governance.

6.6 Taken together, these measures will ensure that the Government can sustain the pace of improvement in public service delivery seen in past spending rounds, and continue to make progress on its goals of sustainable growth and employment, fairness and opportunity, stronger communities and a better quality of life, and a secure and fair world.

THE LONG-TERM OPPORTUNITIES AND CHALLENGES AHEAD

6.7 While much has been achieved in the past ten years, the world is changing rapidly. There are new opportunities and challenges in the decade ahead, which will have far-reaching implications for public services. These include:

- demographic and socio-economic change, with rapid increases in the old age dependency ratio and rising consumer expectations of public services;

- the intensification of cross-border economic competition, with new opportunities for growth, as the balance of international economic activity shifts toward emerging markets such as China and India;

- the rapid pace of innovation and technological diffusion, which will continue to transform the way people live and open up new ways of delivering public services;

- continued global uncertainty with ongoing threats from international terrorism and conflict and the continued imperative to tackle global poverty; and

- increasing pressures on natural resources and the global climate, requiring action by governments, businesses and individuals to maintain prosperity and improve environmental care.

6.8 To inform the long-term decisions to be made in the 2007 CSR, the Government has engaged with businesses, voluntary organisations, think-tanks and the academic community to develop a detailed picture of these challenges and opportunities. The Government published key findings of this work in *Long-term opportunities and challenges for the UK: analysis for the 2007 CSR* in November 2006.

6.9 Meeting these challenges will require innovative cross-departmental policy responses and sustained investment in key areas. As set out in Budget 2006, the Government has been taking forward a series of cross cutting reviews whose findings will inform the plans set out in the 2007 CSR. Progress on each of these reviews is set out below.

Demographic and socio-economic change **6.10** The Government has been examining a number of areas to ensure it continues to build on its progress towards increasing fairness and social justice, as set out in Chapter 5, in the face of continuing demographic and socio-economic change over the decade ahead:

- the *Mental Health and Employment Review* is considering options for improving employment outcomes for people with mental health conditions. The consultations have identified the need for an holistic approach for individuals focusing on employers, the NHS and the employment system. The right support will help many of the adults excluded from the world of work due to mental illness to return to, and remain in, employment, benefiting their health and the wider economy. Further details are set out in Chapter 4;

- building on the Government's response to Kate Barker's *Review of Housing Supply*,[1] the *Supporting Housing Growth Review* is considering a number of reforms to ensure new housing is supported by the necessary public infrastructure such as schools, roads and hospitals, and thereby better respond to the demographic pressures on the supply of housing. Further details are set out in Chapter 3; and

- the *Children and Young People's Review* is examining how to secure further improvement in outcomes for the youngest in our society. Interim findings are set out in Box 6.1.

---

[1] *Review of Housing Supply*, HM Treasury and the Office of the Deputy Prime Minister, March 2004.

Box 6.1 Children and Young People Review

The Government's aim is to ensure that every child, regardless of circumstances, gets the best start in life and ongoing support they need to fulfil their potential. The Children and Young People Review was set up to examine the progress made in improving outcomes for children and young people and what further action needs to be taken as part of the 2007 CSR and beyond.

The review has received evidence from over 200 organisations and held consultation events with parents, young people, academics and practitioners from public and voluntary services. In January 2007 the review published a discussion paper setting out the evidence collected and the review's analysis.[2] The review has found that *Every child matters*, the Government's programme of reform of children's services, is bringing about significant improvements and identifies a number of areas where more can be done to ensure the potential of all children is fulfilled. In particular, the review identifies the need for further progress in raising educational attainment, building social and emotional skills and helping parents to support their child's development. Under the umbrella of this review, three sub-reviews have identified the following priorities:

- **a strategy for youth services:** to go further to develop high quality, accessible positive activities, ensuring young people have more say in what is provided;

- **support for disabled children:** to ensure more responsive public services, empowering disabled children and their families to influence their own provision, encouraging earlier intervention and best practice support, and better support where needs are complex; and

- **support for families caught in a cycle of low achievement:** to ensure more effective, coordinated whole-family support, helping the minority of children experiencing the poorest outcomes.

The review will complete its work with recommendations on policy priorities in spring 2007.

6.11 The number of older people, particularly those aged over 85, is expected to rise sharply over coming years with significant implications for public services, such as long-term care for the elderly. Recent reports from Derek Wanless for the King's Fund, the Joseph Rowntree Foundation, and others have made important contributions to the debate around the future of social care provision, which will also be informed by individual budgets, Partnerships for Older People Projects, direct payments and the In Control programme. In assessing proposals, as part of the long-term vision of the 2007 CSR, the Government will consider whether they are affordable, whether they are consistent with progressive universalism, and whether they promote independence, dignity, well-being and control in line with *Improving the Life Chances of Disabled People,* the White Paper *Our Health, Our Care, Our Say,* and the National Service Framework for Older People.

Changing global economy **6.12** The steps set out in Chapters 2, 3 and 4 to entrench macroeconomic stability, raise productivity growth and increase employment opportunity for all are essential in order to ensure every individual and business is able to seize the opportunities presented by an increasingly competitive and integrated global economy. To make further progress over the 2007 CSR period:

- the *Leitch Review of Skills,* published in December 2006, set out ambitions for the skills profile the UK should aim to achieve by 2020, together with a range of policy recommendations for improving the UK's skills base. Further details on the steps the Government is taking in response to the review are set out later in this chapter and in Chapter 3;

---

[2] *Policy review of children and young people: a discussion paper,* HM Treasury and the Department for Education and Skills, January 2007.

- the *Eddington Transport Study*, published in December 2006, set out criteria for securing the maximum long-term benefit from transport investment for economic productivity, stability and growth. The Government is taking forward these recommendations and will set out its proposals to deliver the major reforms to the planning, funding and delivery of transport interventions in the CSR, as set out in Chapter 3;

- in order to ensure that all regions and localities within England can share the benefits of economic growth in the decade ahead, the Government is reviewing the effectiveness of sub-national interventions on economic development and the regeneration and renewal of deprived areas. Further details are set out in Chapter 3; and

- the *Barker Review of Land Use Planning*, published in December 2006, shows how planning policy can better deliver economic growth and prosperity alongside other sustainable development goals. The Government welcomed the review, and will be bringing forward reforms this spring via a White Paper. Chapter 3 sets out further details.

Innovation and technological development 6.13 The rapid pace of technological change is set to continue over the decade ahead, creating new opportunities for both businesses and public services. To help harness these opportunities:

- the Sainsbury Review will assess the responsiveness of the science and innovation system to the challenges and opportunities of globalisation, and take a forward look at what more needs to be done to ensure the UK's continued success in wealth creation and scientific research. Chapter 3 sets out further details;

- the Office for Strategic Co-ordination of Health Research (OSCHR) has been established in response to the *Cooksey Review of Health Research Funding*, published in December 2006. OSCHR will work through the Translational Medicine Board (TMB) and the Public Health Research Board (PHRB) to develop and oversee a single, integrated strategy for translational research and public health research, delivering economic and health benefits to the UK; and

- the Government is taking forward the recommendations of the *Gowers Review of Intellectual Property*, published in December 2006, to ensure the UK's intellectual property (IP) system is fit for the digital age. Chapter 3 sets out the details of new reforms to tackle IP crime and greater support for UK businesses to help recognise, protect and maximise the value of their IP.

6.14 To ensure the UK has the skills and science base it needs to prosper in an increasingly competitive global economy, Budget 2007 announces an early CSR07 settlement for the Department of Trade and Industry's (DTI) ring-fenced science budget and the Department for Education and Skills (DfES), which together will ensure that total investment in the public science base will rise by an annual average rate of 2.5 per cent in real terms over the CSR07 period, meeting the commitment in the *Ten Year Science and Innovation Investment Framework*. These early settlements provide long-term certainty for the research community, and will deliver resources to meet a range of priorities over the CSR period, including further investment to support excellent research, increase the economic impact of the science base and implement the recommendations of the Sainsbury and Cooksey Reviews. Further details are set out in Chapter 3.

Continued global uncertainty 6.15 While the UK has faced terrorist threats in the past, the global reach, capability and sophistication of international terrorist groups places the current threat on a scale not previously encountered. Global security in the decade ahead will be shaped by a range of factors, including international responses to poverty, future conflicts and areas of instability. As part of its response to these challenges, a review of the delivery of the Government's counter-terrorism and security strategies will inform the 2007 CSR.

Environmental pressures and climate change 6.16 The *Stern Review on the Economics of Climate Change*[3], published in October 2006, examined the consequences of climate change in both developed and developing countries, and the specific implications for the UK. It showed that climate change is a serious and urgent challenge, which requires an urgent global response. The costs of mitigating the effects of climate change are significant but manageable, and can be minimised through international and co-ordinated action. Chapter 7 sets out the Government's programme of action to tackle climate change and other environmental policies.

EMBEDDING A CULTURE OF VALUE FOR MONEY

6.17 To ensure that historic increases in investment are translated into better outcomes across public services, the Government has taken a series of steps to drive improvements in delivery and ensure maximum value for money for the taxpayer. The 2004 Spending Review set out the Government's ambition to achieve annual efficiency gains of over £21 billion by 2007-08. **Against this ambition departments and Local Authorities have reported annual efficiency gains worth over £15 billion to the end of December 2006.**

6.18 Table 6.1 shows the gains reported by departments and Local Authorities to date. A full breakdown of departmental progress towards efficiency and relocation targets will be available on the Office of Government Commerce (OGC) website, the day after the Budget.[4] Further information will be available in departmental reports, due later in the year.

Table 6.1: Public sector efficiency savings

	Efficiency targets	Reported delivery
Department		
Education and Skills	4,350	1,622
Health	6,470	4,449
Transport	785	532
Communities and Local Government (previously ODPM)	620	756
Home Office	1,970	2,118
Constitutional Affairs	290	244
Crown Prosecution Service	34	70
Defence	2,830	1,869
Foreign and Commonwealth Office	120	69
International Development	310	259
Trade and Industry	380	354
Environment, Food and Rural Affairs	610	411
Culture, Media and Sport	260	183
Work and Pensions	960	1,005
Northern Ireland Office	90	69
Chancellor's Departments	550	293
Cabinet Office	25	11
Other Departments	31	35
Local Government	6,450	4,538
Total efficiency savings[1,2] **rounded to nearest £10m**	**21,480**	**15,580**

[1] Total forecast is sum of targets, less overlap of £5,650m efficiencies across central and local government.
[2] Total reported delivery is sum of delivery, less overlap of £3,305m efficiencies across central and local government.

---

[3] *Stern Review on the Economics of Climate Change*, Cambridge University Press, October 2006.
[4] http://www.ogc.gov.uk/efficiency.asp

Measuring efficiency **6.19** The National Audit Office's (NAO) February 2006 report into the Government's efficiency programme recognised the challenges of verifying and validating efficiency data.[5] In its recently published second report, the NAO notes the good progress made by the OGC in addressing these measurement issues.[6] The Government expects this progress to continue, and the OGC will do further work to tackle the remaining measurement challenges during the final year of the programme, including by encouraging greater use of departmental internal auditors and through further engagement with the NAO and the Audit Commission. Building on the NAO's recommendations regarding the current programme, savings delivered by the CSR07 value for money programme will be measured net of implementation costs.

Workforce reductions **6.20** Alongside efficiency gains, departments are continuing to reform their workforces to deliver better services. The NAO report noted that workforce reductions to date were broadly robust and their analysis of the systems underpinning workforce reporting offered substantial assurance on the reductions being made. At the end of December 2006 departments had reported workforce reductions of over 50,800, strong progress towards the target of 70,600 reductions in the civil service and military posts in administrative and support roles. In addition, the Department for Work and Pensions and Her Majesty's Revenue and Customs have reallocated over 9,700 jobs to front line posts to date.

Table 6.2: Workforce reduction across departments

Department	Reductions	Reallocations to front line roles	Total reduction
Department for Work and Pensions	21,398	6,667	28,065
Ministry of Defence	12,421	0	12,421
HM Revenue & Customs	8,504	3,036	11,540
Other departments	8,565	0	8,565
Total	50,888	9,703	60,591

Lyons relocations **6.21** The 2004 Spending Review also announced the Government's ambition to relocate substantial numbers of public sector employees outside the high cost areas of London and the South East and help boost regional economies. At the end of December 2006 departments had reported 11,068 relocations, over halfway towards the target of 20,000 by 2010. Through relocation and better management of the civil estate, over 2 million square feet of office space previously used by government was released to the market in London and the South East in the first half of the 2004 Spending Review period.

Transforming government procurement **6.22** Building on the Gershon recommendations, the Government is taking further steps to maximise the value of procurement, as set out in *Transforming government procurement* published in January 2007. This sets out reforms to government procurement which will support the delivery of world class public services, improve value for money and help to reduce costs for both the public sector and private contractors.[7] The reform programme will raise the standard and profile of a more flexible Government Procurement Service and will be led by a smaller, higher calibre, more focused Office of Government Commerce (OGC).

---

[5] *Progress in Imposing Government Efficiency*, NAO, February 2006.

[6] *The Efficiency Programme: A Second Review of Progress*, NAO, February 2007.

[7] Details of a survey on the allocation of public sector procurement by business size are available on the DTI's website www.dti.gov.uk.

Value for money in the 2007 CSR

Releasing resources for new priorities   6.23   To continue to improve front-line service delivery and release the resources needed to respond to new long-term challenges, the 2007 CSR will go beyond the ambition set out in the 2004 Spending Review efficiency programme by:

- deepening the government-wide efficiency programme in the operational areas established by the Gershon Review, with greater engagement of frontline professionals to identify opportunities for service improvements;

- taking a fundamental look at the way that government spends money on programmes and policies ten years on from the first CSR, through a set of zero-based reviews of departments' baseline expenditure;

- delivering a step-change in the management of the public sector asset base, taking forward the recommendations of the Lyons Review of Asset Management; and

- reviewing the opportunities for transforming service delivery across government, looking at how the channels through which services are delivered can be made more efficient and responsive to the needs of users.

6.24   The 2006 Pre-Budget Report set out the baseline ambition of 3 per cent savings per year across central and local government. Since then, departments have been refining their value for money plans for the CSR07 years, and this Budget announces that all of the savings delivered under the CSR07 value for money programme will be net of implementation costs and cash-releasing, thereby maximising resources available to improve frontline services and fund new priorities.

Early CSR07 settlements   6.25   Strong progress in departments' value for money preparations has enabled a number of departments to agree early spending settlements for the 2007 CSR period which deliver continued service improvements at reduced cost:

- Budget 2006 announced early settlements for the Department for Work & Pensions, HM Revenue & Customs, HM Treasury and the Cabinet Office, which will see their budgets fall by 5 per cent a year in real terms over the CSR07 period; and

- the 2006 Pre-Budget Report announced a 2007 CSR settlement for the Department for Constitutional Affairs, which will reduce its budget by 3.5 per cent per year in real terms, and also announced 5 per cent annual real reductions in the spending plans for five smaller departments (National Savings & Investments, the Food Standards Agency, the Privy Council Office, the Government Actuary's Department and the Central Office of Information); and

- this Budget announces that the Attorney General's Departments (AGDs) have already agreed to deliver ambitious value for money reforms over the CSR07 period, enabling them to continue improving services within overall budgets that will fall by 3.5 per cent per year in real terms. Further details are set out later in the chapter. This Budget also announces an early 2007 CSR settlement for the Office of Fair Trading which will reduce its budget by 5 per cent a year in real terms over the 2007 CSR period. Further details are set out in Chapter 3.

Value for money savings

6.26   These settlements embed ongoing value for money improvements into departments' medium-term expenditure planning and lay the foundations for a CSR focussed on meeting the challenges of the decade ahead. The Government has set aside over £1 billion in modernisation funding for the early settlements announced to date, enabling these departments to release a total of over £2 billion in nominal savings over the three years of the CSR 07 period and to embed ongoing efficiencies for the longer term.

Administration budgets

6.27   Controls on departments' administration budgets help to drive efficiency in the running of government itself and maximise the resources that are delivered to the frontline. By harnessing the potential of new technologies and driving through operational efficiencies in the running of departmental business, the Government is able to make further progress in reducing the proportion of taxpayers' money that is spent on the administration of departments. Having frozen administration budgets in nominal terms over the 2004 Spending Review period to ensure that all additional expenditure goes directly to frontline services, the 2006 Pre-Budget Report announced that the Government will go further over the 2007 CSR period with 5 per cent annual real reductions in administration budgets across departments, releasing over £1 billion a year by 2010-11, and reducing the proportion of public spending spent on administration to a new record low.

Public sector pay

6.28   The Government's sustained investment in public services has increased pay for frontline staff and widespread recruitment and retention problems are largely a thing of the past. This has supported the expansion of frontline workforces to help drive improvements in public service delivery. There are now 92,000 more teaching assistants, 36,000 more teachers and 85,000 more nurses than in 1997.

6.29   Over the 2007 CSR period controlling pay spending will be essential in delivering value for money from public spending and keeping inflationary pressures in check. The Government has made clear that pay settlements must be consistent with the achievement of the CPI inflation target of 2 per cent and demonstrated this commitment by announcing on 1 March 2007 that the overall headline awards for Pay Review Body groups in 2007-08 are to be less than the 2 per cent inflation target, averaging 1.9 per cent, the lowest level of awards in over 10 years. In preparation for the 2007 CSR, key departments will prepare pay and workforce plans setting out how they will achieve the Government's objectives on pay policy and service delivery throughout the period.

Varney review

6.30   Sir David Varney's review *Service Transformation: A better service for citizens and businesses, a better deal for the taxpayer* was published alongside the 2006 Pre-Budget Report. This review emphasises the Government's commitment to continually procure and make use of technology in the most effective way, to maximise benefit for citizens and businesses. The review's recommendations are being taken forward through the Service Transformation Delivery Plan, which is being developed under the leadership of Sir Gus O'Donnell and will be published alongside the 2007 CSR. As part of this, a feasibility study into a single point of contact change of circumstance service, led by the Secretary of State for Work and Pensions, was initiated in January 2007.

E-services

6.31   To realise the full potential of the internet to provide a key means for citizens and businesses to access government services 24 hours-a-day, 7 days a week, and to achieve possible savings of £400 million by the end of 2010-11:

- the single access websites, Businesslink.gov and Directgov, will be strengthened and responsibility for the Business.gov programme will shift to HMRC from 2 April 2007, and work will be carried out to consider moving Directgov to the Department for Work and Pensions from the beginning of the 2007 CSR period; and

- the Government will aim to rationalise substantially the number of its websites, with 551 already identified for closure.

Citizen and business contact 6.32 To ensure citizens and businesses receive faster and better services when accessing government through the telephone or face-to-face:

- all publicly funded contact centres will be required to undergo formal published accreditation by December 2008, aiming to deliver £400 million savings through improvements by 2010-11;

- the implementation of the cross-government estate management strategy – High Performing Property – will now incorporate the use of local office estate across departments. Rationalisation of the local office network, establishment of one-stop-shop local offices and an increased use of mobile services within local communities could result in savings of £250 million by the end of 2010-11; and

- a department led 'Citizen and Business Contact Council' will promulgate benchmarks for contact performance and drive greater efficiencies.

Strengthening citizen insight 6.33 As envisaged by Sir David Varney, citizen and business insight must become central to the design and delivery of public services. The Citizen Insight Forum will be expanded and strengthened to promote and extend the skills and capability of public services to take account of citizens and businesses experience in the design and delivery of public services.

CAPITAL AND ASSETS

Capital in the CSR 6.34 In order to take full advantage of the unprecedented increase in investment over the last decade, the 2007 CSR will adopt a more strategic approach to asset management, driving better value for money and encouraging efficient management of the Government's existing asset base. Consistent with the recommendations of the Lyons Review of Asset Management, the focus of this new approach is the development of a unique Asset Management Strategy (AMS) for each department. These will be published following the conclusion of the 2007 CSR, increasing transparency and accountability in the management of the Government's assets.

Asset management strategy 6.35 Departments' AMS will demonstrate that they have in place an effective management framework, which actively maximises the value of their existing assets and provides a strategic context for future investments. They will provide an account of the systems and procedures in place to ensure:

- assets are adequately maintained and efficiently utilised to deliver high performing public services;

- surplus assets no longer required for service delivery are disposed of; and

- future investment decisions are based on a more complete assessment of the condition and performance of the existing asset base.

A zero-based approach to capital budgeting 6.36 In the 2007 CSR, departments are bidding for their capital budgets from a zero base, splitting their bid into capital to maintain the capability of their existing asset stock and capital to fund new investment. As part of their AMS, departments will provide an account of both the evolution of the asset stock resulting from any proposed spending and how that evolution ensures that the capital stock at the end of the period will better meet policy objectives. This will ensure that public resources are used more effectively and directed to those areas where it is most needed.

Asset disposals

National Asset Register **6.37** A key tool for helping the government to improve asset management practice in the 2007 CSR is the updated National Asset Register (NAR), which was published in January 2007. The NAR, which provides information on over £300 billion worth of the Government's assets, held in over 370 different government bodies, constitutes the most comprehensive list of central government assets and maintains the UK's position at the forefront of international best practice in public sector asset management. This information will help the Government fulfil its commitment to retain only those assets required for public service delivery and to realise the full potential of its asset base in the 2007 CSR.

6.38 In their AMS, departments will outline plans for the disposal of surplus assets as well the procedures in place to ensure all surplus assets have been identified. To date, disposals of over £12 billion have been achieved towards the fixed asset disposal target of £30 billion. Ongoing asset disposals will help ensure that not only will the focus on improving the management of public sector assets continue, but that the increases in public sector investment in recent years will be maintained.

Fixed assets **6.39** Strong progress is being made across government in the disposal of surplus fixed assets:

- the Ministry of Defence disposed of £231 million worth of surplus RAF sites over 2006-07, as part of its strategic programme of estate rationalisation in greater London. In addition they have disposed of Halton Hospital, the Queensgate site and land at Wainscott. This progress will continue into the CSR07 period, with plans to dispose of over £400 million worth of surplus assets in 2007-08;

- Local Authorities have secured asset sales (including housing) totalling £9.4 billion in 2004-05 and 2005-06;

- since the 2006 Budget, the Scottish Executive has disposed of surplus property worth over £100 million, including £24 million at the Scottish Agricultural Agency site and £74 million by health boards. The Welsh Assembly has disposed of £105 million of surplus assets, and with its agencies, is expected to generate up to a further £180 million from asset disposals during the next financial year, while Northern Ireland Departments' have disposed of £80 million worth and have plans for a further £200 million by 2008; and

- the British Rail (Residuary) Board disposed of over £39 million worth of surplus assets over 2006-2007 including Hudson House in York for £12 million, the former British Rail records office at Paddington for £5.2 million and a goods yard in Tunbridge Wells for £5 million.

Public corporations **6.40** The Government will continue to work with departments and local authorities to consider the potential sale options of public corporations, trading funds and financial assets where:

- they are no longer required to meet the Government's public service objectives;

- the private sector can generate operational efficiencies in the ongoing management of assets and services (through a sale or Public Private Partnership structure); and

- resources are released from a sale that can be reinvested in public services.

6.41   The Government continues to explore other asset disposals, including the potential sale of part of its stake in British Energy through a capital markets transaction, continuing to seek to realise value from its stake in Urenco and finalising the sale of the Tote. As part of the 2007 CSR, the Treasury will be working with departments to realise the disposal of other public corporations, trading funds and assets where it is economically productive and represents value for money. Additionally, the Government is working with London and Continental Railways to develop restructuring options for the company that could be implemented once section two of the Channel Tunnel Rail Link comes into service.

Financial assets   **6.42**   The Government is also examining the financial assets it holds to identify those where private sector ownership may represent better value for money. Following the reforms to tuition fees in 2006, this Budget announces a programme of student loan sales, resuming sales originally started in the late 1990's. These sales will raise around £6 billion by the end of 2010-11.

Intangible assets   **6.43**   Since the publication of Professor Cave's Independent Audit of Spectrum Holdings,[8] the Government has undertaken an extensive work programme to identify spectrum which can be released. Alongside Budget, the Government is publishing *The Forward Look,* which sets out the progress made and the next steps towards releasing surplus public sector spectrum to the market. The MoD has begun the process of auditing all its spectrum holdings, to identify which spectrum can be released and when, and has examined the first three priority bands. Auditing of the first band will be completed this summer, the next two by the end of the year, and the remainder of the 23 priority bands identified by the Cave Review in spring 2008. By May 2008 the MoD will compile a database of spectrum use of the bands identified by the Cave Review and will publish a detailed implementation plan setting out MoD's future spectrum requirements and plans for the sale of those bands that can be released. It will start releasing spectrum in 2008 with a significant proportion to be released in 2009 and 2010. The Government is undertaking digital switchover in order to ensure optimal use of spectrum. Ofcom is consulting on a proposal that the spectum released by switchover should be auctioned on an open basis during 2008-09. The Government supports this proposal which is consistent with its established policy.

SETTING THE ENVELOPE FOR THE 2007 CSR

6.44   The historic increases in investment in public services of the last decade have been delivered alongside a strong economy and sound public finances. The Government's fiscal rules have been central to this achievement, ensuring that the public finances are prudently managed over the economic cycle and that spending and taxation impact fairly between generations – removing the past discrimination against investment and ensuring that borrowing for investment is conducted in a sustainable way. Further details on the fiscal rules can be found in Chapter 2.

6.45   However the world is changing rapidly with new opportunities and challenges ahead, which will transform both the environment in which public services operate and UK's role in the world. To ensure the UK continues to prosper in an increasingly competitive global economy, the Government must entrench the stability secured in the UK for the decade ahead.

6.46   The Government's ambitious value for money programme, will release resources to meet these challenges, with net cash-releasing savings of at least 3 per cent per year being delivered across all of Government, real reductions in administration costs of at least 5 per cent per year across departments and pay settlements consistent with 2 per cent CPI inflation

---

[8] *Independent Audit of Spectrum Holdings.* Professor Martin Cave, December 2005. Available at: www.spectrumaudit.org.uk

target. Combined with reforms to transform the delivery of public services, these savings will enable the Government to sustain the pace of improvement in frontline public services seen in previous spending rounds and focus additional investment on key priorities, within a framework that entrenches the macro-economic stability secured in the past decade.

Spending plans for the 2007 CSR
6.47 Consistent with the Government's strict fiscal rules, Budget 2007 confirms the firm overall spending envelope for the 2007 CSR period, 2008-09, 2009-10 and 2010-11, locking in historic increases in investment since 1997 while allowing total public spending to increase by an average of 2 per cent per year in real terms with:

- current spending increasing by an average of 1.9 per cent per year in real terms; and

- net investment rising to $2^{1}/_{4}$ per cent of GDP compared with $^{1}/_{2}$ per cent of GDP in 1997-98, locking in the step change in investment over the past decade.

6.48 Final plans for the split between Departmental Expenditure Limit (DEL) and Annually Managed Expenditure (AME) spending will be set at the time of the CSR.

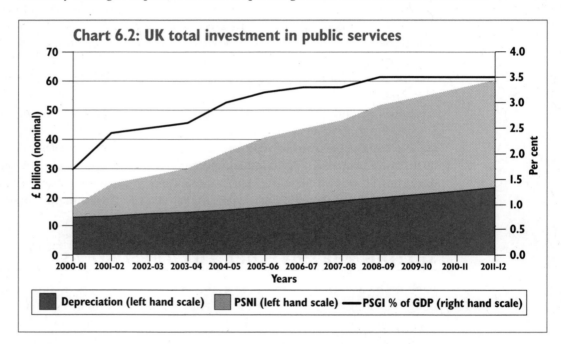

Chart 6.2: UK total investment in public services

TRANSFORMING THE DELIVERY OF PUBLIC SERVICES

6.49 Recognising that increased resources alone are not enough to transform the performance of public services, the sustained increases in investment of the last ten years, have been matched with ambitious reforms to support the efficiency, delivery and accountability of public services. The 2007 CSR will build on these reforms, ensuring increased resources are combined with measures to build the capacity of public services to deliver the outcomes necessary for the UK to meet the challenges and opportunities of the decade ahead.

Developing the performance management framework

Evolution of **6.50** The 1998 CSR laid the foundations for a modernised public spending framework and
framework for the first time the Government set out the key objectives it expected investment and reform
to deliver. Since then, Public Service Agreements (PSAs) have played a vital role in galvanising
public service delivery and achieving major improvements in outcomes.

6.51 The 2007 CSR will build on this approach driving ambitious improvements in priority
areas while developing the supporting performance management framework, to ensure a
user-focused, devolved approach to public service delivery. The performance management
framework in the CSR07 period will include:

- a comprehensive set of Strategic Objectives for each department;

- a focussed set of PSAs which articulate the Government's highest priority
outcomes for the spending period and will typically span several
departments;

- a single, cross-departmental Delivery Agreement for each PSA, developed in
consultation with front-line workers and users, supported by a basket of
national, outcome-focused indicators;

- an emphasis on central coordination working in synergy with greater
bottom-up accountability, local flexibility and user responsiveness; and

- a premium on the use of high quality, timely data while freeing up the
frontline by reducing low value data burdens.

Departmental **6.52** Each department will agree and publish a new, comprehensive set of Strategic
Strategic Objectives at the CSR. Departments will use these objectives to manage and report on
Objectives performance and to inform resourcing decisions, ensuring a more holistic, coherent and
better aligned and framework for performance and financial management across the board.

PSAs – highest **6.53** Alongside Departmental Strategic Objectives, a new set of PSAs will set out the
priority highest priority outcomes for the Government for the CSR 07 period, with less than a third of
outcomes the number of PSAs than in the current spending review period. Recognising that delivery of
the Government's highest priority outcomes requires public services to adopt collaborative
approaches across organisational boundaries, both at Whitehall and the frontline, these PSAs
will not be constrained by departmental boundaries but will reflect a government wide set of
priorities, articulating the most important areas for collective action.

Delivery **6.54** To ensure coherent cross–departmental working as well as buy-in throughout the
Agreements delivery chain, each cross-cutting PSA will be underpinned by a single, published Delivery
Agreement setting out plans for delivery, the role of each organisation in the delivery chain,
and how progress towards the outcome will be measured and strengthening accountability at
all levels. Departments are working together to draw up Delivery Agreements involving local
authorities, frontline professionals, such as teachers and nurses, and service users so that
frontline expertise informs the definition, measurement and delivery of priorities.

National level **6.55** Delivery Agreements will set out a small basket of national, outcome-focussed
indicators indicators that will be used to measure progress on each PSA. Indicators will be selected and
developed in consultation with frontline professionals to ensure that they are appropriate
and effective. Precise targets and minimum standards will continue to be key levers for
improvement but will give more weight to the priorities of individual areas and communities
– focusing action where there is most need for improvement.

Responsive **6.56**   To ensure frontline deliverers genuinely take account of local and individual needs,
public services PSA Delivery Agreements will incorporate mechanisms that enable citizens to have a real say
in the decisions that affect their experience of public services and enable them to hold those
services more directly to account. To further enhance accountability for service delivery the
Government will take steps to provide citizens with greater access to timely data on the
performance of local services. This will increase the transparency of service provision,
enabling greater bottom-up pressure to improve services and giving users a more robust basis
on which to make decisions.

Good quality **6.57**   The availability of good quality, timely data at all levels in the delivery chain is critical
data & reduction to drive strong accountability and improved outcomes in public services. The Government
in unnecessary has a crucial role to ensure that all data it asks for the frontline, which goes wider than just
burdens that related to PSAs, is proportionate, appropriate and collected efficiently. While data on
national and local priorities must be made available on a consistent, coherent and high
quality basis to citizens, this needs to be coupled with a sustained reduction in unnecessary
bureaucracy and data burdens across public sector delivery systems.

6.58   The Government will therefore – working closely with the Better Regulation Executive
– examine the scope for building on its intention to reduce wider administrative burdens on
business by 25 per cent, by reducing wider the cost to frontline service deliveries of central
data burdens by a similar amount. As part of this, it will look to establish a mechanism at the
heart of Government to manage the future flow of data.

Financial **6.59**   The Government needs to use high value performance data in combination with
Accounting from appropriate financial data. The annual financial statements of government departments and
the 2007 CSR other entities in the public sector are currently prepared using accounting policies based on
period UK Generally Accepted Accounting Practice. In order to bring benefits in consistency and
comparability between financial reports in the global economy and to follow private sector
best practice, this Budget announces that from the first year of the CSR period these
accounts will be prepared using International Financial Reporting Standards (IFRS)
adapted as necessary for the public sector.

6.60   This Budget also announces the Government's intention that Whole of Government
Accounts will now be published for the first time for the 2008-09 financial year. This revised
timetable is to allow time to complete the alignment of local and central government
accounting policies and to enable WGA to be prepared on the new IFRS basis.

Third sector

6.61   The third sector has a key role to play in delivering public services that are innovative
and responsive to the needs of users and communities. The third sector's often close
relationships with the users of its services enables it to promote 'co-production' of outcomes,
where users are equal partners with professionals in transforming services to suit their needs.
It can also promote accountability, by providing a challenge and advocacy role on behalf of
citizens at the margins of society. Placing the third sector at the heart of reforms to public
service delivery will require a new approach to commissioning and procurement embracing
its multiple roles in shaping and delivering services. The Office of the Third Sector will work
in partnership with the Improvement and Development Agency on a national programme to
train 2,000 of those who commission public services on how better to involve the third sector.

6.62 The *Review of the future role of the third sector in social and economic regeneration*, launched in Budget 2006 to inform the 2007 CSR, is examining the role of the third sector in shaping public services. The 2006 Pre-Budget Review set out the Government's commitment to make three year funding the norm rather than the exception for third sector organisations over the 2007 CSR period. The review is also examining how the public sector can learn from the third sector's innovative approaches to delivering public services, and how to build a more robust evidence base on the value of the third sector contributes to improving public service outcomes, beyond narrow economic ones. Chapter 5 sets out further details

---

Box 6.6 Putting citizens' views at the centre of public services

The 2007 CSR needs to be informed by a wide public debate about the right policies and priorities for Government in the face of the long-term challenges and opportunities facing the UK. Therefore, in preparation for the CSR, the Government is taking steps to engage the public by:

- **seeking the public's views on the challenges and opportunities facing the UK** – in preparation for the CSR the Government has been listening to citizens' views on the challenges and opportunities of the decade ahead, consulting over 2000 third sector organisations, service users, front-line professionals, businesses, unions, think-tanks, academics and members of the public;

- **engaging the public on key policy priorities** – the Cabinet's policy review process, assessing the long-term policy choices facing the UK, has engaged citizens on key cross-cutting policy challenges through a national deliberative process; and

- **consulting service users and front line professionals on delivery planning** – the Government will ensure that the Delivery agreements for the Public Service Agreements established in the 2007 CSR are informed by the views and expertise of front line professionsals and service users.

In addition, the Government plans to build on the efforts of the last ten years to achieve a step-change in the engagement of citizens in the ongoing design, delivery and governance of their local public services, making services more accountable to their users and more personalised to individual needs and preferences. The Government will therefore take steps in the 2007 CSR to:

- **ensure 'customer satisfaction' is a key priority for front line professionals** – the Government will use customer satisfaction indicators in its performance management framework, to ensure service deliverers pay proper attention to user experience;

- **restructure service delivery around the user** – the Government will implement the conclusions of Sir David Varney's review of service transformation, which highlighted the importance of providing services in a way that is more convenient for citizens and businesses;

- **strengthen citizens' voice in local services** – building on measures such as tenant management organisations and parent canals in schools, the Government will take further steps to integrate user voice in the design, delivery and governance of local services; and

- **empower services users through information** – the Government will take steps to promote greater provision of real time date, giving citizens a more robust basis on which to exercise choice and hold services to account.

Local government

6.63 Local government has an increasingly important role to play in the delivery of complex public service outcomes. The Local Government White Paper, published in October 2006, sets out how the Government intends to strengthen the role of local government, and increase local flexibility to deliver better outcomes across communities.

6.64 The Treasury, the Department for Communities and Local Government and other departments will continue working with the Local Government Association and local authorities in order to ensure that a sustainable and deliverable CSR07 settlement for local services and taxpayers is achieved.

Lyons Inquiry **6.65** Sir Michael Lyons has today published his report on the role and funding of local government *Place-shaping: a shared ambition for the future of local government*. The Government welcomes this substantial work, which contains many ideas for strengthening the role of local government to help build a stronger and fairer society.

6.66 The Government agrees with the report that more needs to be done by central and local government alike to enhance the ability of councils to deliver for their local communities. Building on the recent Local Government White Paper this provides a framework that the Government will take forward in the 2007 CSR. In particular, the Government agrees that with more freedom in the allocation of their budgets, local councils can play a much fuller role in building strong communities. **Therefore the Government will set out a clear target to reduce specific grants and ring fenced funding and examine the scope to minimise complex and time-consuming reporting and data provision as part of the CSR.**

6.67 The Government also agrees with the report's analysis on the crucially important role of local government in driving economic prosperity. The review of sub-national economic development and regeneration, which will report for the CSR, will examine this issue and further details are set out in Chapter 3. **The Government will examine how the local government grant system could give local authorities greater rewards for delivering increased economic prosperity in their areas, through reform of the Local Authority Business Growth Incentives scheme and will bring forward proposals before the summer.**

6.68 The report also makes a number of recommendations relating to council tax. It concludes that council tax should be retained as at least part of the local government finance system. However there remain a number of problems with it, including strong public feelings due to its perceived unfairness, and the fact that it has to be raised every year to increase revenue, having no automatic link to increased prosperity. The Government agrees with this analysis and is committed to ensuring that council tax payers get a fair deal. Council tax rises have been significantly below the historic average over the last few years. **The Government will continue to use capping powers over the coming years to ensure that council tax rises are affordable. The Government also remains committed not to revalue council tax for the lifetime of this Parliament given the disruption to individuals and families that such change might cause. In the absence of revaluation it is not feasible to change the banding structure of council tax. Alongside council tax, the Government will consider the analysis in Sir Michael's report on other potential financing options for the medium to long term.**

6.69 Finally, to improve the fairness of council tax relative to income, Sir Michael proposes improvements to council tax benefit (CTB) and measures aimed at increasing its take up. The Government agrees that local councils can do much more to encourage CTB take up and wants to work with the Local Government Association to boost the performance of all councils on this measure. **The Government will consider the wider proposals on CTB in light of practicalities and affordability alongside priorities for the tax and benefit systems as a whole.**

6.70 Sir Michael proposes reforms to the system of business rates. These recommendations, which the Government will be taking forward, are set out in Chapter 3 and include modernisation of Empty Property Relief and examining the options for a supplementary business rate.

6.71 The report also makes a number of recommendations on charging and other local taxes. The Government will consider charging for waste in its forthcoming waste strategy. The Government also agrees with the report that if national road pricing policy were to be rolled out in the future, central government would need to bring any existing schemes into the wider context of national road pricing policy. Finally, the report recommends that the Government should consult on the costs and benefits of providing a permissive power for local authorities to levy taxes on tourism. As Sir Michael points out, a robust evidence base has not been developed to support the introduction of such taxes. Therefore, the Government does not intend to introduce a tourist tax.

DELIVERING ON PRIORITIES

Increased funding for eduction
6.72 Since 1997 the Government has made children and young people's services, education and training a priority for increased investment. Spending on education in the UK has more than doubled in nominal terms in the past ten years supporting significant improvement in outcomes. In an increasingly competitive global economy, educational success is now more important than ever. The Government is committed to further improving outcomes for children and ensuring all adults have the opportunity to upskill and progress in the changing labour market.

6.73 Budget 2007 announces an early CSR07 settlement for the Department for Education and Skills which sees education spending in England rise by 2.5 per cent a year in real terms (5.3 per cent a year in nominal terms) on average between 2007-08 and 2010-11. UK education spending as a proportion of GDP is projected to increase from 4.7 per cent in 1996-97 to 5.6 per cent by 2010-11. The total DfES Departmental Expenditure Limits will increase by £3.3 billion in 2008-09, £6.6 billion in 2009-10 and £11.2 billion in 2010-11, compared to 2007-08. The settlement allows the Government to take a significant further step towards meeting its ambition that all pupils have access to the levels of support and opportunity currently available to pupils in the independent sector – with total schools resource and capital funding rising from under £2,500 per pupil in 1997-98, to £4,800 in 2005-06, £5,550 in 2007-08 and over £6,600 in 2010-11 (equivalent to £5,800 in 2005-06 prices).

6.74 The details of this settlement are set out below:

Table 6.3: 2007 CSR education spending plans

£ million	2007-08	2008-09	2009-10	2010-11
Resource DEL budget	57,050	60,088	62,912	66,378
of which near cash	56,215	59,003	61,687	65,063
Near cash additions over baseline	–	2,788	5,472	8,848
Total capital budget (Capital DEL plus PFI)	8,315	8,565	9,065	10,165
of which PFI	*1,320*	*1,320*	*1,320*	*1,320*
Capital DEL additions over baseline	–	250	750	1,850
Total DEL	**64,010**	**67,298**	**70,622**	**75,188**
Total education (England) £ billion	63.7	66.9	70.0	74.4

Table 6.4: Education spending in the UK[1]

£ billion	2005-06	2006-07	2007-08	2008-9	2009-10	2010-11
Total UK education	67.4	71.1	77.4	81.1	84.8	90.0
UK education as a proportion of GDP (per cent)	5.4	5.4	5.6	5.6	5.6	5.6

[1] UK education measured consistent with international definitions from the UK classifications of the functions of government (COFOG). Actual outturns are subject to spending decisions by local authorities and devolved administrations.

6.75   In addition to the extra resources being allocated for education over the CSR07 period, DfES is also taking significant steps to deliver better value for money in education, training and children's services, releasing resources for investing in further improving outcomes. These include:

- the DfES Centre for Procurement Performance (CPP) rolling out innovative e-Procurement systems that will both deliver savings to the taxpayer and improve choice and convenience for schools:

- schools realising savings associated with falling pupil rolls, including through a reduction in surplus places, and recycling excessive levels of school balances for more productive use across the system; and

- reducing the significant variation in the cost and effectiveness of local authority provision for looked after children by improving the way in which they are planned and commissioned.

6.76   The sustained high levels of investment in education since 1997 have been matched with far-reaching reforms that have supported a step change in the quality of provision and substantial improvements in results:

- almost all 3 and 4 year olds benefiting from free early years education;

- improved results at all Key Stages. 58.5 per cent of pupils achieved 5 GCSEs at grades A* to C in 2006, up from 45.1 per cent in 1997, and where English and Maths are included, 45.3 per cent of pupils now achieve 5 GCSEs at grades A* to C, up from 35.6 per cent in 1997;

- post-16 staying on rates have risen significantly and the proportion of 19 year olds attaining level 2 qualifications has risen by over 5 percentage points between 2004 and 2006; and

- the proportion of economically active adults with at least a level 2 qualification increased by over 9 percentage points between 1997 and 2006, with over 1.6 million people achieving a Skills for Life qualification to improve their basic literacy, numeracy and language skills since 2001.

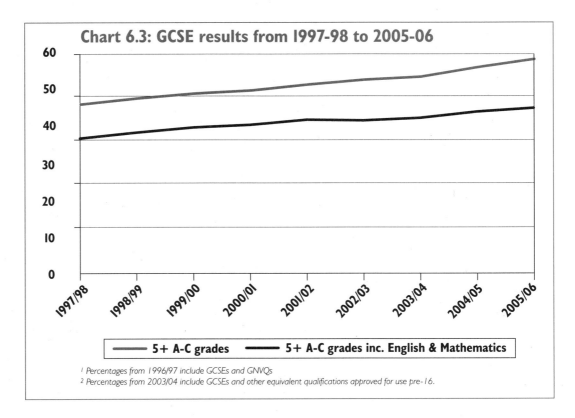

Chart 6.3: GCSE results from 1997-98 to 2005-06

Legend: ——— 5+ A-C grades   ——— 5+ A-C grades inc. English & Mathematics

¹ Percentages from 1996/97 include GCSEs and GNVQs
² Percentages from 2003/04 include GCSEs and other equivalent qualifications approved for use pre-16.

6.77 The investment allocated to education over the 2007 CSR period will build on these significant improvements and enable the Government to pursue its ambitions across a range of programmes, as set out below.

Childcare and early years **6.78** As set out in Chapter 5, to ensure every child has the best start in life and the ongoing support they and their families need to fulfil their potential, the Government will meet and build on the commitments set out in the Ten Year Strategy for Childcare. This includes delivering a nationwide network of 3,500 Sure Start Children's Centres, one in every community, by 2010 and extending the weekly entitlement for 3 and 4 year olds to early education to 15 hours by 2010, with a long-term goal of 20 hours a week.

Schools **6.79** This settlement will allow schools to take the next steps in raising attainment for all and narrowing the persistent attainment gaps that exist across the system. This will include making a reality of personalised learning and delivering on the Government's commitment to ensure all schools provide a full offer of extended services by 2010.

> **Box 6.7 Personalisation for all**
>
> Personalisation is about fulfilling potential. It means every child supported to learn and achieve in the way that is most effective for them. The Government is committed to building on the recommendations of the Teaching and Learning in 2020 Review group, chaired by Christine Gilbert, to ensure all pupils benefit from an increasingly personalised approach. This CSR 07 settlement provides substantial additional resources to support this vision. The Government expects that, over the CSR, every pupil should have access to a single member of staff – for example a learning guide, a class teacher, a form tutor or a Director of Studies – who is able to co-ordinate a package of support that best helps that pupil. This should include:
>
> - working with that pupil to identify their long term aspirations and guide them on the best choice of subjects, especially after the age of 14;
>
> - agreeing individual targets for their learning across the curriculum, and monitoring progress on a subject by subject, and term by term basis;
>
> - identifying and arranging any additional support that the pupil needs to develop within class and out of school hours, both in academic subjects and in the development of social and emotional skills;
>
> - identifying and tackling any wider barriers to progress, linking in with the *Every Child Matters* agenda; and
>
> - ensuring frequent and effective communication with parents to report on progress and advise on the best ways they can help with their child's learning.

6.80 Children who are behind in their studies can often benefit from additional support to help them catch up. The Pre-Budget Report announced that the *Every Child a Reader* programme, which provides intensive one – one support for six year old children that are the furthest behind in literacy, will be rolled out nationally, to benefit over 30,000 children a year by 2010-11. **Budget 2007 further announces funding to provide an average of 10 hours of one to one teacher-led tuition for over 300,000 under-attaining pupils a year in English by 2010-11, and 300,000 under-attaining pupils a year in Maths.**

6.81 There are now over 4,000 schools, almost 1 in 5 offering the full core offer of extended services. However, the Training and Development Agency has concerns about the workload involved in developing and maintaining extended activities – in particular building the effective links with local agencies, businesses and other educational institutions on which a full menu of activities and services depends. To support the delivery of the Government's commitment that all schools should provide extended hours services by 2010, this Budget announces additional funding which, together with significant existing levels of resource across the system, will be sufficient to support extended service co-ordinators in secondary schools and clusters of primary schools.

6.82 Providing access to the community is a core part of the Government's vision for extended schools. Academies aim both to raise standards for pupils and provide first class facilities for wider use in areas of particular deprivation, and the settlement allows the Department for Education and Skills to continue to make good progress in rolling out the programme. Budget 2007 announces that the Government will remove VAT constraints for current academies and all those planned for the future. These changes will further strengthen the effectiveness and value for money of the Academies programme as it continues to move forward.

14-19 year olds **6.83**   The Government will make further progress in increasing the number of young people continuing in education and training after the end of the compulsory school age, building the foundation to improve the skills of young people. This CSR07 settlement will allow the Government to reform the 14-19 curriculum as set out in the 14-19 Education and Skills White Paper, providing a system where all young people can learn in ways which motivate and engage them in learning, providing the skills to participate in further and higher education and employment. The CSR settlement will provide the foundation for all young people to be entitled to study the 14 lines of specialised diplomas and participate in an apprenticeship scheme from 2013.

6.84   As set out in Chapters 3 and 5, to continue progress in re-engaging young people not in education or training back into learning, the Government will extend Activity and Learning Agreement pilots into the CSR07 period.

Adult skills **6.85**   The Government is making progress in improving the skills of the UK workforce. As detailed in Chapter 3, the interim targets for improving the basic skills of the adult population and reducing the number of adults in the workforce who lack a first, full Level 2 qualification have both been recently achieved. The additional resources provided in the CSR07 settlement will allow the Government to build on this progress and make a good start towards the world-class skills ambitions set out in the Leitch Review of Skills.[1]

Higher education **6.86**   As set out in Chapter 3, Budget 2007 also announces an early settlement for the 2007 **& science** CSR years for the Department of Trade and Industry's ring-fenced science budget. Together with the early settlement for the Department for Education and Skills, this will ensure that total investment in the public science base will rise by an annual average rate of 2.5 per cent in real terms over the CSR period, meeting the commitment in the ten-year framework, further details set out in table 6.5. These early settlements provide long-term certainty for the research community and will deliver resources to meet a range of priorities over the CSR period, including further investment to support excellent research, increase the economic impact of the science base and implement the recommendations of the Sainsbury and Cooksey Reviews.

Table 6.5: Public investment in the UK science base

£ million	2007-08	2008-09	2009-10	2010-11	Average annual real growth over the CSR %
DTI Science Budget Departmental Expenditure Limits[1]	3,383	3,525	3,746	3,971	2.7
DfES funding for research and knowledge transfer in English Universities Departmental Expenditure Limits	1,655	1,710	1,775	1,926	2.4
Total UK science spending[2]	**5,397**	**5,608**	**5,903**	**6,287**	**2.5**
UK science spend as a % GDP	**0.39**	**0.39**	**0.39**	**0.39**	

[1] *Full resource budgeting basis, net of depreciation.*
[2] *Actual outturns are subject to spending decisions by the devolved administrations. Excludes non cash items.*

---

[6] *Prosperity for all in the global economy – world-class skills*, Leitch Review, December 2006. Available at www.hm-treasury.gov.uk

Olympics budget   **6.87**   The 2012 Olympic and Paralympic Games will be an outstanding celebration of sport and culture inspiring a generation of children and providing a lasting legacy for some of the most deprived London communities, with benefits for the whole country. The Government has announced a robust funding package for the Olympics together with a fully funded programme contingency. The contingency will be tightly controlled to ensure that the Olympic Delivery Authority delivers value for money while being able to meet the absolute deadline. The funding package provides additional contributions from the Government, the Lottery and the Mayor of London, while safeguarding Lottery provision for the third sector and maintaining the London council tax contribution at the current level.

Strengthening the fight against crime and terrorism

6.88   The first responsibility of government is to protect its citizens and ensure their security – safeguarding the nation against terrorist attacks, cutting crime, bringing offenders to justice and managing them effectively to reduce re-offending. A range of complex and interconnected trends and risks, both at home and abroad, will shape the safety and security of UK citizens over the decade.

Meeting the   **6.89**   Whilst the UK has faced terrorist threats in the past, the global reach, capability and
terrorist   sophistication of international terrorist groups places the current threat on a scale not
challenge   previously encountered. Since 11 September 2001, the protection of the UK and its people from international terrorism has been a top priority for the Government. This has been reflected both by reprioritisation of existing resources and by very substantial increases in departmental budgets. In total, spending on security and intelligence across departments will be over £2¼ billion by 2007-08, more than double the amount spent before 11 September 2001.

6.90   This Budget announces a further £86.4 million for the Security and Intelligence Agencies to accelerate the ongoing development of their counter-terrorism capabilities. The review of the delivery of the Government's counter-terrorism and security strategies announced in Budget 2006 is also ongoing, and its final conclusions will be set out as part of the 2007 CSR.

CSR07   **6.91**   The Government recognises that the fight against crime and terrorism requires a
settlements for   sustained focus and effective co-operation across organisational boundaries. In order to
the criminal   provide the long-term certainty needed to drive forward improvements across the criminal
justice system   justice system:
departments

- Budget 2006 announced an early CSR07 settlement for the Home Office which maintains its 2007-08 budget in real terms up to 2010-11 – locking in the 75 per cent real terms increase in funding which the department has received since 1997-98, and enabling it to continue an ambitious programme of reform in policing, immigration, offender management and other areas of departmental business; and

- the 2006 Pre-Budget Report announced an early settlement for the DCA which provided over £100 million of modernisation funding, enabling the department to take forward a series of investments and reforms to improve the efficiency and effectiveness of the justice and legal aid systems, within an overall budget which will reduce by 3.5 per cent per year in real terms over the CSR07 period.

Attorney **6.92** This Budget completes the early settlements for the criminal justice system by
General's announcing that the Crown Prosecution Service (CPS) and other Attorney General's
Departments Departments (AGDs) have identified ambitious value for money reforms that enable them
to maintain service improvements within an overall budget that reduces by 3.5 per cent per
year in real terms over the CSR07 period. With £19 million of modernisation funding
provided as part of this settlement, the AGDs will now be able to take forward a series of
reforms including:

- workforce modernisation, which will deliver greater productivity and working
  time flexibility so that the CPS can continue to meet the 24/7 operational
  requirements of the police through the joint CPS/police charging scheme;

- improved CPS performance in Magistrates' courts by streamlining
  Magistrates' court processes to increase timeliness and encourage offenders
  to plead guilty at the first hearing; and

- better case management, through improved use of IT and more joined-up
  working with the police.

Prisons **6.93** As part of the Home Office's long-term objective to ensure that more offenders are
caught, punished and prevented from re-offending, the Home Secretary announced in July
2006 plans to expand prision capacity by 8,000 places by 2012, with an extra 2,500 places on
stream by the end of 2007. Resources provided to the Home Office over the SR04 and 2007
CSR periods provide the investment and long-term funding needed to drive forward this
building programme.

Military **6.94** In addition to action to strengthen security at home, the Government believes it has
operations both an interest and a responsibility to promote peace and stability abroad. Conflict and
instability elsewhere have the potential to enhance the risk to the UK. International peace
support operations continue to play a key role in global stability. The United Kingdom's
continued engagement in these operations is an important component in achieving the
Government's foreign, defence and development policy objectives. **Budget 2007 announces
£400 million of provision for the special reserve in 2007-08 as a prudent allowance against
continuing international commitments in Iraq, Afganistan and elsewhere, and further
allocates £200 million from the reserves in 2007-08 to support ongoing peacekeeping
activity across the world.** Cost and provision will be reviewed at the time of the 2007 Pre-
Budget Report.

PROTECTING THE ENVIRONMENT

The Government is committed to delivering a strong economy based not just on high and stable levels of growth, but also on high standards of environmental stewardship. This Budget responds to the Stern Review on the Economics of Climate Change and sets out the next stage in the Government's strategy for tackling climate change both domestically and globally, including:

- **that the Government will launch a competition to develop the UK's first full-scale demonstration of carbon capture and storage, the result of which will be announced next year;**

- **an increase in fuel duty rates of 2 pence per litre (ppl) from 1 October 2007, and increases in the next two years of 2ppl and 1.84ppl respectively;**

- **announcing car vehicle excise duty rates for the next three years,** including rates for the most polluting cars rising to £400 and rates for clean cars in band B falling to £35;

- **a review to examine the vehicle and fuel technologies which over the next 25 years could help 'decarbonise' road transport;**

- a package of measures to support biofuels including **extending the 20 pence per litre biofuels duty differential to 2009-10;**

- **a rise in climate change levy rates from 1 April 2008** in line with current inflation;

- that from 1 October 2007 **all new zero-carbon homes costing up to £500,000 will pay no stamp duty, with zero-carbon homes costing in excess of £500,000 receiving a reduction in their stamp duty bill of £15,000;**

- **an intention that, by the end of the next decade, all householders will have been offered help to introduce energy efficient measures with the aim that, where practicably possible, all homes will have achieved their cost-effective energy efficiency potential;**

- **increasing funds available through the Low Carbon Buildings Programme** to a total of over £18 million to help meet the demand from households for microgeneration technologies; and

- **a £800 million international window for the Environmental Transformation Fund** to finance overseas development projects that deliver both poverty reduction and environmental benefits in developing countries.

The Budget also reports on the Government's strategy for tackling other environmental challenges including:

- **an increase from 1 April 2008 in the standard rate of the landfill tax by £8 a tonne per year, until at least 2010-11;** and an increase in the lower rate of the landfill tax from £2 per tonne to £2.50 per tonne from 1 April 2008; and

- **an increase in the aggregates levy rate to £1.95 per tonne from 1 April 2008.**

Sustainable development **7.1** The Government is committed to delivering strong, stable and sustainable economic growth. To achieve this aim it is crucial to take care of the natural environment and the resources on which economic activity depends. Economic growth need not be at the expense of the environment. Instead it must be based on the principles of sustainable development: integrating economic prosperity with environmental protection and social equity.

Long term challenges **7.2** Growth in economies and populations is putting greater pressure on the environment and greater demand on the world's natural resources. Managing this pressure has been identified as a key long-term challenge, as set out in *Long-term opportunities and challenges: analysis for the 2007 Comprehensive Spending Review*[1], published on 27 November 2006. The report assesses how growth has led to increasing levels of degradation, potentially threatening the future benefits derived from the environment. It points to a number of key areas for further action over the coming decade and beyond, including:

- *climate change* – the most pressing environmental issue the world faces, which requires a coordinated, international response so that the worst effects can be avoided at manageable cost. Some climate change is already inevitable, so the UK and other countries will also need to adapt;

- *rising levels of waste* – municipal, commercial and industrial waste streams are expected to increase steadily, at a time when the UK is committed to reducing the volume of waste sent to landfill;

- *water scarcity and water quality* – changes to the UK's climate and demographics will lead to increased pressure on water supplies in some areas, particularly south-east England. Pollution from diffuse and point sources continues to put the quality of water bodies at risk; and

- *biodiversity* – eco-systems with greater biological diversity are more adaptable and resilient to external shocks and changes. Biodiversity also plays an important regulatory role, underpinning the healthy functioning of the environment as well as having a cultural value.

Government intervention **7.3** Every section of society – business, individuals and government – has a role to play in helping meet the UK's climate change and other environmental goals. For its part, the Government recognises it is required to take action where market failures prevent long-term economic and environmental consequences from being taken into account in decision-making. A key aim of government intervention is to encourage behavioural change, particularly with regard to the use of energy, waste and water. Investment to increase efficiency in these areas is often a cost-effective option for businesses and households, but short-term cost considerations, lack of information or awareness and market failures can create barriers to the take-up of more efficient alternatives. Intervention can correct these market failures, ensuring the implementation of the 'polluter pays' principle where environmental costs are fully internalised in economic decisions.

Principled approach **7.4** *Tax and the Environment*, published by HM Treasury in 2002, set out the detail of how environmental policy should be developed. In the 2005 Pre-Budget Report, the Government reiterated the principles which underpin decisions about whether government intervention is needed and if so, what that action should be:

- the decision to take action must be evidence-based;

---

[1] *Long-term opportunities and challenges: analysis for the 2007 Comprehensive Spending Review*, HM Treasury, November 2006.

- any intervention to tackle environmental challenges must take place at the appropriate level – international, national or local;

- action to protect the environment must take account of wider economic and social objectives;

- action on the environment must be part of a long-term strategy;

- the right instrument must be chosen to meet each particular objective; and

- where tax is used, it will aim to shift the burden of tax from 'goods' (e.g. employment) to 'bads' (e.g. pollution).

7.5 Within this framework, it is essential that the Government uses the most effective instrument to achieve its aims. For instance, regulation or voluntary agreements can be most effective where there are a limited number of polluters, or where, for example, market failures make product standards for energy or water efficiency the most cost-effective instrument of behavioural change. Spending measures may have a role to play where the polluter cannot afford to reduce pollution, or where equity or distributional issues make a tax or similar measure unacceptable. Fiscal measures can tackle external environmental costs, such as pollution, through reflecting such costs in prices and encouraging the behavioural changes needed to move to a more sustainable economy. Indeed, as highlighted in its *Statement of Intent on Environmental Taxation*, published in 1997, the Government believes that fiscal measures can be an important part of a wider package of measures, and is committed to reforming the tax system to shift the burden from 'goods' to 'bads'. Overall, it is crucial that environmental policy is the outcome of balanced decision-making. All intervention by the Government to meet environmental aims must also take account of the impact of any action on its wider economic and social objectives, including macroeconomic stability, business competitiveness, social inclusion and reducing fuel poverty.

Commission for Environmental Markets and Economic Performance **7.6** The Government believes that a green economy can also be a growing economy, and that there are new opportunities for UK business, commerce and science. That is why a new Commission for Environmental Markets and Economic Performance (CEMEP) was set up in November 2006 with a remit to examine the likely growth of global markets in environmental goods and services over the next 20 years, and the current and potential comparative advantage of UK firms in this area. The Commission is chaired by the Secretaries of State for the Environment, Food and Rural Affairs, and Trade and Industry, and is made up of experts from business, NGOs, academia and trade unions. It will investigate how government and business can stimulate employment and productivity in sectors with a significant contribution to environmental outcomes and resource productivity. These recommendations should ensure that the UK is well placed to take advantage of growing markets in environmental technologies and services. The Commission is due to report to the Government before summer 2007.

Progress to date on environmental challenges

7.7 The UK has made significant progress on all its environmental priorities, while maintaining strong economic growth. On climate change, the UK's contribution to the EU's commitments under the Kyoto Protocol is to reduce greenhouse gas emissions by an average of 12.5 per cent compared with 1990 levels over the years 2008 to 2012, taking emissions trading into account. On this basis, UK greenhouse gas emissions fell by 18.8 per cent by 2005, making the UK one of the few countries on track to meet its Kyoto commitments. On the same basis, UK carbon dioxide emissions in 2005 were approximately 11 per cent lower than 1990 levels. Following the measures announced in the Climate Change Programme and

Energy reviews, projections suggest that by 2010 the UK could reduce greenhouse gas emissions by over 23 per cent compared to 1990. Carbon intensity, which measures the level of carbon dioxide emissions against gross domestic product (GDP), has also improved by 55 per cent since the early 1970s at a rate of 2 per cent per year.

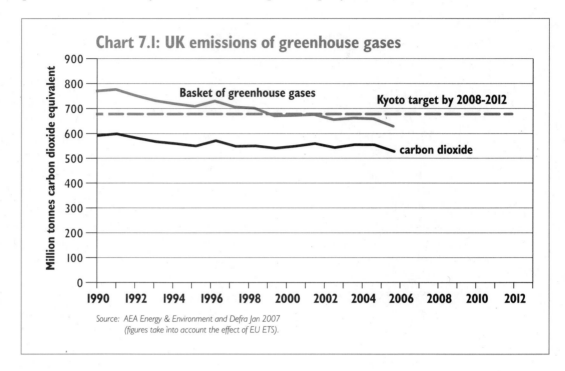

Chart 7.1: UK emissions of greenhouse gases

Source: AEA Energy & Environment and Defra Jan 2007
(figures take into account the effect of EU ETS).

7.8   Good progress has also been made in other areas. On air quality, between 1997 and 2004, nitrous oxide emissions were reduced by 24 per cent and sulphur dioxide emissions were reduced by 49 per cent. Between 1997-98 and 2005-06, the quantity of waste going to landfill fell by 25 per cent and household recycling rates in England increased from around 8 per cent to nearly 27 per cent. Between 2001 and 2005, sales of virgin aggregate in Great Britain reduced by around 18 million tonnes, with an estimated increase in the use of recycled aggregate in England of around 5.5 million tonnes. In 2005, 64 per cent of England's rivers were of good chemical quality, compared with 43 per cent in 1990, and 71 per cent were of good biological quality, up from 60 per cent in 1990.

TACKLING THE GLOBAL CHALLENGE OF CLIMATE CHANGE

Stern Review   7.9   *The Stern Review on the Economics of Climate Change*[2] commissioned by the Chancellor of the Exchequer in July 2005, was set up to understand more comprehensively the nature of the economic challenges of climate change and how they can be met, both in the UK and globally. Published on 30 October 2006, the Review brought together the latest science on climate change, and employed economic methods to assess both the human and environmental impacts of, and responses to, climate change. It examined the consequences of climate change in developed and developing countries and promoted understanding of the costs and benefits involved in meeting the challenge. Since the publication of the Stern Review, the UK has agreed it will support a number of other countries in conducting similar national reviews and Sir Nick Stern will continue in an advisory role to them.

---

[2] *The Stern Review on the Economics of Climate Change*, Oct 2006.

7.10   The Stern Review highlighted that the scientific evidence is now overwhelming: climate change is serious and demands an urgent response. Increasing concentrations of greenhouse gases in the atmosphere will lead to a likely increase in extreme weather events and other impacts of increasing magnitude and severity. If no action is taken to reduce greenhouse gas emissions, global temperatures could rise by over 2 degrees Celsius from pre-industrial levels by 2035 and greenhouse gas concentrations by the end of the century could result in at least a 50 per cent chance that the temperature rise exceeds 5 degrees Celsius during the following decades. This would be equivalent to the change in average temperature from the last Ice Age to today. All countries would be affected by this change in the global climate, with developing countries being hit hardest. The Review concluded that the benefits of bold and early international action far outweigh the economic costs of not acting. The Review estimated that the cost of not taking action could be equivalent to losing between 5 and 20 per cent of annual global consumption whereas the costs of taking action can be limited to around 1 per cent of annual global GDP if the world pursues the optimum policies.

Importance of   **7.11**   Stern argued that an international approach to tackling climate change is essential for **international** both environmental and economic reasons. Climate change is a global environmental **action** problem – all countries emit greenhouse gases, and no one country can make all the necessary cuts alone. For that reason, all countries have to contribute to reducing emissions in line with their common but differentiated responsibilities and capabilities. It is also in the interests of the world economy that it costs no more than is necessary to mitigate climate change, with emissions reduced where most cost effective.

7.12   To avoid the worst impacts of climate change it is necessary to stabilise the concentration of greenhouse gases in the atmosphere at an appropriate level. The Stern Review highlights that global atmosphere concentrations of greenhouse gases are currently at 430 parts per million (ppm) of carbon dioxide equivalent (CO_2e) and are increasing at a rate of at least 2.5ppm per annum. The Review argues that getting below 450ppm will be very difficult and costly, while stabilisation above 550ppm could have disastrous consequences. The Review shows clearly that using the right policies to stabilise within this range would be cost effective relative to the consequences of not acting.

Economic   **7.13**   The Stern Review also considered the use of appropriate economic methodologies for **methodologies** taking the effects of climate change into account in making policy choices. Cost benefit analysis, as it is usually conceived, is appropriate for considering policies which have more marginal effects on overall welfare whereas climate change potentially has very large effects. In addition, use of discount rates which are big enough effectively to put little or no weight on costs for future generations is ethically inappropriate for considering the prudent response to climate change. So the Review both takes account of the scale of the problem and explicitly chooses not effectively to dismiss the welfare of future generations. In doing so it demonstrates that its main conclusions are robust to plausible changes to the main assumptions chosen. Given the very special nature of the climate change problem these developments are unlikely to have an effect on most areas of government analysis and decision making, though consideration is being given to possible consequences. In particular, the Government is taking forward work on the impacts on the calculation of the social cost of carbon.

Developing the right international framework

7.14   The Stern Review makes clear that coordinated and multilateral action is key to reducing emissions, while keeping costs manageable and avoiding damaging competitiveness. Climate change is an international issue and all countries need to act together to make a difference. Reducing global emissions must be the aim, rather than focusing on reducing emissions from individual countries.

International leadership   **7.15**   The UK has helped to build international consensus on the need to tackle climate change, and has driven forward multilateral action to reduce emissions. This leadership has been at both an EU and global level, and has involved engagement with developed and developing countries. The UK has supported the UN Framework Convention on Climate Change (UNFCCC) and the Kyoto Protocol, which provide the world with an international framework within which all governments can work together towards global emissions reductions in an equitable manner. The UK Government also championed action on climate change through its G8 and EU presidencies during 2005. The Gleneagles Summit in July 2005 achieved significant progress with the adoption of an Action Plan and a continuing Dialogue among the world's 20 largest energy-using economies. And in response to the UK's initiative at Hampton Court in October 2005, the EU has adopted a joined-up approach to energy and climate change for the first time.

The EU and the G7   **7.16**   The Commission's Strategic Energy Review (SER) was published on 10 January 2007 and at a landmark summit on 8-9 March 2007, European Heads of State agreed to support this comprehensive package of proposals putting Europe at the head of global leadership on energy and climate change, which could accelerate international agreement on a post-Kyoto framework. European Heads of State agreed to a binding EU-wide target to reduce greenhouse gases by 20 per cent by 2020 compared to 1990. Moreover, the European Union undertook to achieve a 30 per cent reduction in emissions by 2020, as part of a wider international agreement. Further targets were agreed on renewables, biofuels, energy efficiency, and on carbon capture and storage.

7.17   A key conclusion of the Stern Review was the need for Economic and Finance Ministries to be involved in climate change policy. Over the coming months, therefore, Ministers from HM Treasury and the Department of Trade and Industry (DTI) as well as the Department of Environment, Food and Rural Affairs (Defra) will undertake a series of joint visits to European countries to underline the need to translate Europe's ambitions into policy proposals. These visits will include meetings with their counterparts in Germany and Poland, as well as Portugal and Slovenia – the holders of the next two EU presidencies. At the G7 Finance Ministers conference on 9-10 February, the major economies also recognised the key role of market-based policy responses to the challenge of climate change.

Clean Energy Investment Framework   **7.18**   The Clean Energy Investment Framework is a direct response by the multilateral development banks to the Gleneagles Action Plan. It is designed to facilitate greater public and private investment in cleaner and more efficient energy focusing on the provision of access to energy in developing countries, the transition to a low-carbon economy and the need to adapt to climate risks, particularly in the poorest countries. The UK has called on the multilateral development banks to adopt a collaborative approach that could lead to the development of a unified global investment framework; and for the development banks to jointly set out a level of ambition for the scale of investment that could be mobilised through their frameworks. A conference on financing clean energy through public-private partnership was held in London on 13-14 March, bringing together the development banks, the private sector and the public sector to initiate work on how best to leverage investment.

Deforestation   **7.19**   The Stern Review highlighted that deforestation is responsible for 18 per cent of world greenhouse gas emissions, and prompt action to tackle deforestation is a critical and cost effective part of the global response to climate change. Sustainable forestry management has the potential to deliver many economic benefits for local communities as well as wider environmental gains. Since the publication of the Stern Review, the UK Government has been involved in discussions with Brazil, Papua New Guinea, Costa Rica, Germany (as President of the G8), the World Bank and other countries on how resources can be mobilised for sustainable forestry.

7.20 The Congo Basin has the second largest tropical forest in the world. Already some 1.5 million hectares of forest are lost each year and deforestation in the Congo is expected to accelerate if action is not taken, adding hundreds of millions of tons of carbon emissions. As announced in Chapter 5, in the 2007 Comprehensive Spending Review the Government will create a new international window of the Environmental Transformation Fund (ETF) with £800 million of overseas development assistance to support development and poverty reduction through environmental protection, and to help developing countries respond to climate change. The Government will allocate £50 million from the fund to support proposals made by ten Congo Forest countries to help them protect the Congo Basin's forests and people. Chapter 5 provides more detail.

The Stern Review Policy Framework

7.21 Box 7.1 outlines the main elements of the mitigation framework set out by the Stern Review. Within this framework, the Stern Review makes clear that governments should have the flexibility to choose the most appropriate levers to address specific market failures. This is in line with the UK Government's principled approach to taking action to protect the environment.

Box 7.1: The Stern Review on the Economics of Climate Change – Policy Framework

The Stern Review identified three key elements of an appropriate mitigation policy response:

- **pricing carbon through trading, tax or regulation** – ensuring that emissions reductions are delivered in the most cost-effective way to reflect the marginal damage caused by emissions which rises over time as the stock of greenhouse gases grows;

- encouraging research, development, demonstration and deployment to bring forward a range of **low carbon technologies**; and

- measures to encourage long-term **behavioural change and overcome barriers,** particularly on energy efficiency where there may be remaining market failures in the move to a low carbon economy.

The Stern Review also highlights the need for adaptation to the unavoidable impacts of climate change. This will be important in all countries but especially developing countries that will be hit soonest and hardest.

7.22 The UK's 2006 Climate Change Programme and Energy Reviews set out how both new and existing policies will enable the Government to move towards its targets for reducing greenhouse gas emissions. Box 7.2 highlights that, since 1997, the Government's approach has included all three elements of the Stern framework in its efforts to tackle climate change, employing an innovative range of measures at both international and national level. In addition, the forthcoming Energy White Paper will also bring forward an ambitious package of further measures to meet the twin challenges of energy security and tackling climate change.

7.23   On 13 March 2007, the Government published a draft Climate Change Bill which would put into statute the UK's targets to reduce carbon dioxide emissions, through domestic and international action, by 60 per cent by 2050 and 26-32 per cent by 2020, against a 1990 baseline. It would require the Government to set binding limits on aggregate carbon dioxide emissions over five-year carbon budget periods, beginning with the period 2008-2012, with at least three successive budgets always set. A Committee on Climate Change would be set up as an independent statutory body to advise the Government on the emissions reductions pathway to 2050, and on the level of carbon budgets. The Government would also have a duty to report annually to Parliament on the UK's progress towards the 2020 and 2050 targets and in relation to meeting its carbon budgets.

Box 7.2: Highlights of Government action since 1997 to tackle climate change:

Pricing carbon:

- strong support for the EU ETS, including setting stretching national caps in Phase I and Phase II and publishing the UK Emissions Trading Vision Paper which set out the UK's proposals for Phase III.

Encouraging innovation and research, development, demonstration and deployment of low carbon technologies:

- leading international collaboration such as through the Renewable Energy and Energy Efficiency Partnership (REEEP), the Southern Africa biofuels taskforce and the EU-sponsored Near Zero Emissions Coal project with China;

- increasing funding to around £800 million by 2008 to support environmental R, D and D and developing public-private partnerships through the Energy Technologies Institute and the UK Energy Research Partnership; and

- supporting the development and deployment of new energy sources through the Renewables Obligation, the Renewable Transport Fuel Obligation and the Low Carbon Buildings Programme to support microgeneration.

Removing barriers to behavioural change and encouraging energy efficiency:

- supporting international initiatives to improve energy efficiency such as the EU Energy Efficiency Action Plan; the International Framework Agreement on Energy Efficiency; and the 1-Watt Initiative;

- encouraging energy efficiency in businesses through: the climate change levy and climate change agreements; the Carbon Trust; and enhanced capital allowances for energy-saving technologies;

- encouraging energy efficiency in households through the Energy Efficiency Commitment; the Energy Saving Trust; new building regulations; reduced VAT rates for energy-saving materials and microgeneration technologies; Warm Front; and the Landlords Energy Saving Allowance; and

- encouraging fuel efficiency in the transport sector through reforms to vehicle excise duty and company car tax.

Carbon pricing

7.24 The first element of the policy framework for responding to climate change set out in the Stern Review is to create a carbon price, through tax, emissions trading or regulation, to reflect the marginal damage caused by emissions, which rises over time as the stock of greenhouse gases grows. Over time, the aim should be to work towards a common price across sectors and countries to ensure that emissions reductions are delivered in the most cost-effective way.

EU ETS 7.25 The EU, with a strong lead from the UK, has taken the world's most significant step towards carbon pricing by establishing the EU Emissions Trading Scheme (EU ETS), which keeps emissions within fixed limits while allowing emissions to be reduced at least cost through trading. The EU ETS is the UK's principal carbon pricing instrument, capping half of the EU and UK's emissions.

7.26 In November 2006, the European Commission took an important decision on ten member states' proposed plans for EU ETS Phase II (2008-12). The Commission requested reductions in the total number of allowances in nine of the ten member states' plans (that is, all but the UK's), and the Commission has now made decisions on a further four national allocation plans (NAPs). Taken together these decisions will ensure greater scarcity in Phase II and reinforce the scheme's long-term credibility. The UK NAP for Phase II covers more activities than Phase I, covering approximately 52 per cent of UK emissions. The plan commits the UK to limiting its contribution to emissions to 246 million tonnes of carbon dioxide (equivalent to an overall emission reduction of 29 million tonnes of carbon dioxide ($MtCO_2e$), or 8 million tonnes of carbon (MtC) per year below business as usual), with 7 per cent of allowances being allocated through the use of auctioning.

7.27 In October 2006, the Government published its vision for the long-term future of emissions trading, with the aim of developing the EU ETS as the basis of a global carbon market and forging an EU agreement to a post-2012 framework. The UK's key proposals are to:

- set a new European-wide emissions reduction target from 1990 levels of 30 per cent by 2020 and then at least 60 per cent by 2050, providing greater long-term certainty for business. As set out above, member states have now agreed to a 20 per cent reduction by 2020 and have indicated their willingness to commit to an additional 10 per cent conditional on other countries taking similar action;

- foster a deeper, more liquid market by considering expansion of EU ETS to cover more sectors and gases;

- move towards more auctioning of allowances in future phases; and

- extend the scheme beyond Europe – first, by guaranteeing that credits from Clean Development Mechanism projects in developing countries will be valid for compliance in EU ETS beyond 2012, which will enable not only financial flows but technology transfer to the world's poorest countries, and second, by enabling similar schemes in other countries, such as those being developed in Japan, Australia, the North Eastern American states and California, to trade with the European scheme.

7.28 Following the 2006 Pre-Budget Report, the UK Government has held discussions with other EU member states to build a consensus on the need to provide long-term certainty on EU ETS. Other member states subsequently reaffirmed their commitment to the central role of emission trading in the EU's long-term strategy for reducing greenhouse gas emissions in the conclusions of the 8-9 March 2007 European Council meetings. The Netherlands and Sweden have also affirmed their commitment to the specific proposals in the UK's vision paper. In addition, UK business, environmental NGOs and the Government published a manifesto for the EU ETS in March 2007 which emphasised the importance of a stable and predictable trajectory of emissions reduction targets in the EU ETS, and called on European industry, NGOs and governments to press member states to secure a sound basis for the future of the carbon trading market.

Building a global carbon market

7.29 Over the last few years, a new market in global emissions reduction has developed from trading in allowances created under the EU ETS, schemes in other countries and the flexible mechanisms of the Kyoto Protocol – the Clean Development Mechanism and Joint Implementation. However, to secure the full benefits of cost-effective global emissions reduction, this developing market needs to evolve, achieving greater scale and liquidity, long-term visibility, and the convergence of currently separate schemes and elements.

7.30 London is already the pre-eminent centre for this new global market. In March 2007, the Chancellor met leading City trading firms who agreed to identify ways to create greater scale and innovation in global carbon markets. **Budget 2007 announces a UK proposal to host an international conference later this year on the developing global carbon market, focusing on how to link schemes in different countries and enhance trading with developing nations.** London's leading position on carbon finance will also be assisted by the announcement extending the Investment Manager Exemption (IME) to include certain instruments for carbon trading (more details can be found in chapter 5).

7.31 The first step towards expanding the EU ETS to other countries was achieved at the meeting of EU Finance Ministers in November 2006, when the European Free Trade Area – Iceland, Liechtenstein, Norway and Switzerland – agreed in principle to being included in the EU ETS. The UK has also been working with California on the creation of an emissions trading market to meet their ambitious long-term emissions reduction targets, and has held discussions with other US states that are also developing schemes. Building on the partnerships with France and New Zealand announced at the 2006 Pre-Budget Report, the Government has had discussions on linking and other issues with the federal Australian Task Group on emissions trading, which is due to report in May. Engagement has also begun with Mexico, who are keen to work with the UK on scaling up and improving the Clean Development Mechanism and on carbon trading in Latin America. In India, the first meeting of the Indo-UK Economic and Financial Dialogue in January also agreed to joint working on how investment can address the challenge of climate change. The UK will continue to work with the European Commission and other member states to forge links with other countries to deepen and strengthen international emissions trading.

Aviation in the EU ETS

7.32 Climate change in general is an international challenge that will affect all countries but aviation in particular is an international industry operating across country borders and reducing emissions from aviation requires a multilateral solution. Globally, carbon dioxide from aviation is responsible for around 1.6 per cent of total greenhouse gas emissions, but this level is set to increase as other sectors reduce emissions while demand for air travel rises. The UK aviation sector currently emits 5.5 per cent of the UK's total carbon dioxide output – and this could rise to 15 per cent by 2030. Aircraft are also responsible for high-altitude emissions of nitrogen oxides (NOx), and for the formation of cirrus clouds and contrails, which means that the total climate change effect of all aviation emissions is two to four times greater than the effect of carbon dioxide emissions alone. The Government's policy, as set out in the 2003 White Paper *The Future of Air Transport*[3], and supported by the Stern and Eddington Reviews, is to ensure that aviation pays the external costs it imposes on society at large according to the 'polluter pays' principle.

7.33 The UK has long argued for changes to the international laws which prevent the taxation of fuel used on international flights, but this process will inevitably take time. That is why the Government's priority over the last few years has been to work to include aviation within the EU ETS. Adding aviation to the scheme will improve the liquidity of the market and ensure that the aviation sector plays its part in delivering real carbon reductions across Europe. The UK continues to make progress to facilitate, at an international and European level, inclusion of aviation in EU ETS and the Commission legislative proposal for inclusion by 2011 recently received broad support from member states.

Pricing emissions outside the EU ETS   **7.34** The EU ETS already covers approximately half of UK emissions including all emissions from electricity generation, and forms the central component in the Government's domestic policy framework to tackle climate change. In sectors not currently covered by the EU ETS, national measures can play a part in pricing carbon. Governments should choose the most appropriate policies to achieve this taking account of economic, social and other factors. Given that different sectors have different characteristics, consideration of these factors leads to different approaches being adopted in different sectors.

Surface transport   **7.35** Surface transport is the second largest source of carbon dioxide emissions in the UK and, due in part to sustained economic growth, emissions from it are set to continue growing until around 2015, before falling thereafter. UK transport emissions are primarily priced through a taxation framework – mainly through fuel duty – which provides incentives to individuals and business to drive less and use other modes of transport. In setting fuel duty rates, the Government also takes into account other external costs of motoring, such as congestion and air pollution, and the need to maintain sound public finances.

Fuel duty   **7.36** It is the Government's policy that fuel duty rates should rise each year at least in line with inflation as the UK seeks to reduce polluting emissions and fund public services. **Budget 2007 sets out fuel duty rates for the next three years. Main fuel duty rates for 2007-8 will increase by 2 pence per litre (ppl), with these changes in rates deferred until 1 October 2007. Main fuel duty rates will then rise by 2ppl on 1 April 2008 and 1.84ppl on 1 April 2009. By 2009-10, main fuel duty rates will still remain 11 per cent lower in real terms than they were in 1999. In addition, the Government today announces an increase in duty for 2007-8 of 2ppl for rebated oils, also from 1 October, maintaining the differential between main and rebated fuel duty rates. Rebated oils rates will then rise by the same proportions as main duty rates in the subsequent two years.** More detail on rebated oils is in Chapter 5.

---

[3] *The Future of Air Transport*, Department for Transport, December 2003.

Technology policy

7.37   Carbon pricing should help bring forward low carbon technologies by providing a market incentive. However, the Stern Review also highlighted the need for additional technology policies to accelerate the shift to new or improved technologies in key sectors such as power generation and transport. These accompanying policies will be essential to avoid locking in high carbon emission levels from long-lived capital stock (such as electricity generation plants) and to keep costs low as constraints on greenhouse gas emissions become tighter. Innovative environmental technologies may also suffer from similar market failures to those in other technologies, such as spillover effects and public good externalities. As with other responses to climate change, it is important that the UK works together with other countries to develop new technologies. But, in technology there are also real opportunities for UK leadership and advantage.

Energy Technologies Institute

7.38   Budget 2006 launched the Energy Technologies Institute (ETI) to deliver a step change in the funding, strategic direction and outcome of UK energy science and technology. The Institute, which will be fully operational in 2008, will be a 50:50 public:private partnership, with the aspiration of raising £100 million per year for UK-based energy research, design, demonstration and development; a total of £1 billion over a ten-year period. BP, Shell, E.ON UK, EDF, Caterpillar, Rolls-Royce and Scottish and Southern Energy have committed to contribute a total of £312.5 million over ten years from 2008. The Institute intends to expand private sector membership further, to match the Government's commitment to provide up to £50 million per year over a ten-year period. The Institute will primarily occupy the ground between the longer-term research funded by the UK's Research Councils and the deployment of proven technologies. It will provide funding for universities, SMEs and other firms, and international collaborations to accelerate the development and movement of promising technologies from the laboratories to commercial application.

Technologies in the energy supply sector

7.39   As set out in the 2006 Energy Review, the Government aims to promote a diverse energy supply, including renewable energy, new carbon abatement technologies to reduce emissions from fossil fuels and, subject to consultation, nuclear power. The Government's role is to provide the right incentives to allow the market to invest in this range of technologies, using policies such as the Renewables Obligation, and, importantly, a long-term carbon price created by the EU ETS.

Carbon capture and storage

7.40   Carbon capture and storage (CCS) could reduce the carbon dioxide emissions from fossil fuel power stations by as much as 90 per cent. The Government made clear in the Energy Review that the next logical step for CCS would be building a full-scale demonstration plant, subject to it being cost-effective. Since the 2006 Pre-Budget Report, the DTI has appointed consulting engineers to look robustly at the costs of a CCS plant based in the UK, and help the Government ascertain whether supporting one through a challenge fund or other mechanism would provide value for money. **The Government announces today that it will launch a competition to develop the UK's first full-scale carbon capture and storage demonstration, the result to be announced next year. When operational early in the next decade, this will make the UK a world leader in this globally important new technology.** Further details of the competition will be announced in the forthcoming Energy White Paper.

7.41   At the Spring Council in March 2007, the UK successfully pushed for a greater EU commitment to developing carbon capture and storage and EU leaders called for the Commission to develop a mechanism to stimulate the construction and operation by 2015 of up to 12 demonstration plants, and for member states and the Commission to work towards the necessary technical, economic and regulatory framework to bring environmentally safe CCS to deployment in new fossil-fuel power plants, if possible by 2020. The UK is continuing to work with the Norwegian Government through the North Sea Taskforce on transporting and storing carbon dioxide beneath the North Sea, with the outcome to be published by July 2007. The Government has also established a cross Government task force to look at a range of issues related to the regulation of CCS in the UK including licensing of offshore CO_2 storage and responsibility for the long term liability. A consultation on this will be launched later this year. In November 2006 the London Convention was amended to allow carbon dioxide to be stored in geological formations below the sea, a major step towards enabling the implementation of CCS. The UK is now working towards a similar amendment in June 2007 for the OSPAR (Oslo-Paris) convention which governs North East Atlantic waters and restricts CCS in a similar way. In addition, the Stern Review highlighted the particularly important role that CCS technology could play in lowering carbon emissions in fast-growing economies with growing fossil fuel consumption such as China and India. The UK is leading the joint EU-China project to build a commercially viable Near Zero Emissions Coal (NZEC) power plant in China.

Microgeneration   **7.42**   Microgeneration technologies, such as solar heating and micro-wind, have the potential to contribute to both improved energy security and lower carbon emissions. To encourage their deployment the Government has reduced VAT on microgeneration installations and introduced grant support through the Low Carbon Buildings Programme (LCBP). Budget 2006 announced an additional £50 million to fund a second phase of the LCBP with the aim of stimulating the market for microgeneration technologies so that they can be commercially supplied to the market at a lower price than at present. **The Government today announces that it will allocate a further £6 million – making a total investment of over £18 million – to Phase One of the Low Carbon Buildings Programme for households.** DTI will discuss the future operation of the scheme with the industry. This final tranche of funding for Phase One will aid the transition to a more mature market for microgeneration which, from April 2008, will include support from Phase 3 of the Energy Efficiency Commitment.

7.43   Many small, distributed generators produce more electricity than they need. This excess electricity can be sold ('exported') to suppliers in order to earn some extra income for the generator, and supply a small amount of electricity to the grid. Energy suppliers are working on the rewards they offer to microgenerators who export their surplus electricity to the grid. If they do not make offers by this summer, the Climate Change and Sustainable Energy Act 2006 gives Government the powers to require suppliers to do so. This will ensure that homes can benefit fairly from the export of electricity. **The Government will ask Ofgem to examine how green homes can benefit more from the prices paid to them when they become not just sources of clean energy for themselves but sell it back to the grid.** In addition, as announced in the Pre-Budget Report, Finance Bill 2007 will legislate so that, where an individual householder installs microgeneration technology in their home for the purpose of generating power for their personal use, any payment or credit they receive from the sale of surplus power is not subject to income tax, and they are not required to include it on their income tax return. **Budget 2007 announces that, for these same individuals, any Renewables Obligation Certificates acquired in respect of electricity generated from microgeneration technologies installed on their property will not give rise to an income tax or capital gains tax charge.**

Alternative transport technologies   **7.44**   Alternative fuel and vehicle technologies have the potential to deliver significant environmental benefits. To push forward technological development, the EU established voluntary agreements with car manufacturers to reduce the average level of carbon dioxide (CO_2) per grammes per kilometre (g/km) for new cars to 140 g/km by 2008-9. Discussions on the detail of a successor regime to the voluntary agreements are currently being held. The European Commission recently published its 'CO_2 from cars' communication, which calls for new mandatory targets for average new car CO_2 to be reduced to 130 g/km by 2012. Coupled with vehicle improvements, for example, tyre pressure monitoring systems, and an increase in the use of biofuels, the Commission proposed that the overall target should be to reduce average new car CO_2 to 120 g/km by 2012. The Government's view is that the objective beyond 2012 should be to reduce average new car emissions to 100 g/km of CO_2.

7.45 The Chancellor has asked Professor Julia King, Vice-Chancellor of Aston University and former Director of Advanced Engineering at Rolls-Royce plc, working with Sir Nicholas Stern, to lead a review to examine the vehicle and fuel technologies which over the next 25 years could help to 'decarbonise' road transport, particularly cars. The Review will draw upon expertise in industry, both in the UK and internationally, and across Government, in the Department for Transport (DfT), Defra, DTI and HM Treasury. It will feed into the work of the Energy Technologies Institute. The Secretary of State for Transport will set out the terms of reference for the Review shortly.

Alternative fuels **7.46** The Alternative Fuels Framework, published in the 2003 Pre-Budget Report, affirmed the need for fiscal incentives to reflect environmental benefits of new fuels and committed the Government to a three-year rolling guarantee for biofuel and road fuel gas duty rates, offering certainty to support investment. For aviation, the Government recognises that in the short term there are limited options for using alternative fuels in aircraft, but will continue to explore the areas where Government support may be appropriate.

Renewable **7.47** To encourage the development of biofuels the Government is introducing from 2008
Transport Fuel a Renewable Transport Fuel Obligation (RTFO), which will require transport fuel suppliers to
Obligation ensure a set percentage of their sales are from a renewable source. Budget 2006 announced that the level of obligation would be set at 2.5 per cent in 2008-09 and 3.75 per cent in 2009-10, before reaching 5 per cent in 2010-11. This will deliver net savings of around 1 MtC per year by 2010. The Government intends the level of the Obligation to rise above 5 per cent after 2010-11, provided that three critical factors are met: robust sustainability and carbon standards; a new fuel quality standard at EU level to ensure existing and new vehicles can run on biofuel blends higher than 5 per cent; and the costs being acceptable to the consumer and the wider economy. To encourage the use of the most environmentally-friendly biofuels, the Government will require transport fuel suppliers to report on the carbon saving and sustainability of the biofuels they supply. Work on developing a framework for these reporting schemes, led by the Low Carbon Vehicle Partnership, is progressing well. This work is being taken forward in close partnership with the Dutch Government and the European Commission with the aim of demonstrating how such systems could be developed on an EU-wide basis. The Government is also continuing to press the European Commission to develop urgently mandatory minimum standards for carbon and sustainability at EU level.

Biofuels duty **7.48** Fuel duty differentials have been in place for biodiesel since 2002 and bioethanol
differential since 2005. Budget 2007 announces the extension of the 20ppl biofuels duty incentive until 2009-10, offering further certainty to the industry. In addition, the RTFO buy-out price – the price paid by fuel suppliers who fail to meet their obligation for the first year of the RTFO – will be set at 15ppl in 2009-10. As set out in Budget 2006, the combination of duty incentive and buy-out price is guaranteed at 35 ppl in 2008-09 and 2009-10 but will reduce to 30 ppl in 2010-11. In line with the Alternative Fuels Framework, the Government will announce the level of the duty differential for 2010-11 in Budget 2008 but expects that the emphasis will move from the duty incentive towards the buy-out price as the principal support mechanism in future years. The Government's intention is that the level of the RTFO buy-out price should be sufficiently high to ensure that obligated suppliers do not routinely resort to using it, and so will keep the level of the buy-out price under review.

Modernisation and deregulation of biofuels   **7.49**   At Budget 2006 the Government announced that it would review the definition of biodiesel in the Hydrocarbon Oil Duties Act 1979 to ensure that environmentally friendly fuels continue to receive recognition through the duty system. The review concluded that the definition should be kept under active review as new fuels and approaches emerge. HM Revenue and Customs (HMRC) also issued at the 2006 Pre-Budget Report further guidance on testing biodiesel against the current definition. Following consultation, HMRC will relax requirements for small biofuels producers to register and submit returns and reduce the requirement for all but the largest producers from monthly to quarterly returns.

Biogas duty differential   **7.50**   The Government recognises that using gas produced from a renewable source ("biogas") can deliver significant climate change and environmental benefits. Biogas used as a road fuel already benefits from a duty incentive of over 40ppl. The Government today announces that it will extend the duty incentive for biogas at least at its current level until 2011-12, providing certainty to the industry. Future decisions on the biogas duty incentive will take account of the incentives offered for biogas through the Renewable Transport Fuel Obligation, alongside other issues.

High blend biofuels   **7.51**   Bioethanol is typically used in blends of 5 per cent. However it can be used in blends of up to 85 per cent (E85), if the vehicle has been either designed specifically, or has been modified to use the fuel. Following the commitment in the 2006 Pre-Budget Report to consider the case for introducing an incentive in company car tax to support the take-up of vehicles capable of using high-blend bioethanol E85, the Budget announces a 2 per cent company car tax discount for such vehicles from April 2008.

Biomass in fuel production   **7.52**   The Government will also continue to support innovative types of biofuel production, especially where these could result in biofuels with greater life cycle emissions benefits, or fuels which can be mixed with fossil fuels at higher blends. As announced at the 2006 Pre-Budget Report, the Government has extended the 20ppl fuel duty differential to the use of biomass in conventional fuel production to encourage the development of this technology.

Extending biofuels to other uses   **7.53**   Following the announcement in the 2006 Pre-Budget Report of action to encourage the use of biofuels off-road, the Government has laid legislation to reduce the duty rate for biofuels mixed with rebated gas oil in approved pilot projects. It expects two such projects in the railway sector to begin shortly and will monitor the results closely. To further encourage the off-road use of biofuels, the Government today announces that it intends to permanently reduce the current duty rate for biofuel/rebated gas oil mixtures with the new rate to be determined in the light of the outcome of the pilots and other factors.

Enhanced Capital Allowances for biofuels   **7.54**   At Budget 2006 the Government applied for State aid approval for an enhanced capital allowance (ECA) scheme to support the most carbon-efficient biofuels plant. Following discussions with the European Commission over the summer the Government launched a further stakeholder discussion process with interested parties in October 2006 to update them on progress and gather views on the best way forward. The consultation process is now complete, and in light of the responses, the Government will re-apply for State aid clearance and, subject to that, will introduce a 100 per cent first-year allowance for biofuels plant that meet certain qualifying criteria, and which make good carbon balance inherent in their design, as proposed. In addition, as announced in Chapter 3, the Government will also introduce a payable enhanced capital allowance for companies not in taxable profit to ensure both profit and loss making firms have an incentive to invest in the cleanest biofuels plant. The Government will continue to monitor the development of innovative and lower-carbon biofuels production methods, and consider the most effective form of on-going support.

International collaboration on biofuels   **7.55**   The UK has initiated a joint taskforce with Brazil, South Africa and Mozambique to promote the development of a sustainable regional biofuels industry in Southern Africa. This will bring together key partners, including the World Bank and local industries, with leading experts from Brazil, to promote the production and use of biofuels in the region and to enhance South-South technology transfer. And, in advance of the EU-US Summit on 30 April this year, the Government will propose the establishment of an EU-US taskforce to facilitate the exchange of skills, knowledge and research and development on biofuels, including the development of 'second-generation' biofuels.

Road fuel gases   **7.56**   Road fuel gases, such as compressed natural gas (CNG) and liquefied petroleum gas (LPG), can deliver carbon and air quality benefits over conventional road fuels. In line with the Alternative Fuels Framework and previous practice, the Government today announces that it will maintain the CNG differential with main road fuels in 2009-10, and will decrease the LPG differential by a further 1ppl. Changes will be made to both rates before then in line with announcements at previous Budgets and Pre-Budget Reports.

Sulphur-free fuels   **7.57**   Sulphur-free fuels offer local air quality benefits, while helping new engine technologies work more efficiently. Following consultation by the Department for Transport (DfT), regulations will be brought forward to ensure the widespread availability of sulphur-free diesel and sulphur-free 'super' grades of petrol. The regulations will enter into force in late 2007. In advance of that, HMRC will bring forward deregulatory changes to the definition of ultra-low sulphur diesel in the Hydrocarbon Oil Duties Act 1979, to assist the industry in delivering sulphur-free fuels at lower cost.

Overcoming barriers and changing behaviour

7.58   The third essential element in the policy framework identified by the Stern Review are measures to overcome barriers and encourage long-term behavioural change, particularly on energy and fuel efficiency where there may be remaining market failures such as asymmetries of information. The policy response must ensure delivery of cost-effective measures which would not otherwise have been delivered by carbon pricing, thereby enabling a lower carbon price.

International action on energy efficiency   **7.59**   The UK is committed to action at EU and international levels to raise the efficiency of energy using products and is leading the international task force established at Gleneagles to reduce stand-by power to 1 Watt (the IEA 1-Watt initiative). As there is a clear advantage in coordinating action at an EU level, the UK Government welcomes the inclusion of the EU Energy Efficiency Action Plan in the Commission's broader Strategic Energy Policy for Europe agreed at the March 2007 summit, and will be encouraging the Commission to maintain this level of ambition in implementing these measures later this year.

Business energy efficiency   **7.60**   Growing awareness of climate change issues, alongside the introduction of key Government policies, has led to many more companies contributing towards emissions reductions and taking action to improve their energy efficiency. The Government is committed to implementing a coherent policy framework that supports these actions and has sought to complement the EU ETS with a range of national measures to improve business energy efficiency, in particular the climate change levy package.

Climate change levy   **7.61**   The UK's tax to encourage business energy efficiency – the climate change levy (CCL) – was introduced in 2001 to encourage businesses to reduce energy demand and subsequently the EU made it a requirement for all member states to tax the business use of energy. The CCL was accompanied by a 0.3 percentage point cut in employer national insurance contributions (NICs) resulting in a net reduction in tax liability for business. The levy, and parallel taxes in other EU countries, provide an important complement to the EU

ETS by incentivising firms to improve energy efficiency and so supporting achievement of the EU ETS cap. Independent analysis by Cambridge Econometrics[4] estimated that the levy will deliver cumulative savings of 16.5 MtC to 2005. By 2010, the levy will be saving around 3.5 MtC a year, well above initial estimates, and will have reduced energy demand in the commercial and public sector by nearly 15 per cent a year compared with if the levy package had not been in place. As announced in Budget 2006, having kept CCL at its original level for its first six years, CCL rates will increase in line with inflation from 1 April 2007 to maintain the levy's environmental impact. The Government expects that the rates of the levy will at least keep pace with inflation over time. Therefore, the Government announces today that, from 1 April 2008, the rates of CCL will increase in line with current inflation. As stated in the 2006 Pre-Budget Report, the Government will continue to consider the case for reforms to the CCL within the context of the development of EU ETS Phase III after 2012.

Climate change levy simplification   **7.62**   The Government also announces today a package of changes to simplify the operation of the CCL. This includes simplifying how relief is applied to energy-intensive businesses that sign climate change agreements. This will align procedures with other reliefs, and remove an unnecessary and redundant provision, allowing levy relief to be provided where certification is received after the supply, and removing the requirement on customers to notify suppliers before it is destined for export or onward supply.

Climate change agreements   **7.63**   Over 50 energy intensive sectors are now able to benefit from an 80 per cent discount in CCL in return for signing climate change agreements (CCAs), under which firms agree to improve energy efficiency and/or reduce emissions. When introduced alongside the levy in 2001, CCAs were forecast to save 2.5 MtC a year but these targets have already been exceeded by an extra 2.4 MtC. Indeed, CCAs have increased carbon savings above the level that would have been achieved if all firms paid the full CCL rates. By 2010, it is estimated that CCAs will deliver savings of around 2.8 MtC per year. Regular reviews of existing CCAs by Defra continue to ensure that the energy efficiency improvements and emissions reductions delivered by the agreements are maximised.

Enhanced capital allowances and the Carbon Trust   **7.64**   Alongside the CCL and CCAs, the Government also introduced enhanced capital allowances for energy-saving technologies, with over 14,000 approved products now eligible for support. The Government has commissioned an independent review of the effectiveness of the ECA for energy-saving technology, which will be published later this year. As announced in Chapter 3, the Government will also introduce a payable enhanced capital allowance for companies not in taxable profit to ensure both profit and loss making firms have an incentive for energy-saving technology. Increased funding for the Carbon Trust, which provides businesses with advice on improving their energy efficiency as well as interest-free loans to fund capital energy-saving projects such as lighting, insulation and boilers, was also part of the CCL package. In 2004-05, the Carbon Trust worked with over 2,800 organisations, resulting in cost savings of £200 million for business.

Regional Development Agencies and the environment   **7.65**   Budget 2006 announced that the Financial Secretary and Richard Ellis, chair of the East of England Development Agency, would chair a group comprising of representative business organisations, Regional Development Agencies (RDAs) and the Carbon Trust, to examine how to ensure firms have access to the information they need to improve energy efficiency. In response to the findings of the group, the 2006 Pre-Budget Report announced that the Government will seek to streamline and coordinate services as part of the wider programme to reduce the complexity of business support and better tailor services to business needs. The RDAs will promote streamlined advice on resource efficiency delivered through Business Links. In total, the advice, support and incentives available from Business Links and the RDAs for environmental improvement and innovation, including for small

---

[4] *Modelling the Initial Effects of the Climate Change Levy*, Cambridge Econometrics, March 2005, available at www.hmrc.gov.uk

businesses, will rise from £140 million this year to £240 million next year. To support small and medium-sized businesses on energy efficiency, each of the nine English RDAs will pilot in 2007-08 a streamlined business resource efficiency advice service, through Business Links. This will include on-site audits of resource efficiency, delivered consistent with, and coordinated through, the Business Support Simplification Programme.

Large non-energy intensive organisations

7.66   In the 2006 Energy Review, the Government highlighted the potential for further cost-effective carbon savings from large non-energy-intensive organisations, such as supermarkets and financial institutions. This sector of the economy is already covered by some policy measures, such as the CCL and the carbon price established by the EU ETS. A consultation was launched in October 2006 to examine measures that could improve energy efficiency in this sector and set out possible policy options, including a mandatory trading scheme and voluntary benchmarking and reporting amongst others. The consultation closed at the end of January. The Government is considering responses and will publish its conclusions in the Energy White Paper.

Household energy efficiency

7.67   Households account for over a quarter of UK energy consumption and carbon emissions. Many energy efficiency measures can reduce emissions cost-effectively but are not taken up due to a variety of market failures – particularly cavity wall, loft and hot water cylinder insulation, draught proofing, efficient boilers and heating controls. The main mechanism to encourage the take up of energy efficiency measures in this sector is the Energy Efficiency Commitment (EEC), which requires energy suppliers to achieve targets for installing efficiency measures in the household sector. Suppliers typically achieve these targets by providing discounts to homeowners on a range of energy saving materials, including loft and cavity wall insulation. Low income households can also receive energy saving products free of charge. The EEC should deliver savings of nearly 1 MtC a year by 2010. The Government believes that activity in the third phase of the EEC (2008-11) could save a further 0.9-1.2 MtC a year by 2010, while recognising that the scheme needs to remain cost-effective and practical and that the overall policy framework needs to continue to take account of wider social considerations. Alongside the EEC, the Warm Front and Decent Homes programmes provide insulation and other energy efficiency measures free to low income households and in the social housing sector. Warm front provides grants for up to a maximum of £2,700, or £4,000 if oil central heating is required. Pensioners who do not currently have central heating can receive a £300 discount when installing a new system.

7.68   Later this year Energy Performance Certificates will be introduced giving all homes at the point of sale an energy efficiency rating and will provide householders with clear information and advice about how to improve it. The forthcoming Energy White Paper will set out the Government's proposals for improvements to billing information and for the roll-out of smart metering and visual display units over the next decade. Based on consultation with major banks and building societies, the Government anticipates that these measures and improved energy advice and information have the potential to create a market for 'green' financial products designed to help householders invest in energy efficiency and microgeneration installations. Through all the above measures, the Government's intention is that, by the end of the next decade, all householders will have been offered help to introduce energy efficiency measures, with the aim that, where practically possible, all homes will have achieved their cost-effective energy efficiency potential.

Code for sustainable homes

7.69   It is also essential that new homes are constructed to high standards of sustainability. In December 2006, the Department for Communities and Local Government introduced the Code for Sustainable Homes which, building on the higher energy efficiency standards introduced in April 2006 through building regulations, sets out new national standards for sustainability in homebuilding and challenges developers to go further in meeting these standards[5]. To ensure that the planning system plays an appropriate role in reducing carbon emissions, the Government has consulted on a new Planning Policy Statement (PPS) on Climate Change to be published later this year. This will aim to integrate climate change considerations fully into the planning process.

Zero-carbon homes 7.70   Alongside the Code for Sustainable Homes, in December 2006 the Government published a consultation, *Building a Greener Future*[6], setting out the Government's ambition for moving towards zero-carbon new housing. This included a commitment to progressively incorporate the Code's standards on energy efficiency into future building regulations, to ensure that, within a decade, all new homes will be zero carbon. The Pre-Budget Report announced that the Government would introduce a time-limited stamp duty exemption for the vast majority of new zero-carbon homes. Budget 2007 announces that from 1 October 2007 all new homes meeting the zero carbon standard costing up to £500,000 will pay no stamp duty, and zero-carbon homes costing in excess of £500,000 will receive a reduction in their stamp duty bill of £15,000. The relief will help kick-start the market for new highly efficient technologies in homes, both for the fabric of the building and in the use of microgeneration ahead of 2016, and sets a gold standard for green homes. The exemption will be time limited for 5 years until 30 September 2012, but before the end of the time limit the Government will review the effectiveness of the relief and consider the case for an extension, which could include introducing other qualifying criteria such as requiring a proportion of recycled materials and restricting carbon used in manufacture of materials and construction.

Energy Efficient Windows 7.71   Energy efficient windows have a major role to play in reducing household energy use and increasing the energy efficiency of existing homes. The Government supports the development of energy efficient glazing technology, and welcomes the introduction of the British Fenestration Rating Council's Window Energy Rating System, which has been endorsed by the Energy Saving Trust. The Government will carefully monitor the progress of this rating system and developments in the market, and will work with the industry and manufacturers to explore the case and scope for incentives to encourage the installation of energy efficient glazing.

Private rented sector 7.72   A particular market failure exists in the private rented sector where cost savings from energy efficiency investments are difficult for landlords to recover in increased rent. In Budget 2004, the Government took action to correct this market failure by introducing the Landlords Energy Saving Allowance (LESA), which provides an allowance of up to £1,500 for landlords who invest in cavity wall and loft insulation. LESA has since been extended to solid wall and hot water system insulation as well as draught proofing. The 2006 Pre-Budget Report announced the expansion of LESA, and the Government will now legislate in the 2007 Finance Bill for the extension of the existing sunset clause from 2009 to 2015, the application of the allowance to per property rather than per building, ensuring smaller properties have access to the full allowance, and the addition of the acquisition and installation of floor insulation as a qualifying investment. The Government is also seeking State aid approval to extend the availability of LESA to all corporate landlords.

Low energy lighting 7.73   The EU's Energy-using Products (EuP) Framework Directive will bring forward measures to improve the efficiency of a range of electronic and energy-using products within the EU. Under the EuP Directive, member states have agreed to establish, by 2009, new European legislation to increase the efficiency of light bulbs. Working with UK manufacturers, retailers and trade associations, the UK Government aims to become by

---

[5] *Code for Sustainable Homes*, DCLG, December 2006.

[6] *Building a Greener Future – Consultation Document*, DCLG, December 2006.

2011 the first European country to phase out the use of inefficient general lamp standard (GLS) light bulbs, where an efficient alternative exists. This will reduce UK carbon emissions by up to 1.2 MtC a year by 2020 and lead to a saving of around £30 on average household energy bills. To encourage the purchase of low energy light bulbs, the Government has this month written to European Finance Ministers and the European Commission to recommend the introduction of a reduced VAT rate for energy efficient products.

Consumer electronics 7.74   As announced at Budget 2006, the Government is also working in partnership with major retailers and the Energy Saving Trust in advance of EU regulation, to introduce voluntary schemes in the retail sector to encourage the purchase of more energy efficient alternatives in consumer electronics, and therefore raise the energy efficiency of electrical products. This has the potential to reduce UK carbon emissions by up to a further 1.7 MtC a year by 2020 and lead to a saving of around £45 on average household bills.

Public sector energy efficiency 7.75   The public sector has an important role to play in setting an example to encourage all individuals, households and firms to improve their energy efficiency and limit their environmental impact. All government departments are committed to producing focused action plans to reduce carbon emissions and to renew them annually. In June 2006, the Government announced that all central government's office estate is to be carbon neutral by 2012, and set new targets for energy efficiency, water, waste and biodiversity. At the local authority level, a best value energy efficiency indicator requires local authorities to address their energy consumption.

Fuel efficiency of vehicles 7.76   Chart 7.3 shows a substantial decrease in average carbon emissions from new cars per kilometre travelled every year for the last decade. Innovation in car manufacturing to improve the fuel efficiency of cars, and incentives for people to purchase less polluting vehicles have both contributed to this.

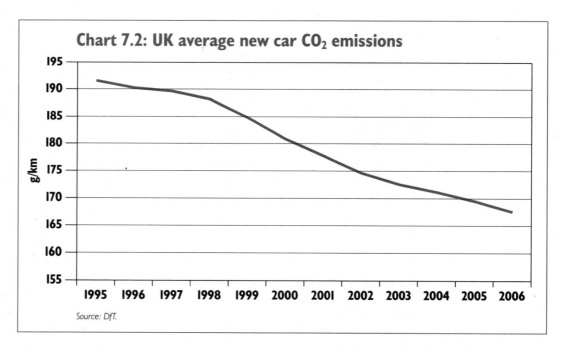

Chart 7.2: UK average new car CO_2 emissions

g/km

Source: DfT.

Vehicle excise duty 7.77   Vehicle excise duty (VED) for cars was reformed in 2001 and is now based on graduated carbon dioxide bands, giving a clear signal to motorists to choose more fuel efficient vehicles. Fuel efficiency labels matching the graduated VED structure were introduced into car showrooms in 2005, raising consumer awareness of the potential fuel savings that can be achieved by choosing a lower carbon dioxide emission vehicle. In addition, on 11 March 2007, the DfT launched a climate change communications campaign to promote smarter driving by providing consumer information to encourage the purchase of greener cars.

7.78 As with fuel duty rates, the Government today announces VED rates for this year and the next two years to further sharpen environmental signals to motorists to purchase more fuel efficient vehicles and continue to support the development of low-carbon market, including:

- raising the rate for the most polluting cars (band G) to £300 in 2007-08 and £400 in 2008-09; and reducing the rate for low-carbon band B cars to £35 in 2007-08, with that rate then frozen for the subsequent two years;

- raising the rates for graduated bands C-E, cars registered before 2001 and all light goods vehicles by £5 in each of the next three years;

- raising the rates for graduated band F by £10 in 2007-08, then £5 in each of the subsequent two years;

- in 2007-08 only, freezing the rates for motorbikes in the lower band with higher bands increasing by £1-£2; and freezing VED rates for Heavy Goods Vehicles (HGV), Special Types Vehicles, Combined Transport Vehicles and all vehicle categories that are linked to the basic goods rate;[7] and

- aligning the VED rates for petrol and diesel cars as the differential in nitrogen oxides and particulate matter emissions for new cars is expected to fall to close to zero once Euro V and VI emission standards become mandatory.

- Changes to this year's VED rates take effect from 22 March 2007. All changes in subsequent years take effect from licenses commencing 1 April in the respective year.

Company car tax **7.79** Company car tax (CCT) was reformed in 2002 and is now based on carbon emissions, encouraging the take up of more fuel efficient cars. These changes are forecast to deliver significant carbon savings of between 0.4 and 0.9 MtC per year by 2020. To further promote more fuel efficient vehicles, Budget 2006 announced that from 6 April 2008, the emissions corresponding to the lower threshold rate of 15 per cent will be reduced from 140g of carbon dioxide per kilometre to 135g of carbon dioxide per kilometre. The Government also created a new lower 10 per cent band for company cars with carbon dioxide emissions of 120g per kilometre or less from 6 April 2008. The Government today announces that the thresholds for the 2009-10 percentage charge rate will be frozen at 2008-09 levels.

7.80 Budget 2006 announced that HMRC would review the taxation of employee car ownership schemes (ECOS) and the benefits employees derive from them, with a view to possible changes. HMRC has undertaken extensive discussions with business during summer 2006 and January 2007, which demonstrated there are a number of different ECOS schemes, and that there is a noticeable interaction between the tax treatment of ECOS, tax-free mileage allowances (AMAPs) and rates of company car tax, which may have contributed to the popularity of ECOS. Furthermore, the review has suggested that the more structured ECOS schemes make extensive use of AMAPs to reduce their tax and NICs liabilities, which may provide a potential incentive to drive a greater number of business miles. Therefore, ahead of the Pre-Budget Report, the Government will consider the case for changing the structure of AMAPs to align the tax/NICs treatment and to ensure that rates and thresholds are set at an

---

[7] The basic goods rate is equal to lorry VED band A. VED rates for the following vehicle categories are currently linked to this rate: Buses, Trade Licences, Special Vehicles, Private HGVs, Small Island Vehicles and Recovery Vehicles.

appropriate level to promote environmentally friendly business travel.

Company car fuel   **7.81**   The company car fuel benefit charge – paid by employees who drive company cars and receive free fuel for private use – was reformed in 2003 to align it with the environmental principles of the company car tax system. Budget 2007 announces that the fixed figure on which the company car fuel benefit charge is based will be maintained at £14,400 in 2007-08. As announced in the 2005 Pre-Budget Report, the VAT fuel scale charge, which is a simplified scheme for taxing the private use of road fuel, will, from 1 May 2007 be based on a car's carbon dioxide rating. Budget 20007 announces that the VAT fuel scale charge will increase in line with fuel pump prices from 1 May 2007.

Capital allowances for cars   **7.82**   As outlined in Chapter 5, the Government has been developing proposals for modernising relief for capital expenditure on business cars with the aim of providing incentives to business to purchase cleaner cars. This could build on the existing 100 per cent first-year allowance for very low emission cars and recent reforms to VED and company car tax. More detail is released in a consultation update document, *Modernising tax relief for business expenditure on cars*, and the Government will continue to engage with business.

Vehicle emission standards   **7.83**   The Euro IV emissions standards for small vans became mandatory from 1 January 2007, and therefore, newly registered vans are no longer eligible for the reduced rate of VED. However, the discount will remain for the lifetime of vans meeting the Euro IV requirements registered before 1 January 2007. The EU has recently reached agreement in principle on the Euro V and VI emission standards for cars and small vans, with the regulation likely to come into force towards the end of the year. Euro V and VI will become mandatory from 1 January 2011 and 1 September 2015 respectively. The Government will consider the case for incentivising the early uptake of Euro V and subsequently Euro VI technology through company car tax and other instruments. An incentive for Euro VI take-up cannot be provided until Euro V is mandatory.

7.84   As announced at 2006 Pre-Budget Report the Government has considered options for providing incentives for the early uptake of lorries and buses that meet the Euro V emission standard before it becomes compulsory in November 2009. The Government announces today that a renewed scheme of Reduced Pollution Certificates for lorries and buses that meet the Euro V standards before they become mandatory in 2009 will come into force from October 2007. The nature of the scheme will be similar to the one that existed prior to October 2006 for Euro IV vehicles. Details of Government support to improve the targeted enforcement on hauliers who break road safety and other laws is in Chapter 3.

Air passenger duty   **7.85**   The Government believes that air passenger duty plays a valuable role in ensuring that passengers understand and acknowledge the environmental costs of their actions. The resultant behaviour change can deliver significant climate change benefits: the decision announced in the 2006 Pre-Budget Report to increase the rates of air passenger duty from 1 February 2007 will deliver climate change savings equivalent to around 0.75 MtC per year by 2010-11. The aviation industry has suggested to Government that the way in which air passenger duty defines different classes of travel may not always send the appropriate environmental signal and may cause market distortions, for example for "business class only" flights and "premium economy"-type seats. The Government is open to introducing changes to the definition, but only if it can be done on a broadly revenue neutral basis. The Government will discuss further with industry how this can be achieved.

Adaptation

International adaptation **7.86** The Stern Review also emphasises the importance of adaptation as some impacts of climate change are no longer avoidable. In particular, assistance to developing countries is crucial in ensuring that the changing climate does not adversely impact on growth nor undermine poverty reduction in these regions, as they will be most affected by the effects of climate change. The UK has already contributed £10 million over three years to the Special Climate Change Fund and the Least Developed Countries Fund for Climate Change. The UK also has schemes underway to develop coherent approaches to climate risk screening and assessment worldwide, and to improve the quality and availability of climate risk data in Africa.

Domestic adaptation **7.87** Climate change will have mixed effects on the UK. The UK will experience hotter, drier summers and warmer, wetter winters, which could lead to increased frequency of flooding. The Government's Foresight report identified a range of costs from 2 to 27 times current spending levels by the 2080s, depending on emissions trajectories and the choices made about the balance between defences to mitigate flooding and the costs of dealing with floods when they do happen. The Government is working with the Association of British Insurers on a project looking at what more can be done to encourage greater uptake of property-level flood protection measures and resilient repair of properties after a flood – both important adaptations for preparing the country's housing stock for the impacts of increased flood risk. In addition, the Government is also currently developing an Adaptation Policy Framework, which consider how to ensure a more comprehensive approach to adaptation policy across Government, and bring greater transparency to this area.

IMPROVING WASTE MANAGEMENT

7.88 Since 1997, the Government has introduced a number of measures to develop more sustainable waste management practices, reduce the UK's reliance on landfill and ensure that waste producers consider the full costs of the disposal of waste when making decisions, including increasing the standard rate of landfill tax and introducing the Landfill Allowance Trading Scheme for local authorities. These measures aim to ensure that the UK will meet its international obligations, including those under the EU Landfill Directive. Defra will publish a comprehensive review of its Waste Strategy this May.

Landfill tax **7.89** The landfill tax increases the price of waste sent to landfill, encouraging more sustainable ways of managing waste. The tax – working alongside other measures – has been successful with overall quantities of waste recorded at landfill sites registered for the tax falling from around 96 million tonnes in 1997-98 to around 72 million tonnes in 2005-06, a reduction of around 25 per cent. The UK is on track to meet its 2010 targets under the Landfill Directive, although subsequent targets in 2013 and 2020 remain challenging.

7.90 The standard rate of landfill tax applying to active wastes (those that give off emissions) has been increased by £3 per tonne in each of the last two years as part of the Government's aim of reaching a rate of £35 per tonne. As announced at the 2006 Pre-Budget Report, the rate will increase by a further £3 per tonne to £24 per tonne from 1 April 2007. The Government also stated it would consider whether the standard rate needed to increase more steeply from 2008, or go beyond the £35 per tonne commitment. In order to encourage greater diversion of waste from landfill and more sustainable waste management options, the Government today announces that, from 1 April 2008 and until at least 2010-11, the standard rate of landfill tax will increase by £8 per tonne each year. The lower rate applying to inactive waste will also increase from £2 to £2.50 per tonne from 1 April 2008.

7.91   Revenue from the increasing rates of landfill tax has been recycled to business in England through Defra's Business Resource Efficiency and Waste programme (BREW). The Government acknowledges the good work of many of the projects funded by BREW and this programme will continue in 2007-08. Additional tax revenue from business as a result of the increase in the landfill tax escalator announced in this Budget will be recycled to business through the reductions in corporation tax also announced today (set out in more detail in Chapter 3). Spending plans for BREW and other environmental programmes will be set out as part of Defra's settlement in the 2007 Comprehensive Spending Review (CSR) later this year. The Government has also recycled additional revenue from local authorities, as a result of increases in landfill tax, back to the sector to help fund improvements in local waste management. A joint waste review, carried out by Defra, DCLG and HM Treasury, working closely with local authorities, is identifying ways in which local and central government can work together to improve waste management over the 2007 CSR period. This work will inform Defra's Waste Strategy and the steps taken in the CSR to enable local authorities to improve waste management and help meet the shared commitments in this area.

7.92   The Government has published today a consultation document regarding the support provided to encourage the remediation of contaminated land (further detail can be found in chapter 3). As part of this consultation, the Government is seeking views on whether the existing exemption from landfill tax for waste arising from contaminated land should end, with the revenue redirected into other measures such as enhanced land remediation tax relief.

Landfill
Communities
Fund

7.93   The Landfill Communities Fund, previously known as the Landfill Tax Credit Scheme, redresses some of the environmental costs of landfill by improving the environment in the vicinity of landfill sites. Budget 2006 announced an increase in the value of the fund to £60 million a year. It also issued a challenge to private and voluntary sector partners in the fund to use the additional money to support opportunities for young people to volunteer on environmental projects. The Government today announces that the value of the fund will be increased by £5 million to £65 million for 2007-08. It will also be amending the regulations in order to reduce the administrative burden on environmental bodies and simplify the operation of the fund. The Government will consider the case for further increases in the value of the Landfill Communities Fund from 2008-9 onwards.

Enhanced Capital
Allowances for
waste

7.94   The Government has continued to examine the potential to introduce an ECA scheme to support new waste management facilities. This work has focused on developing options to encourage investment in developing markets for the outputs (for example, solid refuse fuel) of new waste treatment facilities. The Government today announces that it intends to review the classes of equipment that can qualify for ECAs for good quality heat and power (CHP) to ensure that the scheme includes all necessary equipment for CHP facilities to use solid refuse fuel.

IMPROVING WATER EFFICIENCY AND QUALITY

Investment in
water-efficient
technologies

7.95   Enhanced capital allowances to support business investment in designated water efficient technologies were introduced in 2003 and currently cover more than 700 approved products. For 2007, the Government will add a further three technology classes: vehicle wash water reclaim units, efficient industrial cleaning equipment, and water management equipment for mechanical seals. The Government has also agreed to consult on a proposal to oblige water companies in areas of serious water stress to consider compulsory metering alongside other measures in drawing up long-term plans for managing water resources. As announced in Chapter 3, the Government will also introduce a payable enhanced capital allowance for companies not in taxable profit to ensure both profit and loss making firms have an incentive for utilising water-efficient technology.

Water pollution from agriculture 7.96 The Government is currently assessing a range of possible policy options to tackle diffuse water pollution from agriculture (DWPA), and remains committed to ensuring that the costs of such pollution do not fall on water customers. The Government will consult later this year on the most cost-effective options for dealing with DWPA and continues to keep options for using economic instruments under review. The Government has also embarked on a rolling two-year programme to develop the voluntary initiative to tackle pollution from pesticides.

PROTECTING THE UK'S COUNTRYSIDE AND NATURAL RESOURCES

Biodiversity 7.97 The Government is committed to ensuring that the UK's natural resources are managed prudently. In particular, it aims to improve biodiversity and land use. The conservation of biodiversity is one of the goals of the Government's Environmental Stewardship scheme, a recently introduced agri-environment scheme which provides funding to farmers and other land managers in England who deliver effective environmental management on their land. Nearly 28,000 Environmental Stewardship agreements, covering over 4 million hectares of English farmland, are now in place.

Aggregates levy 7.98 The aggregates levy was introduced in 2002 to ensure that the external costs associated with the exploitation of aggregates are reflected in the price of aggregate, and to encourage the use of recycled aggregate. There is strong evidence that the levy is achieving its environmental objectives, with sales of primary aggregate down and production of recycled aggregate up. In Budget 2006, the Government confirmed that it expects that the levy rate will at least keep pace with inflation over time. **The Government announces today that the levy will increase from £1.60 per tonne to £1.95 per tonne from 1 April 2008, to take account of inflation since the introduction of the levy. The Government also announces the introduction of an exemption from the levy for aggregate arising from the construction and maintenance of railways, tramways and monorails.** This is in line with the exemption already in existence for aggregate to build and maintain highways and waterways.

Table 7.1: The Government's policy objectives and Budget measures

Sustainable Development Indicator and recent trend data	Recent Government Measures

Tackling Climate Change

Targets
Joint Defra/DTI/DfT PSA target – reduce greenhouse gas emissions to 12.5 per cent below 1990 levels in line with Kyoto commitment and move towards a 20 per cent reduction in carbon dioxide emissions below 1990 levels by 2010.

Progress
UK greenhouse gas emissions were 15.3 per cent below 1990 levels in 2005.[1] Carbon dioxide emissions fell by 5.4 per cent during this period.

- Climate Change Programme, Defra, March 2006.
- UK Emissions Trading Scheme, Defra, August 2001.
- Energy Efficiency Commitment, Defra, April 2002 and April 2005.
- Renewables Obligation, DTI, April 2002 and December 2003.
- Energy Review, DTI, July 2006.
- Energy Efficiency – the Government's Plan for Action, Defra, April 2004.
- EU ETS Phase I began January 2005, EU ETS Phase II UK National Allocation Plan (NAP) published March 2007.
- Energy Efficiency Commitment 2 introduced April 2005.
- Bio-energy Capital Grant Scheme, Defra, Dec 2006.
- Package of fiscal measures, including climate change levy (see Table 7.2).

Air Quality

Targets
Joint Defra/DfT PSA – to improve air quality by meeting the Air Quality Strategy for seven key air pollutants between 2003 and 2010.

Progress
Results for 2006 show average UK urban background levels of particulate pollution (PM_{10}) decreased from 31 micrograms per cubic metre in 1996 to 24 micrograms in 2006. Urban ozone levels increased from 48 micrograms per cubic metre to 61 micrograms over the same period, due to the reduction in other urban pollutants which tend to suppress ozone. The average number of days with moderate or higher air pollution decreased from 48 to 41 in urban areas and increased from 41 to 57 in rural areas between 1996 and 2006[2].

- Air Quality Strategy DETR January 2000 and Addendum, Defra February 2003, and Review, Defra 2004-06, Review of Air Quality Strategy due April 2006.
- Implementation of Integrated Pollution, Prevention and Control regime, Defra 2002-2007.
- Air Transport White Paper, DfT, December 2003.
- Ten Year Plan for Transport, DETR July 2000, and Future of Transport White Paper, July 2004.
- Continued support for local air quality management system.
- Negotiation and implementation of EU air quality directives and international agreements 2004-06.
- Review of the Transport Energy Grant Programmes, DfT 2004-06.
- Fiscal measures including fuel differentials for less polluting fuels (see Table 7.2).

Improving Waste Management

Targets
Defra PSA – enable at least 25 per cent of household waste to be composted or recycled in 2005-06.
Landfill Directive target to reduce the volumes of biodegradable municipal waste disposed of at landfill to 75 per cent of 1995 levels by 2010, 50 per cent by 2013, and 35 per cent by 2020.

Progress
Around 27 per cent of household waste in England was recycled or composted in 2005-06. 12.4 million tonnes of BMW was sent to landfill in 2005/6, 81% of England's total allowance for this first year of the Landfill Allowances Trading Scheme.

- Waste Strategy 2000, DETR, May 2000.
- Waste Implementation Programme, Defra, 2002.
- Reform of the Waste Minimisation and recycling challenge fund.
- Landfill allowance (trading) schemes enacted by the Waste and Emissions Trading (WET) Act 2003.
- Business resource and efficiency waste programme (BREW) 2004.
- Waste Strategy review consultation published by Defra in Feb 2006.
- Landfill tax and related measures (see Table 7.2).

Regenerating the UK's towns and cities

Targets
ODPM PSA 5: 60 per cent of housing development to be on previously developed land.
ODPM PSA 1: Work with departments to help meet PSA floor targets to deliver neighbourhood renewal and tackle social inclusion.
ODPM PSA 8: Deliver cleaner, safer and greener public spaces.

Progress
In 2004, 72 per cent of new housing was on previously developed land, including conversions increasing from around 54 per cent in 1990.[3]
Latest data shows the gap between the most deprived areas and the rest of the country has narrowed on several key indicators, including health, crime and education.
There are currently 22 Urban Regeneration Companies in the UK.

- Sustainable Communities "building the future" launched in February 2003.
- Feb 2005 Planning Policy Statement 1 placed sustainability for the first time as a core principle of the planning system.
- SR04 made available £525m a year through the Neighbourhood Renewal Fund to tackle deprivation in the most deprived areas and maintained commitment to New Deal For Communities programmes.
- SR04 announced Safer and Stronger Communities Fund providing single funding stream to improve liveability.
- National Nuisance Vehicle Strategy launched in November 2004.
- Feb 2005 English Partnerships launched pilot programme with 12 local authorities to tackle England's legacy of derelict and brownfield land, to bring 66,000 hectares of brownfield land into beneficial use.
- Budget 2005 announced the Local Enterprise Growth Initiative to increase investment and enterprise in the most deprived areas.
- Package of fiscal measures including contaminated land tax credit (see Table 7.2).

---

[1] The six main greenhouse gases are: carbon dioxide, methane, nitrous oxide, hydrofluorocarbons, perfluorocarbons and sulphur hexafluoride.

[2] Air quality indicator for sustainable development, 2006 (provisional): statistical release, Defra, 2006.

[3] Land in use change in England. Residential Development to 2004 (January 2006).

Table 7.1: The Government's policy objectives and Budget measures (continued)

Sustainable Development Indicator and recent trend data	Recent Government Measures
Protecting the UK's countryside and natural resources	

Sustainable Development Indicator and recent trend data	Recent Government Measures
Targets Defra PSA – positive trends in the Government's headline indicators of sustainable development (includes wildlife, river water quality, land use). Water Framework Directive – requires achievement of good chemical and ecological status in surface water by 2015. *Progress* • Farmland birds almost halved between 1977 and 1993. However, declines have reduced in recent years and 2004 populations were virtually unchanged from 1993. • Woodland birds fell by about 24 per cent between 1975 and 1992. Since then, however, populations have remained broadly constant. • In 2005 about 64 per cent of rivers in England were rated as having good chemical quality and approximately 71 per cent of English rivers were of good biological quality.	• Rural White Paper, DETR, November 2000. • Cap Reform Agreement 2003. • Strategy for Sustainable Farming and Food, Defra, December 2002. • Environmental Stewardship Schemes, Defra, 2005. • Regulations transposing the Water Framework Directive came into force 2 January 2004. • Developing measures to promote catchment-sensitive farming (Defra-HMT consultation), June 2004. • England Rural Development Programme. • Environmental Stewardship, England's new agri-environment scheme, launched March 2005. • Aggregates levy and aggregates levy sustainability fund (see table 7.2). • Pesticide Strategy, 2006. • In 2006, Sites of Special Scientific Interest land in target condition rose to 72 per cent.

Table 7.2: The environmental impacts of Budget measures

Budget measure	Environmental impact
Climate Change and Air Quality	
Climate change levy package	Climate change levy is estimated to deliver annual emissions savings of over 3.5 million tonnes of carbon (MtC) by 2010[1].
	Climate change agreements are estimated to deliver annual emissions savings of 2.8 MtC by 2010.
	Total CCL package including CarbonTrust, is estimated to deliver annual emissions savings of over 7.5 MtC by 2010.
Fuel duty	Fuel duty increases announced for 2007-10 expected to result in carbon savings of 0.16 MtC a year by 2010-11.
Fuel duty differentials including: – to facilitate a market switch: • From leaded to unleaded; • From low sulphur to ultra-low sulphur diesel (ULSD); • From low sulphur to ultra-low sulphur petrol (ULSP). – to encourage growth in the use of more environmentally-friendly fuels: • Road fuel gases; • biodiesel (20ppl differential); • bioethanol (20ppl differential).	The shift to ULSP from ordinary unleaded is estimated to have reduced emissions of nitrogen oxide by 1 per cent, carbon monoxide by 4 per cent and volatile organic compounds by 1 per cent per year[2]. The shift to ULSD from ordinary diesel is estimated to have reduced emissions of particulates by 8 per cent and nitrogen oxides by up to 1 per cent per year. The road fuel gas differential has reduced emissions of particulates and nitrogen oxides, which has helped to improve local air quality. The increased use of biodiesel and bioethanol will reduce CO_2 emissions overall typically around 50 per cent per litre of biofuel used.
Support for biofuels	The Renewable Transport Fuel Obligation (RTFO) to be introduced from 2008-09 is expected to save 1 MtC by 2010[3].
Rebated fuels	Maintaining the differential with main road fuels in 2007-08 will reduce levels of fraud, and will deliver small CO_2 and local air pollution benefits through increased use of less polluting fuels and less use of rebated fuels, which are more polluting.
Vehicle excise duty (VED)	The sharpening of environmental signals will help deliver 0.1-0.17 MtC reduction in CO_2 emissions by 2020. Numbers of vehicles in 3 lowest CO_2 emission graduated VED bands is forecast to grow significantly in the longer term in part due to VED reform.
Company car tax (CCT)	CO_2 emissions savings of reformed CCT system estimated to be 0.2 to 0.3 MtC in 2005, forecast to rise to between 0.4 and 0.9 MtC per year by 2010[4].
Company car fuel benefit charge	The number of company car drivers getting free fuel for private use has fallen by around 600,000 since 1997, partly as a result of reforms to the company car tax system in April 2002 and changes to the fuel benefit rules in April 2003, helping to reduce levels of CO_2 emissions, local air pollutants and congestion[5].
VAT fuel scale charge	The reforms are expected to deliver a small reduction in CO_2.
Air passenger duty (APD)	Doubling of rates announced in 2006 Pre Budget Report will result in a reduction of carbon of 0.2 to 0.5 MtC by 2010/11, with a central estimate of 0.3 MtC. When the effect of non-CO2 emissions at high altitude is taken into account doubling rates has a climate change impact equivalent to saving 0.5 to 1.25 MtC emitted on the ground, with central estimate of 0.75 MtC.
Landlords Energy Saving Allowance (LESA)	Small reduction of carbon emissions.
Reduced rate of VAT on professionally-installed energy saving materials and microgeneration (from 17.5% to 5%)	Small reduction of carbon emissions.
Reduced rate of VAT on domestic fuel and power (from 8% to 5%)	Estimated to increase carbon emissions by 0.2 million tonnes by 2010[6].

[1] *Modelling the Initial Effects of the Climate Change Levy, Cambridge Econometrics, available at www.hmrc.gov.uk.*
[2] *Using NETCEN emissions models – further detail on methodology used is provided in NETCEN's January 2000 report 'UK Road Transport Emissions Projections'.*
[3] *Department for Transport modelling.*
[4] *HMRC modelling.*
[5] *HMRC modelling.*
[6] *HMRC modelling.*

Table 7.2: The environmental impacts of Budget measures (continued)

Budget measure	Environmental impact
Household energy efficiency	The Energy Efficiency Commitment from 2002-2008 is expected to reduce emissions by around 1 MtC a year by 2010. The next phase, from 2008-2011, could save an additional 1.2 MtC a year by 2010, with subsequent supplier obligation saving an additional 3-4 MtC a year by 2020. Improving home insulation could contribute about 2 MtC a year. Other measures also have a significant impact e.g. building regulation improvements in 2002 and 2006 are expected to reduce emissions by about 1.5 MtC a year by 2010.
Warm front and other fuel poverty programmes	Estimated carbon savings of 0.4 MtC a year by 2010.
Zero-Carbon Homes	Overall savings from both the regulation and tax incentive estimated to be 1.2 MtC by 2020.
Energy efficient initiatives for consumer electronics and low energy lighting	Phasing out the use of inefficient GLS lightbulbs could reduce UK carbon emissions by up to 1.2 MtC a year by 2020. Encouraging more energy efficient consumer electronics has the potential to save up to 1.7 MtC a year by 2020.
Low Carbon Buildings Programme	Carbon savings by 2010 around 0.01 MtC per year.
Carbon capture and storage	Carbon capture and storage demonstration expected to deliver savings of between 0.25-1.0 MtC per year by 2020.
Improving Waste Management	
Landfill tax	Between 1997-98 and 2005-06, the total quantity of waste disposed to landfill sites registered for landfill tax fell by 25 per cent, while the amount of active waste disposed to landfill fell by 14 per cent[7]. The Landfill tax is expected to save up to 0.2 MtC a year by 2010.
Landfill communities fund	Landfill tax credits scheme (now the landfill communities fund) has provided £759 million for projects since its introduction.
Regenerating the UK's towns and cities	
Contaminated land tax credit	Bringing forward remediation of contaminated land.
Capital allowances for flats over shops	Bringing empty space over shops back into the residential market, while reducing the pressure for new greenfield development.
Reforms to VAT on conversion and renovation	Reduced pressure on greenfield site development.
Protecting the UK's countryside and natural resources	
Aggregates levy and aggregates levy sustainability fund	An 8 per cent reduction in sales of aggregates between 2001 and 2005. Reductions in noise and vibration, dust and other emissions to air, visual intrusion, loss of amenity and damage to wildlife habitats.
Enhanced capital allowances for water efficiency technologies	More sustainable use of water by business.

[7] Data at www.uktradeinfo.com.

A ILLUSTRATIVE LONG-TERM FISCAL PROJECTIONS

> To safeguard long-term economic growth and ensure inter-generational fairness it is important that Budget decisions are consistent with the long-term sustainability of the public finances. The illustrative long-term fiscal projections presented in this annex provide an assessment of the long-term sustainability of the Government's fiscal policies over the period up to 2036-37, in line with the requirements of the *Code for fiscal stability*. The key points are:
>
> - the UK remains well placed to deal with potential future spending pressures due to ageing and other factors;
>
> - given the projected profile for tax revenue and transfers, current public consumption can grow at around assumed GDP growth after the medium term while meeting the Government's golden rule; and
>
> - public sector net investment can grow broadly in line with the economy without jeopardising the sustainable investment rule.
>
> This conclusion concurs with the findings of the 2006 *Long-term public finance report*, which provides a more detailed examination of the long-term public finances. The report finds that, on a range of assumptions and using a number of techniques, the UK's fiscal position is sustainable in the long term on the basis of current policies, and that the UK is well placed relative to many other developed countries to face the challenges ahead. However, the Government remains vigilant to future risks and is not complacent about the long-term challenges posed by an ageing population. It will therefore continue to update and report on assessments of long-term fiscal sustainability.

A.1   The Government's fiscal policy framework, as set out in the *Code for fiscal stability*,[1] is designed to ensure transparent, long-term decision-making. Fiscal policy is set to ensure sustainable public finances, with consideration to the short, medium and long term. Long-term fiscal sustainability helps to promote long-term economic growth and ensures that financial burdens are not shifted to future generations.

Illustrative long-term fiscal projections   A.2   To assess the sustainability and inter-generational impact of fiscal policy, the Code requires the Government to publish illustrative long-term fiscal projections. In principle, fiscal projections can be either "top-down" or "bottom-up". A top-down approach imposes high-level constraints on the fiscal aggregates and then shows the combinations of spending and taxation that could meet those constraints. A bottom-up approach does not impose any high-level constraints on expenditure or revenue raising; it looks at how long-term trends, for example projected demographic changes, could affect future spending and revenue if current policy were to remain unchanged. It therefore demonstrates the potential effects of long-term pressures on the fiscal aggregates if no public spending and tax policy assumptions were made.

A.3   The illustrative long-term fiscal projections presented in this annex take a top-down approach, where the Government's fiscal rules are imposed as a constraint. The illustrative projections then show by how much current expenditure and investment will be able to grow, given certain assumptions regarding government revenues, transfer payments and capital depreciation.

---

[1] *Code for fiscal stability*, HM Treasury, 1998.

A.4 To complement and enhance the illustrative projections, the Government has published the Long-term public finance report each year since 2002, most recently alongside the 2006 Pre-Budget Report.[2] The report primarily takes a bottom-up approach; it examines long-term challenges for the public finances and provides a comprehensive assessment of the sustainability of the public finances.

LONG-TERM SOCIO-ECONOMIC AND OTHER TRENDS

A.5 Declining fertility rates and increases in life expectancy over past decades have led to a general ageing of the population in the UK and throughout most of the developed world. The median age of the UK population increased from 34.1 years in 1971 to 38.8 years in 2005. The latest official UK principal population projections were produced by the Government Actuary's Department (GAD) in October 2005.[3] Details of these 2004-based population projections are given in the 2006 *Long-term public finance report*.

A.6 Based on the latest principal projections, the UK's population will increase from around 60 million today to around 68 million by the mid 2030s. The population structure is also projected to change substantially. Chart A.1 shows the wide variations between the projected changes in size of different age groups, with the oldest age group projected to more than double in absolute size over the next 30 years, while the 0-15 years and 16-54 years age groups remain more or less stable. The median age of the UK population is projected to rise to 43.4 years by 2036.

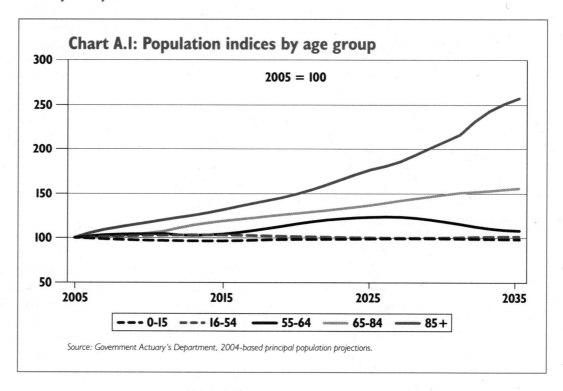

Chart A.1: Population indices by age group

2005 = 100

Source: Government Actuary's Department, 2004-based principal population projections.

A.7 The composition of the population will change as a result. The share of the population aged 16 to 64 years is projected to fall by around 5½ percentage points between now and 2035. At the same time the share of people aged 65 years and over is projected to rise

---

[2] 2006 *Long-term public finance report: an analysis of fiscal sustainability*, HM Treasury, December 2006.

[3] http://www.gad.gov.uk/Population/index.asp. Also note that on 31 January 2006 responsibility for producing official population projections for the UK passed to the Office for National Statistics (ONS), which intends to issue the next full set of population projections later in 2007.

by around 8 percentage points over this period, and the share of those aged 85 years and over is projected to rise by just over 2 percentage points, from its present level of around 2 per cent. By contrast the share of children (those aged up to 15 years) in the total population is projected to fall.

A high degree of **A.8**   Any long-term projection is subject to a high degree of uncertainty. To deal with this
uncertainty uncertainty, GAD has produced high and low variants around the principal projections, using alternative fertility, longevity and net migration assumptions. The variants differ markedly from the principal projections, and suggest that governments should attempt to plan for a wide range of potential outcomes. To this end, a cautious approach to assessing the long-term sustainability of the public finances is taken below.

Other long-term **A.9**   However, demographic change is only one of a number of trends that may have a
trends significant impact upon public finances in the future. In November 2006 the Government published *Long-term opportunities and challenges for the UK: analysis for the 2007 Comprehensive Spending Review.*[4] That document looks in turn at five areas of change that the Government will have to confront in the decade ahead:

- demographic and socio-economic change, with rapid increases in the old-age dependency ratio on the horizon, and rising consumer expectations of public services;

- the intensification of cross-border economic competition, with new opportunities for growth, as the balance of international economic activity shifts toward emerging markets such as China and India;

- the rapid pace of innovation and technological diffusion, which will continue to transform the way people live and open up new ways of delivering public services;

- continued global uncertainty with ongoing threats of international terrorism and global conflict and the continued imperative to tackle global poverty; and

- increasing pressures on our natural resources and global climate, requiring action by governments, businesses and individuals to maintain prosperity and improve environmental care.

METHODOLOGY AND ASSUMPTIONS

A.10   As stated above, the illustrative long-term fiscal projections are generated using a so-called top-down modelling approach. "Top-down" refers to the fact that a number of high-level assumptions are imposed on the model, which constrain the evolution of specific fiscal aggregates. For the illustrative long-term fiscal projections the high-level assumptions are that a) the tax to GDP ratio remains constant after the medium term, b) the Government's golden rule holds in every year after the medium term and c) the Government's sustainable investment rule is met in every year over the projection period of 30 years. The golden rule is assumed to hold in every year after the medium term because it is not possible to project an economic cycle beyond the medium-term horizon.

---

[4] *Long-term opportunities and challenges for the UK: analysis for the 2007 Comprehensive Spending Review*, HM Treasury, November 2006.

A.11   The illustrative projections incorporate long-term social security projections provided by the Department for Work and Pensions, which cover pension and non-pension social transfers. Using this information and projections of debt interest payments to calculate total transfer spending, it is possible to calculate how much money the Government has left out of total current expenditure for current consumption, i.e. current expenditure on goods and services. Current consumption covers, among other things, current spending on health, education, law and order, and defence. These illustrative top-down projections are complemented by the bottom-up projections provided in the Long-term public finance report, which provide an indication of future demand pressures on public spending.

A.12   Up to and including 2011-12, the end of the medium-term forecast period, the long-term illustrative projections are based on the fiscal forecasts and assumptions presented in Chapter C of the Financial Statement and Budget Report (FSBR). Beyond that, it is assumed that the Government will leave current policy unchanged in the future, in the sense that the tax to GDP ratio will remain constant and Government will meet its fiscal rules. This should not be interpreted as meaning that policy will not change over time; the assumption is used so that the long-term projections do not pre-judge future government policy.

Economic assumptions **A.13**   Table A.1 sets out the economic assumptions that underlie the long-term fiscal projections after 2011-12. To deal with the uncertainty involved in projecting long-term trends, cautious assumptions are used. Productivity is assumed to grow by $1^3/_4$ per cent a year from 2012-13, which is $^1/_4$ per cent lower than the neutral view of productivity growth. This is in line with the "lower productivity" scenario used in the 2006 *Long-term public finance report*.

Table A.1: Cautious assumptions for real GDP growth and its components

Year	2012-13 to 2016-17	2017-18 to 2026-27	2027-28 to 2036-37
Productivity	$1^3/_4$	$1^3/_4$	$1^3/_4$
Employment	$^1/_4$	0	0
Real GDP	**2**	$1^3/_4$	$1^3/_4$

Source: HM Treasury.

A.14   The illustrative projections use the so-called "cohort" method to project gender- and age-specific employment rates and total employment levels beyond the medium term. The growth rates for productivity and employment generate the growth rates for GDP from 2012-13 onwards. The employment projections take into account the increases to the State Pension age proposed in the Pensions Bill currently before Parliament.[5] Box A.1 gives a summary of how this modelling has been done. For a more detailed explanation of the cohort method and how the proposed pensions reforms have been incorporated, see the 2006 *Long-term public finance report*.

A.15   After combining the productivity assumption and employment projection, the resulting GDP projection is substantially lower than that which has been recorded on average over the last ten years, reflecting a cautious approach to projecting long-term fiscal aggregates. Indeed, it is significantly lower than the cautious assumption of trend growth of $2^1/_2$ per cent over the medium term used for the medium-term public finance projections.

---

[5] For further details see the White Paper *Security in retirement: towards a new pensions system*, Department for Work and Pensions, May 2006.

Box A.1: Adjusting for the proposed increase in the State Pension age

The increase in the State Pension age proposed in the Pensions Bill currently before Parliament could be expected to have some effect on labour market behaviour. On the one hand, it might be that the increase influences the behaviour of people only at the age where they would previously have been eligible for a state pension. On the other hand, people could adjust their behaviour at younger ages, in anticipation of having to wait longer to claim the State Pension.[a] The chart below shows these two possible behavioural responses (the lower and upper profiles respectively), compared to the participation rate profile without any reform.

The middle variant represents an average of these two possible behavioural responses, and therefore provides a reasonable estimate of the likely labour market effect of the proposed increase in the State Pension age.[b] This middle variant is used for the GDP projection underlying the illustrative long-term fiscal projections.

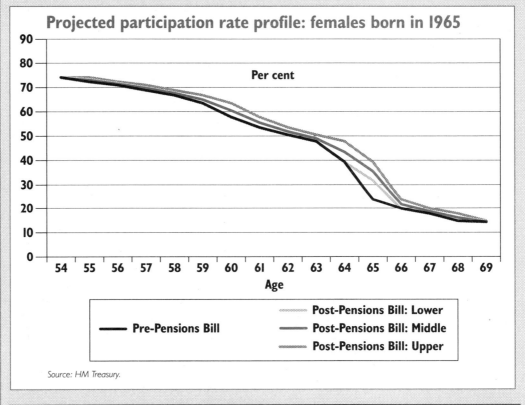

Projected participation rate profile: females born in 1965

Source: HM Treasury.

[a] Historical data indicate that participation rates typically begin to fall significantly from the age of 55 onwards. It is therefore reasonable to assume that this is the earliest age at which the State Pension age begins to affect behaviour.
[b] The effect of the State Pension age on labour market participation using the middle variant is broadly in line with estimates of the labour market effect of the State Pension age produced in a study by the Office for National Statistics. See *Labour Force Projections 2006-2020*, Office for National Statistics, January 2006.

Taxation and spending assumptions

A.16   For the period up to and including 2011-12, the illustrative long-term fiscal projections are based on the forecasts and assumptions presented in Chapter C of the FSBR. Beyond the medium-term horizon, the projections could be described as a "what if" scenario. They describe what might happen if high-level policy settings in 2011-12 were to continue throughout the rest of the projection period. For example, it is assumed that the Government continues to raise the same amount of revenue as a proportion of GDP as in 2011-12, offsetting possible changes in tax bases by changing policy in a revenue-neutral way. By assumption, the golden rule is met, with the current budget in balance at all times. This implies that the sum of total current expenditure and depreciation is also assumed to be constant, as a share of GDP, from 2012-13 onwards.

A.17   Current public consumption is calculated as total current expenditure less transfers. Transfers mainly consist of social security spending (e.g. basic State Pension and Disability Living Allowance) and debt interest payments. The latter are calculated using the projected debt stock and a long-term interest rate, which is assumed to equal the implicit average interest rate between 2007-08 and 2011-12. Under the assumption that the current budget is in balance, the change in the absolute level of public sector net debt reflects changes in public sector net investment. As in previous illustrative long-term projections, the share of public sector net investment in GDP is reset at 1.8 per cent beyond the medium term.

ILLUSTRATIVE PROJECTIONS

A.18   Chart A.2 shows the projected evolution of total current expenditure, transfers, current consumption and net debt as a share of GDP between 2006-07 and 2036-37, given the assumptions stated above.

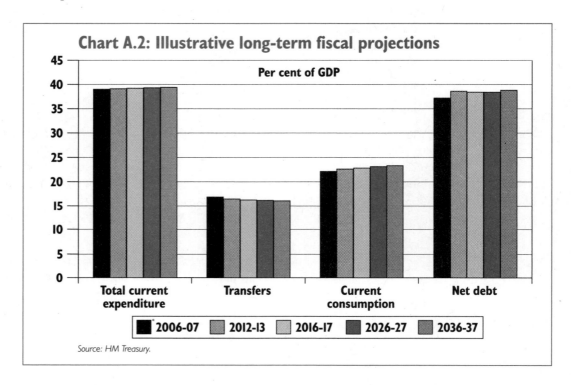

Chart A.2: Illustrative long-term fiscal projections

Per cent of GDP

Legend: 2006-07 2012-13 2016-17 2026-27 2036-37

Source: HM Treasury.

A.19   Total current expenditure is projected to increase between 2006-07 and 2011-12. Given the assumptions stated above, total current expenditure remains more or less stable beyond the medium term. Transfers are projected to fall from 16.9 per cent in 2006-07 to 16.1 per cent by 2036-37, while current consumption is projected to increase from 22.6 per cent in 2012-13 to 23.3 per cent in 2036-37. Hence current consumption can grow at around assumed GDP growth, after the medium term, while still meeting the fiscal rules.

A.20   Starting from 38.6 per cent in 2012-13, net debt is projected to remain broadly stable, reaching 38.8 per cent by 2036-37, consistent with the sustainable investment rule.

A.21   The illustrative long-term fiscal projections presented here complement the analysis presented in the 2006 *Long-term public finance report*. The report projects the independent evolution of individual age-related spending items such as state pensions and long-term care, and then uses a broad range of techniques, assumptions and modelling approaches to assess long-term sustainability based on the bottom-up projections. The report demonstrates that the UK fiscal position is sustainable in the long term on the basis of current policies and that the UK is well placed relative to many other developed countries to face the challenges ahead. In reality, spending on individual items does not grow independently or without constraints, as governments impose high-level fiscal policy decisions. The top-down approach used in the illustrative long-term fiscal projections presented here reflects the way in which Government draws up its budget, taking into account its fiscal rules. In this sense the bottom-up and top-down projections are complementary.

Sensitivity analysis   **A.22**   Long-term projections of any type are inevitably subject to a high degree of uncertainty. The outcome of any projection exercise depends on the underlying assumptions. These include population projections and assumptions regarding, among other things, productivity, revenue, labour market participation and social security spending. It is important to determine the sensitivity of baseline projections to changes in the assumptions. The 2006 *Long-term public finance report* illustrates the effect of different interest rate and productivity assumptions and includes a more detailed discussion of the uncertainty surrounding long-term projections.

INTERNATIONAL COMPARISONS

Population ageing: a global phenomenon   **A.23**   The UK is not alone in facing an ageing population, and many countries are projected to age more rapidly than the UK. Chart A.3 shows that a number of EU Member States are projected to observe an increase in the demographic old-age dependency ratio[6] between 2005 and 2050 in excess of 30 percentage points. This includes four of the new Member States that joined the EU in 2004 (Czech Republic, Poland, Slovakia and Slovenia), as well as Bulgaria and Romania, who joined in 2007.

---

[6] The demographic old-age dependency ratio shows the number of people aged 65 years and over relative to the number of people aged 16 to 64 years.

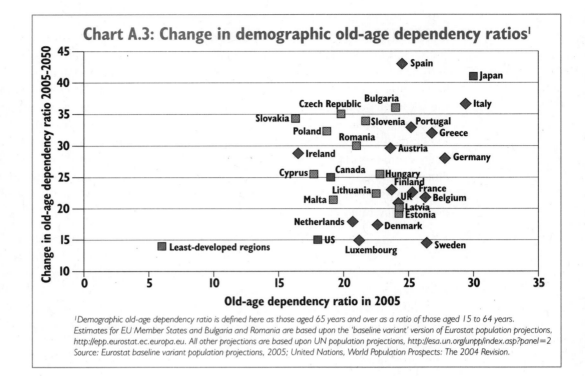

Chart A.3: Change in demographic old-age dependency ratios[1]

[1]Demographic old-age dependency ratio is defined here as those aged 65 years and over as a ratio of those aged 15 to 64 years. Estimates for EU Member States and Bulgaria and Romania are based upon the 'baseline variant' version of Eurostat population projections, http://epp.eurostat.ec.europa.eu. All other projections are based upon UN population projections, http://esa.un.org/unpp/index.asp?panel=2 Source: Eurostat baseline variant population projections, 2005; United Nations, World Population Prospects: The 2004 Revision.

A.24 Similar trends are expected for most other developed countries. Chart A.3 shows that Japan's population is projected to age significantly, with the old-age dependency ratio increasing by 41 percentage points between 2005 and 2050. By contrast, the US population is projected to age relatively moderately. The chart also shows the projected change for least developed regions,[7] illustrating that population ageing is not a phenomenon limited to developed countries. Many developing and middle-income countries will also experience substantial population ageing over the coming decades, albeit, in many cases, from a lower starting point. For example, India's demographic old-age dependency ratio is projected to rise from 8 per cent in 2005 to 22 per cent by 2050.

EU A.25 In February 2006, the EU's Economic Policy Committee (EPC) published detailed findings on the impact of an ageing population on future spending trends.[8] It found that age-related spending is projected to rise substantially in some EU Member States if existing policies remain unchanged (see Chart A.4).[9] Across the EU as a whole, age-related spending is projected to increase to around 27 per cent of GDP by 2050. Chart A.4 indicates that projected spending pressures are not confined to the existing EU15, with many of the recently acceded Member States projected to observe increases in age-related expenditure between now and 2050. Based on the EPC projections, age-related spending for the UK is projected to remain below the EU average throughout the projection period, reaching just over 23 per cent of GDP by 2050. As can be seen from the chart, this is broadly equal to the current EU average.

---

[7] As defined by the United Nations. See http://esa.un.org/unpp/definition.html.

[8] *The impact of ageing on public expenditure: projections for the EU25 Member States on pensions, health care, long-term care and unemployment transfers (2004-2050)*, European Union Economic Policy Committee, February 2006. The ECOFIN Council has given a mandate to the EPC to update its age-related expenditure projections by the autumn of 2009.

[9] Age-related spending comprises spending on pensions, health, long-term care, education and unemployment benefits in these projections.

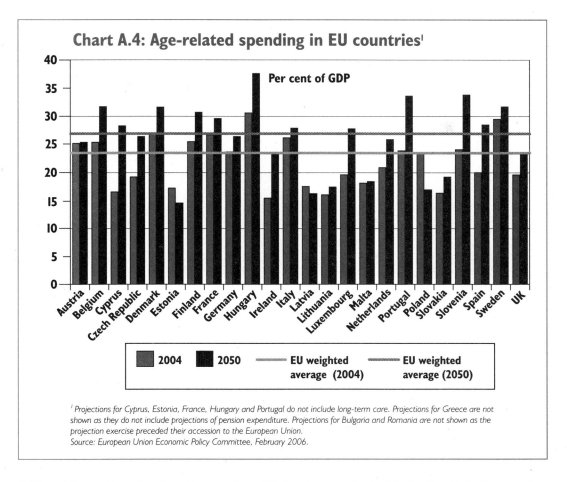

Chart A.4: Age-related spending in EU countries[1]

Per cent of GDP

Legend: ■ 2004 ■ 2050 —— EU weighted average (2004) —— EU weighted average (2050)

[1] Projections for Cyprus, Estonia, France, Hungary and Portugal do not include long-term care. Projections for Greece are not shown as they do not include projections of pension expenditure. Projections for Bulgaria and Romania are not shown as the projection exercise preceded their accession to the European Union.
Source: European Union Economic Policy Committee, February 2006.

Other developed countries

A.26   Many other developed countries will also have to deal with the fiscal challenges that arise from an ageing population. For example, projections published by the Japanese Ministry of Finance suggest a rise in social security benefits from 23.9 per cent to 26.1 per cent of GDP between 2006 and 2025.[10] Its already high level of debt makes Japan's sustainability challenge more difficult. A report published by the New Zealand Treasury uses both the top-down and bottom-up approaches to assess New Zealand's long-term fiscal position.[11] It projects a public spending increase of 7 percentage points between 2005 and 2050. Rising health spending drives most of the increase. Similarly, the Australian Government Productivity Commission has projected an increase in fiscal pressure (the extent to which government spending outpaces revenue growth) in Australia of 5.7 percentage points of GDP between 2003-04 and 2044-45.[12]

CONCLUSIONS

A.27   The illustrative fiscal projections presented in this annex complement the detailed findings presented in the 2006 *Long-term public finance report,* which show that the UK's public finances are broadly sustainable over the long term. The UK is also well placed to face future challenges relative to many other developed countries. The Government can continue to meet the golden rule and the sustainable investment rule throughout the projection period, while allowing current public consumption and public sector net investment to grow at around the assumed rate of GDP growth.

---

[10] See *Current Japanese Fiscal Conditions and Issues to be Considered,* Ministry of Finance, Japan, 2006.
[11] *New Zealand's Long-term Fiscal Position,* New Zealand Treasury, June 2006.
[12] *Economic Implications of an Ageing Australia,* Australian Government Productivity Commission, March 2005.

A.28   However, even with the use of prudent and cautious assumptions, a wide range of unforeseen developments and spending pressures could arise over the projection period. The Government will therefore continue to update and report on its assessments of long-term fiscal sustainability, both through regular publication of the Long-term public finance report alongside the Pre-Budget Report and through the illustrative long-term fiscal projections presented with each Budget, so as to ensure that all fiscal policy decisions are set within a sustainable long-term framework.

Financial Statement and Budget Report

BUDGET POLICY DECISIONS

A.1   The Economic and Fiscal Strategy Report (EFSR) explains how the measures and other decisions announced in Budget 2007 build on those already introduced to advance the Government's long-term goals. This chapter of the Financial Statement and Budget Report (FSBR) brings together in summary form all the measures and decisions that affect the Budget arithmetic that have been announced since Budget 2006 and gives their estimated effect on government revenues and spending to 2009-10. This chapter also includes a summary of the main rates and allowances for the personal tax and benefit system, the business tax system, Value Added Tax (VAT), environmental taxes, and other indirect taxes.[1]

A.2   The appendices to this chapter provide additional information on Budget measures:

- Appendix A1 provides details of tax changes and other policy decisions which were announced in Budget 2006 or earlier, but which take effect from or after April 2007;

- Appendix A2 explains in detail how the effects of the Budget measures on government revenues are calculated; and

- Appendix A3 provides estimates of the costs to the Government of some of the main tax allowances and reliefs.

BUDGET POLICY DECISIONS

A.3   Table A1 summarises the Budget 2007 measures and their effects on government revenues and spending. These include tax measures, national insurance contributions (NICs) measures, measures that affect Annually Managed Expenditure (AME), and additions to Departmental Expenditure Limits (DEL). Measures that are financed from existing DEL provisions are not included.

---

[1] The contents of the brackets after each measure in this chapter refer to the line in Tables A1 and A2 where its costs or yield is shown. The symbol '-' indicates that the proposal has no Exchequer effect until at least 2010-11. The symbol '*' indicates that the effect is negligible, amounting to less than £3 million a year.

Table A1: Budget 2007 policy decisions

		(+ve is an Exchequer yield)		£ million
	2007-08 indexed	2008-09 indexed	2009-10 indexed	2007-08 non-indexed
Corporate tax reform				
1 Main rate of Corporation Tax reduced to 28%	−140	−1,385	−2,230	−140
2 General plant and machinery capital allowances at 20%	0	+1,490	+2,270	0
3 Long-life plant and machinery capital allowances at 10%	0	−210	−380	0
4 Integral fixtures capital allowance at 10%	0	+70	+200	0
5 Industrial Buildings Allowance: phased abolition	0	+75	+225	0
6 Small Companies Rate of Corporation Tax phased to 22%	+10	+370	+820	+10
7 One-year extension of 50% First Year Allowances for small enterprises	−35	−250	+80	−35
8 New Annual Investment Allowance at £50,000	0	−30	−920	0
9 R&D tax credit increase to 130%	0	−40	−90	0
10 SME R&D tax credit increase to 175%	0	−30	−60	0
11 Payable Enhanced Capital Allowances	0	−20	−40	0
12 Reform of Venture Capital Schemes	0	+30	+30	0
13 VAT: revalorisation of registration and deregistration thresholds	0	0	0	−5
Personal tax reform				
14 Income Tax: indexation of starting and basic rate limits	0	0	0	−870
15 Remove starting rate of Income Tax on non-savings income	0	+7,320	+8,630	0
16 Increase Age Allowances by £1,180 and raise for 75s and over to £10,000	0	−810	−950	0
17 Increase Child Tax Credit by £150 above indexation	0	−880	−1,020	0
18 Raise the threshold of the Working Tax Credit by £1,200	0	−1,310	−1,310	0
19 Increasing the Tax Credit withdrawal rate by 2 per cent	0	+600	+620	0
20 Income Tax and NICs: phased alignment of higher thresholds	0	+1,110	+1,490	0
21 Income Tax and NICs: raising the higher rate threshold and upper earnings limit	0	0	−250	0
22 Basic rate of Income Tax reduced to 20 pence	0	−8,090	−9,640	0
23 Working Tax Credit continued for 4 weeks after leaving work	−10	−15	−20	−10
Supporting families and communities				
24 Raising the ISA cash limit by £600 and the overall limit by £200	0	−15	−50	0
25 Benefit simplification	0	−5	*	0
26 VAT: reduced rates on products for the elderly	−5	−10	−10	−5
Modernising the tax system				
27 Extension of the dividend tax credit	0	−5	−15	0
28 VAT: reduced rate for smoking cessation products	−10	*	0	−10
29 Energy Products Directive: expiry of derogation	0	+10	+30	0
30 Abolition of Small Consignments' Relief for excise duties	+5	+5	+5	+5
31 Gift aid: increase in benefits	0	−5	−5	0
32 Sale and repurchase agreements: tax treatment	+40	+60	+60	+40
33 VAT: non-business use of assets	+10	+15	+20	+15
34 General insurers' reserves: transitional relief	0	−70	−20	0
Protecting tax revenues				
35 Life insurance companies: financing arrangements	+120	+165	+165	+120
36 Loss-buying	+30	+45	+50	+30
37 VAT: countering missing trader fraud	+50	+45	+35	+50
38 Strengthening the disclosure regime	+15	+30	+30	+15

Table A1: Budget 2007 policy decisions

	(+ve is an Exchequer yield)			£ million
	2007-08 indexed	**2008-09 indexed**	**2009-10 indexed**	**2007-08 non-indexed**
Duties changes				
39 Alcohol duties: revalorise beer, wine and sparkling wine, freeze spirits	−20	−15	−10	+210
40 Tobacco duties: revalorise	0	0	0	+40
41 Gaming duties: changes to duty bands and rates	+30	+35	+35	+35
Property				
42 Rationalisation of empty property relief	0	+950	+900	0
Protecting the environment				
43 Expansion of Enhanced Capital Allowances for water-efficient technologies	*	*	−5	*
Supporting a clean and efficient transport system				
44 VED: enhancing environmental incentives	+125	+220	+280	+230
45 Road fuel duties: increases from 1 October 2007	−380	+490	+660	+480
46 Rebated oils duties: increases from 1 October 2007	+50	+125	+135	+65
47 Biofuels: extension of differential to 2009-10	0	0	+10	0
48 Road fuel gas: continuation of differentials to 2009-10	0	0	+5	0
49 Renewal of reduced pollution certificate scheme for lorries	0	0	−5	0
Protecting the UK's natural resources				
50 Aggregates levy: encouraging the sustainable use of resources	−10	+40	+45	0
Improving waste management				
51 Landfill tax: supporting recycling	0	+175	+325	0
Other policy decisions				
52 Special reserve	−400	0	0	−400
TOTAL POLICY DECISIONS	**−525**	**+280**	**+125**	**−130**
Negligible				
MEMO ITEM				
Resetting of the AME margin	−1,000			

A.4   Table A2 summarises the impact on government revenues and spending of other measures introduced since Budget 2006, including those measures announced in the 2006 Pre-Budget Report.

Table A2: Other measures announced since Budget 2006

			(+ve is an Exchequer yield)			£ million
			2007-08 indexed	**2008-09** indexed	**2009-10** indexed	**2007-08** non-indexed
		Increasing employment opportunity for all				
a	†	Increase in Housing Benefit disregard	-5	-	-	-5
b		Housing Benefit subsidy rate for temporary accommodation	+10	-	-	*
c	†	Supporting people into work through extending the job grant	-5	-	-	-5
		Building a fairer society				
d	†	Indexation of the Working Tax Credit	0	0	0	-420
e	†	July renewal deadline for Child and Working Tax Credits[1]	+60	+20	+10	+60
f	†	Indexation of income tax allowances	0	0	0	-1,280
g	†	Indexation of national insurance rates and limits	0	0	0	-345
h	†	Tackling Managed Service Companies	+350	+450	+250	+350
i	†	Film tax reliefs: transitional arrangements	-20	-20	*	-20
j	†	Life assurance companies reform	-15	-20	-10	-15
k	†	Simplification of general insurers' reserves	0	+130	+150	0
l	†	VAT: partial exemption special method	+20	+20	+25	+20
m		VAT: supplies by health professionals	+5	+5	+10	+5
n	†	Construction Industry Scheme deduction rates	+250	-10	-20	+250
o	†	Increasing travellers' allowance from outside the EU	-15	-15	-15	-15
		Protecting revenues				
p	†	Controlled Foreign Companies: repeal of public quotation exemption	+125	+160	+160	+125
q	†	Tackling avoidance using structured finance arrangements	+15	+15	+15	+15
r	†	Countering corporation tax avoidance	+180	+195	+195	+180
s	†	Life assurance companies: valuation rules	+95	+95	+95	+95
t	†	Stamp Duty Land Tax anti-avoidance	+75	+70	+70	+75
u	†	Countering CGT avoidance	+70	+130	+120	+70
v		Avoidance by partnerships using sideways loss relief	+400	+300	+60	+400
w		Countering avoidance by financial traders	+30	+45	+50	+30
		Protecting the environment				
x	†	Air passenger duty rates[2]	+1,000	+1,100	+1,200	+1,000
y	†	Fuel duties: revalorise main rates from 7 December 2006	0	0	0	+630
z	†	Fuel duties: maintain the differential for rebated oils from 7 December 2006	0	0	0	+85
aa	†	Fuel duties: maintain the differential for biofuels from 7 December 2006	0	0	0	+5
ab	†	Rebated oils: changes to excepted vehicle schedule	-5	0	0	-5
ac	†	Extension of the Landlords Energy Saving Allowance	0	-10	-10	0
		Other policy decisions				
ad	†	Direct payments to schools	-155	-	-	-155
		TOTAL POLICY DECISIONS	+2,465	+2,660	+2,355	+1,130

* Negligible.

† Announced in the 2006 Pre-Budget Report.

- Included within the current spending growth assumption from 2008-09 onwards.

[1] AME spending element included within the current spending growth assumption from 2008-09 onwards.

[2] The costing assumes revalorisation annually from 1 April 2008.

PERSONAL TAX AND SPENDING MEASURES

Income Tax

Bands, rates and personal allowances

A.5   As announced in the 2006 Pre-Budget Report, all income tax personal allowances will be increased by statutory indexation for 2007-08. (f)

A.6   The starting and basic rate limits for 2007-08 are increased with statutory indexation and there are no changes to the income tax rates this year. (14)

A.7   As announced at Budget 2004, the lifetime allowance for tax privileged pension schemes will be £1.6 million in 2007-08. The annual allowance will be £225,000 for 2007-08.

Table A3: Bands of taxable income 2007-08

2006-07	£ a year	2007-08	£ a year
Starting rate 10 per cent	0-2,150	Starting rate 10 per cent	0-2,230
Basic[1,2] rate 22 per cent	2,151-33,300	Basic[1,2] rate 22 per cent	2,231-34,600
Higher[2] rate 40 per cent	over 33,300	Higher[2] rate 40 per cent	over 34,600

[1] The rate of tax applicable to interest remains at 20 per cent for income between the starting and basic rate limits.
[2] The rates applicable to dividends are 10 per cent for income up to the basic rate limit and 32.5 per cent above that.

Table A4: Income tax allowances

	£ a year		
	2006-07	2007-08	Increase
Personal allowance			
age under 65	5,035	5,225	190
age 65-74	7,280	7,550	270
age 75 and over	7,420	7,690	270
Married couple's allowance[1]			
aged less than 75 and born before 6th April 1935	6,065	6,285	220
aged 75 and over	6,135	6,365	230
minimum amount[2]	2,350	2,440	90
Income limit for age-related allowances	20,100	20,900	800
Blind person's allowance	1,660	1,730	70

[1] Tax relief for these allowances is restricted to 10 per cent.
[2] This is also the maximum relief for maintenance payments where at least one of the parties is born before 6 April 1935.

Effects on the Scottish Parliament's tax varying powers – statement regarding Section 76 of the Scotland Act 1998

A.8   A one penny change in the Scottish variable rate in 2007-2008 could be worth approximately plus or minus £300 million, and is unaffected by Budget 2007. After the reforms announced in Chapter 5, a one penny change in the Scottish variable rate in 2008-2009 could then be worth approximately plus or minus £370 million, compared with plus or minus £310 million that year without these changes. None of these figures include an estimate of the behavioural impacts of invoking the Scottish variable rate. In HM Treasury's view, an amendment to the Scottish Parliament's tax-varying powers is not required as a result of these changes.

National insurance contributions

A.9   As announced in the 2006 Pre-Budget Report, the national insurance contributions (NICs) thresholds, limits and flat rates will increase in line with statutory indexation for 2007-08. There will be no change to NICs rates for employers and employees, or to the rate of profit-related NICs paid by the self-employed. (g)

Table A5: Class 1 national insurance contribution rates 2007-08

Earnings[1] £ per week	Employee (primary) NICs rate[2] per cent	Employer (secondary) NICs rate[3] per cent
Below £87 (LEL)	0	0
£87 to £100 (PT/ST)	0[4]	0
£100 to £670 (UEL)	11	12.8
Above £670	1	12.8

[1] The limits are defined as LEL – lower earnings limit; PT – primary threshold; ST – secondary threshold; and UEL – upper earnings limit.

[2] The contracted-out rebate for primary contributions in 2007-08 is 1.6 per cent of earnings between the LEL and UEL for contracted-out salary-related schemes (COSRS) and contracted-out money purchase schemes (COMPS).

[3] The contracted-out rebate for secondary contributions is 3.7 per cent of earnings between the LEL and UEL for COSRS and 1.4 per cent for COMPS. For COMPS, an additional age-related rebate is paid direct to the scheme following the end of the tax year. For appropriate personal pensions, the employee and employer pay NICs at the standard, not contracted-out rate. An age- and earnings-related rebate is paid direct to the personal pension provider following the end of the year.

[4] No NICs are actually payable but a Class 1 NIC is treated as having been paid in respect of earnings between LEL and PT to protect benefit entitlement.

Table A6: Self-employed national insurance contribution rates 2007-08

Annual profits[1] £ per year	Self-employed NICs	
	Class 2 £ per week	Class 4 per cent
Below £4,635 (SEE)	0[2]	0
£4,635 to £5,225 (LPL)	£2.20	0
£5,225 to £34,840 (UPL)		8
Above £34,840		1

[1] The limits are defined as LPL – lower profits limit; and UPL – upper profits limit.

[2] The self-employed may apply for exemption from paying Class 2 contributions if their earnings are less than, or expected to be less than, the level of the Small Earnings Exception (SEE).

Modernising the personal tax and benefit system

A.10   From 6 April 2008, the 10 pence starting rate will be removed for earned income but will continue to be available for savings income and capital gains. (15)

A.11   From 6 April 2008, the additional age-related income tax allowances for those aged 65 and over will rise by £1,180 above indexation. By April 2011, the age-related allowance for those aged 75 and over will increase to £10,000. (16)

A.12   From 6 April 2008, the child element of the Child Tax Credit will be increased by £150 a year above earnings indexation. (17)

A.13   From 6 April 2008, the income threshold at which the Working Tax Credit is received in full will be increased by £1,200 to £6,420 per year. (18)

A.14   From 6 April 2008, the rate at which tax credits are withdrawn will increase from 37 per cent to 39 per cent. (19)

A.15   From 6 April 2008, the threshold of earnings above which people pay 1 per cent NICs (the upper earnings limit, UEL) will increase by £75 per week. The following year the UEL will be aligned with the point at which the higher rate of tax becomes payable. The upper profits limit (UPL) rises with the UEL. (20)

A.16   From 6 April 2009, the higher rate threshold will be increased by £800 above indexation. (21)

A.17   From 6 April 2008, the basic rate of income tax will be reduced from 22 pence to 20 pence. (22)

A.18   From 6 April 2007, HMRC will introduce a four-week run-on of entitlement to Working Tax Credit from the day a claimant ceases to work over 16 hours. (23)

Other personal taxes, benefits and spending measures

Tax credits   **A.19**   As announced in the 2006 Pre-Budget Report, the renewal period for Child and Working Tax Credit will be reduced from five to four months from July 2007. (e)

Working Tax Credit   **A.20**   As announced in the 2006 Pre-Budget Report, all the elements of Working Tax Credit rise in line with indexation for 2007-08. (d)

Table A7: Working and Child Tax Credits rates and thresholds

	2007-08 £ a year
Working Tax Credit	
Basic element	1,730
Couples and lone parent element	1,700
30 hour element	705
Disabled worker element	2,310
Severe disability element	980
50+ Return to work payment (16-29 hours)	1,185
50+ Return to work payment (30+ hours)	1,770
Childcare element of the Working Tax Credit	
Maximum eligible cost for one child	£175 per week
Maximum eligible cost for two or more children	£300 per week
Per cent of eligible costs covered	*80%*
Child Tax Credit	
Family element	545
Family element, baby addition	545
Child element	1,845
Disabled child element	2,440
Severely disabled child element	980
Income thresholds and withdrawal rates	
First income threshold	5,220
First withdrawal rate (per cent)	*37%*
Second income threshold	50,000
Second withdrawal rate (per cent)	*6.67%*
First threshold for those entitled to Child Tax Credit only	14,495
Income disregard	25,000

Managed Service Companies   **A.21**   As announced in the 2006 Pre-Budget Report, with effect from 6 April 2007 for tax and 6 August 2007 for NICs, those working through Managed Service Companies (MSCs) will pay employed levels of tax and NICs, with the MSC obliged to operate pay as you earn (PAYE) and deduct tax and Class 1 NICs. Where the MSC is unable to pay its PAYE or NICs liability, debts arising from Royal Assent may be transferred to appropriate third parties. (h)

Dividend tax credit: non-UK dividends

A.22   From 6 April 2008, the non-payable dividend tax credit will be extended to dividends from non-UK resident companies, subject to certain conditions. A person will qualify for the non-payable dividend tax credit if they have less than a 10 per cent shareholding in the distributing non-UK resident company and in total they receive less than £5,000 per year of dividends from non-UK resident companies. (27)

Individual Savings Accounts

A.23   From 6 April 2008 the Individual Savings Account (ISA) annual investment limit will rise to £7,200, with a maximum of £3,600 in cash. (24)

A.24   As announced in the 2006 Pre-Budget Report, a package of reforms to the ISA regime will be implemented from 6 April 2008. (*)

Building Society bonuses

A.25   Regulations were laid on 1 December 2006 with effect from 1 January 2007, ensuring that Building Society bonuses that are paid to holders of Child Trust Fund accounts or ISAs can be paid directly into the account free of tax. This does not affect the tax treatment of demutualisation bonuses. (*)

Pensions tax simplification

A.26   A package of technical improvements will be introduced to ensure that the pensions tax rules continue to meet the original intentions of the regime. (*)

A.27   An individual's entitlement to tax relief on pension contributions will be removed where these are used to fund personal term assurance policies. For contributions under occupational pension schemes, this will apply where the insurer received the application for the policy on or after 29 March 2007. For contributions under other registered pension schemes, this will apply where the insurer received the application for the policy on or after 14 December 2006. (*)

A.28   As announced in the 2006 Pre–Budget Report, changes will be introduced to the tax regime for alternatively secured pensions (ASPs) with effect from 6 April 2007 to bring practice in line with policy intention and ensure tax privileged pension funds are used to secure an income in retirement, whilst meeting the needs of those with principled religious objections to annuities. (-)

Housing and Council Tax benefits

A.29   As announced in the 2006 Pre-Budget Report, the earnings disregard in Housing Benefit and Council Tax Benefit will rise in line with inflation to £15.45 with effect from 6 April 2007. (a)

A.30   From 1 April 2007 the maximum amount of Housing Benefit subsidy payable on temporary accommodation to local authorities outside London will be frozen, and the maximum amount payable to London local authorities will be reduced. (b)

Child benefit

A.31   The rate of child benefit for the eldest child will rise above standard uprating to a total value of £20 per week from 6 April 2010. (-)

Job grant for benefit claimants

A.32   As announced in the 2006 Pre-Budget Report, from 6 December 2006 Jobseeker's Allowance claimants aged under 25 who had children when they moved into work after being unemployed for six months or more will receive entitlement to the Job Grant of £100 or £250. (c)

Armed Forces Redundancy Scheme

A.33   A measure will be introduced with effect from 6 April 2006 to ensure that payments under the 2006 Armed Forces Redundancy Scheme will be tax-free in the same way as payments under the 1975 scheme. (-)

Homes abroad owned through companies

A.34   Draft legislation will be published later this year which will ensure that individuals who have or will purchase a home abroad through a company will not face a benefit in kind tax charge on their private use of the property. When legislation is introduced it will apply to future and past tax years. (*)

Benefit
simplification

A.35 A package of alignment measures will be introduced during 2007-08 to streamline rules on benefit payment periods, the backdating period for Disability Living Allowance and Attendance Allowance forms, the treatment of rental income and termination payments. (25)

CHARITIES AND COMMUNITIES

Gift aid **A.36** With effect from 6 April 2007, the value of benefits that donors may receive as a result of a donation made within the gift aid regime will increase to 5 per cent of the donation for those donating £1000 or more, with the upper limit on benefits received increasing to £500. (31)

Charities and
educational
institutions

A.37 A measure will be introduced with effect from 6 April 2007 to ensure that salary costs are correctly deducted when an employer seconds an employee to a charity or educational institution. (-)

TAXES ON CHARGEABLE GAINS, INHERITANCE TAX, ASSETS AND PROPERTY

Capital gains tax **A.38** The capital gains tax annual exempt amount is increased in line with statutory indexation to £9,200 from 6 April 2007. (-)

Tax regime for
trusts

A.39 As announced on 9 October 2006, with effect from 6 April 2006, a measure will be introduced amending a minor omission in the 2006 Trust Modernisation legislation for payments for the buy back of company shares. In addition, as announced on 9 February 2007, with effect from 6 April 2007, a measure will be introduced amending a minor omission for chargeable event gains on some types of life insurance. (*)

Inheritance tax **A.40** As announced at Budgets 2005 and 2006, the inheritance tax (IHT) nil-rate band allowance will increase to £300,000 in 2007-08, £312,000 in 2008-09 and £325,000 in 2009-10. Budget 2007 announces the IHT nil-rate band will increase to £350,000 in 2010-11. (-)

A.41 A measure will be introduced, with effect from 21 March 2007 to ensure that, in certain situations, people can elect back into the inheritance tax regime after the normal self assessment deadline, rather than incurring the pre-owned assets charge. (-)

SDLT:
simplification

A.42 [A measure will be introduced with effect from Royal Assent which will reduce the amount of Stamp Duty Land Tax (SDLT) paid in many cases where property is exchanged between connected persons by no longer treating these exchanges as linked transactions. (-)

A.43 A measure will be introduced with effect from Royal Assent, allowing payment of Stamp Duty Land Tax to be made separately from submission of the land transaction return. In addition, provision will be made to allow for electronic submission of the Stamp Duty Land Tax self certificate. (*)

SDLT: shared
ownership trusts

A.44 A measure will be introduced with effect from Royal Assent to extend relief for shared ownership leases to shared ownership trusts. (*)

SDLT: surplus
school land

A.45 A measure will be introduced with effect from 25 May 2007 to modify relief for transfers of surplus school land. (*)

Stamp duty on shares A.46 As announced in the 2006-Pre Budget Report, regulations came into effect on 1 February 2007 exempting from stamp duty reserve tax (SDRT) purchases of shares in non-UK resident exchange traded funds. (*)

Empty property relief A.47 The empty property relief in national non-domestic rates is to be reformed from 1 April 2008 so that office and retail premises receive 100 per cent relief for a three month period and industrial and warehouse premises receive 100 per cent relief for a six month period when first falling empty. Relief will end for property remaining empty beyond these periods. Charities will be exempt from the effects of this reform. (42)

Sinking funds A.48 From 6 April 2007, a relief from the 40 per cent trust rate of tax on income arising from service charges and sinking funds held by private sector landlords on trust will take effect. (*)

BUSINESS TAXES, TAXATION OF FINANCIAL SERVICES AND SPENDING MEASURES

Modernising the corporate tax system

Corporation tax rates A.49 The main rate of corporation tax will be set at 28 per cent for the financial year 2008-09. The small companies' rate will be set at 20 per cent for the financial year 2007-08; 21 per cent in 2008-09; and 22 per cent in 2009-10. (1) (6)

Capital allowances A.50 Capital allowances for plant and machinery investment will be reduced from 25 per cent to 20 per cent from April 2008. (2)

A.51 Capital allowances for long-life plant and machinery investment will be increased from 6 per cent to 10 per cent from April 2008. (3)

A.52 Fixtures that are integral to a building will be seperately identified and will receive a new capital allowance rate of 10 per cent from April 2008. (4)

Industrial buildings allowance A.53 The industrial buildings allowance will be removed in stages between 2008-2011. The allowance will be reduced to 3 per cent for the financial year 2008-09, 2 per cent for 2009-10, 1 per cent for 2010-11 and 0 per cent from April 2011. (5)

Capital allowances for small enterprises A.54 The capital allowances for small enterprises will continue to be 50 per cent in the financial year 2007-08. (7)

Annual Investment Allowance A.55 An Annual Investment Allowance of £50,000 per annum for plant and machinery investment will be introduced from April 2008. (8)

R&D tax credits A.56 Subject to state aids approval, the enhanced deduction element of the SME R&D tax credits will increase from 150 per cent to 175 per cent from April 2008. The value of the payable credit available will remain broadly at its current value of 24 per cent of qualifying expenditure. The rate of company R&D tax credit will increase from 125 per cent to 130 per cent from April 2008. (9) (10)

Enhanced capital allowances A.57 Payable enhanced capital allowances for energy-efficient and water-efficient technology – and for biofuels plant which make good carbon balance inherent in their design – will be introduced from April 2008. Loss-making companies investing in energy and water efficient technology, and in the cleanest biofuels plant will be able to claim a payable cash credit. (11)

Tax based venture capital schemes   **A.64**   From Royal Assent, companies receiving funding under the Enterprise Investment Scheme (EIS) and the Corporate Venturing Scheme (CVS) will be subject to an employee headcount of fewer than 50 and an investment tranche size limit of £2 million per year. These limits will also apply to companies receiving investments from Venture Capital Trusts (VCTs) from funds raised on or after 6 April 2007. In addition, a number of technical improvements to the schemes will be made. (12)

Other business taxes, taxation of financial services and spending measures

Film tax   **A.58**   The European Commission gave final state aid clearance for the cultural test, which acts as the gateway to the new film tax relief. To ensure continuity in film tax relief during the transition to the new system, Section 42 relief for films was extended until 31 December 2006. The new film tax relief commenced from 1 January 2007. (i)

A.59   A measure will be introduced allowing companies to elect out of the film rules. Such an election applies to all films starting principal photography in the accounting period for which it is made, and in all subsequent periods. (*)

Securitisation companies   **A.60**   A measure will be introduced to amend legislation relating to securitisation companies, to take effect from Royal Assent. (-)

HMRC online services   **A.61**   Following Lord Carter's Review of HMRC's Online Services, the Government will introduce a package of measures to encourage the use of electronic filing and payment, starting with self-assessment from 31 October 2008. (*)

Companies: early filing   **A.62**   As announced in the 2006 Pre-Budget Report, a package of measures will be introduced to encourage companies to file their tax returns early, and to send their accounts to Companies House simultaneously. (*)

Construction Industry Scheme   **A.63**   As announced in the 2006 Pre-Budget Report, the new Construction Industry Scheme will commence on 6 April 2007 with deduction rates of 20 per cent for those registered for net payment and 30 per cent for those not registered in the scheme. (n)

Community investment tax relief   **A.64**   Regulations will be introduced setting out a revised criteria of accreditation for the Community Investment Tax Relief (CITR) scheme. Following this change, from the third anniversary of accreditation, at least 75 per cent of CITR funds must be 'on average' rather than 'at all times' onward-invested in relevant investments. (*)

North Sea Oil taxation   **A.65**   As announced in the Pre-Budget report 2006, from 1 July 2007, oil and gas fields will be removed from the charge to Petroleum Revenue Tax if they are redeveloped following full decommissioning. (*)

UK stock exchanges   **A.66**   As announced on 20 February 2007, the Government will no longer require transactions in shares admitted to trading on a regulated market under EU Markets in Financial Instruments Directive (MiFID) to be reported to that market, or intermediaries to be members of that market, in order for intermediaries to benefit from stamp duty relief, to take effect from 1 November 2007. The Government is also modernising the definition of 'recognised stock exchange' for tax purposes to allow shares traded on other markets regulated under MiFID to benefit from the same tax arrangements that currently only apply to listed shares which are traded on the London Stock Exchange. (-)

Offshore Funds tax regime   **A.67**   The restriction on the structure of multi-tiered funds in the Offshore Funds regime will be removed. This will take effect for accounting periods beginning on or after 1 January 2007. There will also be minor changes to assist with the practical application of the regime, including: amending the definition of an Offshore Fund, effective for accounting periods beginning on or after 1 January 2007; and the treatment of losses on disposal of units or shares for losses arising on or after 6 April 2007 for income tax payers, and on or after 1 April 2007 for corporation tax payers. (-)

Property Authorised Investment Funds   **A.68**   The Government has been continuing to consider the taxation position for Authorised Investment Funds investing in property. A framework for taking this issue forward can be found on HM Treasury website. (*)

Investment Manager Exemption   **A.69**   The group of activities considered eligible for the Investment Manager Exemption will be extended to include certain instruments for carbon trading. This extension is intended to be effective from 12 April 2007. (-)

Islamic finance   **A.70**   A measure will be introduced to clarify the taxation of alternative finance securitisations, to take effect from 1 April 2007 for companies and 6 April 2007 for individuals. (-)

A.71   As announced in October 2006, regulations will be introduced to extend the Community Investment Tax Relief scheme to include Islamic financial products. (*)

General insurers' reserves   **A.72**   As announced in the 2006 Pre-Budget Report, the existing complex tax rules dealing with the reserves of general insurance companies and Lloyd's will be repealed, subject to transitional rules, and replaced. The detail of the transitional rule and the basis for replacement accounts-based rules are now announced. The new rules will have effect for periods of account ending on or after Royal Assent. (k) (34)

Lloyd's   **A.73**   As announced in the 2006 Pre-Budget Report, a measure will be introduced, effective for Lloyd's corporate members whose final underwriting year is 2007 or later, to allow trading losses to be transferred with an underwriting business where there is continuity of ownership. (*)

Life insurance   **A.74**   As announced in the 2006 Pre-Budget Report, five existing categories of long-term business will be merged into a single new category with effect for periods commencing on or after 1 January 2007. (j)

A.75   As announced in the 2006 Pre-Budget Report, the current complex rules for dealing with transfers of business between life insurance companies will be replaced by simplified provisions, including a narrowly targeted anti-avoidance rule and a clearance procedure. Some measures will apply for periods beginning on or after 1 January 2007. Others will apply from an appointed day. The appointed day will be determined after consultation with the industry. (-)

A.76   As announced in principle in the 2006 Pre-Budget Report, a measure is introduced setting out in statute the circumstances in which the profits of a life insurance company will be computed under Case I of Schedule D, rather than under the I minus E basis, with effect from periods commencing on or after 1 January 2007. (-)

A.77   A package of measures will be introduced, with effect from periods commencing on or after 1 January 2007, to modify the treatment of structural assets and correct miscellaneous anomalies among the life insurance tax provisions. (-)

A.78 A package of measures, some announced in the 2006 Pre-Budget Report and some in Budget 2007, will be introduced that allows the tax exemption to be retained on the transfer of existing tax exempt business from friendly societies to life insurance companies and deals with anomalies which can arise on assignment of tax exempt policies. The measures will apply to transfers assignments taking place from Royal Assent and for assignments taking place after 1 January 2007. (-)

A.79 As announced on 18 and 19 December 2006, a package of measures was introduced, with effect from periods ending on or after 31 December 2006, to spread the tax cost where life insurance companies take advantage of the relaxation of the regulatory rules, announced by the Financial Services Authority, to release non-profit reserves. (-)

VALUE ADDED TAX

VAT registration **A.80** From 1 April 2007 the VAT registration threshold will be increased from £61,000 to £64,000 and the deregistration threshold from £59,000 to £62,000. (13)

EU travellers' allowances **A.81** As announced in the 2006 Pre-Budget Report, the tax-free allowance for international travellers returning from trips outside the EU will double to £290 following a decision in November by EU Member States. The new limit is likely to come into force in 2007. (o)

Partial exemption **A.82** As announced in the 2006 Pre-Budget Report, with effect from 1 April 2007, a package of measures will be introduced to strengthen and simplify the partial exemption special method regime. (l)

Non-business use of assets **A.83** A measure will be introduced with effect from 1 September 2007 to regulate VAT accounting on non-business use of assets allocated wholly to business purposes. (33)

Smoking cessation products **A.84** From 1 July 2007, the Government will introduce a reduced VAT rate of 5 per cent for one year for over the counter sales of smoking cessation products. (28)

Health professionals **A.85** As announced on 30 January 2007, certain supplies by health professionals which are not medical care will be liable to VAT at 17.5 per cent from 1 May 2007. (m)

Retention of records **A.86** As announced in the 2006 Pre-Budget Report, VAT record keeping requirements for businesses transferred as a going concern will be brought into line with other tax and regulatory regimes, so that in most cases the seller retains his records. This will have effect from 1 September 2007. (-)

Housing alterations for the elderly **A.87** From 1 July 2007 the rate of VAT for certain home alterations that support the needs of elderly people will be reduced to 5 per cent. (26)

ENVIRONMENTAL AND TRANSPORT TAXES

Climate Change Levy A.88 The rates of Climate Change Levy (CCL) will be indexed from 1 April 2008. (-)

Climate change simplification A.89 A package of measures will be introduced and brought fully into effect by autumn 2007 to simplify aspects of the climate change levy, particularly concerning relief certification. (*)

Zero-carbon homes and stamp duty A.90 A relief from stamp duty land tax will be introduced with effect from 1 October 2007 for new homes built to a zero-carbon standard to be set in regulations. The exemption will be time limited to 30 September 2012. The relief will provide exemption from tax liability when the house costs £500,000 or less and will provide a £15,000 reduction in tax liability to all homes worth more than £500,000. (*)

Vehicle Excise Duty A.91 Graduated Vehicle Excise Duty (VED) rates for band G cars will increase to £300 in 2007-08, £400 in 2008-09 and frozen in 2009-10. Band B reduces to £35 this year, with this rate then frozen for the next 2 years. Band F increases by £10 in 2007-08 and £5 in each of the next two years. Rates for Bands C-E, pre-2001 cars and vans, and post-2001 vans will rise by £5 in each of the next three years. VED rates for petrol and diesel cars are aligned. In 2007-08 only, the rates for motorbikes in the lower band will be frozen, with higher bands increased by £1-£2; and rates for heavy goods vehicles (HGV), special types vehicles, combined transport vehicles and all vehicle categories that are linked to the basic goods rate will be frozen. Changes to VED rates for 2007-08 take effect from 22 March 2007. (44)

Lorry Reduced Pollution Certificates A.92 A renewed scheme of Reduced Pollution Certificates for lorries and buses will come into force from 1 October 2007. The nature of the scheme will be similar to the one that existed prior to October 2006 for Euro IV vehicles. (49)

Fuel duties A.93 As announced in the 2006 Pre-Budget Report, with effect from 7 December 2006, an inflation-based rise in main road fuel duty was introduced. With effect from the same date the differentials with biofuels, rebated oils and compressed natural gas duty rates were maintained, and the differential with liquefied petroleum gas was decreased by 1 penny per litre (ppl). (y)(z)(aa)

A.94 With effect from 1 October 2007 there will be a 2ppl increase in man road fuel duties. On 1 April 2008 and 1 April 2009 respectively rates will rise by 2ppl and then 1.84ppl. Consequential changes will be made to road fuel gas and biofuel duty rates in line with previous commitments. (45)

A.95 Road fuel gases differentials were previously announced until 2008-2009. The compresssed natural gas differential will be maintained until 2009-10 and the liquified petroleum gas differential will decrease each year by 1ppl on 1 October 2007, 1 April 2008 and 1 April 2009. (48)

A.96 The 20ppl duty incentive for biofuels is already guaranteed until 2008-09. It will be now extended until 2009-10. (47)

A.97 The differential between main road fuel and rebated oils duties will be maintained in 2007-08. In the subsequent two years rebated oils rates will increase by the same proportions as main road fuel duties. (46)

Second generation biofuels A.98 As announced in the 2006 Pre-Budget Report, the definition of biodiesel is being reviewed to ensure that new second generation biodiesels with environmental benefits are included. (-)

Extending biofuels to other users A.99 As announced in the 2006 Pre-Budget Report, with effect from 1 March 2007, red diesel and biodiesel blends may be used in approved pilot schemes at the red diesel rate (7.69ppl). (*)

Enhanced Capital Allowance for biofuel plants A.100 The Government will re-apply for state aids clearance, and subject to that, will introduce 100 per cent first year allowance for biofuels plant that meet certain qualifying criteria, as proposed. A payable enhanced capital allowance will be introduced for companies not in taxable profit to ensure both profit making and loss making firms have an incentive to invest in the cleanest biofuels plant. (-)

Biomass in fuel production A.101 As announced in the 2006 Pre-Budget Report, the 20ppl fuel differential was introduced on 12 January 2007 to enable a pilot involving the use of biomass in conventional fuel production to go ahead. (-)

Biogas A.102 The duty incentive for biogas used as a road fuel will be extended at least at its current rate until 2011-12. (-)

Company car tax A.103 The thresholds for the 2009-10 minimum percentage charge rate will be frozen at the 2008-09 levels. From 6 April 2008 a 2 per cent CCT discount for company cars capable of using high-blend bioethanol E85 will be introduced. (*)

Fuel benefit charge A.104 The fixed figure on which the company car fuel benefit charge is based will be maintained at £14,400 for 2007-08. (-)

Fuel scale charge A.105 From 1 May 2007, VAT fuel scale charges will be based on carbon dioxide emissions and revalorised in line with pump prices. (-)

Air passenger duty A.106 As announced in the 2006 Pre-Budget Report, air passenger duty rates doubled from 1 February 2007. (x)

A.107 As announced in the 2006 Pre-Budget Report, the scope of the European rates of air passenger duty now includes all signatories to the European Common Aviation Agreement from 1 February 2007. (*)

Aggregates levy A.108 The rate of aggregates levy will increase to £1.95 per tonne from 1 April 2008. (50)

Aggregates levy scope exemption for railways A.109 An exemption from aggregates levy for the aggregate arising from the construction and maintenance of railways, tramways and monorails will be introduced. (*)

Landfill tax A.110 From 1 April 2008, the standard rate of landfill tax will increase each year by £8 per tonne each year until at least 2010-11. The lower rate of landfill tax will also increase to £2.50 per tonne. (51)

Landfill communities fund A.111 The value of the landfill communities fund (previously known as the landfill tax credit scheme) for 2007-08 will increase by £5 million from 1 April 2007. This fund will be worth £65 million for 2007-08. (*)

Enhanced Capital Allowance scheme for waste   **A.112**   There will be a review of the classes of equipment that can qualify for Enhanced Capital Allowances (ECAs) for good quality combined heat and power (CHP) to ensure that the scheme includes all necessary equipment for CHP facilities to use solid refuse fuel. (*)

Microgeneration   **A.113**   As announced in the 2006 Pre-Budget Report, legislation in Finance Act 2007 will confirm that householders installing microgeneration for their personal use will not be subject to income tax on any payment for surplus electricity exported to the grid. For these same householders, Renewables Obligation Certificates acquired in respect of electricity generated from microgeneration technologies on their property will not give rise to an income tax or capital gains tax charge from 6 April 2007. (-)

Landlords Energy Saving Allowance   **A.114**   As announced in the 2006 Pre-Budget Report, subject to state aids approval, the Landlords Energy Saving Allowance will be extended to corporate landlords; there will be an extension to the existing sunset clause from 2009 to 2015; the allowance will be applied per property rather than per building; and the addition of the acquisition and installation of floor insulation will qualify as an investment. (ac)

Rebated oil: excepted vehicles   **A.115**   As announced in the 2006 Pre-Budget Report, from 1 April 2007 changes will take effect to the schedule of excepted vehicles entitled to use rebated oil. (ab)

Energy Products Directive   **A.116**   Following the non renewal of derogations to the Energy Products Directive on fuel used in private air navigation and private boating, the Government will implement the required legislative changes from 1 November 2008. (29)

Enhanced capital allowances   **A.117**   The list of designated water-efficient technologies qualifying for 100 per cent enhanced first-year capital allowances will be expanded during 2007, to include three further technology classes. (43)

Table A8a: VED bands and rates for cars registered after 1 March 2001 (graduated VED)

	CO$_2$ emissions VED band	2007-08[1] alternative (g/km)	standard fuel	2008-09 alternative fuel	standard fuel	2009-10 alternative fuel	standard fuel
A	100 and below	0	0	0	0	0	0
B	101 to 120	15	35	15	35	15	35
C	121 to 150	95	115	100	120	105	125
D	151 to 165	120	140	125	145	130	150
E	166 to 185	145	165	150	170	155	175
F	186 and above[2]	190	205	195	210	200	215
G	226 and above[3]	285	300	385	400	385	400

[1] Rates take effect from 22 March 2007.
[2] Cars registered before 23 March 2006.
[3] Cars registered on or after 23 March 2006.

Table A8b: VED bands and rates for private and light goods vehicles registered before 1 March 2001 (pre-graduated VED)

Engine size	2007-08[1]	2008-09	2009-10
1549cc and below	115	120	125
Above 1549cc	180	185	190

[1] Rates take effect from 22 March 2007.

OTHER INDIRECT TAXES AND DUTIES

Tobacco duty **A.118** From 6pm on 21 March 2007, tobacco duty rates will be indexed to maintain the real price of tobacco. (40)

Table A9: Changes to tobacco duties

	Effect of tax[1] on typical item (increase in pence)	Unit
Cigarettes	11	packet of 20
Cigars	4	packet of 5
Hand-rolling tobacco	11	25g
Pipe tobacco	7	25g

[1] *Tax refers to duty plus VAT.*

Alcohol duties **A.119** Excise duty on spirits will be frozen; rates on beer, wine, sparkling wine and cider will be indexed, from 26 March 2007. (39)

Table A10: Changes to alcohol duties

	Effect of tax[1] on typical item (increase in pence)	Unit
Beer	1	Pint of beer @ 4.2% abv
Wine	1	175ml glass typical strength
Wine	5	75cl bottle typical strength
Sparkling wine	7	75cl bottle typical strength
Spirits	0	70cl bottle @ 37.5% abv
Spirits-based RTDs	0	275ml bottle @ 5.4% abv
Cider	1	Litre of cider typical strength
Sparkling cider	5	75cl bottle typical strength

[1] *Tax refers to duty plus VAT.*

Betting and gaming duties **A.120** Gaming duty bands are increased in line with inflation and rates have been changed for accounting periods starting on or after 1 April 2007: the 2.5 per cent starting is abolished; the 12.5 per cent rate increases to 15 per cent; and a new rate of 50 per cent is introduced on gross yield from gaming in excess of £10 million. (41)

A.121 Remote gaming will be brought within the scope of gambling taxation at the rate of 15 per cent on an operator's gross profits. In addition, participation fees for remote gaming will not be liable to VAT. (*)

A.122 Changes to align Amusement Machine Licence Duty categories with a DCMS Order will come into effect from midnight 21 March 2007. The rates of Amusement Machine Licence Duty will be frozen. (-)

A.123 A measure will be introduced, with effect from Royal Assent and another appointed day, making consequential amendments to the Betting and Gaming Duties Act, the Finance Act 1993, and the Finance Act 1997 to ensure the scope and charging provisions of the betting and gaming duties are preserved. (-)

Small consignments relief **A.124** A measure will be introduced with effect from Royal Assent to repeal the UK relief from duty for small, non-commercial consignments of excise goods. (30)

PROTECTING TAX REVENUES

Controlled Foreign Companies rules A.125   As announced in the 2006 Pre-Budget Report, with effect from 6 December 2006, measures were introduced to amend the Controlled Foreign Companies (CFC) rules following the European Court of Justice (ECJ) judgment in Cadbury Schweppes, and to remove the public quotation exemption to prevent specific avoidance. (p)

Structured finance A.126   A measure to tackle avoidance involving structured finance schemes was announced on 6 June 2006 and enacted in Finance Act 2006. (q)

Six year limitation period for direct tax claims A.127   As announced in the 2006 Pre-Budget Report, legislation will be introduced to ensure that the limitation period for the recovery of direct tax paid by reason of mistake of law is six years from the date of payment. The provision will have retrospective effect, but will not disturb the entitlement of those who have secured what amounts to a final judgment in their favour prior to 6 December 2006. (-)

Sideways loss relief A.128   As announced on 2 March 2007, and with effect from that date, measures to counter avoidance will be introduced which prevent individuals using trading partnerships generating losses that can be claimed as sideways loss relief. (v)

Insurance premium tax A.139   A measure will be introduced, with effect from 22 March 2007, amending the Insurance Premium Tax definition of "premium" to prevent exploitation of a potential loophole. (*)

Life policies and commissions A.130   A measure will be introduced to prevent avoidance of tax using schemes involving life policies and commission arrangements. This applies to new policies made on or after 21 March 2007 and to existing policies if certain variations or exercises of options are made on or after that day. (-)

Stamp Duty on Shares A.131   As announced in the 2006 Pre-Budget Report, a package of measures will be introduced with effect from 1 November 2007 to ensure that reliefs for stamp duty on shares and Stamp Duty Reserve Tax continue to operate effectively following implementation of the EU Markets in Financial Instruments Directive (MiFID). (*)

Stamp Duty Land Tax A.132   As announced in the 2006 Pre-Budget Report, a package of measures was introduced, with effect from 6 December 2006 to counter schemes designed to avoid Stamp Duty Land Tax. (t)

Capital gains tax A.133   As announced in the 2006 Pre-Budget Report, a measure was introduced with effect from 6 December 2006 to counter schemes involving the creation and use of artificial capital losses to avoid tax. (u)

Disclosure of tax avoidance schemes A.134   As announced in the 2006 Pre-Budget Report, new powers will be introduced, with effect from Royal Assent, for HMRC to investigate a scheme where there are reasonable grounds to believe a promoter has failed to comply with a statutory disclosure obligation. (38)

Corporate capital loss and gain buying A.135   A measure will be introduced with effect from 22 March 2007, amending one of the targeted anti-avoidance rules on buying corporate gains and losses to ensure that it works as intended. (-)

A.136   A measure will be introduced, with effect from 6 March 2007, to prevent avoidance of tax on corporate gains using schemes involving options. (-)

Life insurance A.137   A measure will be introduced with effect from periods commencing on or after 1 January 2007 to simplify and strengthen the tax law relating to certain financing arrangements utilised by life insurance companies. (35)

A.138 As announced in the 2006 Pre-Budget Report, a measure was introduced with effect from 6 December 2006 to ensure that any difference between the fair value of an asset held in an insurance company's long-term insurance fund and the admissible value of the asset under the regulatory rules is brought into account when the asset leaves the long-term insurance fund. (s)

Penalties for incorrect returns **A.139** A measure will be introduced, with effect from 1 April 2009, to align penalties across income tax, national insurance contributions, corporation tax and VAT. (-)

Joint and several liability **A.140** A measure will be introduced with effect from 1 May 2007 to extend the Joint and Several Liability provisions introduced in 2003 to counter MTIC fraud. Also from Royal Assent a power will be introduced to amend the circumstances in which VAT-registered businesses are presumed to have reasonable grounds to suspect that VAT will go unpaid to HMRC. (37)

Employee benefit trusts **A.141** A measure will be introduced with effect from 21 March 2007 to prevent schemes side-stepping anti-avoidance legislation relating to employee benefit trusts. (-)

Sale and repurchase agreements **A.142** A new accounts-based regime for taxing sale and repurchase (repo) agreements for companies will be introduced to replace the current rules. The measure will take effect from a date to be determined by Treasury Order. (32)

Financial products **A.143** As announced in the 2006 Pre-Budget Report, a package of measures was introduced, with effect from 6 December 2006, to prevent avoidance of tax using schemes involving financial products. Further measures were announced and effective from 6 and 7 March 2007. (r) (w)

Double taxation relief **A.144** As announced in the 2006 Pre-Budget Report, measures were introduced to prevent companies from avoiding the effect of legislation in Finance Act 2005 on the basis that the tax in respect of which double taxation relief is being claimed is UK tax rather than foreign tax. The changes apply to schemes where there is any action (or failure to act), any relevant tax is paid, or any relevant income is received, on or after 6 December 2006. (r)

Sale of lessor companies **A.145** As announced on 22 November 2006, measures were introduced with effect from that date to counter schemes which are intended to undermine legislation introduced in Finance Act 2006. Measures countering further schemes are announced with effect from 21 March 2007. (-)

Loss-buying **A.146** A measure will be introduced to prevent companies buying the trading losses of corporate members of Lloyd's who are leaving the market and with which they have no previous economic connection. The measure will be effective for changes in the ownership of corporate members on 21 March 2007. (36)

ADDITIONAL SPENDING AND DEBT MANAGEMENT DECISIONS

2007 Comprehensive Spending Review

A.147 Budget 2007 sets firm overall departmental spending limits for the 2007 Comprehensive Spending Review (CSR) period of 2008-09, 2009-10 and 2010-11. This allows current spending to increase by an average of 1.9 per cent per year over three years and maintain net investment at $2^1/_4$ per cent of GDP. Final plans for DEL and AME spending will be set in the Comprehensive Spending Review. Budget 2007 announces that education spending will rise 2.5 per cent a year in real terms (5.3 per cent in nominal terms) on average over the CSR period.

Annually Managed Expenditure

A.148 In line with usual practice, Budget 2007 sets the Annually Managed Expenditure (AME) margin to £1 billion in 2007-08.

Special reserve

A.149 Budget 2007 allocates £400 million to the special reserve in 2007-08 to make provision for the continuing costs of military operations in Iraq and Afghanistan and other international commitments. (52)

Schools standards grant

A.150 The 2006 Pre-Budget Report announced a further £130 million direct to schools in England in 2007-08, including to support personalised teaching and extended services. These additions mean that direct payments to schools will rise to an average of £200 per pupil for primary schools and £225 per pupil for secondary schools. (ad)

BUDGET POLICY DECISIONS: APPENDICES

APPENDIX AI: MEASURES ANNOUNCED IN BUDGET 2006 OR EARLIER

AI.I   This appendix sets out a number of tax, benefit and other changes which were announced in Budget 2006 or earlier and which will take effect from April 2007 or later. The revenue effects of these measures have been taken into account in previous economic and fiscal projections.

Table AI.I: Measures announced in Budget 2006 or earlier which take effect from April 2007 or later

		(+ve is an Exchequer yield)			£ million
		2007-08 indexed	**2008-09** indexed	**2009-10** indexed	**2007-08** non-indexed
a	VAT Cash Accounting: increase in threshold for eligibility	−120	0	0	−120
b	VAT: Countering Missing Trader Intra Community fraud	+135	+155	+120	+135
c	Extension of paid maternity leave to 9 months	−385	−385	−385	−385
d	NICs quinquennial review of contracted-out rebates	+25	+75	+175	+15
e	Enhanced capital allowances for the cleanest biofuels production plants	0	−30	−20	0
f	Extending the scope of R&D tax credits	−15	−40	−40	−15
g	Work focussed interviews for lone parents	−20	0	0	−20
h	Child Tax Credit: uprate child element in line with earnings in 2008-09 and 2009-10	0	−230	−520	0
i	Inheritance tax: Increase threshold to £312k in 2008-09, £325k in 2009-10, and indexation thereafter	0	−10	−50	0
j	Business Premises Renovation Allowance	−20	−30	−30	−20
k	Broader definition of registered childcare	−35	−85	−130	−35
l	Climate Change Levy revalorisation	0	0	0	+20
	TOTAL POLICY DECISIONS	**−435**	**−580**	**−880**	**−425**

VAT cash accounting   **AI.2**   As announced in the 2005 Pre-Budget Report, the turnover below which businesses are eligible for cash accounting is to be increased from £660,000 to £1.35m. This will take effect from 1 April 2007. (a)

Missing Trader Intra Community fraud   **AI.3**   As announced in Budget 2006, and following receipt of the necessary derogation from EU law, from 1 June 2007, a change of VAT accounting procedure (the reverse charge) for certain goods, in order to counter MTIC fraud will be introduced. The costing has been revised to reflect a significant reduction in fraud levels, the revised start date, and a change in the coverage of the measure, which will apply to business-to-business transactions greater than £5,000 involving mobile telephones and computer chips. (b)

Statutory Maternity Pay   **AI.4**   As announced in the 2004 Pre-Budget Report, paid maternity leave will be extended to 9 months from April 2007. (c)

National insurance contributions Al.5   As announced on 1 March 2006, from April 2007 the reduction in total employer and employee NICs for individuals in defined benefit occupational schemes who have contracted out of the state second pension will increase from 5.1 per cent to 5.3 per cent. For individuals in defined contribution pension schemes who have contracted out, the NICs rebate below the age-related cap will increase by between 0.5 per cent and 1.9 per cent, while the cap will be reduced from 10.5 per cent to 7.4 per cent. (d)

Capital allowance for biofuel production Al.6   As announced in the 2005 Pre-Budget report, subject to state aids approval, the Government will establish an Enhanced Capital Allowance scheme for the cleanest biofuels production plant. (e)

R&D tax credits Al.7   As announced in Budget 2006, legislation will be introduced in Finance Act 2007 to extend the SME R&D tax credit scheme to companies with between 250 and 500 employees. The legislation will be activated at a later date subject to state aids approval from the European Commission and once activated the extension is expected to apply to R&D expenditure from 1 April 2007. (f)

Lone parents Al.8   As announced in Budget 2006, from April 2007 all lone parents who have been on benefit for at least a year will, at a minimum, be required to attend a Work Focused Interview every six months. (g)

Child Tax Credit Al.9   As announced in Budget 2006, the child element of the Child Tax Credit will increase at least in line with average earnings up to and including 2009-10. (h)

Inheritance tax Al.10   As announced at Budget 2005, the nil-rate band for inheritance tax will rise faster than statutory inflation to £300,000 for new tax charges arising on or after 6 April 2007. As further announced at Budget 2006, it will continue to rise above forecast inflation to £312,000 in 2008-09, and £325,000 in 2009-10. (i)

Business Premises Renovation Allowance Al.11   Businesses Premises Renovation Allowance (BPRA) will come into effect from 11 April 2007. This scheme will provide 100 per cent capital allowances for the costs of renovating business property that has been vacant for at least a year, in a deprived area as defined by the UK Assisted Areas map. The reduced costing for 2007-08 reflects the delayed implementation. (j)

Registered childcare Al.12   In the context of the Childcare Act 2006, from April 2007 there will be a new Voluntary Ofsted Childcare Register. This will broaden the scope for new types of care to be Ofsted registered. (k)

Climate Change Levy Al.13   As announced at Budget 2006, with effect from 1 April 2007 the rates of the Climate Change Levy will increase in line with inflation. (l)

APPENDIX A2: EXPLAINING THE COSTING

A2.1   This appendix explains how the Exchequer effects of the Budget measures are calculated. In the context of these calculations, the net Exchequer effects for measures may include amounts for taxes, national insurance contributions, social security benefits and other charges to the Exchequer, including penalties.

Calculating the costings

A2.2   The net Exchequer effect of a Budget measure is generally calculated as the difference between applying the pre-Budget and post-Budget tax and benefit regimes to the levels of total income and spending at factor cost expected after the Budget. The estimates do not therefore include any effect of the tax changes themselves on overall levels of income and spending. However, they do take account of other effects on behaviour where they are likely to have a significant and quantifiable effect on the cost or yield and any consequential changes in revenue from related taxes and benefits.

A2.3   These may include estimated changes in the composition or timing of income, spending or other tax determinants. For example, the estimated yield from increasing the excise duty on spirits would include the change in the yield of VAT and other excise duties resulting from the new pattern of spending. The calculation of the expected effect of changes in duty rate on consumer demand for excise goods assumes that any change in duty is passed on in full to consumers. Where the effect of one tax change is affected by implementation of others, the measures are normally costed in the order in which they appear in Tables A1, A2 and A1.1.

A2.4   The non-indexed base columns shown in Tables A1, A2 and A1.1 show the revenue effect of changes in allowances, thresholds and rates of duty, including the effect of any measures previously announced but not yet implemented, from their pre-Budget level. The indexed base columns strip out the effects of indexation by increasing the allowances, thresholds and rates of duty in line with their forecast assumptions.

A2.5   A policy which has been previously announced but not yet implemented is also stripped out of the indexed numbers. The indexed base has been calculated on the assumption that:

- income tax and national insurance allowances and thresholds, and the single person, couple, lone parent and disabled worker elements of the Working Tax Credit, inheritance tax nil-rate band allowance threshold and the capital gains tax annual exempt amount all increase in line with the Retail Price Index (RPI) to the September prior to the Budget;

- the child element of the Child Tax Credit rises in line with the annual increase in average earnings in the year to the second quarter prior to the Budget, until 2009-10;

- air passenger duty, climate change levy, aggregates levy, vehicle excise duty, fuel, tobacco and alcohol duties all rise in line with the projected annual increase in the RPI to the third quarter following the Budget; and

- VAT thresholds and gaming duty bands rise in line with the increase in the RPI to the December prior to the Budget.

A2.6   Implementation dates are assumed to be: Budget day for fuel and tobacco duties; the first Monday after Budget day for alcohol duties; May for amusement machine licence duty; July for insurance premium tax, and April for all other taxes, duties and tax credits, including air passenger duty from 2008.

A2.7   The yields of measures that close tax avoidance loopholes or tackle tax fraud represent the estimated direct Exchequer effect of the measures with the existing level of activity.

A2.8   These costings are shown on a National Accounts basis. The National Accounts basis aims to recognise tax when the tax liability accrues irrespective of when the tax is received by the Exchequer. However, some taxes are scored on a receipts basis, principally due to the difficulty in assessing the period to which the tax liability relates. Examples of such taxes are corporation tax, self-assessment income tax, inheritance tax and capital gains tax. This approach is consistent with other Government publications.

Notes on individual Budget measures

VAT: cash accounting **A2.9**   The cost of this measure has been revised since Budget 2006 to take into account new assumptions on projected take up following recent external research.

Zero-carbon homes and stamp duty **A2.10**   The Exchequer cost is expected to rise to around £15 million by 2011-12.

General insurers' reserves **A2.11**   The Exchequer yield is expected to reduce gradually to zero by 2013-14.

APPENDIX A3: TAX ALLOWANCES AND RELIEFS

A3.1   This appendix provides estimates of the revenue cost of some of the main tax allowances and reliefs.

A3.2   Tax reliefs can serve a number of purposes. In some cases they may be used to assist or encourage particular individuals, activities or products, and so may be an alternative to public expenditure. In this case they are often termed 'tax expenditures'. There may, for example, be a choice between giving a tax relief as an allowance or deduction against tax, or by an offsetting cash payment.

A3.3   Many allowances and reliefs can reasonably be regarded (or partly regarded) as an integral part of the tax structure – so called 'structural reliefs'. Some do no more than recognise the expense incurred in obtaining income. Others reflect a more general concept of 'taxable capacity'. The personal allowances are a good example: to the extent that income tax is based on ability to pay, it does not seek to collect tax from those with the smallest incomes. However, even with structural reliefs of the latter kind, the Government has some discretion about the level at which they are set. Many other reliefs combine both structural and discretionary components. Capital allowances, for example, provide relief for depreciation at a commercial rate as well as an element of accelerated relief. It is the latter element which represents additional help provided to business by the Government and is a 'tax expenditure'.

A3.4   The loss of revenue associated with tax reliefs and allowances cannot be directly observed, and estimates have to be made. This involves calculating the amount of tax that individuals or firms would have had to pay if there were no exemptions or deductions for certain categories of income or expenditure, and comparing it with the actual amount of tax due.

A3.5   The estimates in Table A3.1 below show the total cost of each relief. The classification of reliefs as tax expenditures, structural reliefs and those elements combining both is broadbrush and the distinction between the expenditures and structural reliefs is not always straightforward. In many cases the estimated costs are extremely tentative and based on simplifying assumptions and must be treated with caution. The figures make no allowance for the fact that changes in tax reliefs may cause people to change their behaviour. This means that figures in Table A3.1 are not directly comparable with those of the main Budget measures shown earlier in this chapter.

A3.6   Estimation of behavioural effects is difficult. The sizes of behavioural changes will obviously depend on the measure examined and possible alternative behaviours. For example, removing the tax privileges of a form of saving may just lead people to switch to another tax-privileged form of saving.

A3.7   The estimated costs of reliefs and allowances given in Table A3.1 are costed separately and cannot be added up to give a meaningful total. The combined yield of withdrawing two related allowances could differ significantly from the sum of individual costs. Similarly the sum of the costs of component parts of reliefs may differ from the total shown.

A3.8   The Government regularly publishes estimates of tax expenditures and reliefs. Largely because of the difficulties of estimation, the published tables are not comprehensive but do cover the major reliefs and allowances. The figures are shown on a full-year accruals basis unless otherwise specified and only reliefs with an estimated annual costs of at least £50 million are shown. The costs of minor tax reliefs can be found on the HM Revenue and Customs website. More details on individual tax allowances and reliefs can be found in the HM Treasury publication, *Tax ready reckoner and tax reliefs*, published alongside the 2006

Pre-Budget Report.

Table A3.1 Estimated costs of principal tax expenditures and structural reliefs

	£ million	
	2005-06	**2006-07**
TAX EXPENDITURES		
Income tax		
Relief for:		
Approved pension schemes	14,300	16,300
Share Incentive Plan	250	280
Approved savings-related share schemes	120	140
Enterprise Management Incentives	110	120
Approved Company Share Option Plans	170	190
Personal Equity Plans	450	475
Individual Savings Accounts	1,350	1,625
Venture Capital Trusts	325	75
Enterprise Investment Scheme	160	140
Professional subscriptions	80	80
Rent a room	100	100
Exemption of:		
First £30,000 of payments on termination of employment	800	800
Interest on National Savings Certificates including index-linked certificates	110	150
Premium Bond prizes	170	200
Income of charities	1,100	1,200
Foreign service allowance paid to Crown servants abroad	90	95
First £8,000 of reimbursed relocation packages provided by employers	300	300
Life assurance premiums (for contracts made prior to 14 March 1984)	55	50
Personal Tax Credits	4,400	4,600
Corporation tax		
R&D tax credits	440	450
Income tax and corporation tax		
Small budget film tax relief	420	240
Large budget film tax relief	280	240
National insurance contributions		
Relief for:		
Share Incentive Plan	170	190
Approved savings-related share schemes	80	90
Approved company share-option plans	50	60
Employer contributions to approved pension schemes		
Capital gains tax		
Exemption of gains arising on disposal of only or main residence	13,000	15,000

Table A3.1: Estimated costs of principal tax expenditures and structural reliefs

	£ million	
	2005-06	**2006-07**
Inheritance tax		
Relief for:		
Agricultural property	210	240
Business property	320	370
Exemption of transfers to charities on death	460	530
Value added tax		
Zero-rating of:		
Food	10,500	10,800
Construction of new dwellings (includes refunds to DIY builders)	7,200	7,700
Domestic passenger transport	2,200	2,250
International passenger transport (UK portion)	100	100
Books, newspapers and magazines	1,600	1,650
Children's clothing	1,200	1,250
Water and sewerage services	1,200	1,200
Drugs and supplies on prescription	1,150	1,200
Supplies to charities	200	200
Ships and aircraft above a certain size	600	650
Vehicles and other supplies to disabled people	400	450
Reduced rate for:		
Domestic fuel and power	2,200	2,200
Certain residential conversions and renovations	150	150
Energy-saving materials	50	50
Women's sanitary products	50	50
STRUCTURAL RELIEFS		
Income tax		
Personal allowance	40,200	42,000
Corporation tax		
Life companies reduced rate of corporation tax on policy holders' fraction of profit	1,050	1,250
Income tax and corporation tax		
Double taxation relief	10,000	10,000
National insurance contributions		
Contracted-out rebate occupational schemes:		
Rebates deducted at source by employers	7,200	7,500
Rebates paid by the Contributions Agency direct to the scheme	200	200
Personal and stakeholder pensions	2,400	2,200

Table A3.1: Estimated costs of principal tax expenditures and structural reliefs

	£ million	
	2005-06	**2006-07**
Value added tax		
Refunds to:		
Northern Ireland government bodies of VAT incurred on non-business purchases under the Section 99 refund scheme	300	350
Local Authority-type bodies of VAT incurred on non-business purchases under the Section 33 refund scheme (includes national museums and galleries under the Section 33A refund scheme)	7,150	7,750
Central government, health authorities and NHS Trusts of VAT incurred on contracted-out services under the Section 41(3) refund scheme	3,900	4,750
RELIEFS WITH TAX EXPENDITURE AND STRUCTURAL COMPONENTS		
Income tax		
Age-related allowances	2,400	2,400
Reduced rate for savings	200	210
Exemption of:		
British Government securities where owner not ordinarily resident in the UK	1,230	1,230
Child Benefit (including one parent benefit)	1,090	1,130
Long-term incapacity benefit	220	230
Industrial disablement benefits	60	60
Attendance allowance	120	120
Disability living allowance	360	370
War disablement benefits	60	70
War widow's pension	30	30
Corporation tax		
Small companies' reduced corporation tax rate	3,970	4,500
Starting rate of corporation tax	430	0
Exemption for gains on substantial shareholdings	260	260
Income tax and corporation tax		
Capital allowances	18,200	19,400
Of which:		
First year allowances for SMEs	380	620
Enhanced capital allowances for energy saving technology	170	130
Accelerated capital allowances for Enterprise Zones	120	40
Capital gains tax		
Indexation allowance and rebasing to March 1982	300	280
Taper relief	4,620	6,020
Exemption of:		
Annual exempt amount (half of the individual's exemption for trustees)	2,000	2,300
Gains accrued but unrealised at death	690	710

Table A3.1: Estimated costs of principal tax expenditures and structural reliefs

	£ million	
	2005-06	**2006-07**
Petroleum revenue tax		
Uplift on qualifying expenditure	80	110
Oil allowance	790	860
Safeguard: a protection for return on capital cost	40	50
Tariff receipts allowance	80	50
Exemption for gas sold to British Gas under pre-July 1975 contracts	40	60
Inheritance tax		
Nil-rate band for chargeable transfers not exceeding the threshold	10,400	11,300
Exemption of transfers on death to surviving spouses	2,000	2,200
Stamp Duty Land Tax		
Exemption of transfers of land and property where the consideration does not exceed the £120,000 threshold in 2005-06 and the £125,000 threshold in 2006-07 and non-residential land and property where the consideration does not exceed the £150,000 threshold	520	580
Exemption of all residential transfers in designated disadvantaged wards where the consideration exceeds £120,000 in 2005-06, £125,000 in 2006-07 but does not exceed £150,000	50	50
Transfers to charities	120	120
Group relief	1,510	1,530
Transfers to registered social landlords	60	60
National insurance contributions		
Reduced contributions for self-employed not attributable to reduced benefit eligibility (constant cost basis)	1,700	1,800
Value Added Tax		
Exemption of:		
Rent on domestic dwellings	3,150	3,350
Supplies of commercial property	150	150
Private education	300	300
Health services	850	900
Postal services	500	500
Burial and cremation	100	100
Finance and insurance	3,950	4,200
Betting and gaming and lottery duties	1,250	1,350
Small traders below the turnover limit for VAT registration	900	950
Vehicle Excise Duty		
Exemption for disabled motorists	160	170

The UK economy grew by 2¾ per cent in 2006, as forecast in the 2006 Pre-Budget Report, and has now expanded for 58 consecutive quarters, the longest unbroken expansion on record. The rebalancing of domestic demand gathered pace during 2006, with business investment ending the year growing at the fastest rate for eight years. In its latest report on the UK, the IMF described this recent macroeconomic performance as "impressive".

The world economy grew at 5 per cent in 2006, a faster rate than at any time since 1990, and is expected to remain strong in 2007. With the G7, and particularly the euro area economies, recording stronger growth in the final quarter of 2006, the outlook for UK export market growth in 2007 appears slightly stronger than at the time of the Pre-Budget Report. This should support the rebalancing of domestic and external demand in the UK.

Following five consecutive quarters of slightly above-trend growth, the UK economy is estimated to have ended 2006 operating close to its trend level, although there remains evidence of some slack in the labour market. As expected, the temporary rise in unemployment during 2006 has abated, with the claimant count measure falling in seven of the past eight months and the broader Labour Force Survey measure falling in the final quarter of the year.

Inflation has risen further since the 2006 Pre-Budget Report, with the rise continuing to be largely attributable to energy and food prices. The contribution of energy prices to overall inflation is expected to fall quite sharply during 2007. Despite inflation having moved above target, monetary policy has kept inflation expectations firmly anchored and earnings growth has remained subdued.

The Budget 2007 economic forecast is little changed from that of the 2006 Pre-Budget Report:

- GDP is forecast to grow by 2¾ to 3¼ per cent in 2007. With the small negative output gap expected to have closed early in 2007, growth is expected to remain close to trend at 2½ to 3 per cent in 2008 and 2009; and

- CPI inflation is expected to return to target in the second half of 2007.

INTRODUCTION[1,2]

B.1 This chapter discusses recent economic developments and provides updated forecasts for the UK and world economies in the period to 2009. It begins with an overview of developments and prospects in the world economy, which sets the global context for recent developments and prospects in the UK. It then outlines the UK economic forecast, before concluding with a more detailed discussion of sectoral issues, the components of growth and risks surrounding the forecast.

---

[1] The UK forecast is consistent with output, income and expenditure data to the fourth quarter of 2006 released by the Office for National Statistics (ONS) on 23 February 2007. This release also contained revisions to earlier quarters of 2006, which the Treasury has carried through to other National Accounts series that the ONS has not yet revised, in particular sectoral saving and borrowing. A fully consistent National Accounts dataset to the fourth quarter will be published by the ONS on 28 March. A detailed set of charts and tables relating to the economic forecast is available on the Treasury's internet site (http://www.hm-treasury.gov.uk). Copies can be obtained on request from the Treasury's Public Enquiry Unit (020 7270 4558).

[2] The forecast is based on the assumption that the exchange rate moves in line with an uncovered interest parity condition, consistent with the interest rates underlying the economic forecast.

THE WORLD ECONOMY

Overview

B.2   The world economy grew at a faster rate in 2006 than at any time since 1990, with GDP growth of 5 per cent, reflecting a pick-up in G7 activity and continued strength in emerging markets. This was the third consecutive year of growth around 5 per cent. Global growth is expected to slow slightly in 2007, though to remain high by historical standards at $4^3/_4$ per cent.

B.3   Since 2003, world output growth has been driven by the US and Asia, particularly China. In 2006, GDP growth in the US remained above trend, despite a considerable contraction in residential investment. The euro area recovery strengthened and became more broad-based, while growth in Japan remained firm. In 2007, G7 activity is expected to moderate towards trend rates. Growth in the emerging markets is expected to ease somewhat from the very high rates of recent years.

Table B1: The world economy

	Percentage change on a year earlier, unless otherwise stated			
		Forecast		
	2006	**2007**	**2008**	**2009**
World GDP	5	$4^3/_4$	$4^3/_4$	$4^1/_2$
Major 7 countries[1]:				
Real GDP	$2^3/_4$	$2^1/_2$	$2^1/_2$	$2^1/_2$
Consumer price inflation[2]	$1^1/_2$	2	2	2
Euro area GDP	$2^3/_4$	$2^1/_4$	$2^1/_4$	$2^1/_4$
World trade in goods and services	$9^3/_4$	$7^3/_4$	$7^1/_2$	7
UK export markets[3]	$8^1/_2$	7	$6^1/_2$	$6^1/_4$

[1] *G7: US, Japan, Germany, France, UK, Italy and Canada.*

[2] *Per cent, Q4.*

[3] *Other countries' imports of goods and services weighted according to the importance of imports from the UK in those countries' total imports.*

B.4   World trade growth has recovered strongly over the past five years, rising from zero growth in 2001 to $9^3/_4$ per cent in 2006. The weaker path of US GDP growth since the second quarter of 2006 has not resulted in a softening of world trade growth. This is because the moderation in US demand has been largely contained to residential investment, while final demand in Asia and Europe has remained strong. Against this background, only a modest slowdown in world trade growth is forecast.

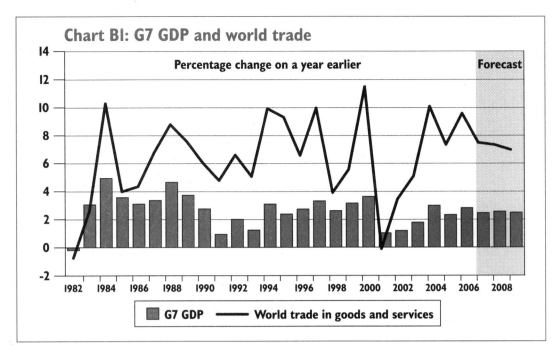

Chart BI: G7 GDP and world trade

Percentage change on a year earlier

Forecast

G7 GDP ■ — World trade in goods and services

B.5   In recent years, persistent gaps between domestic demand and production growth across regions of the world have coincided with a widening of current account imbalances. In particular, the US current account deficit in 2006 reached 6½ per cent of GDP, while across Asia, parts of Europe and the oil-producing countries, surpluses have grown large. The risk of a disorderly unwinding of global current account imbalances remains, but there have been some recent signs of rebalancing. Exchange rate adjustment is ongoing, with the dollar having fallen around 20 per cent in real terms over the past five years and the euro having risen by a similar amount, while more recently the balance of world growth has shifted slightly towards Europe.

B.6   Recent falls in headline inflation rates in the G7 have reflected developments in energy prices. Core inflation has remained broadly stable, and low by historical standards. Monetary authorities across the developed world have continued to respond to inflationary pressures. Since the 2006 Pre-Budget Report, interest rates have been raised by the Bank of England, the Bank of Japan and the European Central Bank.

B.7   After the 2006 Pre-Budget Report, asset prices around the world continued to rise strongly, with a number of stock markets reaching all-time highs. However, in some less liquid, more specialised credit markets, the price of risk began to rise. Since late February, global financial markets have experienced a period of volatility. It is too early to draw conclusions as to what has driven recent financial market movements. It is possible that the period of volatility will be brief, similar to that in May and June 2006, but it is also possible that it could reflect a reaction to a general under-pricing of risk, a factor that has been highlighted by, among others, the Governor of the Bank of England.[3] The risk from such a correction becoming sustained remains, and is discussed further in paragraph B.100.

G7 activity

B.8   GDP growth in the G7 picked up in 2006, to 2¾ per cent from 2¼ per cent in 2005. The expansion is expected to continue this year, albeit at a slightly more moderate pace of 2½ per cent.

---

[3] See, for example, *Speech by Mervyn King, Governor of the Bank of England. At a dinner for Kent business contacts*, 16 January 2006. Available at: http://www.bankofengland.co.uk/publications/speeches/2006/speech263.pdf.

United States **B.9** The US economy grew at an above-trend rate in 2006 despite a sharp fall in housing-related activity. New housing construction in the US is relatively sensitive to house prices, so the moderation in house price growth that began over a year ago was soon followed by a contraction in residential investment. Since the second half of 2005, the negative contribution to GDP growth from falling residential investment has been offset by solid growth in private consumption and business investment, which together account for over 80 per cent of demand in the US economy. Net trade made a small positive contribution to GDP growth in 2006, supported by the effect of a weaker dollar and strong world demand.

B.10 Growth in 2006 as a whole, at $3^1/_4$ per cent, was slightly stronger than in 2005, but growth eased through the year. More moderate rates of growth are set to continue in 2007, largely as was expected at the time of the 2006 Pre-Budget Report. Continued solid gains in the labour market, particularly via service sector employment, and rising real incomes should support consumption growth. Business investment growth is expected to moderate in 2007, from the six-year high reached in 2006. Finally, a mildly more positive outlook for net exports in the US should feed through to GDP growth.

Euro area **B.11** Growth in the euro area continued to strengthen during 2006, supported by a solid pick-up in business investment and, to a lesser extent, private consumption. Strong job creation, most notably in the finance and business services sector, helped to drive down the unemployment rate by close to 1 percentage point in 2006. The euro area unemployment rate has fallen to its lowest level since the inception of the euro in 1999, though it remains high by international standards. The broadening of growth towards domestic demand has been accompanied by rising rates of import growth in by far the UK's largest export market.

B.12 Within the euro area, there has been a rebalancing of growth among Member States. Growth in Germany, Europe's largest economy, has picked up to its fastest rate since 2000. Revisions to euro area National Accounts data, alongside strong growth in the fourth quarter, suggest the economy is carrying more momentum into 2007 than was apparent at the time of the 2006 Pre-Budget Report. With euro area trend growth generally estimated to be around 2 per cent, growth of $2^3/_4$ per cent in 2006 represents a cyclical upswing. Over the forecast horizon, the recovery is expected to continue, albeit at rates of growth that are closer to trend. Fiscal consolidation measures, particularly in Germany, but also in Italy, are expected to slow domestic demand growth temporarily in these countries in the first half of 2007.

Japan **B.13** Extensive revisions to Japan's National Accounts data in December 2006 led to significant changes in the measured level and composition of GDP growth. The economy is now estimated to have grown by $2^1/_4$ per cent in 2006, up only slightly from 2 per cent in 2005, with exports and business investment continuing to provide most of the momentum. Private consumption growth slowed in line with weaker real income growth, despite continued low rates of unemployment. In 2007, the Japanese economy is expected to grow slightly above its trend rate, which is generally estimated to be between $1^1/_2$ and 2 per cent.

Box B1: Government policy on EMU

The Government's policy on membership of the single currency was set out by the Chancellor in his statement to Parliament in October 1997. In principle, the Government is in favour of UK membership; in practice, the economic conditions must be right. The determining factor is the national economic interest and whether, on the basis of an assessment of the five economic tests, the economic case for joining is clear and unambiguous. An assessment of the five economic tests was published in June 2003. This concluded that: *"since 1997, the UK has made real progress towards meeting the five economic tests. But, on balance, though the potential benefits of increased investment, trade, a boost to financial services, growth and jobs are clear, we cannot at this point in time conclude that there is sustainable and durable convergence or sufficient flexibility to cope with any potential difficulties within the euro area."*

The Chancellor's statement to the House of Commons on 9 June 2003 on UK membership of the European single currency set out a reform agenda of concrete and practical steps to address the policy requirements identified by the assessment. The Budget reports on progress including:

- the introduction in December 2003 of a symmetric inflation target as measured by the Consumer Prices Index (CPI). CPI inflation has been within 1 percentage point of its target since its inception;

- reforms to increase housing supply and measures to improve consumer access to housing finance, described further in Chapter 3; and

- reforms at national, regional and local level to enhance the flexibility of labour, capital and product markets in the UK. Chapters 3 and 4 provide further detail.

As part of the policy of 'prepare and decide', the Government coordinates appropriate euro preparations across the UK economy. The Government also supports business in dealing with the euro as a foreign currency. Further information is available on the Treasury's euro website (www.euro.gov.uk).

On the Stability and Growth Pact, the Government continues to emphasise the need for a prudent interpretation of the Pact as described in Budget 2006. The reforms to the Pact agreed in March 2005 rightly place a greater focus on the avoidance of pro-cyclical policies, and on achieving low debt levels and thereby enhancing the long-term sustainability of public finances, with the flexibility for low debt countries such as the UK to invest in the provision of much needed public services. The Government continues to work closely with Member States and EU institutions, as the success of the reforms will depend on how they are implemented. It is also essential to recognise the importance of national frameworks and national ownership of fiscal policy.

In his statement to the House of Commons on 9 June 2003, the Chancellor committed the Government to an annual review of progress. The Government does not propose a euro assessment to be initiated at the time of this Budget. The Treasury will again review the situation at Budget time next year, as required by the Chancellor's June 2003 statement.

Emerging markets and developing economies

B.14   Emerging market economies continued to grow rapidly during 2006, supported by strong trade growth, buoyed by the resilience of the US economy and, in some cases, high commodity prices. Despite recent financial market volatility, interest rate spreads on emerging market sovereign debt, a measure of the relative risk that investors associate with these countries, remain low, in part reflecting improved macroeconomic fundamentals. As the global environment remains supportive, emerging markets' GDP growth is expected to continue at high rates, although it is likely to moderate slightly in 2007.

Emerging Asia   **B.15**   Growth in emerging Asia was at a 10-year high in 2006, buoyed by rapid expansions in China and India. Recent momentum is expected to continue in 2007.

China   **B.16**   In 2006, the Chinese economy grew by almost 11 per cent, slightly above market expectations, and contributing around a third of world growth.[4] There are some signs that private consumption growth is picking up, although investment remains the largest contributor to GDP growth. Net exports provided a positive contribution to growth in 2006, as China's trade surplus continued to expand rapidly. Inflation picked up to 2.7 per cent in February 2007, from 0.9 per cent a year earlier, partly as a result of higher food prices. The Chinese Government has continued to implement measures aimed at reining back rapid fixed investment and credit growth, including a series of increases to commercial banks' reserve requirements at the central bank.

India   **B.17**   In India, GDP has been revised up significantly for the period between 2004 and 2006, and is now estimated to have grown at an average annual rate of close to 9 per cent. The combination of brisk consumer demand, strong credit growth, and industrial capacity constraints has resulted in a marked increase in inflation, to more than 6 per cent in February 2007. Economic growth in India is widely forecast to moderate towards more sustainable rates from 2007 onwards.

Russia   **B.18**   In 2006, growth in Russia continued to be strong, with GDP expanding by more than 6 per cent for the fourth consecutive year. Consumption growth remained rapid, while investment surprised on the upside after recovering from the slowdown in 2005. High commodity prices continued to contribute to a large current account surplus. Inflation in Russia has eased, but remains relatively high at $8^{1}/_{4}$ per cent in the year to January 2007.

Emerging Europe   **B.19**   As in the euro area, growth in emerging Europe in 2006 was slightly stronger than expected at the time of the 2006 Pre-Budget Report. Growth continues to be driven by strong domestic demand, boosted by the positive impact on trade from stronger euro area growth. The recent expansion has been accompanied by a moderate pick-up in inflation across the region.

---

[4] China accounted for around a third of world GDP growth when the world's economies are weighted according to the 'purchasing power parity' (PPP) measure of their exchange rate, rather than market exchange rates. PPP exchange rates take account of the different prices of non-traded goods and services across countries – for example, a haircut or train journey will tend to be much cheaper in China than in the UK – and is therefore the appropriate measure when considering economic welfare. When weighted according to market exchange rates, a measure more appropriate for companies doing business across borders, China's share of world GDP growth is considerably lower.

Box B2: Growth in the new EU Member States

One of the marked features of European economic growth over the past decade is the rapid growth of the Central and Eastern European countries that recently joined the European Union (EU).[a] Since 1996, growth in these new Member States, known as the accession 10 (A10), has averaged almost $4\frac{1}{2}$ per cent a year, compared with $2\frac{1}{4}$ per cent in the 'old' EU Member States. The phenomenon of less mature economies, with lower per capita GDP, catching up with developed market economies, as in the EU (chart a), is a familiar one. In the case of the A10, the catch-up process followed economic reforms that started in the early 1990s, and are still ongoing. The reforms have supported growth by facilitating the reallocation of resources to more productive use. Importantly, they have raised the return to capital, which has encouraged strong investment, both domestic and foreign.

While clearly positive for the A10 countries themselves, this rapid growth also has positive implications for the UK. One obvious channel is through increased trade. A common tool used to analyse trade flows is the so-called gravity model, based on the intuition that trade between two countries will rise in line with geographical proximity, economic size and income levels. Such models do well in describing actual trade flows. Strong growth and rising income levels in the A10 should therefore be expected to be positive for UK exports. This is borne out by the evidence: the share of UK exports going to the A10 increased from less than 1 per cent in 1992 to $1\frac{1}{2}$ per cent in 1999, and reached $2\frac{1}{4}$ per cent by 2005. In fact, UK exports to the A10 as a group have grown at a similar rate as those to China, and somewhat faster than those to India, and accounted for a larger share of UK exports in 2005 than either of those economies (chart b). Strong growth in the A10 also provides investment opportunities for UK companies: the stock of UK FDI in the A10 reached around £6 billion in 2005, while earnings on that investment approached $£\frac{3}{4}$ billion.

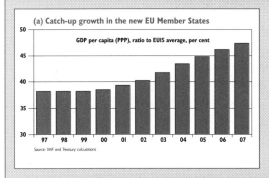

(a) Catch-up growth in the new EU Member States

Source: IMF and Treasury calculations

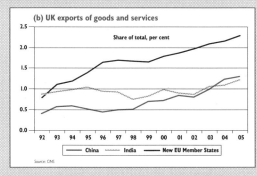

(b) UK exports of goods and services

Source: ONS

[a] The Czech Republic, Estonia, Hungary, Latvia, Lithuania, Poland, Slovakia and Slovenia joined in May 2004, along with Cyprus and Malta; Romania and Bulgaria joined in January 2007.

Latin America   **B.20**   GDP growth in Latin America in 2006 was comfortably above its historical average. The downward trend for interest rates spreads on sovereign debt for the majority of Latin American countries continued in 2006. A number of countries took steps to reduce their external vulnerabilities by modifying their debt profiles. Inflation rates remain high in a number of countries, most notably Venezuela, where the rate increased to more than 20 per cent on a year earlier in February 2007.

Africa and the   **B.21**   The latest estimates of growth in 2006 across Africa and the Middle East show GDP to
Middle East   have expanded at a rate above its historical average. As in recent years, strong global demand for oil and non-fuel commodities continued to drive economic activity. It is widely forecast that the region will continue to grow at similar rates in 2007.

World trade

B.22   Stronger than expected global economic activity over the past year has been reflected in world trade, which is now estimated to have grown by $9^3/_4$ per cent in 2006. World trade growth is expected to slow in 2007, to a rate of $7^3/_4$ per cent, with weaker contributions from all regions. From 2008 onwards, world trade is expected to grow at rates in line with the average of the past 20 years.

B.23   In parallel with developments in world trade, growth in UK export markets in 2006 was stronger than expected at the time of the 2006 Pre-Budget Report. The forecast for UK export market growth has also been revised up slightly from 2007 onwards, owing to stronger growth in the G7, and particularly the euro area economies which together account for 50 per cent of UK exports. While US demand has moderated, the impact on UK exports is expected to be limited since the moderation has been largely confined to residential investment.

B.24   World trade growth has been consistently stronger than UK export market growth in recent years due to the different composition of these two aggregates. Over the past four years, Asia contributed close to half of total world trade growth, but, given Asia's relatively small share in UK exports, only about a quarter of UK export market growth. The extent to which G7 economies have benefited from the recent growth boom in China and India has varied. Proximity and export composition explain the relatively high level of demand from China as a share of total demand for Japanese and German output, while on this score the UK ranks fourth in the G7. In the case of demand from India, the UK ranks first among the G7 countries, in part reflecting the relatively high share of services exports in the UK's trade with India. Other emerging economies are also important markets for the UK, in particular the new accession countries in Eastern Europe described in Box B2, which together currently represent a larger export market for the UK than either China or India.

Oil and commodity prices

B.25   Since the beginning of 2007, the price of a barrel of Brent crude oil, the European standard, has averaged around $58, remaining below the average price in 2006 of $66, but considerably above the 10-year average of around $32.

B.26   After the 2006 Pre-Budget Report, oil prices initially fell because of unusually warm winter temperatures in North America and Europe, before rebounding as normal weather conditions resumed and OPEC production cuts took effect. The average of independent forecasts for Brent oil prices in 2007 has fallen almost $2 a barrel since December 2006, reflecting a slight easing of perceived market tightness as growth of supply is expected to outpace growth of demand. The outlook for oil prices remains sensitive to geo-political, regulatory and weather-related risks in the major producer and consumer nations.

B.27   Non-fuel commodity prices remain high. The major price indices for industrial metals, which, as noted in the 2006 Pre-Budget Report, tend to be positively correlated with the global business cycle, are currently at broadly similar levels to those prevailing at the time of the Pre-Budget Report. The price of some metals, notably lead, nickel and tin, have continued to rise strongly, while others, including copper and zinc, have eased from the peaks of 2006. Agricultural commodities also experienced significant price increases in the second half of 2006, particularly for grains and cattle. These increases coincided with rising food price inflation in a number of countries, including the UK.

G7 inflation

B.28   In recent months, movements in G7 headline inflation have reflected changes in energy prices, which have fallen from the high levels of a year ago. This downward effect has been most noticeable in the US, where the headline consumer price index is particularly sensitive to changes in oil prices. Favourable developments in energy prices have been somewhat offset by higher food prices across most G7 economies. In Japan, which suffered consumer price deflation between 1999 and 2005, negative headline inflation rates have been absent since May 2006.

B.29   Core inflation, excluding energy and food prices, remains elevated in the US, despite dipping briefly in the final quarter of 2006. In Europe, core inflation has picked up recently, though this partly reflects the 3 percentage point VAT increase in Germany in January 2007. Core inflation rates across the G7 are low by historical standards, while they remain negative in Japan.

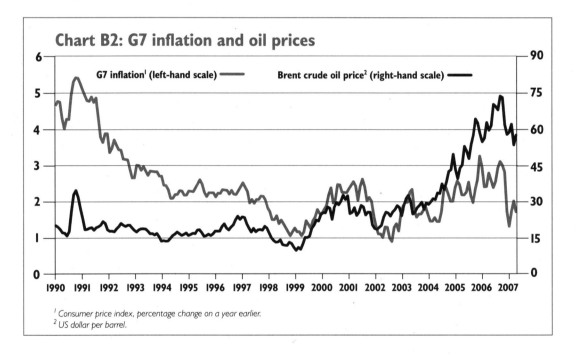

Chart B2: G7 inflation and oil prices

^{1} *Consumer price index, percentage change on a year earlier.*
^{2} *US dollar per barrel.*

THE UK ECONOMIC FORECAST

The Treasury's approach to economic forecasting

B.30   The Treasury's approach to forecasting macroeconomic developments accords with the 'growth cycle approach' favoured by many policymakers. At the heart of this approach is an estimate of the economy's 'trend' level and rate of growth, which provides the foundation for analysis of cyclical movements around that trend, the output gap, and developments in the components of demand. The Treasury's analysis of trend growth and the output gap is therefore central to the economic forecast that underpins the setting of fiscal policy. The trend growth assumption provides the medium-term anchor for the forecast. The current output gap estimate, and assessment of the economy's momentum through analysis of the individual income and expenditure components, inform judgement on the short-term path of the economy back to trend.

B.31   The Treasury assesses trend growth in the economy on the basis of non-oil gross value added (GVA) rather than overall GDP because, while the oil and gas sector affects output, it has little direct impact on capacity pressures in the rest of the economy, and hence the sustainable level of non-oil activity or employment.

B.32   The Office for National Statistics (ONS) compiles estimates of non-oil GVA in the National Accounts, but its trend level is not directly observable and must therefore be estimated. A wide variety of methods are available for decomposing the level of output into its trend and cyclical components.[5] The Treasury's approach begins with the identification of 'on-trend' points, drawing on evidence from a broad range of economic indicators.[6] The rate of trend output growth in completed past cycles is then estimated as the average growth rate between adjudged start and end-of-cycle on-trend points.

B.33   A different approach is required for estimating trend growth during the latest incomplete cycle and over the forecast horizon because the end-of-cycle on-trend point is in the future, and hence inherently uncertain. The Treasury's approach is to decompose the change in trend output over past cycles into changes in four components: output per hour; average hours worked per worker; the employment rate; and working-age population. The next section contains a discussion of developments in these components and how they inform the overall trend growth estimate since the 2001 on-trend point.

B.34   For any assumed trend rate of growth and trend level of output at a previous on-trend point, it is straightforward to calculate the size of the output gap implied by the latest National Accounts data on actual output. However, it is important to evaluate the plausibility of the output gap estimate implied by this 'trend growth arithmetic' by assessing the extent to which it is consistent with evidence from a broad range of cyclical indicators. Recent economic developments and an assessment of the cyclical indicators are discussed in the following sections.

B.35   The estimates of trend growth and the latest output gap provide the foundation for the detailed economic forecast. In the short term, the Treasury's judgement on the speed with which the economy will return to trend is informed by analysis of momentum in the key components of growth and their determinants, including assessment of the signals from private sector business survey-based indicators. Once the effects of any recent shocks are forecast to have dissipated and the economy is judged to have returned to trend, growth is generally held at its trend rate and the output gap at zero. That is not to suggest that the growth rate will actually be constant in later periods of the forecast, but rather that future shocks to the economy are as likely to be positive as negative so that, on average, the best forecast of growth once present shocks have worked through will be the trend rate.

Assessment of trend growth

B.36   The Treasury's neutral estimate of the economy's trend rate of growth of output for Budget 2007 remains at $2^3/_4$ per cent a year to the end of the projection period. This is unchanged from the 2006 Pre-Budget Report.[7]

---

[5] See *Trend growth: recent developments and prospects*, HM Treasury, April 2002, and *Evidence on the UK economic cycle*, HM Treasury, July 2005, for further details of the Treasury's approach to estimating trend growth and a discussion of alternative approaches, including statistical filtering techniques and more explicit economic model-based methods.

[6] Details of the indicators monitored by the Treasury can be found in the *Technical note on cyclical indicators*, HM Treasury, December 2005.

[7] For a full discussion of the most recent review of the Treasury's trend growth projections see *Trend growth: new evidence and prospects*, HM Treasury, December 2006.

B.37   Table B2 presents historical estimates of trend output growth and its decomposition for the first half of the current economic cycle and for the previous cycle, together with the forward-looking assumption of trend growth based on projections of its components to the end of the current cycle and beyond.

Table B2: Contributions to trend output growth[1]

	Estimated trend rates of growth, per cent per annum					
	Trend output per hour worked[2, 3]		Trend average hours worked[3]	Trend employment rate[3]	Population of working age[4]	**Trend output**
	Underlying	Unadjusted				
	(1)	(2)	(3)	(4)	(5)	(6)
1986Q2 to 1997H1						
Budget 2006	2.22	2.04	−0.11	0.36	0.24	**2.55**
PBR 2006 and Budget 2007	2.10	1.92	−0.11	0.36	0.24	**2.43**
Over the recent past						
1997H1 to 2001Q3						
Budget 2002	2.14	1.96	−0.37	0.36	0.66	**2.63**
PBR 2002 and Budget 2003	2.35	2.14	−0.47	0.43	0.50	**2.61**
PBR 2003 and Budget 2004	2.65	2.44	−0.47	0.42	0.54	**2.94**
PBR 2004 and Budget 2005	2.70	2.50	−0.43	0.41	0.58	**3.06**
PBR 2005 and Budget 2006	2.79	2.59	−0.44	0.42	0.58	**3.15**
PBR 2006 and Budget 2007	2.81	2.60	−0.44	0.42	0.58	**3.16**
Projection[5]						
2001Q3 to 2006Q4						
Budget 2002	2.10	2.00	−0.1	0.2	0.6	**2¾**
PBR 2002 to Budget 2005	2.35	2.25	−0.1	0.2	0.5	**2¾**
PBR 2005 and Budget 2006	2.25	2.15	−0.2	0.2	0.6	**2¾**
PBR 2006 and Budget 2007[6,7]	2.25	2.15	−0.2	0.2	0.7	**2¾**
2006Q4 onwards						
PBR 2004 and Budget 2005	2.35	2.25	−0.1	0.2	0.3	**2½**
PBR 2005 and Budget 2006	2.25	2.15	−0.2	0.2	0.4	**2½**
PBR 2006 and Budget 2007[6]	2.25	2.15	−0.2	0.2	0.6	**2¾**

[1] *Treasury analysis based on judgement that 1986Q2, 1997H1 and 2001Q3 were on-trend points of the output cycle. Figures independently rounded. Trend output growth is estimated as growth of non-oil GVA between on-trend points for the past, and by projecting components going forward.*

Columns (2) + (3) + (4) + (5) = (6).

Full data definitions and sources are set out in Annex A of 'Trend growth: new evidence and prospects', HM Treasury, December 2006.

[2] *The underlying trend rate is the unadjusted trend rate adjusted for changes in the employment rate, i.e. assuming the employment rate had remained constant.*

Column (1) = column (2) + (1-a).column (4), where a is the ratio of new to average worker productivity levels. The figuring is consistent with this ratio being of the order of 50 per cent, informed by econometric evidence and LFS data on relative entry wages.

[3] *The decomposition makes allowances for employment and hours worked lagging output. Employment is assumed to lag output by around three quarters, so that on-trend points for employment come three quarters after on-trend points for output, an assumption which can be supported by econometric evidence. Hours are easier to adjust than employment, and the decomposition assumes that hours lag output by just one quarter, though this lag is hard to support by econometric evidence. Hours worked and the employment rate are measured on a working-age basis.*

[4] *UK resident household basis.*

[5] *Neutral case assumptions for trend from 2001Q3.*

[6] *Underlying trend assumptions around which the mid-points of the GDP forecast growth ranges from 2006Q4 are anchored.*

[7] *The projection of working-age population is consistent with average growth since 2001Q3. This may change as a result of population data revisions.*

Productivity growth

B.38 Since the latter half of 2005, productivity growth, measured in terms of output per hour worked, has grown at above-trend rates. This is likely to reflect the cyclical response to stronger output growth, since productivity growth tends to fluctuate positively with output growth, and thus the cycle.[8] Annual growth in output per hour worked has averaged almost $2^1/_2$ per cent since the on-trend point in 2001, compared with an unadjusted trend projection of 2.15 per cent. While recognising that uncertainties in the labour market data feed through into uncertainties around the strength of productivity growth, this evidence enhances confidence in the trend projection.

Labour market developments

B.39 In 2006, strong employment growth was accompanied by even stronger labour supply growth reflecting the combination of a fall in the inactivity rate during the first half of the year and ongoing strong growth in the population of working age. Over the past year, working-age employment grew by $^1/_2$ per cent and total employment by $^3/_4$ per cent, the difference being due to the $7^1/_4$ per cent increase in employment of those above the State Pension age. In 2006, private sector employment grew by around 250,000 while public sector employment fell by 25,000. The working-age employment rate remained stable at around $74^1/_2$ per cent through 2006, a little below its assumed trend, while by the end of the year the older workers' employment rate had risen to 11 per cent.

B.40 With employment continuing to rise through 2006 and labour supply growth moderating in the second half, by the end of the year the level and rate of unemployment had begun to fall, as expected at the time of the 2006 Pre-Budget Report. This pattern of solid employment growth and a gradual reduction in unemployment is expected to continue in 2007. Working-age population growth is expected to remain strong: the latest evidence suggests that migration to the UK from new Member States of the EU continued through 2006 at levels somewhat above those seen in 2005.

B.41 Employment growth over the past year has been much stronger among part-time than full-time employees, but average hours worked per week have remained steady at around the same level since late 2003.

B.42 As highlighted in the 2006 Pre-Budget Report, there are uncertainties surrounding official labour market data relating to the measurement of migration flows and growth of the working-age population, and the number of temporary foreign workers in the UK. As part of its work programme aimed at improving migration statistics, the ONS recently published a feasibility study into the production of short-term migration estimates.[9] Based on the information gathered for this study, the ONS estimates that a significant proportion of the disparity between growth in jobs in 2005 as measured by the Labour Force Survey (LFS) and the workforce jobs series "might be explained by an increase in under-coverage of working short-term migrants"[10] in the LFS.

Overview of recent developments

B.43 The UK's macroeconomic policy framework continues to deliver unprecedented growth and stability. GDP in the UK has now expanded for 58 consecutive quarters, the longest unbroken expansion since quarterly National Accounts began more than half a century ago. Over the past 10 years, the UK has enjoyed more stability in terms of GDP growth and inflation than in any decade since the war. Despite recent energy and food-related price rises, discussed below, inflation, on the RPI measure, has remained within a range of $^3/_4$ to $4^3/_4$

---

[8] *See Productivity in the UK 6: Progress and new evidence*, HM Treasury, March 2006.
[9] *Short-term migration feasibility report*, ONS, January 2007.
[10] *Review of workforce job benchmarking*, ONS, March 2007.

per cent over the past 10 years, compared with a range of 1 to 11 per cent in the 1990s, $2^1/_2$ to 22 per cent in the 1980s and 5 to 27 per cent in the 1970s.

GDP growth **B.44** As forecast at the time of the 2006 Pre-Budget Report, the UK economy grew by $2^3/_4$ per cent in 2006. Having expanded at a rate of 0.7 per cent for four consecutive quarters, GDP growth picked up slightly to 0.8 per cent in the fourth quarter of 2006. Minor upward revisions to historical data show that GDP grew by 2 per cent in 2005.

Table B3: Quarterly GDP and non-oil GVA growth

| | Percentage change on previous quarter | | | | | | | |
| | 2005 | | | | 2006 | | | |
	QI	Q2	Q3	Q4	QI	Q2	Q3	Q4
GDP	0.3	0.5	0.5	0.7	0.7	0.7	0.7	0.8
Non-oil GVA	0.4	0.5	0.6	0.7	0.7	0.8	0.7	0.8

B.45 There was a notable degree of rebalancing in the sources of domestic demand in the economy in 2006. Nominal consumer spending has been trending down relative to nominal GDP for the past five years. Real household and government consumption, which had grown faster than the overall economy during the first half of this decade, grew in 2006 at rates below that of the whole economy, at $2^1/_4$ and 2 per cent respectively. Offsetting that, whole economy investment grew by 6 per cent, significantly above the 3 per cent average of the first half of the decade. Signs of a rebalancing of domestic and external sources of demand in 2006 were more tentative: despite the strongest export growth since 2000, net trade subtracted $^1/_2$ a percentage point from GDP growth, in line with the average of the earlier years of this decade.

Inflation **B.46** Consumer price inflation picked up during 2006, almost entirely attributable to the combined effect of higher energy and food prices, the former driven by higher oil and wholesale gas prices, and the latter by the unusually hot summer weather. CPI inflation has continued to rise since the 2006 Pre-Budget Report, from 2.4 per cent in October to a high of 3.0 per cent in December, before falling back to 2.8 per cent in February 2007. Inflation averaged $2^3/_4$ per cent during the fourth quarter of 2006, slightly higher than expected at the time of the Pre-Budget Report, mainly reflecting developments in the prices of seasonal foods. As expected, the contribution of energy prices to CPI inflation remained high at close to 1 percentage point. Despite inflation having picked up, there have been no signs of second-round effects on earnings growth, which has remained subdued. The Government has continued to emphasise the need for pay settlements to be consistent with the achievement of the inflation target of 2 per cent.

B.47 In terms of traded goods, import price inflation picked up steadily from a low of -$3^1/_4$ per cent in February 2004 to a peak of $7^1/_4$ per cent in April 2006. In part this pick-up reflected rising oil and metals prices over the period, but even excluding these factors import price inflation increased from -$2^1/_2$ to $3^1/_4$ per cent. Since April 2006, it has fallen back sharply, and goods import prices fell in the year to January 2007. These developments have fed through to producers' input price inflation, which, having peaked at the end of 2005 at 18 per cent, turned negative in the year to January 2007. Manufacturers chose to absorb most of the increase in input prices in margins, and to a lesser extent offset it by reining back earnings growth. Consequently, output price inflation picked up only slightly, from $1^3/_4$ per cent at the end of 2005 to 3 per cent by mid-2006, before falling back to $2^1/_4$ per cent in the year to February 2007.

Monetary and fiscal policy **B.48** Since August 2006, as growth has strengthened and CPI inflation has moved above target, the MPC has acted by raising the Bank Rate on three occasions, the latest being in January 2007. At $5^1/_4$ per cent, interest rates remain low by historical standards, having averaged $11^3/_4$ per cent in the 1980s and $9^1/_2$ per cent in the first half of the 1990s. Market-derived interest rate expectations are for a further $^1/_4$ percentage point increase in 2007. Fiscal policy has been moderately tightened since 2004-05.

Assessment of the output gap

B.49 Since the 2006 Pre-Budget Report, minor revisions to estimates of non-oil GVA growth since the beginning of 2005, alongside estimated growth of 0.8 per cent in the final quarter of 2006, show the economy to have been growing at slightly above-trend rates for five consecutive quarters through to the end of 2006. As a result, the trend growth arithmetic, based on the latest National Accounts data and the Treasury's trend output assumptions, implies only a small negative output gap in late 2006, of around $-^1/_4$ per cent. This is close to estimates from a number of external forecasters, and well within their range.

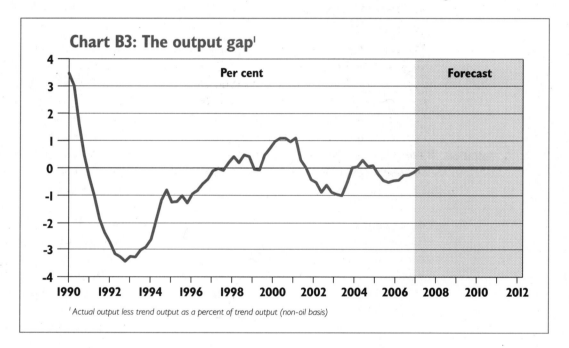

Chart B3: The output gap[1]

[1] Actual output less trend output as a percent of trend output (non-oil basis)

Evidence from cyclical indicators **B.50** The Treasury's assessment of the cyclical position of the UK economy draws on a broad range of economic indicators, including private sector business surveys, labour market indicators and price data. The indicators that have played a formal role in the dating of on-trend points were set out in the *Technical note on cyclical indicators*, published alongside the 2005 Pre-Budget Report. In line with recommendations made by the National Audit Office at that time,[11] Box B3 reports on the Bank of England's Regional Agents' scores, which provide additional information on the cyclical position of the economy and will therefore play a role in the Treasury's future judgements of where the economy stands in relation to trend.

---

[11] See paragraph 74 of the *Audit of assumptions for the 2005 Pre-Budget Report*, National Audit Office, December 2005.

Box B3: The Bank of England's Agents' scores

Since 1997, the Monetary Policy Committee (MPC) of the Bank of England has been able to draw upon a set of quantitative assessments of current economic conditions reported to them by the Bank's twelve regional offices, or Agencies. These 'Agents' scores' cover a broad range of economic factors,[a] including capacity constraints and recruitment difficulties, which are relevant to the Treasury's assessment of the cyclical position of the economy. In January 2006, the Bank began to publish the scores on its website, thereby providing a source of information that has not previously been available to the Treasury in assessing the cyclical position of the economy.

The Agents' scores on capacity constraints in the manufacturing and service sectors were first compiled in January 1998. In terms of labour market slack, an Agents' score on skills shortages was reported between July 1997 and December 2004, and one on recruitment difficulties since then. In its description of the Agents' scores,[a] the Bank advises that these two indicators are comparable. At just under a decade, the time-series for the Agents' scores are shorter than most of the other cyclical indicators the Treasury currently monitors. As such, a degree of caution should be exercised in drawing conclusions from the evidence they present.

The latest Agents' scores, published alongside the minutes of the February MPC meeting, suggest that both the manufacturing and service sectors have been operating at above average rates of capacity utilisation since the middle of 2006. In terms of the labour market, they point to a considerable degree of slack having opened up during the second half of 2005, and some tightening since the third quarter of 2006. Taken together, the Agents' scores appear consistent with the economy currently being close to trend, while pointing to a greater disparity between capacity constraints and labour market slack than is apparent in the other cyclical indicators the Treasury monitors.

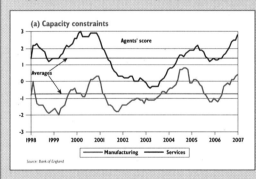

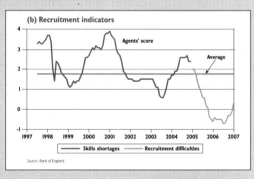

[a] For a general discussion of the Agents' scores, see Ellis, C. and Pike, T. *Introducing the Agents' scores*, Bank of England Quarterly Bulletin, Winter 2005.

B.51   Private sector business surveys of capacity utilisation in the manufacturing and service sectors have recently been at levels close to, and in some cases above, their long-run averages, consistent with the economy being close to trend. By contrast, indicators of recruitment difficulties point to some slack in the labour market, though, as at the time of the 2006 Pre-Budget Report, growth in the labour force appears to be having a differential impact on the availability of specific types of labour. Employers in the service sector are currently reporting difficulties in hiring skilled and clerical labour that are consistent with previous on-trend points, but simultaneously report an increased availability of semi- and unskilled workers. Similarly in the manufacturing sector, while overall recruitment difficulties have eased and remain below levels consistent with on-trend output, employers report varying levels of difficulty in recruiting individuals within different skill-sets.

B.52   Claimant count unemployment, which increased during 2005 and the first half of 2006, has fallen in seven of the past eight months, and is now lower than it was a year ago. Average earnings growth has remained subdued. During 2006 as a whole, private sector earnings growth was $4^{1}/_{4}$ per cent including bonuses, and 4 per cent excluding bonuses, and showed few signs of picking up despite private sector business surveys reporting strong demand for labour. The latest data, covering the three months to January 2007, show whole economy earnings including bonuses up $4^{1}/_{4}$ per cent on a year earlier. Excluding bonuses, whole economy earnings were up just $3^{1}/_{2}$ per cent over the same period. Wage developments have therefore remained consistent with there being some slack in the labour market. More generally, indicators of domestically-generated inflation appear consistent with the economy operating close to trend, with the recent rise in headline inflation dominated by non-cyclical factors.

B.53   On balance, capacity utilisation indicators tend to signal that output is currently close to trend, while labour market indicators point to some ongoing slack suggesting that overall the output gap may be slightly negative. There is, however, a degree of uncertainty about the interpretation of official and private sector business survey indicators of labour market developments at present. Looking further ahead, the ONS is currently engaged in a modernisation programme that aims to deliver better quality National Accounts using modernised systems and methods in the 2008 Blue Book, to be published in September 2008. In the meantime, the scope of revisions to National Accounts data will be limited, which will introduce some temporary additional uncertainty about the path of the economy.[12] One significant improvement that will be implemented in the 2007 Blue Book will be to the measurement of software investment, whereas improvements to the treatment of banking sector output, known as FISIM,[13] will be made in 2008.

GDP and inflation forecasts

Table B4: Summary of forecast[1]

		Forecast		
	2006	**2007**	**2008**	**2009**
GDP growth (per cent)	$2^{3}/_{4}$	$2^{3}/_{4}$ to $3^{1}/_{4}$	$2^{1}/_{2}$ to 3	$2^{1}/_{2}$ to 3
CPI inflation (per cent, Q4)	$2^{3}/_{4}$	2	2	2

[1] See footnote to Table B10 for explanation of forecast ranges.

GDP and the output gap   **B.54**   The latest estimates of GDP and non-oil GVA growth to the fourth quarter of 2006 are consistent with the 2006 Pre-Budget Report forecast. The Budget 2007 GDP growth forecast is unchanged from the Pre-Budget Report: the small negative output gap is expected to have closed early in 2007, and growth is forecast to continue at close-to-trend rates throughout the forecast horizon. This implies GDP growth of $2^{3}/_{4}$ to $3^{1}/_{4}$ per cent in 2007, and $2^{1}/_{2}$ to 3 per cent a year thereafter.

Rebalancing of domestic demand   **B.55**   The rebalancing of domestic demand already evident during 2006 is expected to continue to a somewhat greater degree than was envisaged in the 2006 Pre-Budget Report forecast. Latest estimates of business investment in the second half of 2006 show particularly strong growth, which surprised on the upside, and some of that momentum is expected to carry through into 2007. Private consumption growth, also strong at the end of 2006 following alternately weaker and stronger quarterly growth through the year, is expected to moderate as recent increases in interest rates feed through to disposable income growth and

---

[12] See *Modernising the UK's National Accounts*, ONS, February 2007.

[13] Financial intermediation services indirectly measured.

households' desire to save. The contribution of net trade to GDP growth is expected to remain slightly negative in 2007, but to be neutral thereafter.

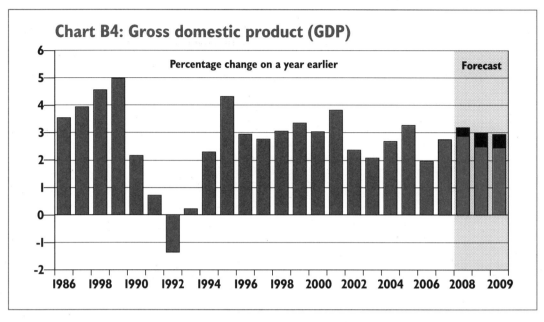

Chart B4: Gross domestic product (GDP)

Percentage change on a year earlier

Forecast

1986 1998 1990 1992 1994 1996 1998 2000 2002 2004 2006 2008 2009

Inflation **B.56** The pick-up in headline inflation over the past year has mainly been attributable to energy and food prices, rather than domestic cyclical pressures, factors that are expected to unwind during 2007. By far the largest contributor to the rise in inflation during 2006 was energy prices, particularly domestic gas and electricity prices. At the time of the 2006 Pre-Budget Report, developments in wholesale gas prices pointed to energy prices stabilising, with their contribution to inflation falling during 2007. Since the Pre-Budget Report, a number of major energy providers have announced significant cuts in utility tariffs that imply the contribution of energy prices to inflation is likely to turn negative by the middle of 2007. Unless harvests prove incrementally worse during 2007 than in 2006, when the unusually hot summer pushed food prices higher, the contribution of food prices to overall inflation should also fall.

B.57 As a result of these expected energy and food-related price developments, CPI inflation is likely to fall quite sharply from its current level, returning to around target in the second half of 2007.

B.58 Inflation expectations remain anchored to the inflation target and earnings growth has remained subdued, suggesting there have been no second-round effects from the recent above-target rates of inflation, although this risk has not yet subsided.

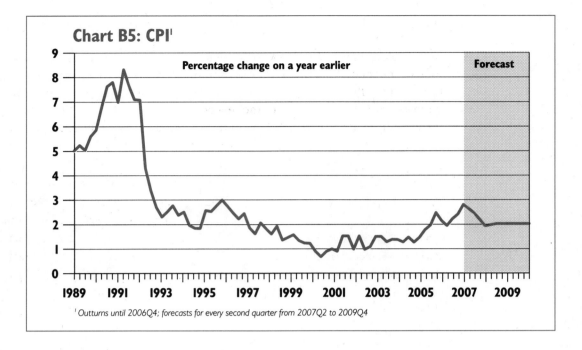

Chart B5: CPI[1]

Percentage change on a year earlier

Forecast

[1] *Outturns until 2006Q4; forecasts for every second quarter from 2007Q2 to 2009Q4*

UK DEMAND AND OUTPUT IN DETAIL

B.59   GDP grew by $2^3/_4$ per cent in 2006, just below the average of the past 10 years, but slightly above the average of the past five years. Within the components of demand, private consumption growth picked up from 2005, but remained slightly below that of the economy as a whole, while business investment picked up sharply, to its strongest rate since 1998. Together, these developments continued, and accelerated, the rebalancing of real domestic demand that began in 2005. The rebalancing of nominal domestic demand, which began earlier, also continued. On the output side of the economy, while the service sector continued to provide the main source of growth in 2006, the manufacturing sector expanded in every quarter of the year, for the first time since 2000.

Table B5: Contributions to GDP growth[1,2]

	Percentage points, unless otherwise stated				
	Average		Forecast		
	2000 to 2005	2006	2007	2008	2009
GDP growth, per cent	$2^3/_4$	$2^3/_4$	$2^3/_4$ to $3^1/_4$	$2^1/_2$ to 3	$2^1/_2$ to 3
Main contributions					
Private consumption	2	$1^1/_2$	$1^1/_2$	$1^1/_2$	$1^1/_2$
Business investment	$^1/_4$	$^3/_4$	$^3/_4$	$^1/_2$	$^1/_2$
Government[3]	$^3/_4$	$^1/_2$	$^3/_4$	$^1/_2$	$^1/_2$
Change in inventories	0	$^1/_4$	0	0	0
Net trade	$-^1/_2$	$-^1/_2$	$-^1/_4$	0	0

[1] *Components may not sum to total due to rounding and omission of private residential investment, transfer costs of land and existing buildings and the statistical discrepancy.*

[2] *Based on central case. For the purpose of projecting public finances, forecasts are based on the bottom of the GDP forecast range.*

[3] *The sum of government consumption and government investment.*

Households and consumption[14]

B.60   Household consumption is the largest expenditure component of GDP, accounting for 64 per cent of the UK economy in nominal terms, having trended down from $66\frac{1}{2}$ per cent in mid-2001. Between 1995 and 2004, as real private consumption grew faster than GDP, it increased steadily as a share of the real economy. Since then, in line with the rebalancing of the economy, consumption's share of real demand has fallen by around $\frac{3}{4}$ percentage points.

Table B6: Household sector[1] expenditure and income

	Percentage change on a year earlier, unless otherwise stated			
		Forecast		
	2006	**2007**	**2008**	**2009**
Household consumption[2]	$2\frac{1}{4}$	$2\frac{1}{4}$ to $2\frac{3}{4}$	$2\frac{1}{4}$ to $2\frac{3}{4}$	$2\frac{1}{4}$ to $2\frac{3}{4}$
Real household disposable income	$1\frac{3}{4}$	$2\frac{1}{4}$ to $2\frac{3}{4}$	$2\frac{1}{4}$ to $2\frac{3}{4}$	$2\frac{1}{4}$ to $2\frac{3}{4}$
Saving ratio[3] (level, per cent)	$5\frac{1}{4}$	$5\frac{1}{2}$	$5\frac{3}{4}$	$5\frac{3}{4}$

[1] Including non-profit institutions serving households.

[2] Chained volume measures.

[3] Total household resources less consumption expenditure as a percent of total resources, where total resources comprise households' disposable income plus the increase in their net equity in pension funds.

Disposable income   **B.61**   Real household disposable incomes in the first three quarters of 2006 grew by $1\frac{1}{2}$ per cent on a year earlier. This was lower growth than in 2005, due to more moderate growth of nominal incomes. The slowdown was almost entirely accounted for by growth of net "property income", the balance between interest and dividends received and paid by households, falling from $17\frac{1}{4}$ per cent to $4\frac{1}{4}$ per cent. Real disposable incomes are expected to grow in a range of $2\frac{1}{4}$ to $2\frac{3}{4}$ per cent throughout the forecast horizon.

Household spending   **B.62**   Private consumption grew $2\frac{1}{4}$ per cent in 2006, slightly above the 2006 Pre-Budget Report forecast. As with retail sales, described below, quarterly growth of consumption in 2006 alternated between weaker and stronger quarters, but averaged 0.7 per cent. Due to the strength of growth in the fourth quarter, private consumption began 2007 at a higher level than was expected at the time of the Pre-Budget Report, with knock-on effects for growth in 2007.

B.63   Private consumption growth is forecast to continue at rates slightly below that of the economy as a whole, reflecting the impact of recent interest rate rises and developments in households' real incomes. Given the slightly tighter interest rate environment currently than at the time of the 2006 Pre-Budget Report, quarterly consumption growth in 2007 is likely to be more moderate. However, the higher starting point for the year leaves the annual growth forecast in 2007 unchanged from the Pre-Budget Report forecast of $2\frac{1}{4}$ to $2\frac{3}{4}$ per cent.

[14] In the National Accounts, private consumption is comprised of final consumption expenditure by households and non-profit institutions serving households (NPISH). Throughout this section, the terms 'household consumption' and 'private consumption' always refer to total final consumption expenditure by households and NPISH.

B.64 Retail sales growth has continued the pattern of fluctuating quarterly growth rates that began in the middle of 2005, with strong growth in the fourth quarter of 2006. Monthly growth rates tend to be particularly volatile over the Christmas period, despite attempts to adjust for seasonal spending patterns, this year rising 1.1 per cent in December but falling 1.8 per cent in January. Since 1986, unadjusted retail sales volumes have typically increased about 20 per cent from November to December, then fallen about 30 per cent in January, presenting obvious seasonal adjustment challenges. These may have been further complicated recently by a shift in the pattern of spending between December and January. December 2006 accounted for the highest proportion of full-year retail sales on record, while January 2007 accounted for the second lowest. The underlying trend in spending may therefore be better represented by a longer-run indicator such as the six-month on previous six months growth rate, which has been running at an annualised rate of 4 per cent or more since August 2006.

Saving ratio **B.65** The household saving ratio is estimated to have declined slightly during 2006, to 5 per cent by the third quarter, but is expected to rise over the forecast period. The GfK consumer confidence survey reports that households' saving intentions remain at high levels, suggesting that a further increase in the saving ratio represents a downside risk to the consumption forecast.

House prices **B.66** As expected at the time of the 2006 Pre-Budget Report, house price inflation picked up during the fourth quarter of 2006 to rates of around 10 per cent on a year earlier, though housing-related indicators have become more mixed since the Pre-Budget Report. As forecast at the time of the Pre-Budget Report, house price inflation is likely to slow during 2007.

B.67 Investment in dwellings has recently risen to around 4 per cent of nominal GDP, which, though rather less than half the ratio of business investment to GDP, is a significant component of demand. In line with other indicators of the housing market, growth of private sector investment in dwellings was strong in the first three quarters of 2006, up 8 per cent on a year earlier. While growth in residential investment is expected to slow, recent momentum and Barker Review commitments[15] are expected to keep growth above that of the economy as a whole throughout the forecast period.

Companies and investment

B.68 Business investment accounts for around 10 per cent of nominal GDP, but its role in the economy extends beyond that. Investment also affects future growth by raising the amount of physical capital available to each worker with which to produce goods and services. Increasing capital intensity is an important driver of labour productivity growth. The contribution of investment to productivity and long-run economic growth is described in more detail in Chapter 3, and in *Productivity in the UK 6: Progress and new evidence* published alongside Budget 2006.

Company **B.69** Companies have a variety of sources from which they can finance investment. These **finances** include internal sources, such as the cashflow generated on their operations or drawdown of accumulated financial assets, and external sources, including bank lending or the issuance of equity or debt to investors. Both sources remain supportive of business investment growth.

---

[15] *The Government's response to Kate Barker's review of housing supply,* HM Treasury, December 2005.

B.70 Profitability, as measured by the net rate of return on capital in the non-financial corporate sector, reached another new record high, of 15^1/$_4$ per cent, in the third quarter of 2006. While that partly reflected extremely high rates of return for companies operating on the UK continental shelf, rates of return remain near record highs in the service sector, and have begun to recover in the manufacturing sector.

B.71 Supportive external financing conditions over recent years have encouraged firms to expand their balance sheets, simultaneously taking on liabilities and building up financial assets. Bank lending to non-financial companies grew at rapid rates during 2006. As a result, capital gearing, a measure of net indebtedness in the corporate sector, has risen to a level that is high by historical standards. However, with interest rates remaining at historically low levels despite recent rises, income gearing, a measure of the ability to service debt, remains well below historic peaks. Since the 2006 Pre-Budget Report, the external financing environment has remained broadly supportive.

Business investment

B.72 Official estimates of business investment growth in 2005 and 2006 are affected by the April 2005 transfer from British Nuclear Fuels Limited (BNFL) to the Nuclear Decommissioning Authority (NDA) of nuclear reactors that were reaching the end of their productive lives. Since BNFL is classified as a public corporation and the NDA is classified within central government, this transfer involved the movement of assets across the boundary between business investment and general government investment. The value of the transfer was negative, reflecting the costs of decommissioning the reactors. The impact on measured business investment growth was therefore positive in 2005 and negative in 2006. However, since this exceptional transfer has no effect on whole economy investment and does not reflect underlying developments in business investment, the following discussion, and the figures in Tables B5 and B7, and those behind Chart B6, exclude its impact.

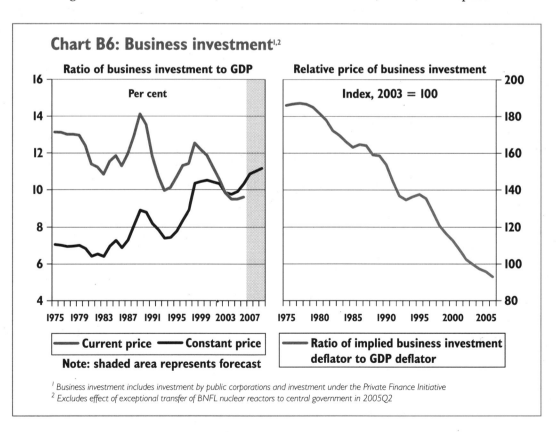

Chart B6: Business investment[1,2]

Ratio of business investment to GDP — Per cent

Relative price of business investment — Index, 2003 = 100

— Current price — Constant price

Note: shaded area represents forecast

— Ratio of implied business investment deflator to GDP deflator

[1] Business investment includes investment by public corporations and investment under the Private Finance Initiative
[2] Excludes effect of exceptional transfer of BNFL nuclear reactors to central government in 2005Q2

B.73   Business investment has now expanded for eight consecutive quarters, the longest continuous expansion for nine years. The 2006 Pre-Budget Report noted upside risks to the investment forecast. Following a stronger than expected final quarter of 2006, with growth of 11 per cent on a year earlier, growth in the year as a whole reached 7 per cent, above the Pre-Budget Report forecast of $5^3/_4$ per cent. The service sector accounted for the majority of business investment growth in 2006, rising $6^1/_4$ per cent on a year earlier, while investment in the manufacturing sector fell 4 per cent, thereby only partly reversing very strong growth of $12^1/_2$ per cent in 2005.

B.74   Much of the momentum in 2006 was accounted for by the non-manufacturing production sector, which includes oil extraction and utilities companies. Given an expected slowdown in capital expenditure by North Sea corporations, the forecast quarterly path of business investment growth in 2007 has only been revised up marginally since the Pre-Budget Report. However, because of the strength of growth in the final quarter of 2006, that translates into a larger upward revision to full-year business investment growth, to $7^1/_4$ to $7^3/_4$ per cent in 2007.

Table B7: Gross fixed capital formation

| | | Percent change on a year earlier | | |
| | | | Forecast | |
	2006	**2007**	**2008**	**2009**
Whole economy[1]	6	$6^1/_2$ to 7	$3^1/_4$ to $3^3/_4$	$3^1/_4$ to $3^3/_4$
of which:				
Business[2,3,4]	7	$7^1/_4$ to $7^3/_4$	$3^3/_4$ to $4^1/_4$	$3^3/_4$ to $4^1/_2$
Private dwellings[2]	8	$3^3/_4$ to $4^1/_4$	$2^3/_4$ to $3^1/_4$	$2^3/_4$ to $3^1/_4$
General government[3,4]	$2^1/_2$	$13^1/_2$	$3^3/_4$	2

[1] Includes costs associated with the transfer of ownership of land and existing buildings.
[2] Private sector and public corporations' non-residential investment. Includes investment under the Private Finance Initiative.
[3] Excludes purchases less sales of land and existing buildings.
[4] Excludes effect of exceptional transfer of BNFL nuclear reactors to central government in 2005Q2.

Government

B.75   Government consumption grew by 2 per cent in 2006, slower than the economy as a whole. As a share of GDP, government consumption has stabilised at around 22 per cent in nominal terms. Measured government investment growth in 2005 and 2006 is subject to the same effects as business investment growth, related to the exceptional transfer of assets from BNFL to the NDA described in paragraph B.72. Excluding this effect, real government investment was up $1^1/_4$ per cent in 2005 and is expected to have grown by $2^1/_2$ per cent in 2006.

Trade and the balance of payments

B.76   As set out in the 2006 Pre-Budget Report, annual growth in recorded exports and imports of goods and services has been severely distorted by activity related to missing trader intra-community fraud (MTIC), which significantly inflated the value of measured goods trade in the first half of 2006.

B.77   While MTIC-related activity should not, in principle, affect official estimates of net trade because the impact on export and import volumes should be equal, inevitable measurement difficulties may in practice carry over to estimates of net trade. Based on detailed trade data supplied by HMRC, the ONS estimates that there were large fluctuations in MTIC-related activity during 2006, in light of which, the ONS continues to advise that, "comparisons of [trade] volumes and prices... should be treated with a great deal of caution."[16]

B.78   The sharp fall in MTIC-related activity through 2006 has a significant effect on the forecast rates of growth of exports and imports in 2007. This is because the forecast abstracts from MTIC effects by assuming that beyond the latest quarter of data, export and import volumes grow in line with underlying trade, excluding MTIC-related activity. The forecast is therefore based on the neutral assumption that the level of MTIC-related activity stays flat at the latest quarterly estimate throughout the forecast. Table B8 presents export and import growth forecasts excluding the effects of MTIC-related activity.

Exports of goods and services   **B.79**   The volume of exports of goods and services excluding MTIC-related activity grew by $6^1/_4$ per cent in 2006, up from 5 per cent in 2005, reflecting a pick-up in underlying goods exports growth to $7^1/_4$ per cent from 5 per cent, and a slight slowdown in the growth of services exports to $4^1/_4$ per cent from $5^1/_4$ per cent.

B.80   The forecast for export growth has been revised up a little from the 2006 Pre-Budget Report, reflecting the slightly stronger outlook for UK export market growth as the balance of world growth has tilted towards Europe. Excluding MTIC-related activity, exports of goods and services are forecast to grow by $5^1/_4$ to $5^3/_4$ per cent in 2007, and by slightly slower rates in 2008 and 2009. While the level of UK exports continues to grow, the forecast assumes that the UK's export market share decreases broadly in line with the average decline since the late 1990s, reflecting the ongoing integration of developing economies into the global economy.

Imports of goods and services   **B.81**   Imports of goods and services excluding MTIC-related activity showed strong growth in 2006, up 7 per cent on a year earlier, mainly reflecting a pick-up in goods imports growth to $8^1/_2$ per cent from 4 per cent in 2005. Growth of services imports slowed from $5^3/_4$ per cent in 2005 to 3 per cent in 2006. With import growth in 2006 having been somewhat stronger than expected at the time of the 2006 Pre-Budget Report, and consistent with stronger expected business investment growth this year, the forecast for import growth in 2007 has been revised up slightly to 5 to $5^1/_2$ per cent. As a result of small revisions to the forecasts for import and export growth, the contribution of net trade to GDP growth is expected to remain negative in 2007, but to be broadly neutral thereafter.

---

[16] *First release: UK trade, January 2007*, ONS, March 2007.

Table B8: Trade in goods and services

	Percentage change on a year earlier					£ billion
	Volumes (excluding MTIC)[1]		Prices[2]			Goods and
					Terms of	services
	Exports	Imports	Exports	Imports	trade[3]	balance
2006	6¼	7	1½	2½	–¾	–55¼
Forecast						
2007	5¼ to 5¾	5 to 5½	0	0	0	–56½
2008	5 to 5½	4¼ to 4¾	2	2	0	–58¼
2009	4½ to 5	4 to 4½	1½	1½	0	–60

[1] Table B10 contains figures including the effects of MTIC-related activity. In 2008 and 2009 export and import growth including and excluding MTIC are the same, reflecting forecast assumptions.

[2] Average value indices.

[3] Ratio of export to import prices.

Sterling and the terms of trade

B.82 In the decade from 1995, the UK's terms of trade, a measure of the volume of imports the UK could purchase through the sale of a given volume of exports, improved steadily. The gains in purchasing power were particularly strong in the second half of the 1990s as sterling appreciated sharply, and in 2002 and 2003, coinciding with the rapid increase in the share of low-cost producers, particularly China, in world trade in goods. The UK's terms of trade subsequently deteriorated in 2005 and 2006, reflecting the sharp increase in the price of certain imported commodities, notably oil and metals. With export and import prices forecast to grow at similar rates, the UK's terms of trade are forecast to remain broadly stable.

Current account

B.83 The UK's deficit on trade in goods widened in 2006 relative to 2005, reaching 6½ per cent of GDP, although the deficit narrowed in the second half of the year compared with the first half. The surplus on trade in services rose from 2 per cent of GDP in 2005 to 2¼ per cent in 2006. Data on the breakdown of services trade to the third quarter of 2006 show that the increased surplus stemmed from strong growth in financial services exports, up 27 per cent on a year earlier in nominal terms, and the unwinding of the negative impact of Hurricane Katrina-related payments on insurance exports. The overall trade deficit in 2006 was 4¼ per cent of GDP, up from 3¾ per cent in 2005.

B.84 Significant income surpluses continued to offset the deficit on trade in goods and services in 2005 and 2006. The latest data show the income surplus running at 2¼ per cent of GDP in 2005 and over the first three quarters of 2006. The composition of the income surplus changed slightly between 2005 and 2006, with a larger surplus on income related to foreign direct investment (FDI), up from 3½ to 4 per cent of GDP, offset by a larger deficit on 'other investment' income, up from 1¼ to 1¾ per cent of GDP. 'Other investment' is largely comprised of flows through the financial sector, i.e. bank deposits and lending. Box B4 discusses the relationship between developments in the UK's international investment position and the income surplus.

B.85 The UK's current account deficit is expected to have risen from 2½ per cent of GDP in 2005 to 3 per cent of GDP in 2006, mainly reflecting developments in the goods trade deficit. From 2007, the current account deficit is expected to stabilise at 2¾ per cent of GDP.

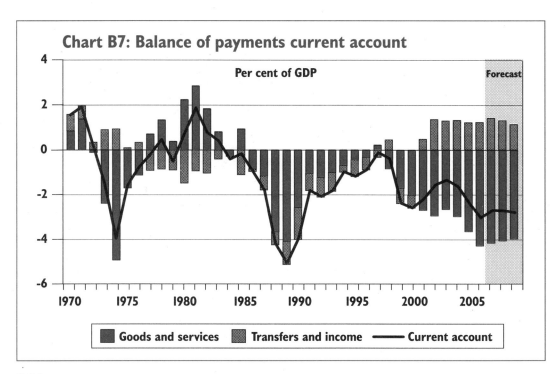

Chart B7: Balance of payments current account

Per cent of GDP

Forecast

Legend: Goods and services — Transfers and income — Current account

Foreign direct investment

B.86 The latest estimates show that the UK attracted a £108 billion inflow of FDI in 2005, around half of which was accounted for by the restructuring of Shell Transport and Trading and Royal Dutch Petroleum into Royal Dutch Shell. That represented a record high for the UK in both cash terms and relative to GDP and, according to the UN's 2006 *World Investment Report*, was the highest inflow ever recorded by a European country, and made the UK the world's largest recipient of inward FDI. Very strong inflows continued in the first three quarters of 2006, reaching almost £64 billion. That was a similar amount to the inflow to the US over the same period, and around twice that to China in 2006 as a whole. As a ratio to GDP, the stock of inward investment in the UK, at around 37 per cent in 2005, was almost three times higher than that in the US, twice that in Germany and a third higher than the ratio in France. The UK also has a larger stock of outward FDI as a ratio to GDP than any other major economy.

Box B4: International investment and the UK's income surplus

A key feature of the UK's current account in recent years has been the strong surplus on investment income, which amounted to $2\frac{1}{4}$ per cent of GDP in the first three quarters of 2006. This has been achieved despite the UK's international investment position (IIP) currently showing liabilities exceeding assets by around 19 per cent of GDP. There are two parts to the explanation of the UK's ability to earn net income on its net liability position:

- Firstly, the UK's IIP is not uniform across assets. On the contrary, low-yielding short-term loans and deposits more than account for the UK's net liabilities while the UK has a net asset position in high-yielding foreign direct investment (chart a). Based on the different rates of return that prevail for different types of investment, income flows to and from the UK should roughly balance despite the negative IIP.

- Secondly, while rates of return on portfolio investment and interest-sensitive loans and deposits are similar for the UK's assets and liabilities, UK companies earn a significantly higher return on their direct investment abroad than overseas companies earn on their direct investment in the UK (chart b). Figures for the year to the third quarter of 2006 imply that the rate of return UK companies earned on FDI abroad was around 12 per cent, compared with around $8\frac{1}{4}$ per cent earned by foreign companies on FDI in the UK. As UK companies' stock of investment abroad, £760 billion, is a third larger than that of foreign companies in the UK, £566 billion, the spread between the rates of return translated into net earnings on FDI equivalent to $3\frac{1}{2}$ per cent of GDP over that period.

In terms of the positive yield differential on direct investment, two sectors of the economy play the major role: in 2005, financial services accounted for around 16 per cent of the UK's overseas assets, but 24 per cent of earnings; and mining and quarrying, mainly oil and gas extraction, accounted for $7\frac{1}{2}$ per cent of overseas assets, but 21 per cent of earnings.

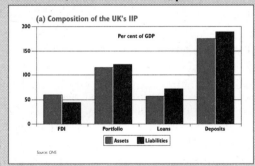

(a) Composition of the UK's IIP

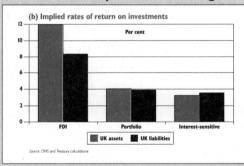

(b) Implied rates of return on investments

Service sector output

B.87   The service sector produces around 75 per cent of UK economic output, a share that has increased continually over the past decade and a half. The service sector as a whole has outperformed the wider economy in each year since 1990, growing by more than 66 per cent during that time. Services make up more than a third of the UK's total exports, a greater proportion than any other G7 economy, and more than double that of Canada, Germany or Japan. In recent years, strong growth in the service sector has been driven by the finance and business services sector, the largest in the UK economy, accounting for around a third of total activity.

B.88   The service sector grew by $3^3/_4$ per cent in 2006, up from 3 per cent in 2005 and above the average for the sector since 2000. Excluding 'government and other services', where the share of public sector activity is high, the service sector grew by $4^1/_4$ per cent in 2006. Growth picked up in the fourth quarter of the year, with activity in wholesale and retail trades expanding at its strongest quarterly rate in almost three years. Private sector business surveys point to continued expansion at similar rates in the first quarter of 2007. For example, monthly indicators of business activity and new business in the service sector compiled by the Chartered Institute of Purchasing and Supply remain well above their long-run averages.

Finance and business services   **B.89**   The finance and business services sector was the main driver of growth in 2006, contributing more than half of the expansion of services output for the second year in succession. Within this sector, the output of other business services, a sector that includes professions ranging from management consultants to private investigators, grew by more than 8 per cent in 2006 as a whole, up from $7^1/_2$ per cent in 2005, with growth strengthening throughout the year.

Distribution   **B.90**   Activity in the distribution sector picked up strongly in the final quarter of 2006, growing by $1^1/_4$ per cent on the previous quarter. On an annual basis, output rebounded from the weakness observed in 2005, to grow by $3^1/_4$ per cent, but remained below the average rate of growth over the past six years, consistent with the more balanced pattern of domestic expenditure seen across the wider economy.

Manufacturing and North Sea output

Manufacturing   **B.91**   Manufacturing accounts for almost 80 per cent of total industrial production and around 14 per cent of whole economy GVA. Manufacturing output grew by $1^1/_2$ per cent in 2006, slightly above the 2006 Pre-Budget Report forecast, buoyed by stronger goods exports to the EU. In particular, production of capital goods grew strongly in 2006, having remained broadly flat in 2005. Monthly private sector business surveys, such as the CBI's *Industrial Trends Survey*, suggest that manufacturing output growth may pick up further in the first quarter of 2007.

North Sea   **B.92**   While manufacturing grew by $1^1/_2$ per cent in 2006, total industrial production output, which includes energy extraction and utilities, was flat, due to an $8^3/_4$ per cent fall in output from the oil and gas sector. A number of temporary factors acted to exacerbate the underlying decline in output from the North Sea. A relatively large new field, 'Buzzard', started production in early 2007, which, along with a number of smaller start-ups in 2007 and 2008, should temporarily boost overall North Sea output.

Independent forecasts

B.93   Since the 2006 Pre-Budget Report, the average of independent forecasts for GDP growth in 2007 has increased from 2.4 per cent to 2.6 per cent. This remains below the Budget forecast range, although some prominent forecasters expect stronger growth than the average: the IMF's latest report on the UK economy, published on 5 March, forecasts growth of 2.9 per cent in 2007, while the Bank of England's February *Inflation Report* forecast, conditioned on market interest rate expectations, showed GDP growth of 3.1 per cent on a year earlier by the fourth quarter of 2007. The latest survey from Consensus Economics[17] shows that the average forecast for GDP growth in 2007 is higher for the UK than for any other G7 economy.

---

[17] *Consensus forecasts*, Consensus Economics Inc., March 2007.

B.94   As with the steady upward shift of the independent average forecast for growth in 2006, the forecast for 2007 has been driven higher by upward revisions to fixed investment growth, from 3.4 per cent at the time of the 2006 Pre-Budget Report to a latest forecast of 4.8 per cent. The average independent GDP growth forecast for 2008 is currently below the Budget forecast range, but one outlier forecast drags down the average, as evidenced by the median forecast of 2.5 per cent being above the mean forecast of 2.3 per cent. In the medium term, independent forecasters expect GDP growth to settle at around 2.6 per cent, in the lower half of the Budget forecast range. In line with the Budget forecast, independent forecasters expect inflation to return to target by the end of 2007 and to remain at target in 2008.

B.95   Treasury forecasts for GDP growth since 1997 have, on average, outperformed the independent consensus. They have also compared well against a sample of forecasters that includes leading international organisations (IMF, OECD, European Commission), research institutes (Oxford Economics, NIESR) and private sector forecasters (Goldman Sachs, HSBC, JP Morgan).[18]

Table B9: Budget and independent[1] forecasts

	Percentage change on a year earlier, unless otherwise stated					
	2007			2008		
	March	**Independent**		**March**	**Independent**	
	Budget	Average	Range	**Budget**	Average	Range
GDP growth	2¾ to 3¼	2.6	1.3 to 3.0	2½ to 3	2.3	−0.3 to 2.9
CPI (Q4)	2	1.9	1.4 to 3.0	2	2.0	1.5 to 2.3
Current account (£ billion)	−37	−36.1	−56.9 to −25.1	−39¼	−37.8	−63.7 to −23.8

[1] 'Forecasts for the UK economy: A comparison of independent forecasts', March 2007.

Forecast issues and risks

B.96   Risks to the Budget 2007 economic forecast appear balanced, given broadly offsetting developments since the 2006 Pre-Budget Report.

Global economy   **B.97**   Growth in the final quarter of 2006 was strong in most of the world's major economies, including the UK, suggesting there is more momentum in these economies, particularly in the euro area, than was apparent at the time of the Pre-Budget Report. Additionally, the strength of growth in Asia, particularly China and India, surprised forecasters once more in 2006, and could do so again in 2007.

B.98   The risk from growing inflationary pressures, noted at the time of the Budget and Pre-Budget Reports in 2006, has yet to recede. G7 economic activity in 2007 is forecast to grow slightly faster than expected at the time of the Pre-Budget Report. Strong growth has been accompanied by increases in core rates of inflation, although they remain low by historical standards. A rise in energy prices, possibly caused by geo-political factors, remains a risk. These developments could prompt G7 central banks to tighten monetary policy further this year. Since the Pre-Budget Report there has been a more marked rise in inflation rates in some emerging markets, notably in India and China, and parts of Latin America and emerging Europe.

---

[18] Treasury analysis based on various issues of *Forecasts for the UK economy: A comparison of independent forecasts*.

B.99   Among the major economies, the US has shown resilience to various shocks over the past four years, but growth could slow further if effects from the weaker housing market were to spill over to the wider economy. In Germany, there is the possibility of a greater than expected impact on domestic final demand following the 3 percentage point increase in VAT in January 2007. However, macroeconomic fundamentals in the euro area have improved, which, coupled with sustained growth momentum, could result in output growth in 2007 that exceeds current expectations.

B.100   Episodes of financial market volatility, such as that experienced in late February and early March this year, represent a further global risk to the outlook. Large and rapid fluctuations in the value of financial assets, possibly reflecting investors' changing attitudes to risk, can have an impact on global growth. These risks may be mitigated to some extent by the development of deeper, more diversified capital markets, and improvements in macroeconomic policy frameworks. In recent years, emerging markets, which tend to be particularly sensitive to developments in global financial markets, have generally improved macroeconomic fundamentals and significantly increased holdings of foreign currency reserves.

B.101   Global current account imbalances remain large. So far the adjustment in some currencies has been orderly, while more recently the balance of world growth has shifted slightly away from the US. However, a disorderly unwinding of these imbalances remains a risk to the global outlook.

B.102   Risks to the multilateral trading system remain, especially from the proliferation of bilateral and regional trade agreements, and increasingly protectionist trade policies. The most powerful signal that can be sent against protectionism is the successful conclusion of the current round of world trade talks. The UK Government continues to work hard with its EU partners, and in the World Trade Organisation, to build on the resumption of full-scale negotiations of the Doha Development Agenda. A firm commitment against protectionism can help to ensure that trade continues to improve living standards across developed and developing economies.

UK economy   **B.103**   A key risk to the UK economic forecast remains the uncertainties over labour market data, and the possibility that if growth in the working-age population has been greater than officially recorded, there may be a greater degree of slack in the economy and thus more scope for growth. The disparities between survey indicators of capacity utilisation and recruitment difficulties, and at different skill levels within the recruitment surveys, add to the uncertainty over how close to trend the economy is currently operating.

B.104   In terms of the components of demand, despite strong growth in consumption at the end of 2006, forecast quarterly consumption growth rates in 2007 have been revised down from the 2006 Pre-Budget Report to reflect developments in interest rates and saving intentions. Risks to the forecast are therefore balanced between the upside risk from recent momentum and the downside risk that developments in households' finances will have a larger than expected impact on consumer spending. While some leading indicators suggest further strength in house price inflation in the short term, house prices remain high in comparison with incomes. The housing market therefore presents upside and downside risks to consumer spending. Business investment ended 2006 with even more momentum than was expected at the time of the Pre-Budget Report. To the extent that internal and external financing conditions remain supportive, and firms' margins recover as input cost pressures ease, there is again scope for investment growth to exceed expectations.

B.105   With inflation expected to remain above target during the first half of 2007, the risk remains that higher rates of actual inflation could feed through to inflation expectations and earnings growth. However, the evidence so far suggests that monetary policy has kept inflation expectations anchored to the inflation target and, while wage settlements growth has picked up a little, there has been no discernable impact on earnings growth.

Table B10: Summary of economic prospects[1]

		Percentage change on a year earlier, unless otherwise stated				
			Forecast[2,3,4]		Average errors from past forecasts[5]	
	2006	2007	2008	2009	2007	2008
Output at constant market prices						
Gross domestic product (GDP)	2¾	2¾ to 3¼	2½ to 3	2½ to 3	¾	½
Manufacturing output	1½	1¾ to 2	1¾ to 2¼	1¾ to 2¼	1¼	1¾
Expenditure components of GDP at constant market prices[6]						
Domestic demand	3	2¾ to 3¼	2½ to 3	2¼ to 2¾	¾	¾
Household consumption[7]	2¼	2¼ to 2¾	2¼ to 2¾	2¼ to 2¾	¾	1
General government consumption	2	2½	2½	2	½	1
Fixed investment	6	6½ to 7	3¼ to 3¾	3¼ to 3¾	2¾	2¼
Change in inventories[8]	¼	−¼ to 0	0	0	¼	¼
Exports of goods and services[9]	11¼	−2½ to −2	4¾ to 5¼	4½ to 5	2¼	3¼
Imports of goods and services[9]	11½	−1¾ to −1½	4¼ to 4¾	4 to 4½	2½	2¾
Exports of goods and services (excluding MTIC)	6¼	5¼ to 5¾	5 to 5½	4½ to 5	–	–
Imports of goods and services (excluding MTIC)	7	5 to 5½	4¼ to 4¾	4 to 4½	–	–
Balance of payments current account						
£ billion	−39¼	−37	−39¼	−42¾	8¾	9¼
Per cent of GDP	−3	−2¾	−2¾	−2¾	¾	¾
Inflation						
CPI (Q4)	2¾	2	2	2	–	–
Producer output prices (Q4)[10]	2	2¼	2	2	1	1½
GDP deflator at market prices	2¼	2¾	2¾	2¾	¼	½
Money GDP at market prices						
£ billion	1288¼	1361 to 1365	1432 to 1443	1506 to 1526	9	8
Percentage change	5¼	5½ to 6	5¼ to 5¾	5¼ to 5¾	¾	½

[1] The forecast is consistent with output, income and expenditure data for the fourth quarter of 2006, released by the Office for National Statistics on 23 February 2007. See also footnote 1 on the first page of this chapter.

[2] All growth rates in tables throughout this chapter are rounded to the nearest ¼ percentage point.

[3] As in previous Budget and Pre-Budget Reports, the economic forecast is presented in terms of forecast ranges, based on alternative assumptions about the supply-side performance of the economy. The mid-points of the forecast ranges are anchored around the neutral assumption for the trend rate of output growth of 2¾ per cent. The figures at the lower end of the ranges are consistent with the deliberately cautious assumption of trend growth used as the basis for projecting the public finances, which is a ¼ percentage point below the neutral assumption.

[4] The size of the growth ranges for GDP components may differ from those for total GDP growth because of rounding and the assumed invariance of the levels of public spending within the forecast ranges.

[5] Average absolute errors for current year and year-ahead projections made in spring forecasts over the past 10 years. The average errors for the current account are calculated as a percent of GDP, with £ billion figures calculated by scaling the errors by forecast money GDP in 2007 and 2008.

[6] Further detail on the expenditure components of GDP is given in Table B11.

[7] Includes households and non-profit institutions serving households.

[8] Contribution to GDP growth, percentage points.

[9] Figures up to and including 2007 are distorted by MTIC.

[10] Excluding excise duties.

Table B11: Gross domestic product and its components

		£ billion chained volume measures at market prices, seasonally adjusted									
		Household consumption[1]	General government consumption	Fixed investment	Change in inventories	Domestic demand[2]	Exports of goods and services	Total final expenditure	*Less* imports of goods and services	*Plus* statistical discrepancy[3]	GDP at market prices
2006		775.3	252.2	207.6	5.6	1240.8	359.0	1599.9	400.6	1.5	1200.7
2007		793.3 to 795.7	258.2	221.2 to 221.9	3.7 to 4.5	1276.4 to 1280.3	350.4 to 351.5	1626.9 to 1631.8	393.6 to 394.8	1.8	1235.1 to 1238.9
2008		810.2 to 816.7	264.4	228.6 to 230.4	3.7 to 5.8	1306.9 to 1317.3	367.5 to 370.4	1674.4 to 1687.7	410.4 to 413.7	1.8	1265.7 to 1275.8
2009		828.8 to 839.4	269.8	235.8 to 238.9	3.5 to 7.0	1337.9 to 1355.1	383.6 to 388.5	1721.5 to 1743.6	426.8 to 432.3	1.8	1296.5 to 1313.1
2006	1st half	384.9	125.5	101.9	4.1	616.5	189.5	806.0	210.5	0.6	596.1
	2nd half	390.4	126.8	105.7	1.5	624.3	169.5	793.9	190.1	0.9	604.6
2007	1st half	394.8 to 395.5	128.5	109.2 to 109.4	1.7 to 1.9	634.2 to 635.4	172.8 to 173.2	807.1 to 808.5	194.4 to 194.7	0.9	613.6 to 614.7
	2nd half	398.5 to 400.2	129.7	112.0 to 112.5	2.0 to 2.6	642.2 to 645.0	177.6 to 178.3	819.8 to 823.3	199.2 to 200.0	0.9	621.5 to 624.1
2008	1st half	402.7 to 405.4	131.4	113.6 to 114.4	2.0 to 2.9	649.7 to 654.1	181.8 to 183.0	831.5 to 837.0	203.3 to 204.7	0.9	629.1 to 633.3
	2nd half	407.5 to 411.3	133.0	115.0 to 116.0	1.7 to 2.9	657.2 to 663.3	185.7 to 187.4	842.9 to 850.6	207.1 to 209.0	0.9	636.7 to 642.5
2009	1st half	412.1 to 416.9	134.3	116.9 to 118.2	1.7 to 3.3	665.0 to 672.7	189.7 to 191.9	854.7 to 864.7	211.3 to 213.7	0.9	644.3 to 651.8
	2nd half	416.6 to 422.5	135.5	119.0 to 120.6	1.8 to 3.7	672.9 to 682.4	193.8 to 196.6	866.7 to 879.0	215.5 to 218.6	0.9	652.1 to 661.3
		Percentage changes on previous year[4,5]									
2006		2¼	2	6	¼	3	11¼	4¾	11½	¼	2¾
2007		2¼ to 2¾	2½	6½ to 7	0	2¾ to 3¼	−2½ to −2	1¾ to 2	−1¾ to −1½	0	2¾ to 3¼
2008		2¼ to 2¾	2½	3¼ to 3¾	0	2½ to 3	4¾ to 5¼	3 to 3½	4¼ to 4¾	0	2½ to 3
2009		2¼ to 2¾	2	3¼ to 3¾	0	2¼ to 2¾	4½ to 5	2¾ to 3¼	4 to 4½	0	2½ to 3

[1] *Includes households and non-profit institutions serving households.*

[2] *Also includes acquisitions less disposals of valuables.*

[3] *Expenditure adjustment.*

[4] *For change in inventories and the statistical discrepancy, changes are expressed as a per cent of GDP.*

[5] *Growth ranges for GDP components do not necessarily sum to the ½ percentage point ranges for GDP growth because of rounding and the assumed invariance of the levels of public spending within the forecast ranges.*

C THE PUBLIC FINANCES

> The Budget 2007 projections for the public finances show that the Government is meeting its strict fiscal rules over the economic cycle:
>
> - the current budget since the start of the current economic cycle in 1997-98 shows an annual average surplus up to 2006-07 of 0.1 per cent of GDP, showing the Government is meeting the golden rule on the basis of cautious assumptions. Beyond the end of the current economic cycle the current budget moves clearly into surplus; and
>
> - public sector net debt is projected to be low and stable over the projection period, stabilising at under 39 per cent of GDP, below the 40 per cent ceiling set by the sustainable investment rule.

INTRODUCTION

C.1   Chapter 2 describes the Government's fiscal policy framework and shows how the projections of the public finances presented in this Budget are consistent with meeting the fiscal rules. This chapter explains the latest outturns and the fiscal projections in more detail. It includes:

- five-year projections of the current budget and public sector net debt, the key aggregates for assessing performance against the golden rule and the sustainable investment rule, respectively;

- projections of public sector net borrowing, the fiscal aggregate relevant to assessing the impact of fiscal policy on the economy;

- projections of the cyclically-adjusted fiscal balances; and

- detailed analyses of the outlook for government receipts and expenditure.

C.2   The fiscal projections continue to be based on deliberately cautious key assumptions audited by the National Audit Office (NAO).

MEETING THE FISCAL RULES

C.3   Table C1 shows five-year projections for the current budget and public sector net debt, the key aggregates for assessing performance against the golden rule and the sustainable investment rule. Outturns and projections of other important measures of the public finances, including net borrowing and cyclically-adjusted fiscal balances, are also shown.

C.4   As explained in Chapter 2, the Government's judgement is that the current economic cycle started in 1997-98. Based on the assumptions used in these projections, the economy is expected to have returned to trend in early 2007.

Table C1: Summary of public sector finances

	Per cent of GDP							
	Outturn		Estimate		Projections			
	2004-05	2005-06	2006-07	2007-08	2008-09	2009-10	2010-11	2011-12
Fairness and prudence								
Surplus on current budget	-1.6	-1.2	-0.7	-0.3	0.2	0.4	0.6	0.8
Average surplus since 1997-1998	0.3	0.2	0.1	0.0	0.1	0.1	0.1	0.2
Cyclically-adjusted surplus on current budget	-1.5	-1.0	-0.5	-0.3	0.2	0.4	0.6	0.8
Long-term sustainability								
Public sector net debt[1]	35.0	36.5	37.2	38.2	38.5	38.8	38.8	38.6
Core debt[1]	34.5	35.8	36.4	37.4	37.7	38.0	38.1	38.0
Net worth[2]	28.8	27.0	25.7	24.9	24.9	24.5	24.4	24.4
Primary balance	-1.7	-1.4	-1.0	-0.8	-0.5	-0.3	0.0	0.2
Economic impact								
Net investment	1.7	1.8	2.0	2.1	2.2	2.2	2.2	2.2
Public sector net borrowing (PSNB)	3.3	3.0	2.7	2.4	2.0	1.8	1.6	1.4
Cyclically-adjusted PSNB	3.2	2.8	2.5	2.4	2.0	1.8	1.6	1.4
Financing								
Central government net cash requirement	3.2	3.3	2.8	2.7	2.0	2.2	1.8	1.8
Public sector net cash requirement	3.2	3.2	2.6	2.6	1.9	2.1	1.6	1.7
European commitments								
Treaty deficit[3]	3.2	2.9	2.8	2.5	2.1	1.9	1.7	1.5
Cyclically-adjusted Treaty deficit [3]	3.1	2.7	2.6	2.5	2.1	1.9	1.7	1.5
Treaty debt ratio[4]	40.5	42.7	43.5	44.3	44.4	44.5	44.4	44.1
Memo: Output gap	0.0	-0.5	-0.2	0.0	0.0	0.0	0.0	0.0

[1] Debt at end March; GDP centred on end March.

[2] Estimate at end December; GDP centred on end December.

[3] General government net borrowing on a Maastricht basis.

[4] General government gross debt measures on a Maastricht basis.

The golden rule **C.5** The projections show that the Government is meeting the golden rule, on the basis of cautious assumptions, with an average annual surplus on the current budget over this economic cycle of 0.1 per cent of GDP. On this basis, and based on cautious assumptions, the Government is meeting the golden rule and there is a margin against the golden rule of £11 billion in this cycle.

C.6 Based on cautious assumptions, the Government will continue to meet the golden rule after the end of this economic cycle with the current budget returning to surplus by 2008-09.

The sustainable **C.7** The sustainable investment rule is also forecast to be met over the current economic **investment rule** cycle. In 1996-97, public sector net debt stood at almost 44 per cent of GDP. The tough decisions on taxation and expenditure taken by the Government, including the decision to use the proceeds from the auction of spectrum licences to repay debt, reduced debt to about 30 per cent of GDP by the end of 2001-02. It is now projected to rise slowly, as the Government borrows modestly to fund increased investment in public services, rising from 37.2 per cent of GDP in 2006-07 to 38.8 per cent in 2010-11, before falling back to 38.6 per cent by 2011-12. The projections for core debt, which exclude the estimated impact of the economic cycle, remain below 38.8 per cent of GDP in the projection period. This is consistent with the fiscal rules, and with the key objective of intergenerational fairness that underpins the fiscal framework.

Net worth **C.8** Net worth is the approximate stock counterpart of the current budget. Modest falls in net worth are expected for the remainder of the projection period from the high level of 28.8 per cent of GDP in 2004-05. At present, net worth is not used as a key indicator of the public finances, mainly due to the difficulties involved in accurately measuring many government assets and liabilities.

C.9 Chart C1 shows public sector net debt and net worth as a per cent of GDP from 1993-94 to 2011-12.

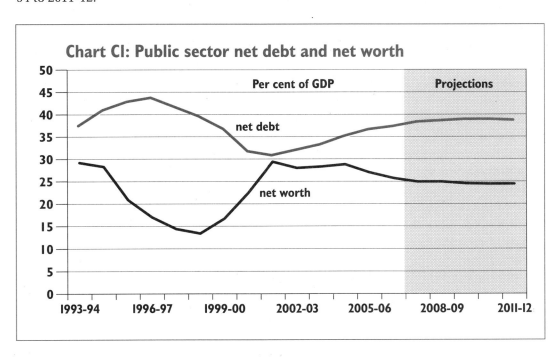

Net investment **C.10** As a result of decisions taken in the 2004 Spending Review public sector net investment is projected to rise from 1¼ per cent of GDP in 2003-04 to 2¼ per cent from 2008-09 onwards. This increase is sustainable and fully consistent with the Government's long-term approach and the fiscal rules, since net debt is being held at a stable and prudent level, below 40 per cent of GDP.

Net borrowing **C.11** Public sector net borrowing has fallen in every year since 2004-05 and is expected to continue to fall in each year of the forecast period, from 3.0 per cent of GDP in 2005-06 to 2.7 per cent in 2006-07, and then to a level of 1.4 per cent of GDP by 2011-12.

Financing **C.12** The central government net cash requirement was 3.3 per cent of GDP in 2005-06. It is projected to fall over the forecast period, reaching a level of 1.8 per cent of GDP by 2011-12.

European **C.13** Table C1 shows the Treaty measures of debt and deficit used for the purposes of the
commitments Excessive Deficit Procedure – Article 104 of the Treaty. The 2007 Budget projections meet the EU Treaty reference value for general government gross debt (60 per cent of GDP) by a considerable margin. The Treaty deficit is expected to be 2.8 per cent of GDP in 2006-07 and is forecast to fall further over the projection period. In addition, the cyclically adjusted level of general government net borrowing is 2.6 per cent of GDP in 2006-07 and falls throughout the projection period, reaching 1.5 per cent of GDP by 2011-12. The projections are therefore consistent with the Government's prudent interpretation of the Stability and Growth Pact.

CHANGES TO THE FISCAL BALANCES

C.14   Table C2 compares the latest estimates for the main fiscal balances with those in Budget 2006 and the 2006 Pre-Budget Report.

Table C2: Fiscal balances compared with Budget 2006 and the 2006 Pre-Budget Report

	Outturn[1]	Estimate[2]	Projections				
	2005-06	2006-07	2007-08	2008-09	2009-10	2010-11	2011-12
Surplus on current budget (£ billion)							
Budget 2006	-11.4	-7.1	1	7	10	12	
Effect of revisions and forecasting changes	-3.7	-1.0	-5	-5 1/2	-5	-4	
Effect of discretionary changes	0.0	0.2	2	2 1/2	2	2	
2006 Pre-Budget Report	-15.1	-7.9	-1	4	7	10	14
Effect of revisions and forecasting changes	0.1	-1.6	-2 1/2	-1 1/2	-1 1/2	-1 1/2	-2
Effect of discretionary changes	0.0	0.0	- 1/2	1/2	0	1/2	1/2
Budget 2007	**-15.0**	**-9.5**	**-4**	**3**	**6**	**9**	**13**
Net borrowing (£ billion)							
Budget 2006	37.1	35.8	30	25	24	23	
Changes to current budget	3.7	0.8	3	3	3	1 1/2	
Changes to net investment	-3.3	0.1	-1	- 1/2	-1	-1	
2006 Pre-Budget Report	37.5	36.8	31	27	26	24	22
Changes to current budget	-0.1	1.6	3	1 1/2	1 1/2	1	1 1/2
Changes to net investment	0.3	-3.4	- 1/2	1	1	0	0
Budget 2007	**37.8**	**35.0**	**34**	**30**	**28**	**26**	**24**
Cyclically-adjusted surplus on current budget (per cent of GDP)							
Budget 2006	-0.3	0.4	0.7	0.7	0.7	0.8	
2006 Pre-Budget Report	-1.0	-0.4	-0.1	0.3	0.5	0.6	0.8
Budget 2007	**-1.0**	**-0.5**	**-0.3**	**0.2**	**0.4**	**0.6**	**0.8**
Cyclically-adjusted net borrowing (per cent of GDP)							
Budget 2006	2.4	1.9	1.6	1.6	1.6	1.5	
2006 Pre-Budget Report	2.8	2.6	2.2	1.9	1.7	1.5	1.3
Budget 2007	**2.8**	**2.5**	**2.4**	**2.0**	**1.8**	**1.6**	**1.4**
Net debt (per cent of GDP)							
Budget 2006	36.4	37.5	38.1	38.3	38.4	38.4	
2006 Pre-Budget Report	36.4	37.5	38.2	38.6	38.7	38.7	38.5
Budget 2007	**36.5**	**37.2**	**38.2**	**38.5**	**38.8**	**38.8**	**38.6**

[1] The 2005-06 figures were estimates in Budget 2006.
[2] The 2006-07 figures were projections in Budget 2006.

Changes between Budget 2006 and the 2006 Pre-Budget Report   **C.15**   In the 2006 Pre-Budget Report, the current budget was revised due to a combination of expenditure and receipts effects. Expenditure was revised up in every year of the projection period. Receipts were revised up in 2006-07 and, mainly due to lower projections of North Sea receipts, down from 2007-08 onwards.

C.16   Overall, the current budget was revised from a deficit of £7.1 billion to a deficit of £7.9 billion in 2006-07. In 2007-08 the deficit was £1 billion compared with a surplus of £1 billion in the Budget 2006 projections. The current budget was projected to return to surplus in 2008-09.

C.17 Public sector net investment was revised down by £3.3 billion in 2005-06, was broadly unchanged in 2006-07, and was slightly lower for subsequent years. These reductions in projected net investment partially offset the reductions in the current budget, but overall net borrowing was revised up.

Changes between the 2006 Pre-Budget Report and Budget 2007 **C.18** The estimated outturn for the current budget in 2006-07 is a deficit of £9.5 billion, compared with a deficit of £7.9 billion projected in the 2006 Pre-Budget Report. The current budget has been revised down by £3 billion compared to the 2006 Pre-Budget Report to a deficit of £4 billion in 2007-08. The downward revisions become smaller in later years, as the current budget returns towards previously projected levels.

C.19 The revisions to the current budget are due to a combination of expenditure and receipts effects. Expenditure is higher in 2007-08 and all subsequent years. Lower than expected North Sea revenues more than account for the shortfall in forecast receipts, before discretionary measures, relative to the 2006 Pre-Budget Report.

C.20 Net investment in 2006-07 has been revised from £28.9 billion at the 2006 Pre-Budget Report to £25.5 billion. This is partly due to departmental underspends against capital budgets and partly because of changes in the treatment of Nigerian debt changes in write-off.

C.21 Discretionary changes since the 2006 Pre-Budget Report include a major package of reforms to the corporate tax system, simplification of the income tax system including removing the starting rate of tax and cutting the basic rate, reforms to tax credits, restricting the tax relief available on empty commercial properties, and other policy decisions. They also include measures to tackle climate change, measures to tackle tax fraud and avoidance, and resetting the AME margin.

FORECAST DIFFERENCES AND RISKS

C.22 The fiscal balances represent the difference between two large aggregates of expenditure and receipts, and forecasts are inevitably subject to wide margins of uncertainty. Over the past ten years, the average absolute difference between year-ahead forecasts of net borrowing and subsequent outturns has been about 1 per cent of GDP. This difference tends to grow as the forecast horizon lengthens. A full account of differences between the projections made in Budget 2004 and Budget 2005, and the subsequent outturns is provided in the *End of year fiscal report*, published alongside the 2006 Pre-Budget Report.

C.23 As explained in Chapter B, the Budget 2007 economic forecast is little changed from the 2006 Pre-Budget Report. UK GDP is expected to grow by $2^3/_4$ to $3^1/_4$ per cent in 2007. Growth is expected to remain close to trend at $2^1/_2$ to 3 per cent a year to the end of the projection period. The rebalancing of domestic demand already evident during 2006 is expected to continue to a somewhat greater degree than was envisaged in the 2006 Pre-Budget Report forecast. Private consumption growth is expected to moderate as recent interest rate rises feed through to disposable income growth and households' desire to save, while business investment growth, which has surprised on the upside recently, is expected to carry some of its recent momentum into 2007.

C.24 Risks to the Budget 2007 economic forecast appear balanced, given broadly offsetting developments since the 2006 Pre-Budget Report. Risks to the consumption forecast are balanced between the upside risk from recent momentum and the downside risk that developments in interest rates and saving intentions will have a larger than expected impact on consumer spending. In terms of business investment, to the extent that internal and external financing conditions remain supportive, and firms' margins recover as input cost pressures ease, there is scope for growth to exceed expectations. With inflation expected to remain above target during the first half of 2007, a risk remains that higher rates of actual inflation could feed through to inflation expectations and earnings growth, although the available evidence suggests there has been no discernable impact on earnings growth thus far.

C.25   A further important source of potential error results from misjudging the position of the economy in relation to trend output. To minimise this risk, the robustness of the projections is tested against an alternative scenario in which the level of trend output is assumed to be one percentage point lower than in the central case. Chart C2 illustrates the Budget projection for this cautious case.

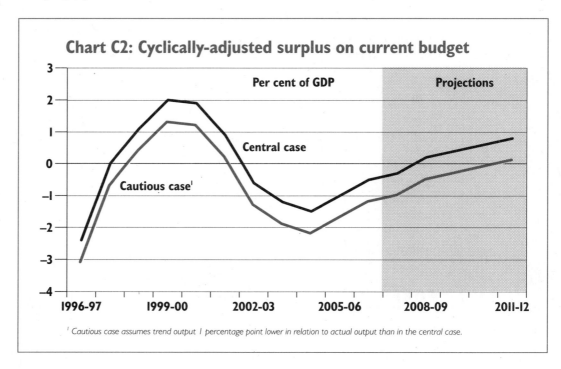

Chart C2: Cyclically-adjusted surplus on current budget

¹ Cautious case assumes trend output 1 percentage point lower in relation to actual output than in the central case.

ASSUMPTIONS

C.26   The fiscal projections are based on the following assumptions:

- the economy follows the path described in Chapter B. The fiscal projections assume that trend growth will be 2½ per cent to 2011-12. In the interests of caution, these projections continue to be based on the assumption that trend output growth will be ¼ percentage point lower than the Government's neutral view;

- there are no tax or spending policy changes beyond those announced in or before this Budget, and the indexation of rates and allowances. Consistent with the *Code for fiscal stability*, the forecast does not take account of measures proposed in this Budget for consultation or other proposals where final decisions have yet to be taken;

- firm Departmental Expenditure Limits (DELs) are as set out in the 2004 Spending Review to 2007-08, adjusted for the impact of policy decisions and reclassifications;

- total Annually Managed Expenditure (AME) programmes to 2007-08 have been reviewed in this Budget.

- although DEL and AME totals for 2008-09 onwards have not yet been determined, Budget 2007 sets firm overall spending limits for the 2007 Comprehensive Spending Review (CSR 07) period. Taking account of time-limited items announced in this Budget, public sector current expenditure is forecast to grow at 2.0 per cent in real terms in 2008-09 , and by 1.9 per cent in 2009-10 and 2010-11, unchanged from the 2006 Pre-Budget Report. This means that, on average, public sector current expenditure is forecast to grow by $2^1/_4$ per cent per year in real terms between 2006-07 and the end of the CSR 07 period. Public sector current expenditure is assumed to grow by 2.0 per cent in real terms in 2011-12;

- the capital expenditure envelope for the CSR 07 period is fixed, based on public sector net investment at $2^1/_4$ per cent of GDP over the period, unchanged from the 2006 Pre-Budget Report. Net investment remains at $2^1/_4$ per cent of GDP in the spending projection for 2011-12; and

- as a result of these decisions on the firm overall limits for current and capital expenditure in the CSR 07 period, Total Managed Expenditure (TME) grows by 2.0 per cent a year on average over the CSR. In each year of the CSR 07 period, TME as a per cent of GDP is broadly unchanged from the 2006 Pre-Budget Report.

Table C3: Economic assumptions for the public finance projections

| | Percentage changes on previous year | | | | | | |
| | Outturn | Estimate | | Projections | | | |
	2005-06	2006-07	2007-08	2008-09	2009-10	2010-11	2011-12
Output (GDP)	2	3	2 3/4	2 1/2	2 1/2	2 1/2	2 1/2
Prices							
CPI	2	2 1/2	2	2	2	2	2
GDP deflator	2	2 1/2	2 3/4	2 3/4	2 3/4	2 3/4	2 3/4
RPI[1] (September)	2 3/4	3 1/2	3 1/2	2 3/4	2 3/4	2 3/4	2 3/4
Rossi[2] (September)	2	3	2 1/4	2 1/2	2 1/2	2 1/2	2 1/4
Money GDP[3] (£ billion)	1,240	1,306	1,378	1,450	1,525	1,604	1,687

[1] Used for revalorising excise duties in current year and uprating income tax allowances and bands and certain social security benefits in the following year.

[2] RPI excluding housing costs, used for uprating certain social security benefits.

[3] Not seasonally adjusted.

C.27 The estimates for 2006-07 are based on all available data within the Treasury and other government departments involved in producing tax and spending forecasts.

The audited **C.28** The key assumptions underlying the fiscal projections are audited by the National
assumptions Audit Office (NAO) under the three-year rolling review process. Details of the audited assumptions are given in Box C1.

C.29 Consistent with the *Code for fiscal stability*, the projections do not take account of decisions where the impact cannot yet be quantified, of measures proposed in this Budget, or where final decisions have yet to be taken. These include:

- further extensions to maternity and paternity leave; and

- further reforms to incapacity benefit.

C.30   The Comptroller and Auditor General has audited the assumptions for forecasting VAT revenues. He concluded that the use of the VAT gap assumption had resulted in forecasts that were cautious in three of the four years of the rolling review period since Budget 2003, and cautious over the period as a whole. The Comptroller and Auditor General was not able to draw a conclusion on the reasonableness of the allowance made in the VAT forecast for the impact of the 2002 VAT Compliance Strategy due to difficulties in identifying the separate contributions of the underlying trend in the VAT gap, the Compliance Strategy, and the impact of legislative measures on VAT receipts.

C.31   The Treasury has adopted a new assumption in Budget 2007 for forecasting VAT receipts, set out in Box C1. HMRC now considers the measures in the original VAT Compliance Strategy to have reached a broadly steady state. Although HMRC is continuing to strengthen its VAT compliance activities, it no longer proposes to make a specific downward adjustment to the VAT gap for compliance related activities in the Budget 2007 assumption.

C.32   The new assumption is based on the 'underlying' VAT gap, which builds in adjustments, where applicable, to take account of the impact of large one-off VAT payments and repayments that relate to past liabilities. This will allow for timing differences that in the past have contributed to volatility in the VAT gap and to errors in the forecast. The Comptroller and Auditor General has audited the revised assumption and concluded that it is a reasonable one for the purposes of forecasting future VAT revenues, and that it will be cautious to the extent that historical trends in the VAT gap are a good indicator of future trends.

C.33   In this Budget, the assumption for forecasting tobacco revenues, that the illicit market share is set at least at the latest published outturn level, has been audited by the Comptroller and Auditor General under the rolling review process for the period since Budget 2003. Due to the absence of firm data for the illicit market share for 2005-06 and 2006-07, it has not been possible to reach a conclusion for the rolling review period as a whole. The Comptroller and Auditor General has therefore reviewed the evidence for 2003-04 and 2004-05, concluding that the assumption has proved cautious in these years.

C.34   Following the agreed postponement of the rolling review process at Budget 2006, HMRC agreed to undertake a review of the process by which the illicit market share was calculated. This work concluded that the underlying data used was no longer robust enough to produce the point estimate of the illicit market share required for the audited assumption. An alternative forecasting methodology was proposed based on an assumption on duty paid clearances, adjusted for timing effects. The Comptroller and Auditor General has audited the revised assumption and concluded that it is a reasonable one, and though there are a number of uncertainties as to how cautious the assumption will be in practice, it introduces an element of caution into the forecast. This revised assumption is set out in Box C1.

C.35   Under the rolling review process, for Budget 2007 the Comptroller and Auditor General has also audited the assumptions relating to factor income shares and government financing. In both cases the review concluded that the assumptions were reasonable and continue to be so for the future.

C.36   The Comptroller and Auditor General reviewed the yield from the Budget 2004 compliance package for direct tax and national insurance contributions and found that the estimated yield from the package was greater than the Treasury's forecasts, and that the forecasts were therefore cautious.

Box C1: Key assumptions audited by the NAO[a]

Trend GDP growth[e]	$2^{1}/_{2}$ per cent a year.
Dating of the cycle[c]	The end date of the previous economic cycle was in the first half of 1997.
Privatisation proceeds[d]	Credit is taken only for proceeds from sales that have been announced.
UK claimant unemployment[b]	Rising slowly to 0.95 million in 2007-08, from recent levels of 0.93 million.[g]
Interest rates[d]	3-month market rates change in line with market expectations (as of 9 March).
Equity prices[e]	FTSE All-share index rises from 3244 (close 9 March) in line with money GDP.
VAT[f]	The underlying VAT gap will rise by 0.5 percentage points per year from the estimated outturn for the current year.
Consistency of price indices[e]	Projections of price indices used to project the public finances are consistent with CPI.
Composition of GDP[f]	Shares of labour income and profits in national income are broadly constant in the medium term.
Funding[f]	Funding assumptions used to project debt interest are consistent with the forecast level of government borrowing and with financing policy.
Oil prices[c]	$58.1 a barrel in 2007, the average for the three months to March 9, and then constant in real terms. This is lower than the $58.6 average of independent forecasts for 2007.
Tobacco[f]	The underlying level of duty paid consumption of cigarettes will be set at least three per cent per year lower than the estimated outturn for the current year.
Budget 2004 compliance and enforcement package[f]	The projected revenue impacts of the Budget 2004 compliance and enforcement package will, for the purposes of the fiscal projections, be reasonable and cautious.

[a] For details of all NAO audits before the 2003 Pre-Budget Report see Budget 2003, 9 April 2003 (HC500).

[b] Audit of Assumptions for Budget 2005, 16 March 2005 (HC452).

[c] Audit of Assumptions for the 2005 Pre-Budget Report, 5 December 2005 (HC707).

[d] Audit of Assumptions for Budget 2006, 16 March 2005 (HC452).

[e] Audit of Assumptions for the 2006 Pre-Budget Report, 5 December 2005 (HC125).

[f] Audit of Assumptions for Budget 2007, 21 March 2007 (HC393).

[g] This is a cautious assumption based on the average of external forecasts and is not the Treasury's central economic forecast.

FISCAL AGGREGATES

C.37   Tables C4 and C5 provide more detail on the projections for the current and capital budgets.

Table C4: Current and capital budgets

	£ billion						
	Outturn	Estimate		Projections			
	2005-06	2006-07	2007-08	2008-09	2009-10	2010-11	2011-12
Current budget							
Current receipts	485.7	517.2	553	586	616	648	682
Current expenditure	484.2	509.0	539	564	590	617	646
Depreciation	16.5	17.7	19	20	21	22	23
Surplus on current budget	**-15.0**	**-9.5**	**-4**	**3**	**6**	**9**	**13**
Capital budget							
Gross investment[1]	39.2	43.2	48	52	55	57	60
Less depreciation	-16.5	-17.7	-19	-20	-21	-22	-23
Net investment	22.7	25.5	29	32	34	35	37
Net borrowing	**37.8**	**35.0**	**34**	**30**	**28**	**26**	**24**
Public sector net debt - end year	**463.4**	**500.0**	**540**	**572**	**607**	**638**	**668**
Memos:							
Treaty deficit[2]	35.8	36.3	35	31	29	27	25
Treaty debt[3]	529.2	567.9	611	644	679	712	744

[1] Includes asset sales, for a breakdown see table C16.
[2] General government net borrowing on a Maastricht basis.
[3] General government gross debt on a Maastricht basis.

Table C5: Current and capital budgets

	Per cent of GDP						
	Outturn	Estimate		Projections			
	2005-06	2006-07	2007-08	2008-09	2009-10	2010-11	2011-12
Current budget							
Current receipts	39.2	39.6	40.1	40.4	40.4	40.4	40.4
Current expenditure	39.1	39.0	39.1	38.9	38.7	38.5	38.3
Depreciation	1.3	1.4	1.4	1.4	1.4	1.4	1.4
Surplus on current budget	**-1.2**	**-0.7**	**-0.3**	**0.2**	**0.4**	**0.6**	**0.8**
Capital budget							
Gross investment[1]	3.2	3.3	3.5	3.6	3.6	3.5	3.5
Less depreciation	-1.3	-1.4	-1.4	-1.4	-1.4	-1.4	-1.4
Net investment	1.8	2.0	2.1	2.2	2.2	2.2	2.2
Net borrowing	**3.0**	**2.7**	**2.4**	**2.0**	**1.8**	**1.6**	**1.4**
Public sector net debt - end year	**36.5**	**37.2**	**38.2**	**38.5**	**38.8**	**38.8**	**38.6**
Memos:							
Treaty deficit[2]	2.9	2.8	2.5	2.1	1.9	1.7	1.5
Treaty debt ratio[3]	42.7	43.5	44.3	44.4	44.5	44.4	44.1

[1] Includes asset sales, for a breakdown see table C16.
[2] General government net borrowing on a Maastricht basis.
[3] General government gross debt on a Maastricht basis.

C.38   Following a deficit of 3 per cent of GDP in 1996-97, current budget surpluses of more than 2 per cent were recorded in 1999-2000 and 2000-01. These surpluses allowed the Government to use fiscal policy to support monetary policy during the economic slowdown in 2001 and 2002, and as a result the current budget moved into deficit. The current budget is expected to remain in deficit until 2007-08 and then move back into surplus in 2008-09, with increasingly larger surpluses in later years, reaching 0.8 per cent of GDP in 2011-12.

C.39   The current budget surplus is equal to public sector current receipts less public sector current expenditure and depreciation. The reasons for changes in receipts and current expenditure are explained in later sections.

C.40   Table C4 also shows that net investment is projected to increase throughout the projection period from £22.7 billion in 2005-06 to £37 billion by 2011-12 as the Government seeks to rectify historical underinvestment in public infrastructure. These increases are sustainable and the Government will still be able to meet its strict fiscal rules, as debt is being held below 39 per cent of GDP, within the 40 per cent limit imposed by the sustainable investment rule.

RECEIPTS

C.41   This section looks in detail at the projections for public sector receipts. It begins by analysing the main determinants of changes in the overall projections since the 2006 Pre-Budget Report, before looking in detail at changes in the projections of individual tax receipts. Finally, it provides updated forecasts for the tax-GDP ratios.

Changes in total receipts since the 2006 Pre-Budget Report

C.42   Total current receipts in 2006-07 are estimated to grow by 6.6 per cent on 2005-06, only slightly below the growth of 6.8 per cent in the 2006 Pre-Budget Report projection, and in line with the growth in provisional outturns for the first 11 months of 2006-07. Table C6 provides a detailed breakdown of the main factors that have led to changes in the overall projections since the 2006 Pre-Budget Report.

Table C6: Changes in current receipts since the 2006 Pre-Budget Report

	£ billion					
	Estimate	**Projections**				
	2006-07	**2007-08**	**2008-09**	**2009-10**	**2010-11**	**2011-12**
Effect on receipts of non-discretionary changes in:						
North Sea taxes	-1 1/2	-2 1/2	-2 1/2	-2 1/2	-2	-1 1/2
Other forecasting changes	1/2	2	1 1/2	1	1	1
Total before discretionary changes[1]	**- 1/2**	**- 1/2**	**-1**	**-1 1/2**	**-1**	**-1**
Discretionary changes[1]	0	0	1 1/2	1 1/2	2	2
Total change[2]	**- 1/2**	**-1**	**0**	**0**	**1**	**1 1/2**

[1] Includes measures announced since the 2006 Pre-Budget Report.

[2] Total may not sum due to rounding.

North Sea taxes **C.43** The impacts on North Sea revenues from changes in the dollar oil price, the dollar-sterling exchange rate, production, and capital and operating expenditure are analysed later in this chapter.

Other forecasting **C.44** A large number of different factors contribute to other forecasting changes and **changes** together are expected to increase current receipts by an average of about £1 billion per year to the end of the projection period.

Tax by tax analysis

C.45 Table C7 shows the changes to the projections of individual taxes since Budget 2006 and the 2006 Pre-Budget Report. Table C8 contains updated projections for the main components of public sector receipts for 2005-06, 2006-07 and 2007-08.

Table C7: Changes in current receipts by tax since Budget 2006 and the 2006 Pre-Budget Report

	£ billion			
	Budget 2006		2006 PBR	
	2006-07	2007-08	2006-07	2007-08
Income tax (gross of tax credits)	2.9	3.1	0.9	1.2
Income tax credits	0.0	0.0	0.0	0.0
National insurance contributions	-1.6	0.7	-0.5	0.9
Non-North Sea corporation tax [1]	-2.6	-2.2	-1.9	-1.4
North Sea revenues	-1.2	-5.5	-1.3	-2.7
Capital taxes [2]	0.1	0.4	-0.1	-0.3
Stamp duty	1.2	1.0	0.6	0.6
Value added tax	0.9	-0.6	1.2	-0.1
Excise duties [3]	-0.5	-0.1	0.0	-0.2
Other taxes and royalties [4]	0.1	1.1	-0.2	-0.1
Net taxes and national insurance contributions	**-0.8**	**-2.1**	**-1.4**	**-2.3**
Other receipts and accounting adjustments	1.6	1.8	0.8	1.5
Current receipts	**0.8**	**-0.2**	**-0.7**	**-0.8**

[1] National accounts measure: gross of enhanced and payable tax credits.

[2] Capital gains tax and inheritance tax.

[3] Fuel, alcohol and tobacco duties.

[4] Includes business rates, council tax and money paid into the National Lottery Distribution Fund, as well as other central government taxes.

Table C8: Current receipts

	£ billion		
	Outturn 2005-06	Estimate 2006-07	Projection 2007-08
HM Revenue and Customs			
Income tax (gross of tax credits)	135.0	146.9	156.9
Income tax credits	-4.5	-4.7	-4.4
National insurance contributions	85.5	88.0	95.1
Value added tax	72.9	77.3	80.0
Corporation tax[1]	42.4	44.9	50.0
Corporation tax credits[2]	-0.5	-0.5	-0.5
Petroleum revenue tax	2.0	2.2	1.6
Fuel duties	23.4	23.6	25.1
Capital gains tax	3.0	3.9	4.6
Inheritance tax	3.3	3.6	4.0
Stamp duties	10.9	13.4	14.3
Tobacco duties	8.0	8.1	8.1
Spirits duties	2.3	2.2	2.3
Wine duties	2.3	2.4	2.5
Beer and cider duties	3.2	3.3	3.4
Betting and gaming duties	1.4	1.4	1.4
Air passenger duty	0.9	1.0	2.1
Insurance premium tax	2.3	2.3	2.4
Landfill tax	0.7	0.8	0.9
Climate change levy	0.7	0.7	0.7
Aggregates levy	0.3	0.3	0.3
Customs duties and levies	2.3	2.3	2.4
Total HMRC	**398.0**	**423.6**	**453.4**
Vehicle excise duties	5.0	5.1	5.6
Business rates	19.9	21.3	22.1
Council tax[3]	21.4	22.4	23.5
Other taxes and royalties[4]	12.7	13.4	14.5
Net taxes and national insurance contributions[5]	**456.8**	**485.7**	**519.2**
Accruals adjustments on taxes	1.4	3.4	2.4
Less own resources contribution to European Commission (EC) budget	-4.3	-4.7	-4.1
Less PC corporation tax payments	-0.2	-0.2	-0.2
Tax credits adjustment[6]	0.6	0.5	0.6
Interest and dividends	6.7	6.0	7.1
Other receipts[7]	24.7	26.5	28.0
Current receipts	**485.7**	**517.2**	**553.0**
Memo:			
North Sea revenues[8]	9.7	9.1	8.1

[1] National Accounts measure: gross of enhanced and payable tax credits.

[2] Includes enhanced company tax credits.

[3] Council tax increases are determined annually by local authorities, not by the Government. As in previous years, council tax figures are projections based on stylised assumptions and are not Government forecasts.

[4] Includes VAT refunds and money paid into the National Lottery Distribution Fund.

[5] Includes VAT and 'traditional own resources' contributions to EC budget.

[6] Tax credits which are scored as negative tax in the calculation of NTNIC but expenditure in the National Accounts.

[7] Includes gross operating surplus and rent; net of oil royalties and business rate payments by local authorities.

[8] Consists of North Sea corporation tax, petroleum revenue tax and royalties.

Income tax and national insurance contributions

C.46 Accrued receipts of income tax and national insurance contributions (NICs) in 2006-07 are expected to be £0.7 billion above their 2006 Pre-Budget Report projection. Relative to the 2006 Pre-Budget Report, both self assessment receipts and PAYE and NIC receipts from wages and salaries have been stronger than expected. Evidence from January and February 2007 suggests that bonus growth is likely to be at least as strong as assumed in the 2006 Pre-Budget Report.

C.47 The continuation of solid employment growth through 2007 should underpin PAYE and NIC receipts in 2007-08. Consistent with the corporation tax forecast, bonuses paid by financial companies are expected to grow in line with the long-term trend growth rate of the financial sector from 2007-08 onwards. In addition, tax on saving income is likely to be higher as a result of higher projected interest rates, as set by the NAO audited assumption. The combination of stronger receipts in 2006-07, faster growth in self-employment income, and the anti-avoidance measure on sideways loss relief should also boost self assessment receipts.

Non-North Sea corporation tax

C.48 Non-North Sea corporation tax receipts are estimated to have grown by about 10 per cent in 2006-07, with strong growth in receipts from both the industrial and commercial sector and financial sector partly offset by a reduction in receipts from the life assurance sector. The latter is mainly a result of falls in bond prices observed in 2006. Receipts in 2006-07 are now estimated to be about £1.9 billion lower than estimated in the 2006 Pre-Budget Report. This is mainly a result of higher than expected repayments in relation to previous years' accounting periods, and companies changing their corporation tax instalment patterns such that a higher proportion of their overall liabilities on 2006 profits were paid in their initial quarterly instalments.

C.49 Corporation tax receipts from onshore companies are forecast to increase by 14 per cent in 2007-08. Growth in receipts from the industrial and commercial sector will benefit from the one-off conversion charge for property firms converting to real estate investment trust status and buoyant receipts from small companies. Given the longer payment lag, such companies will still be paying tax on their 2006 profits. In addition, receipts from the life assurance sector are expected to recover from the falls observed in 2006-07. With the economy back on trend and profit growth in the financial sector expected to return to its long-run trend from 2007 onwards, onshore corporation tax receipts are expected to stabilise at 3.2 to 3.3 per cent of GDP from 2008-09 onwards.

North Sea revenues

C.50 High oil prices have resulted in continuing high profitability for companies engaged in North Sea activity, with recent ONS figures showing that net rates of return on capital employed in the sector remain well above the return for other non-financial companies. However, further increases in capital and operating expenditure within the North Sea, combined with a much greater than expected decline in North Sea production and a strengthening of the dollar–sterling exchange rate, have seen the prospects for North Sea revenues alter significantly since the 2006 Pre-Budget Report, with revenues for 2006-07 likely to be £1.3 billion below the previously forecast level. These various effects are also expected to have an ongoing impact on North Sea revenues throughout the forecast period.

C.51   The forecast for North Sea revenues uses an NAO audited assumption for the dollar oil price linked to the average of independent forecasts for the coming year. As set out in Box C1, this gives a dollar oil price of $58.1 a barrel for 2007, down from the $60.3 a barrel assumed in the 2006 Pre-Budget Report, although similar to the level assumed in Budget 2006. In addition, the appreciation of sterling against the dollar over the past year means that the oil price in sterling terms is markedly below Budget 2006 and the 2006 Pre-Budget Report levels throughout the forecast. This explains over £1 billion of the shortfall in 2007-08 relative to the Budget 2006 projection.

C.52   North Sea production fell by about 10 per cent in 2006, a more pronounced fall than assumed in the Budget 2006 and 2006 Pre-Budget Report forecasts. The steeper fall reflects lower than expected reservoir performance in existing fields, rising maintenance requirements for North Sea infrastructure, delays in the start-up of several new developments and a drop in UK gas demand. Following lower than expected production in 2006, oil companies have reduced their estimates, forward production levels, particularly in 2007 and 2008, and this has been incorporated into the forecast. This explains more than half of the shortfall in 2007-08 receipts relative to the Budget 2006 projection.

C.53   Both operating and capital expenditure, which benefits from capital allowances, by North Sea firms were also substantially higher in 2006 than assumed in either Budget 2006 or the 2006 Pre-Budget Report. North Sea capital expenditure is higher than the projections incorporated into the North Sea revenues forecast made prior to the announcement of the increase in the supplementary charge. The rise in capital expenditure is likely to be a combination of both volume and price increases, with capacity constraints having impacted on rig rates and wages as operators seek to maximise global production. Although supply constraints are forecast to ease, this is likely to take time, so the forecast assumes higher operating and capital expenditure, particularly in 2007 and 2008. These higher levels of expenditure explain around a quarter of the shortfall in 2007-08 relative to the Budget 2006 forecast.

Capital gains tax and inheritance tax   C.54   Initial analysis of self assessment returns suggests that capital gains tax showed robust growth in 2006-07, with receipts up by about 28 per cent on a year earlier. Receipts were buoyed by the strong growth in the equity market in 2005-06 and the continuing effects from the disposal of business assets following the maturing of the business asset taper relief.

Stamp duties   C.55   Receipts from stamp duties in 2006-07 have been revised up by £0.6 billion since the 2006 Pre-Budget Report, primarily because of higher receipts from stamp duty land tax. Receipts have benefited from the strength of the housing market in 2006-07. Growth in stamp duty land tax is likely to slow in 2007-08 with house price inflation likely to moderate during the year. In addition, the forecast assumes that the number of property transactions will stabilise in 2007-08. Stamp duty on shares has benefited from the rise in the equity market through 2006-07. This has helped to offset a fall in the volume of equity trades subject to stamp duty. With equity prices assumed to rise in line with money GDP, growth in stamp duty on shares is also expected to moderate through 2007-08.

VAT receipts **C.56** VAT receipts in 2006-07 are expected to be £1.2 billion above their 2006 Pre-Budget Report projection. In part, this reflects the above-trend growth in the economy in recent quarters and that consumer spending, around two-thirds of the total VAT tax base, was strong in the final quarter of 2006. HMRC's strengthened operational strategy to counter Missing Trader Intra-Community (MTIC) fraud is reflected in the trade statistics which indicate a reduction in the level of attempted fraud during 2006-07. As a result, the VAT gap (the difference between the theoretical liability to tax and actual receipts) is likely to have fallen in 2006-07, offsetting some of the increase in the gap recorded during 2005-06.

C.57 Growth in VAT receipts is likely to slow in 2007-08 as consumer spending growth moderates. The VAT forecast for 2007-08 includes an allowance for increased repayments arising as a result of recent judicial rulings relating to the 3-year cap for making claims of previously overpaid or underclaimed VAT. The Government is appealing these decisions and, if successful, taxpayers would subsequently be required to repay these claims. No allowance is made in the forecast for any such recoveries. Slower growth in VAT receipts in 2007-08 also results from the forecast incorporating a rise in the underlying VAT gap, in line with the NAO audited assumption.

Excise duties **C.58** Receipts of fuel duty are expected to be £0.1 billion below the 2006 Pre-Budget Report projections in both 2006-07 and 2007-08. The decision to raise fuel duty in October 2007 will reduce revenues in 2007-08. Thereafter, the increases in fuel duty announced in Budget 2007 up to 2009-10 will result in higher receipts of fuel duty, compared with the 2006 Pre-Budget Report.

C.59 The forecast for tobacco receipts uses the revised NAO audited assumption. This assumes that the underlying level of duty paid consumption of cigarettes will be set at least 3 per cent lower per year than the estimated outturn for the current year. The Comptroller and Auditor General agreed there were sound reasons for adopting this assumption, and concluded it is reasonable and cautious. The impact on receipts from the smoking ban in enclosed workplaces has been updated and the forecast assumes a loss of revenues of £0.1 billion in 2007-08 and about £0.5 billion in 2008-09. Receipts from alcohol duty are little changed from the 2006 Pre-Budget Report projection.

Council tax **C.60** Council tax increases are determined annually by local authorities, not by the Government. The council tax projections are based on stylised assumptions and are not government forecasts. The projected increase in 2007-08 is based on the latest available estimates released by the Chartered Institute for Public Finance and Accountancy (CIPFA) and the increases for later years on the arithmetic average of council tax increases over the past three years. Since changes to council tax are broadly balanced by changes to locally financed expenditure (LASFE), they have little material impact on the current balance or net borrowing.

Other taxes and receipts **C.61** Interest and dividend receipts are higher than forecast at the 2006 Pre-Budget Report. This reflects the inclusion of the interest accruing on student loans. Future years' forecasts take account of the announced programme of student loan sales, as described in Chapter 6.

Tax-GDP ratio

C.62   Table C9 shows projections of receipts from major taxes as a per cent of GDP. Chart C3 shows the tax-GDP ratio from 1981-82 to 2011-12.

C.63   Table C10 sets out current and previous projections of the overall tax-GDP ratio, based on net taxes and national insurance contributions. The tax-GDP ratio is broadly unchanged from the 2006 Pre-Budget Report projections.

Table C9: Current receipts as a proportion of GDP

	Per cent of GDP						
	Outturn	Estimate			Projections		
	2005-06	**2006-07**	**2007-08**	**2008-09**	**2009-10**	**2010-11**	**2011-12**
Income tax (gross of tax credits)	10.9	11.3	11.4	11.5	11.5	11.6	11.7
National insurance contributions	6.9	6.7	6.9	7.0	7.0	7.0	7.1
Non-North Sea corporation tax[1]	2.8	2.9	3.2	3.2	3.2	3.3	3.3
Tax credits[2]	-0.4	-0.4	-0.4	-0.4	-0.4	-0.3	-0.3
North Sea revenues[3]	0.8	0.7	0.6	0.6	0.6	0.6	0.6
Value added tax	5.9	5.9	5.8	5.9	5.9	5.8	5.8
Excise duties[4]	3.2	3.0	3.0	3.0	2.9	2.9	2.8
Other taxes and royalties[5]	6.8	7.0	7.2	7.2	7.2	7.2	7.2
Net taxes and national insurance contributions[6]	**36.9**	**37.2**	**37.7**	**38.0**	**38.1**	**38.1**	**38.1**
Accruals adjustments on taxes	0.1	0.3	0.2	0.2	0.1	0.1	0.1
Less EU transfers	-0.3	-0.4	-0.3	-0.3	-0.3	-0.3	-0.3
Other receipts[7]	2.6	2.5	2.6	2.5	2.5	2.5	2.5
Current receipts	**39.2**	**39.6**	**40.1**	**40.4**	**40.4**	**40.4**	**40.4**

[1] National Accounts measure, gross of enhanced and payable tax credits.

[2] Tax credits scored as negative tax in net taxes and national insurance contributions.

[3] Includes oil royalties, petroleum revenue tax and North Sea corporation tax.

[4] Fuel, alcohol and tobacco duties.

[5] Includes council tax and money paid into the National Lottery Distribution Fund, as well as other central government taxes.

[6] Includes VAT and 'own resources' contributions to EC budget. Cash basis.

[7] Mainly gross operating surplus and rent, excluding oil royalties.

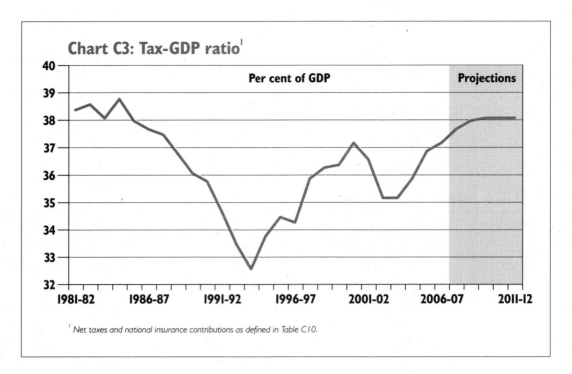

Chart C3: Tax-GDP ratio[1]

Per cent of GDP   Projections

[1] Net taxes and national insurance contributions as defined in Table C10.

Table C10: Net taxes and national insurance contributions[1]

	Per cent of GDP						
	Outturn[2]	Estimate[3]		Projections			
	2005-06	2006-07	2007-08	2008-09	2009-10	2010-11	2011-12
Budget 2006	37.5	38.0	38.5	38.7	38.7	38.7	
2006 Pre-Budget Report	36.9	37.3	37.8	38.1	38.1	38.1	38.1
Budget 2007	**36.9**	**37.2**	**37.7**	**38.0**	**38.1**	**38.1**	**38.1**

[1] Cash basis. Uses OECD definition of tax credits scored as negative tax.
[2] The 2005-06 figures were estimates in Budget 2006.
[3] The 2006-07 figures were projections in Budget 2006.

PUBLIC EXPENDITURE

C.64   This section looks in detail at the projections for public expenditure. The spending projections cover the whole of the public sector, using the National Accounts aggregate Total Managed Expenditure (TME).

C.65   For fiscal aggregates purposes, TME is split into National Accounts components covering public sector current expenditure, public sector net investment and depreciation. For budgeting and other purposes, TME is split into DEL – firm three-year limits for departments' programme expenditure, and AME – expenditure that is not easily subject to firm multi-year limits. Departments have separate resource budgets for current and capital expenditure.

Changes in TME since the 2006 Pre-Budget Report

C.66   The main forecasting changes to TME in the 2004 Spending Review period since the 2006 Pre-Budget Report are to AME, where the totals for 2006-07 and 2007-08 have been revised as a result of changes to the forecasts of individual AME components. The changes in 2006-07 are consistent with the available outturn data for the first 11 months of the year. Central government current expenditure for the first 11 months is 5.6 per cent up on the same period in 2005-06, but spending growth is expected to be slightly lower for the year as a whole, partly because of changes to the monthly profile of grants from central government to local authorities.

C.67   Discretionary changes to TME in the 2004 Spending Review period since the 2006 Pre-Budget Report forecast reflect the Budget 2007 spending measures set out in Chapter A. The allocation to the special reserve increases spending by £0.4 billion in total in 2007-08.

C.68   Public sector current expenditure is expected to be almost £1 billion higher in 2006-07 compared with the 2006 Pre-Budget Report projections. This is more than offset by a fall of £3½ billion in public sector net investment. Current expenditure is expected to be about £2 billion higher in 2007-08 compared to the 2006 Pre-Budget Report. In line with normal practice, the AME margin has been reset to £1 billion. The remaining increase reflects the time-limited increase in the special reserve and forecasting changes to AME components.

C.69   Budget 2007 sets firm overall spending limits for the 2007 Comprehensive Spending Review period. DEL and AME totals for 2008-09 onwards have not yet been determined, but current expenditure growth rates are unchanged from the 2006 Pre-Budget Report projections, taking account of time-limited items announced in this Budget, as set out earlier in this chapter.

C.70   Chart C4 shows TME as a per cent of GDP from 1971-72 to 2007-08.

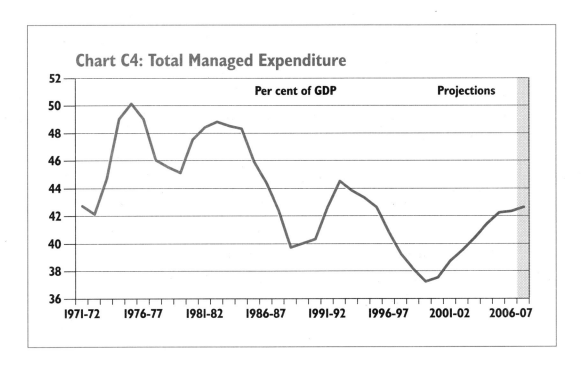

DEL and AME analysis

C.71 Table C11 sets out projected spending on DEL and the main components of AME to the end of the 2004 Spending Review period in 2007-08. Table C12 shows changes since the 2006 Pre-Budget Report.

DEL **C.72** The detailed allocation of DEL is shown in Table C13. In line with previous practice, resource and capital DEL for 2006-07 include an allowance for shortfall reflecting likely underspending against departmental provision.

C.73 Estimated outturn on capital DEL is lower than forecast in the 2006 Pre-Budget Report, partly as a result of classification changes, but also because of lower capital expenditure than planned by the Department for Education and Skills (DfES), Department of Health (DH), and other departments. Estimated outturn for capital expenditure in DEL represents an increase in nominal investment of 12 per cent on 2005-06.

C.74 The latest figures include a number of classification and budgetary changes, which have no impact on National Accounts definitions or TME. The main changes are:

- the movement of Education Maintenance Allowances (EMAs) from AME into DEL in all years, increasing the Department for Education and Skills (DfES) resource budget DEL by about £0.6 billion;

- the movement from DEL into AME of some types of impairments and revaluations of tangible and intangible fixed assets where the causes are independent of departments' management decisions;

- the movement of contributions to international development organisations that are treated as financial transactions in the National Accounts from resource DEL to capital DEL to align more closely the budgeting treatment with the National Accounts treatment;

- adjustments to take account of changes in the Department for Transport's budget for the treatment of London and Continental Railways (LCR). LCR was reclassified by the ONS as a public corporation in February 2006; and

- the movement of profit or loss on asset disposal from resource budgets to capital budgets, which reduces capital budgets and increases resource budgets in both outturn and 2007-08. This better aligns the budgeting treatment with the fiscal framework and improves incentives to dispose of surplus assets.

C.75 Changes in public sector net investment in 2007-08 are a result of revised forecasts for local authority self-financed capital spending, and the updating of local government DEL and DH capital plans to a level consistent with the latest estimates of outturn spending, excluding exceptional items. This reflects changes to the balance of DH capital procurement and technical, classification, and other changes. Capital underspends will be rolled forward as end-year flexibility and NHS and local authority spending plans will be unaffected.

AME **C.76** The main assumptions underpinning the AME forecast are set out in Box C1 and Table C3.

C.77 Social security expenditure is forecast to be slightly lower than expected at the 2006 Pre-Budget Report, mainly because of lower state retirement pension payments. Forecasts of housing benefit, council tax benefit, and Jobseeker's Allowance (caused by lower unemployment assumptions) have also decreased in 2007-08.

Table C11: Total Managed Expenditure 2005-06 to 2007-08

	£ billion		
	Outturn 2005-06	Estimate 2006-07	Projection 2007-08
Departmental Expenditure Limits			
Resource Budget	277.8	293.4	310.0
Capital Budget	34.6	38.8	44.3
Less depreciation	-9.5	-10.5	-10.6
Total Departmental Expenditure Limits	**302.9**	**321.7**	**343.7**
Annually Managed Expenditure			
Social security benefits[1]	127.4	132.0	139.2
Tax credits[1]	15.5	16.2	16.5
Net public service pensions[2]	0.2	1.1	1.7
National Lottery	1.8	1.7	1.6
BBC domestic services	3.2	3.3	3.3
Other departmental expenditure	3.3	3.6	3.1
Net expenditure transfers to EU institutions[3]	4.4	4.7	5.0
Locally-financed expenditure[4]	25.8	25.9	27.8
Central government gross debt interest	25.8	27.4	29.1
Public corporations' own-financed capital expenditure	5.4	4.3	4.6
AME margin	0.0	0.0	1.0
Accounting adjustments[5]	7.6	10.4	10.0
Total Annually Managed Expenditure	**220.5**	**230.5**	**242.9**
Total Managed Expenditure	**523.4**	**552.2**	**586.6**
of which:			
Public sector current expenditure	484.2	509.0	538.6
Public sector net investment	22.7	25.5	29.4
Public sector depreciation	16.5	17.7	18.7

[1] For 2005-06 to 2007-08, child allowances in Income Support and Jobseekers' Allowance (which from 2003-04 are paid as part of the Child Tax Credit) have been included in the tax credits line and excluded from the social security benefits line.

[2] Net public service pensions expenditure is reported on a National Accounts basis.

[3] AME spending component only. Total net payments to EU institutions also include receipts scored in DEL, VAT based contributions which score as negative receipts and some payments which have no effect on the UK public sector in the National Accounts. Latest estimates for total net payments, which exclude the UK's contribution to the cost of EU aid to non-Member States (which is attributed to the aid programme), and the UK's net contribution to the EC Budget, which includes this aid, are (in £ billion):

	2005-06	2006-07	2007-08
Net payments to EU institutions	3.7	2.6	2.6
Net contribution to EC Budget	4.4	3.3	3.3

[4] This expenditure is mainly financed by council tax revenues. See footnote to table C8 for an explanation of how the council tax projections are derived.

[5] Excludes depreciation.

C.78   Forecasts for expenditure on the Child and Working Tax Credits are higher than in the 2006 Pre-Budget Report. Expected average earnings growth for tax credit recipients has been revised down to reflect the high degree of turnover into and out of the system. The most significant component of the 2007-08 increase is upward revisions to child support.

C.79   National lottery figures reflect the latest view on timing of drawdown by the distributing bodies. These estimates are broadly unchanged from the 2006 Pre-Budget Report.

C.80   Other departmental expenditure has increased in 2006-07 and 2007-08, with the net increases largely reflecting some £0.3 billion of additional specific grants being paid to local authorities in respect of additional pensions costs for police and fire services. In 2007-08 there is an additional increase in coal health liabilities, largely reflecting re-profiling of the remaining payments as the schemes wind up. The net increases in other departmental expenditure also includes additional net lending, which is treated as a financial transaction in

Table C12: Changes to Total Managed Expenditure since the 2006 Pre-Budget Report

	£ billion		
	Outturn	Estimate	Projections
	2005-06	2006-07	2007-08
Departmental Expenditure Limits			
Resource Budget	0.8	-1.1	0.1
Capital Budget	-1.2	-3.8	-1.4
Less depreciation	0.8	1.3	0.9
Total Departmental Expenditure Limits	**0.4**	**-3.6**	**-0.5**
Annually Managed Expenditure			
Social security benefits	0.0	-0.1	-0.3
Tax credits	0.0	0.2	0.8
Net public service pensions	0.0	0.2	0.8
National Lottery	0.0	0.0	0.1
BBC domestic services	0.0	0.0	-0.1
Other departmental expenditure	-0.3	0.3	0.3
Net expenditure transfers to EU institutions	0.0	0.5	-1.0
Locally-financed expenditure	0.4	-0.5	0.0
Central government gross debt interest	0.0	0.0	0.8
Public corporations' own-financed capital expenditure	-0.7	-2.7	0.3
AME margin	0.0	0.0	1.0
Accounting adjustments	0.8	3.3	-0.7
Total Annually Managed Expenditure	**0.2**	**1.2**	**2.1**
Total Managed Expenditure	**0.6**	**-2.4**	**1.6**
of which:			
Public sector current expenditure	0.3	0.9	2.0
Public sector net investment	0.3	-3.4	-0.5
Public sector depreciation	0.0	0.1	0.0

the National Accounts, and is therefore offset in the National Accounts adjustments. The transfer of Education Maintenance Allowances into DEL is reflected in the changes to the DEL budget regime described previously.

C.81 Net public service pensions figures are reported on a National Accounts basis, which reflects the differences between the payments to pensioners during the year and contributions received for the main unfunded public service pension schemes. Spending in 2007-08 is expected to be higher than forecast at the 2006 Pre-Budget Report. The increase reflects improvements made to the forecasting methodology.

C.82 Changes to local authority self financed expenditure (LASFE) reflect the limited amount of information available on outturns for local authority expenditure in the first 11 months of 2006-07, which suggest an improvement in the overall fiscal position of local authorities, and changes to the forecasting assumption on council tax increases in 2007-08. Council tax increases are determined annually by local authorities, not by the Government, and since changes to LASFE are broadly balanced by changes to council tax and other income, they have little material impact on the overall fiscal aggregates.

C.83 Net expenditure transfers to EU institutions comprise the Gross National Income (GNI) based contribution less the UK abatement. The net expenditure transfers made in 2006-07 will be higher than expected at the time of the 2006 Pre-Budget Report because of the drawing forward of Member States' 2007 contributions into the first quarter of the year due to the amount of Common Agricultural Policy payments made in that period. Net expenditure transfers are expected to be lower in 2007-08 than forecast in the 2006 Pre-Budget Report due to a reduction in the expected size of the 2008 EC budget, which will reduce the contributions required from Member States.

C.84   The 2006-07 estimate for central government debt interest payments is unchanged from the 2006 Pre-Budget Report. The increase in 2007-08 is due to higher market expectations of interest rates and the use of a more detailed forecasting method, based on a specific analysis of the different types of financing instruments.

C.85   The 2006-07 estimate for public corporations' own financed capital expenditure (PCOFCE) is lower than the 2006 Pre-Budget Report projection, mainly because of changes in the treatment of the write-off of Nigerian debt in the National Accounts. In the 2006 Pre-Budget Report this write-off was scored as a capital grant by Export Credits Guarantee Department (ECGD) in 2006-07, but is now treated as a capital grant by central government, and is included in accounting adjustments. PCOFCE has also been reduced for all years by the classification change to include LCR capital expenditure within capital DEL. PCOFCE has also been revised in line with public corporations' latest spending plans.

C.86   The main accounting adjustments, which reconcile the DEL and AME measures of spending with the National Accounts measure, are shown in Table C14. Changes to the accounting adjustments since the last forecast are mainly due to:

- classification changes to the DEL budget regime, mainly in connection with LCR;

- the change in the National Accounts treatment of the write-off of Nigerian debt, which is now included as an imputed capital grant within National Accounts adjustments and is split between 2005-06 and 2006-07;

- increases in net lending (which is scored within other departmental expenditure but removed in the National Accounts adjustments); and

- changes to the adjustments for non-cash items in resource budgets as a result of changes in the composition of departmental spending.

C.87   Table C15 shows public sector capital expenditure from 2004-05 to 2007-08.

C.88   Table C16 shows estimated receipts from loans and sales of assets from 2005-06 to 2007-08. The figures for sales of fixed assets continue to include housing receipts for local authority housing stocks, even though these have been classified as sales of assets by public corporations. These receipts are included to show a consistent measure of public sector fixed asset sales.

C.89   The figures for sales of financial assets include proceeds in the final quarter of 2005-06 of £0.3 billion from the sale of part of the Government's shareholding in QinetiQ (formerly the Defence Evaluation and Research Agency).

C.90   Table C16 only covers general government and so does not include the sale by British Nuclear Fuels Limited (BNFL) of its Westinghouse subsidiary, which was finalised in October 2006. The proceeds from this sale are included in the public corporation column of Table C20 (public sector net cash requirement). The bulk of the proceeds have been transferred to central government during 2006-07 in two public sector neutral transactions: the repayment of a £0.5 billion BNFL debenture and a special dividend of £1.8 billion. The remaining proceeds are expected to be transferred in 2007-08 and 2008-09.

C.91 The programme of sales of the Department for Education and Skills (DfES) student loan portfolio, announced in Budget 2007, is not included in the table this year as the first sales in this resumed programme will be in 2008-09. As there is a stock of loans suitable for sale, the portfolio to be sold in 2008-09 will include more loans than will be offered in subsequent years.

Table C13: Departmental Expenditure Limits - resource and capital budgets

	£ billion		
	Outturn 2005-06	Estimate 2006-07	Projection 2007-08
Resource Budget			
Education and Skills	25.1	53.6	57.4
Health	76.4	81.1	89.7
of which: NHS	74.2	79.2	87.6
Transport	6.1	6.9	6.7
Department for Communities and Local Government	3.5	3.7	4.3
Local Government	46.2	22.5	22.8
Home Office	12.7	13.2	13.5
Departments for Constitutional Affairs	3.6	3.7	4.0
Law Officers' Departments	0.7	0.7	0.7
Defence	33.4	33.7	32.8
Foreign and Commonwealth Office	1.9	2.0	1.9
International Development	4.1	4.3	4.6
Trade and Industry	5.2	5.8	6.2
Environment, Food and Rural Affairs	2.8	3.3	3.0
Culture, Media and Sport	1.4	1.6	1.6
Work and Pensions	7.8	7.7	7.7
Scotland[1]	20.8	22.3	23.5
Wales[1]	11.0	11.9	12.4
Northern Ireland Executive[1]	6.7	7.2	7.6
Northern Ireland Office	1.2	1.3	1.1
Chancellor's Departments	4.9	5.2	5.0
Cabinet Office	2.2	2.4	2.4
Invest to Save Budget	0.0	0.0	0.0
Reserve	0.0	0.0	0.6
Unallocated special reserve[2]	0.0	0.0	0.4
Allowance for shortfall	0.0	-0.7	0.0
Total Resource Budget DEL	**277.8**	**293.4**	**310.0**
Capital Budget[3]			
Education and Skills	5.7	5.2	7.0
Health	2.2	3.8	4.3
of which : NHS	2.2	3.7	4.2
Transport	5.0	6.5	6.6
Department for Communities and Local Government	5.5	5.4	5.9
Local Government	0.3	0.2	0.1
Home Office	1.0	1.3	1.3
Departments for Constitutional Affairs	0.1	0.2	0.1
Law Officers' Departments	0.0	0.0	0.0
Defence	6.4	7.1	7.6
Foreign and Commonwealth Office	0.1	0.1	0.1
International Development	0.4	0.7	0.6
Trade and Industry	1.2	1.2	1.2
Environment, Food and Rural Affairs	0.8	0.9	0.9
Culture, Media and Sport	0.1	0.2	0.4
Work and Pensions	0.4	0.2	0.1
Scotland[1]	2.4	3.1	3.1
Wales[1]	1.2	1.4	1.6
Northern Ireland Executive[1]	0.8	0.9	1.0
Northern Ireland Office	0.1	0.1	0.1
Chancellor's Departments	0.4	0.3	0.3
Cabinet Office	0.3	0.4	0.3
Invest to Save Budget	0.0	0.0	0.0
Reserve	0.0	0.0	1.5
Allowance for shortfall	0.0	-0.4	0.0
Total Capital Budget DEL	**34.6**	**38.8**	**44.3**
Depreciation	**9.5**	**10.5**	**10.6**
Total Departmental Expenditure Limits	**302.9**	**321.7**	**343.7**
Total education spending	67.4	71.1	77.4

[1] For Scotland, Wales and Northern Ireland, the split between resource and capital budgets is indicative and reflects the consequentials of the application of the Barnett formula to planned changes in UK departments' spending.

[2] This represents provision for the costs of military operations in Iraq and Afghanistan, as well as the UK's other international obligations.

[3] The 2007-08 figures reflect changes including the updating of the Department of Health and local authority DEL capital plans to a level consistent with latest estimates of outturn spending, as set out in paragraph C75. Capital underspends will be rolled forward in end-year flexibility and the NHS and local authorities spending plans will be unaffected.

Table C14: Accounting adjustments

	£ billion		
	Outturn	Estimate	Projection
	2005-06	2006-07	2007-08
Central government programmes	0.0	0.4	0.5
VAT refunds	10.2	10.9	12.5
Central government non-trading capital consumption	6.1	6.5	6.7
Non-cash items in resource budgets and not in TME	-8.2	-8.4	-9.6
Expenditure financed by revenue receipts	0.6	0.6	0.5
Local authorities	4.6	5.0	5.7
General government consolidation	-6.3	-6.5	-6.8
Public corporations	0.5	0.4	0.5
Financial transactions	-0.2	-0.5	-0.4
Other accounting adjustments	0.3	2.0	0.4
Total accounting adjustments	**7.6**	**10.4**	**10.0**

Table C15: Public sector capital expenditure

	£ billion		
	Outturn	Estimate	Projection
	2005-06	2006-07	2007-08
Capital Budget DEL	34.6	38.8	44.3
Locally-financed expenditure	1.2	2.0	1.9
National Lottery	1.0	1.0	0.8
Public corporations' own-financed capital expenditure	5.4	4.3	4.6
Other capital spending in AME	0.8	0.3	0.4
AME margin	0.0	0.0	0.1
Accounting adjustments	-3.8	-3.2	-4.2
Public sector gross investment[1]	**39.2**	**43.2**	**48.0**
Less depreciation	16.5	17.7	18.7
Public sector net investment	**22.7**	**25.5**	**29.4**
Proceeds from the sale of fixed assets[2]	6.1	6.2	6.2

[1] This and previous lines are all net of sales of fixed assets.

[2] Projections of total receipts from the sale of fixed assets by public sector.

PRIVATE FINANCE INITIATIVE

C.92   Under the Private Finance Initiative (PFI), the public sector contracts to purchase services on a long-term basis so as to take advantage of private sector management skills incentivised by having private finance at risk. The private sector has always been involved in the building and maintenance of public infrastructure, but PFI ensures that contractors are bound into long-term maintenance contracts and shoulder responsibility for the quality of the work they do. With PFI, the public sector defines what is required to meet public needs and ensures delivery of the outputs through the contract. Consequently, the private sector can be harnessed to deliver investment in better quality public services while frontline services are retained within the public sector. The Government's position on PFI is set out in the document *PFI: Strengthening Long Term Partnerships*.

C.93 The Government only uses PFI when it is appropriate and where it expects it to deliver value for money. This is based on an assessment of the lifetime costs of both providing and maintaining the underlying asset, and of the running costs of delivering the required level of service. In assessing where PFI is appropriate, the Government's approach is based on its commitment to efficiency, equity and accountability, and on the Prime Minister's principles of public service reform. PFI is only used where it can meet these requirements, and where the value for money it offers is not at the expense of the terms and conditions of staff. The Government is committed to securing the best value for its investment programme by ensuring that there is no inherent bias in favour of one procurement option over another.

C.94 Table C17 shows a breakdown by department of the estimated capital investment in public services resulting from signed PFI contracts. Table C18 shows the estimated total capital value of contracts that are at preferred bidder stage and are expected to reach financial close within the next two years. Under PFI, the public sector contracts for services, including the availability and management of facilities, and not assets. Capital investment is only one of the activities undertaken by the private sector in order to supply these services. The figures in Tables C17 and C18 report the capital value of projects, in order to show investment on a basis comparable with conventional capital procurement.

C.95 Table C19 shows a forecast of the estimated payments for services flowing from signed PFI projects. Actual expenditure will depend on the details of the payment mechanism for each contract when signed. Payments are only projected to fall due in the years shown. Payments may also be lower than those estimated as a result of deductions that can be applied if the supplier fails to meet required performance standards. Variances may also occur as a result of agreed changes to the service requirements that are made during the course of the contract, or because of contractual arrangements that trigger compensation on termination. The fact that capital investment only represents one element of the overall contract means that the figures presented in this table should not be taken to be directly comparable with public sector debt liability.

C.96 In this Budget, the Government sets the local authority PFI credit envelope for the CSR 07 period, in order to provide greater certainty to local authorities on the level of capital investment. PFI credits will be held constant in cash terms at £3.6 billion a year over the CSR 07 period. This will enable local authorities, departments and PFI suppliers to plan for the delivery of PFI projects, while ensuring that payments under local authority PFI contracts remain affordable. Allocations of PFI credits to individual departments will be announced in the 2007 Comprehensive Spending Review.

Table C16: Loans and sales of assets

	£ billion		
	Outturn 2005-06	Estimate 2006-07	Projection 2007-08
Sales of fixed assets			
Central government	1.8	1.6	1.6
Local authorities	1.8	2.4	2.4
Housing Revenue Account[1]	2.5	2.2	2.2
Total sales of fixed assets	**6.1**	**6.2**	**6.2**
Loans and sales of financial assets			
Sale of student loans portfolio[2]	0.0	0.0	0.0
Other loans and sales of financial assets	-1.8	-2.8	-3.7
Total loans and sales of financial assets	**-1.8**	**-2.8**	**-3.7**
Total loans and sales of assets	**4.2**	**3.5**	**2.5**

[1] Capital transactions by local authorities' Housing Revenue Accounts are no longer classified to the local authority sub-sector and so are shown separately.
[2] The programme of sales will resume in 2008-09.

Table C17: Departmental estimate of capital spending by the private sector (signed deals)[1,2,3]

	£ million	
	Projections	
	2006-07	2007-08
Education and Skills[4]	759	454
Health	1,025	1,008
Transport[5]	1,435	1,110
Communities and Local Government	107	140
Home Office	23	20
Constitutional Affairs	15	2
Defence	557	643
Foreign and Commonwealth Office	5	0
Trade and Industry	1	4
Environment, Food and Rural Affairs	128	249
Culture, Media and Sport	38	12
Work and Pensions	46	55
Scotland	595	618
Wales	0	20
Northern Ireland Executive	98	114
Chancellor's Departments	2	2
Total	**4,834**	**4,450**

[1] Investment in assets scored on the public sector balance sheet also score as public sector net investment.
[2] PFI activity in local authority projects is included under the sponsoring central government department.
[3] Figures do not include PFI projects undertaken by public corporations.
[4] Excludes private finance activity in educational institutions classified to the private sector.
[5] Includes estimates of the capital expenditure for the London Underground Limited Public Private Partnership (LUL PPP) PFI contracts in the years that investments are expected to take place.

Table C18: Estimated aggregated capital value of projects at preferred bidder stage[1,2]

	£ million	
	Projections	
	2006-07	2007-08
Education and Skills	253	417
Health	340	2,299
Transport	0	56
Department for Communities and Local Government	334	160
Home Office	62	0
Defence	3,278	1,501
Environment, Food and Rural Affairs	0	332
Culture, Media and Sport	0	60
Scotland	704	94
Wales	0	38
Northern Ireland Executive	122	465
Total	**5,093**	**5,420**

[1] Figures based on departmental returns.

[2] These figures are the total capital value of projects; the actual annual capital spending figures will be lower, as capital spending on large projects is typically spread over several years.

Table C19: Estimated payments under PFI contracts - March 2007 (signed deals)[1]

£ billion			
Projections			
2006-07	6.9	2019-20	5.8
2007-08	7.3	2020-21	5.9
2008-09	7.8	2021-22	5.5
2009-10	8.2	2022-23	5.4
2010-11	8.5	2023-24	5.4
2011-12	8.6	2024-25	5.4
2012-13	8.7	2025-26	5.2
2013-14	8.8	2026-27	5.0
2014-15	8.8	2027-28	4.8
2015-16	8.8	2028-29	4.5
2016-17	8.9	2029-30	4.2
2017-18	8.2	2030-31	3.8
2018-19	5.8	2031-32	3.4

[1] The figures between 2006-07 and 2017-18 include estimated payments for the LUL PPP PFI contract. These contracts contain periodic reviews every 7.5 years and therefore the service payments are not fixed after 2009-10.

Table C20: Public sector net cash requirement

	£ billion							
	2006-07				2007-08			
	General government				General government			
	Central government	Local authorities	Public corporations	Public sector	Central government	Local authorities	Public corporations	Public sector
Net borrowing	**34.8**	**1.6**	**-1.4**	**35.0**	**33.2**	**2.0**	**-1.5**	**33.7**
Financial transactions								
Net lending to private sector and abroad	2.7	0.0	-2.0	0.7	3.6	0.1	-0.3	3.4
Cash expenditure on company securities	0.2	-0.1	-2.4	-2.3	0.1	0.0	0.0	0.1
Accounts receivable/payable	1.9	0.0	0.0	1.9	2.9	0.2	0.0	3.1
Adjustment for interest on gilts	-1.3	0.0	0.0	-1.3	-4.1	0.0	0.0	-4.1
Miscellaneous financial transactions	-2.0	0.5	0.9	-0.5	-0.4	0.0	-0.4	-0.8
Own account net cash requirement	36.3	2.0	-4.9	33.4	35.2	2.3	-2.1	35.4
Net lending within the public sector	0.7	-1.2	0.5	0.0	2.4	-1.6	-0.8	0.0
Net cash requirement[1]	**37.0**	**0.8**	**-4.4**	**33.4**	**37.6**	**0.7**	**-3.0**	**35.4**

[1] *Market and overseas borrowing for local government and public corporation sectors.*

FINANCING REQUIREMENT

C.97   Table C20 presents projections of the net cash requirement by sector, giving details of financial transactions that do not affect net borrowing (the change in the sector's net financial indebtedness) but do affect its financing requirement.

C.98   Table C21 updates the financing arithmetic for both 2006-07 and 2007-08 in line with the updated fiscal forecasts. The central government net cash requirement (CGNCR) for 2006-07 is now forecast to be £37.0 billion, a decrease of £4.2 billion from the 2006 Pre-Budget Report forecast of £41.2 billion. The net financing requirement is expected to be £54.8 billion, a reduction of £4.2 billion from the 2006 Pre-Budget Report. It is also £4.2 billion below total financing, resulting in an increase of £4.2 billion in the forecast level of the Debt Management Office's (DMO's) short-term cash position at end March 2007.

C.99   The forecast for the CGNCR for 2007-08 is £37.6 billion. Gross gilt redemptions are £29.2 billion and National Savings and Investments' net contribution to financing is estimated to be £2.8 billion. This means that the net financing requirement for 2007-08 is forecast to be £59.8 billion. The DMO will aim to meet this net financing requirement by:

- gross gilt issuance of £58.4 billion; and

- an increase in the Treasury bill stock to £17.0 billion.

C.100   Gross gilt issuance will continue to be skewed towards long-conventional and index-linked gilts. In 2007-08, issuance in long-conventional gilts is forecast to be £23.4 billion (or 40 per cent of total issuance) and issuance in index-linked gilts is forecast to be £15.0 billion (or 26 per cent of total issuance).

Table C21: Financing requirement forecast

| | £ billion | | | |
| | 2006-07 | | | 2007-08 |
	April 2006 Revised Remit[1]	December 2006 Pre-Budget Report	March 2007 Budget	March 2007 Budget
Central government net cash requirement	41.2	41.2	37.0	37.6
Gilt redemptions	29.9	29.9	29.9	29.2
Restructuring nuclear liabilities[2]	0.0	-3.8	-3.5	0.0
Financing for the Official Reserves	0.0	0.0	0.0	0.0
Buy-backs[3]	0.0	0.2	0.2	0.0
Planned short-term financing adjustment[4]	-3.6	-3.3	-3.3	-4.2
Gross Financing Requirement	67.5	64.2	60.3	62.6
less				
Assumed net contribution from National Savings and Investments	3.0	5.2	5.5	2.8
Net Financing Requirement	64.5	59.0	54.8	59.8
Financed by:				
1. Debt issuance by the Debt Management Office				
(a) Treasury bills	1.5	-3.5	-3.5	1.4
(b) Gilts	63.0	62.5	62.5	58.4
2. Other planned changes in short-term debt[5]				
Change in Ways & Means	0.0	0.0	0.0	0.0
3. Unanticipated changes in short-term cash position[6]	**0.0**	**0.0**	**4.2**	**0.0**
Total financing	64.5	59.0	59.0	59.8
Short-term debt levels at end of financial year				
Treasury bill stock in market hands[7]	20.6	15.6	15.6	17.0
Ways & Means	13.4	13.4	13.4	13.4
DMO net cash position[8]	0.2	0.5	4.7	0.5

[1] The financing arithmetic in Budget 2006 was revised on 24 April 2006 to reflect outturn data for 2005-06.

[2] Proceeds from the disposal of financial assets in the Nuclear Liabilities Investment Portfolio (NLIP) held by British Nuclear Fuels Limited (BNFL). There has been a small reduction in the value since the 2006 Pre-Budget Report reflecting improved information on the composition of the liquidation proceeds.

[3] Purchases of "rump" gilts which are older, small gilts, declared as such by the DMO and in which Gilt-edged Market Makers (GEMMs) are not required to make two-way markets. The Government will not sell further amounts of such gilts to the market but the DMO is prepared, when asked by a GEMM, to make a price to purchase such gilts.

[4] To accommodate changes to the current year's financing requirement resulting from: (i) publication of the previous year's outturn CGNCR; (ii) an increase in the DMO's cash position at the Bank of England; and / or (iii) carry over of unanticipated changes to the cash position from the previous year.

[5] Total planned changes to short-term debt are the sum of: (i) the planned short-term financing adjustment; (ii) Treasury bill sales; and (iii) changes to the level of the Ways & Means advance.

[6] A negative (positive) number indicates an addition to (reduction in) the financing requirement for the following financial year.

[7] The DMO has operational flexibility to vary the end-financial year stock subject to its operational requirements from 2007-08.

[8] There is an increase in the DMO's net cash position at the Bank of England of £0.3 billion (reflecting a move from an end-day target balance of £0.2 billion prior to the implementation of the Bank of England's money market reforms to an average daily target balance of £0.5 billion) in 2006-07.

C.101   Full details of the DMO's financing remit including further information on the structure of gilts issuance and the gilt auction calendar for 2007-08 can be found in the *Debt and reserves management report 2007-08* which is published alongside the Budget and is available on HM Treasury's website.

ANALYSIS BY SUB-SECTOR AND ECONOMIC CATEGORY

C.102   Table C22 shows a breakdown of general government transactions by economic category for 2005-06 to 2007-08. Table C23 shows a more detailed breakdown for public sector transactions by sub-sector and economic category for 2005-06, 2006-07 and 2007-08. The latest data published by the ONS for 2005-06 (and the first quarter of 2006-07) reflect revisions to both the classification and timing of the write off of part of Nigeria's Paris Club debt owed to the Export Credits Guarantee Department (ECGD).

C.103   The Nigerian debt write-off had originally been scored in the National Accounts as an imputed capital grant of £2.3 billion from the public corporation sector (ECGD is a trading body and so is classified to this sector for National Accounts purposes) with an offsetting imputed repayment of the relevant loans. The transaction has now been re-routed to the central government (CG) sector as the UK Government, rather than ECGD, was the principal in the decision to write off the debt. It has also been scored in two stages, one of £1.1 billion (33 per cent of eligible debt) in October 2005 when the bilateral agreement was signed and £1.2 billion (34 per cent of eligible debt) in April 2006 when the International Monetary Fund (IMF) Board signed off on the first review of Nigeria's IMF Programme. As a result the impact on public sector net borrowing is now split between 2005-06 and 2006-07, rather than all falling in the latter year. The remaining 33 per cent of eligible debt was repaid in cash, in January 2006 and April 2006.

Table C22: General government transactions by economic category

	£ billion		
	Outturn	**Estimate**	**Projection**
	2005-06	**2006-07**	**2007-08**
Current receipts			
Taxes on income and wealth	180.3	194.9	211.1
Taxes on production and imports	159.5	168.7	178.4
Other current taxes	28.7	30.0	31.7
Taxes on capital	3.3	3.6	4.0
Compulsory social contributions	85.4	90.3	95.6
Gross operating surplus	12.1	13.1	13.8
Rent and other current transfers	2.0	2.3	2.3
Interest and dividends from private sector and abroad	4.8	5.4	6.6
Interest and dividends from public sector	2.6	3.0	2.9
Total current receipts	**478.7**	**511.4**	**546.3**
Current expenditure			
Current expenditure on goods and services	274.7	288.4	306.5
Subsidies	6.4	6.9	6.8
Net social benefits	143.8	148.8	157.1
Net current grants abroad	-0.5	0.6	0.2
Other current grants	33.3	35.9	37.1
Interest and dividends paid	26.2	27.9	29.7
AME margin	0.0	0.0	0.9
Total current expenditure	**483.9**	**508.7**	**538.3**
Depreciation	12.1	13.1	13.8
Surplus on current budget	**-17.3**	**-10.3**	**-5.7**
Capital expenditure			
Gross domestic fixed capital formation	6.5	24.5	29.0
Less depreciation	-12.1	-13.1	-13.8
Increase in inventories	0.0	0.0	0.0
Capital grants (net) within public sector	13.1	1.3	0.4
Capital grants to private sector	12.6	14.9	15.2
Capital grants from private sector	-1.5	-1.5	-1.5
AME margin	0.0	0.0	0.1
Net investment	**18.6**	**26.1**	**29.4**
Net borrowing[1]	**35.9**	**36.4**	**35.1**
of which:			
Central government net borrowing	32.9	34.8	33.2
Local authority net borrowing	3.0	1.6	2.0
Gross debt (Maastricht basis)			
Central government	469.1	506.9	548.9
Local government	60.1	60.9	61.6

[1] Although this is based on the ESA95 definition of general government net borrowing (GGNB), the projections are identical to GGNB calculated on a Maastricht definition.

Table C23: Public sector transactions by sub-sector and economic category

	£ billion			
	2005-06			
	General government			
	Central government	Local authorities	Public corporations	Public sector
Current receipts				
Taxes on income and wealth	180.3	0.0	-0.2	180.1
Taxes on production and imports	159.3	0.2	0.0	159.5
Other current taxes	8.1	20.6	0.0	28.7
Taxes on capital	3.3	0.0	0.0	3.3
Compulsory social contributions	85.4	0.0	0.0	85.4
Gross operating surplus	6.1	6.0	8.0	20.1
Rent and other current transfers	1.9	0.0	0.0	2.0
Interest and dividends from private sector and abroad	3.8	1.0	1.8	6.7
Interest and dividends from public sector	3.8	-1.3	-2.6	0.0
Total current receipts	**452.1**	**26.6**	**7.0**	**485.7**
Current expenditure				
Current expenditure on goods and services	166.5	108.2	0.0	274.7
Subsidies	4.7	1.7	0.0	6.4
Net social benefits	128.4	15.4	0.0	143.8
Net current grants abroad	-0.5	0.0	0.0	-0.5
Current grants (net) within public sector	102.3	-102.3	0.0	0.0
Other current grants	33.3	0.0	0.0	33.3
Interest and dividends paid	25.8	0.4	0.3	26.6
AME margin	0.0	0.0	0.0	0.0
Total current expenditure	**460.3**	**23.5**	**0.3**	**484.2**
Depreciation	6.1	6.0	4.4	16.5
Surplus on current budget	**-14.3**	**-3.0**	**2.3**	**-15.0**
Capital expenditure				
Gross domestic fixed capital formation	-6.8	13.3	21.8	28.3
Less depreciation	-6.1	-6.0	-4.4	-16.5
Increase in inventories	0.0	0.0	-0.2	-0.2
Capital grants (net) within public sector	20.6	-7.5	-13.1	0.0
Capital grants to private sector	11.3	1.3	0.0	12.6
Capital grants from private sector	-0.4	-1.1	0.0	-1.5
AME margin	0.0	0.0	0.0	0.0
Net investment	**18.6**	**0.0**	**4.1**	**22.7**
Net borrowing	**32.9**	**3.0**	**1.8**	**37.8**

Table C23: Public sector transactions by sub-sector and economic category

	£ billion			
	2006-07			
	General government			
	Central government	Local authorities	Public corporations	Public sector
Current receipts				
Taxes on income and wealth	194.9	0.0	-0.2	194.7
Taxes on production and imports	168.5	0.2	0.0	168.7
Other current taxes	8.5	21.5	0.0	30.0
Taxes on capital	3.6	0.0	0.0	3.6
Compulsory social contributions	90.3	0.0	0.0	90.3
Gross operating surplus	6.5	6.6	8.5	21.6
Rent and other current transfers	2.3	0.0	0.0	2.3
Interest and dividends from private sector and abroad	3.9	1.5	0.6	6.0
Interest and dividends from public sector	3.5	-0.5	-3.0	0.0
Total current receipts	**482.1**	**29.3**	**5.8**	**517.2**
Current expenditure				
Current expenditure on goods and services	176.3	112.2	0.0	288.4
Subsidies	5.1	1.9	0.0	6.9
Net social benefits	132.8	16.1	0.0	148.8
Net current grants abroad	0.6	0.0	0.0	0.6
Current grants (net) within public sector	106.4	-106.4	0.0	0.0
Other current grants	35.9	0.0	0.0	35.9
Interest and dividends paid	27.4	0.5	0.3	28.3
AME margin	0.0	0.0	0.0	0.0
Total current expenditure	**484.4**	**24.3**	**0.3**	**509.0**
Depreciation	6.5	6.6	4.6	17.7
Surplus on current budget	**-8.8**	**-1.5**	**0.9**	**-9.5**
Capital expenditure				
Gross domestic fixed capital formation	10.1	14.4	5.2	29.7
Less depreciation	-6.5	-6.6	-4.6	-17.7
Increase in inventories	0.0	0.0	0.0	0.0
Capital grants (net) within public sector	9.6	-8.3	-1.3	0.0
Capital grants to private sector	13.1	1.7	0.1	15.0
Capital grants from private sector	-0.3	-1.2	0.0	-1.5
AME margin	0.0	0.0	0.0	0.0
Net investment	**26.0**	**0.1**	**-0.6**	**25.5**
Net borrowing	**34.8**	**1.6**	**-1.4**	**35.0**

Table C23: Public sector transactions by sub-sector and economic category

	£ billion			
	2007-08			
	General government			
	Central government	Local authorities	Public corporations	Public sector
Current receipts				
Taxes on income and wealth	211.1	0.0	-0.2	210.9
Taxes on production and imports	178.2	0.2	0.0	178.4
Other current taxes	9.1	22.6	0.0	31.7
Taxes on capital	4.0	0.0	0.0	4.0
Compulsory social contributions	95.6	0.0	0.0	95.6
Gross operating surplus	6.7	7.1	9.2	23.0
Rent and other current transfers	2.3	0.0	0.0	2.3
Interest and dividends from private sector and abroad	4.9	1.6	0.6	7.1
Interest and dividends from public sector	3.8	-0.8	-2.9	0.0
Total current receipts	**515.7**	**30.7**	**6.6**	**553.0**
Current expenditure				
Current expenditure on goods and services	185.3	121.2	0.0	306.5
Subsidies	4.7	2.0	0.0	6.8
Net social benefits	139.7	17.4	0.0	157.1
Net current grants abroad	0.2	0.0	0.0	0.2
Current grants (net) within public sector	114.8	-114.8	0.0	0.0
Other current grants	37.1	0.0	0.0	37.1
Interest and dividends paid	29.1	0.6	0.3	30.0
AME margin	0.9	0.0	0.0	0.9
Total current expenditure	**511.9**	**26.4**	**0.3**	**538.6**
Depreciation	6.7	7.1	4.9	18.7
Surplus on current budget	**-2.9**	**-2.8**	**1.4**	**-4.3**
Capital expenditure				
Gross domestic fixed capital formation	13.3	15.8	5.2	34.2
Less depreciation	-6.7	-7.1	-4.9	-18.7
Increase in inventories	0.0	0.0	0.0	0.0
Capital grants (net) within public sector	11.0	-10.6	-0.4	0.0
Capital grants to private sector	12.8	2.4	0.1	15.3
Capital grants from private sector	-0.2	-1.3	0.0	-1.5
AME margin	0.1	0.0	0.0	0.1
Net investment	**30.2**	**-0.8**	**-0.1**	**29.4**
Net borrowing	**33.2**	**2.0**	**-1.5**	**33.7**

HISTORICAL SERIES

Table C24: Historical series of public sector balances, receipts and debt

	Per cent of GDP								
	Public sector current budget	Cyclically adjusted surplus on current budget	Public sector net borrowing	Cyclically adjusted public sector net borrowing	Public sector net cash requirement	Net taxes and national insurance contributions	Public sector current receipts	Public sector net debt[1]	Public sector net worth[2]
1970-71	6.9		-0.6		1.2	36.5	43.5		
1971-72	4.2		1.1		1.4	35.2	41.6		
1972-73	2.0	2.5	2.8	2.3	3.6	32.8	39.2		
1973-74	0.4	-0.8	4.9	6.1	5.8	32.1	39.8		
1974-75	-0.9	-2.5	6.6	8.1	9.0	34.8	42.5	52.1	
1975-76	-1.4	-1.7	7.0	7.3	9.2	35.5	43.1	53.8	
1976-77	-1.1	-0.6	5.5	5.1	6.4	35.4	43.5	52.3	
1977-78	-1.3	-1.2	4.3	4.2	3.7	34.3	41.7	49.0	
1978-79	-2.5	-2.4	5.1	4.9	5.2	33.3	40.4	47.1	
1979-80	-1.8	-1.7	4.1	4.0	4.7	33.7	40.9	43.9	
1980-81	-3.0	-1.5	4.9	3.4	5.2	35.8	42.7	46.0	
1981-82	-1.3	2.5	2.3	-1.5	3.3	38.4	46.1	46.2	
1982-83	-1.4	2.9	3.0	-1.3	3.2	38.6	45.8	44.8	
1983-84	-2.0	1.8	3.8	0.1	3.2	38.1	44.7	45.1	
1984-85	-2.1	0.9	3.7	0.7	3.1	38.8	44.6	45.3	
1985-86	-1.2	0.5	2.4	0.7	1.6	38.0	43.5	43.5	
1986-87	-1.4	-1.2	2.1	1.9	0.9	37.7	42.4	41.0	
1987-88	-0.4	-1.7	1.0	2.3	-0.7	37.5	41.4	36.8	73.4
1988-89	1.7	-0.9	-1.3	1.3	-3.0	36.8	41.0	30.5	78.9
1989-90	1.5	-1.4	-0.2	2.6	-1.3	36.1	40.2	27.7	70.7
1990-91	0.3	-1.2	1.0	2.6	-0.1	35.8	39.2	26.2	60.2
1991-92	-2.0	-1.5	3.8	3.4	2.3	34.7	38.8	27.4	52.8
1992-93	-5.7	-3.8	7.6	5.7	5.9	33.5	36.9	32.0	39.9
1993-94	-6.4	-4.2	7.8	5.6	7.1	32.6	36.0	37.3	29.2
1994-95	-4.8	-3.4	6.3	4.9	5.3	33.8	37.1	40.8	28.3
1995-96	-3.4	-2.5	4.7	3.9	4.3	34.5	37.8	42.7	20.9
1996-97	-2.8	-2.3	3.5	3.0	2.9	34.8	37.3	43.6	17.0
1997-98	-0.1	0.0	0.8	0.7	0.2	35.9	38.4	41.6	14.3
1998-99	1.2	1.1	-0.5	-0.3	-0.7	36.3	38.6	39.3	13.4
1999-00	2.3	2.0	-1.7	-1.5	-0.9	36.4	38.9	36.6	16.6
2000-01	2.5	1.9	-2.1	-1.5	-3.8	37.2	39.6	31.7	22.6
2001-02	1.1	0.9	0.0	0.2	0.4	36.6	38.7	30.7	29.4
2002-03	-1.1	-0.6	2.3	1.9	2.4	35.2	37.2	32.0	28.0
2003-04	-1.6	-1.2	3.0	2.6	3.5	35.2	37.4	33.1	28.3
2004-05	-1.6	-1.5	3.3	3.2	3.2	35.9	38.1	35.0	28.8
2005-06	-1.2	-1.0	3.0	2.8	3.2	36.9	39.2	36.5	27.0

[1] At end-March; GDP centred on end-March.

[2] At end-December; GDP centred on end-December.

Table C25: Historical series of government expenditure

	£ billion (2005-06 prices)				Per cent of GDP			
	Public sector current expenditure	Public sector net investment	Public sector gross investment[1]	Total Managed Expenditure	Public sector current expenditure	Public sector net investment	Public sector gross investment[1]	Total Managed Expenditure
1970-71	180.6	34.5	55.2	235.7	32.8	6.3	10.0	42.8
1971-72	189.4	30.0	51.8	241.2	33.5	5.3	9.2	42.7
1972-73	197.8	28.9	51.7	249.5	33.4	4.9	8.7	42.1
1973-74	216.7	32.4	57.8	274.4	35.3	5.3	9.4	44.7
1974-75	239.9	34.9	61.7	301.6	39.0	5.7	10.0	49.0
1975-76	244.9	34.2	61.2	306.1	40.1	5.6	10.0	50.1
1976-77	251.7	28.1	56.0	307.7	40.1	4.5	8.9	49.0
1977-78	248.2	19.2	47.4	295.6	38.6	3.0	7.4	46.0
1978-79	255.4	16.7	45.5	301.0	38.6	2.5	6.9	45.5
1979-80	261.7	15.6	44.8	306.5	38.5	2.3	6.6	45.1
1980-81	269.5	12.5	42.2	311.8	41.1	1.9	6.4	47.5
1981-82	281.6	6.7	36.2	317.8	42.9	1.0	5.5	48.4
1982-83	287.8	10.6	39.2	327.0	42.9	1.6	5.9	48.8
1983-84	296.8	12.9	41.4	338.2	42.6	1.9	5.9	48.5
1984-85	304.8	11.3	38.5	343.3	42.9	1.6	5.4	48.3
1985-86	305.3	8.8	33.7	339.1	41.3	1.2	4.6	45.9
1986-87	310.1	5.3	30.4	340.5	40.5	0.7	4.0	44.4
1987-88	313.6	4.8	28.4	342.1	38.9	0.6	3.5	42.4
1988-89	306.1	2.9	26.5	332.6	36.5	0.3	3.2	39.7
1989-90	308.1	10.8	34.1	342.2	36.0	1.3	4.0	40.0
1990-91	310.2	11.7	33.0	343.2	36.4	1.4	3.9	40.3
1991-92	328.4	15.3	33.2	361.7	38.7	1.8	3.9	42.6
1992-93	344.5	15.9	33.4	377.9	40.5	1.9	3.9	44.5
1993-94	354.5	12.6	30.0	384.5	40.4	1.4	3.4	43.8
1994-95	365.7	13.0	30.3	395.9	40.0	1.4	3.3	43.3
1995-96	370.2	13.0	29.9	400.0	39.4	1.4	3.2	42.6
1996-97	370.1	6.8	22.2	392.3	38.5	0.7	2.3	40.8
1997-98	368.5	6.3	21.2	389.7	37.0	0.6	2.1	39.2
1998-99	368.9	7.7	21.9	390.8	36.0	0.7	2.1	38.1
1999-00	374.9	6.2	20.5	395.4	35.2	0.6	1.9	37.2
2000-01	393.3	4.6	19.2	412.4	35.8	0.4	1.7	37.5
2001-02	405.8	12.3	27.0	432.8	36.3	1.1	2.4	38.7
2002-03	424.3	14.4	29.6	453.9	37.0	1.3	2.6	39.5
2003-04	445.9	16.2	31.5	477.4	37.7	1.4	2.7	40.4
2004-05	464.2	20.7	36.4	500.6	38.4	1.7	3.0	41.4
2005-06	484.2	22.7	39.2	523.4	39.1	1.8	3.2	42.2

[1] Net of sales of fixed assets.

CONVENTIONS USED IN PRESENTING THE PUBLIC FINANCES

Format for the public finances

The June 1998 Economic and Fiscal Strategy Report (EFSR) set out a new format for presenting the public finances that corresponded more closely to the two fiscal rules. The three principal measures are:

- the surplus on current budget (relevant to the golden rule);
- public sector net borrowing; and
- the public sector net debt ratio (relevant to the sustainable investment rule).

These measures are based on the National Accounts and are consistent with the European System of Accounts 1995 (ESA95). Estimates and forecasts of the public sector net cash requirement (formerly called the public sector borrowing requirement) are still shown in the FSBR, but they are given less prominence.

The fiscal rules are similar to the criteria for deficits and debt laid down in the EU Treaty but there are important definitional differences:

- UK fiscal rules cover the whole public sector, whereas the Treaty deficit and debt only includes general (i.e. central and local) government;
- the fiscal rules apply over the whole economic cycle, not year to year;
- the current budget excludes capital spending, which is included in the Treaty deficit measure; and
- the UK debt measure is net of liquid assets, whereas the Treaty measure uses gross debt.

From February 2000 the Treaty deficit moved to being reported on an ESA95 basis.

National Accounts

C104   The National Accounts record most transactions on an accruals basis, including most taxes. Corporation tax, self assessment income tax and some other HMRC taxes are scored on a cash basis due to practical difficulties. The National Accounts also impute the value of some transactions where no money changes hands, for example non-trading capital consumption.

C105   Full details of the sources for each table are included in Budget 2007: data sources, available on the Treasury's internet site, and on request from the Treasury's Public Enquiry Unit (020 7270 4558).

C106   The outturn figures are based on series published in the monthly Public Sector Finance release, last published on 20 March 2007.

C107   The principal measures drawn from the National Accounts are described below.

Fiscal aggregates

C108   The current budget, formerly known as the current balance, measures the balance of current account revenue over current expenditure, including depreciation. The definition of the current budget presented in this chapter is very similar to the National Accounts concept of net saving. It differs only in that it includes taxes on capital (mainly inheritance tax) in current rather than capital receipts. The current budget is used to measure progress against the golden rule. The actual measure is the average surplus on the current budget expressed as a ratio to GDP over the economic cycle.

C109 Public sector net borrowing, formerly known as the financial deficit in the UK National Accounts, is the balance between expenditure and income in the consolidated current and capital accounts. It differs from the public sector net cash requirement in that it is measured on an accruals basis and because certain financial transactions (notably net lending and net acquisition of other financial assets, which affect the level of borrowing but not the public sector's net financial indebtedness) are excluded from public sector net borrowing but are included in the public sector net cash requirement.

C110 Public sector net debt is approximately the stock analogue of the public sector net cash requirement. It measures the public sector's financial liabilities to the private sector and abroad, net of short-term financial assets such as bank deposits and foreign exchange reserves.

C111 General government gross debt, the Treaty debt ratio, is the measure of debt used in the European Union's Excessive Deficit Procedure. As a general government measure, it excludes the debt of public corporations. It measures general government's total financial liabilities before netting off short-term financial assets.

C112 Public sector net worth represents the public sector's overall net balance sheet position. It is equal to the sum of the public sector's financial and non-financial assets less its total financial liabilities. The estimates of tangible assets are subject to wide margins of error, because they depend on broad assumptions, for example about asset lives, which may not be appropriate in all cases. The introduction of resource accounting for central government departments will lead in time to an improvement in data quality, as audited information compiled from detailed asset registers becomes available.

Public sector receipts

C113 Net taxes and national insurance contributions (NTNIC) is a measure of net cash payments made to the UK government and differs in several respects from the National Accounts measure of total public sector current receipts (PSCR). A reconciliation between the two aggregates is given in the lower half of Table C8. The main adjustments are:

- accruals adjustments, mainly on income tax, national insurance contributions and VAT, are added to change the basis of figures from cash to National Accounts accruals;

- payments of customs duties and agricultural and sugar levies that are collected by the government, but then paid to the EU, are subtracted as they do not score as government receipts in the National Accounts. These receipts make up the traditional own resources element of net payments to the EU;

- tax paid by public corporations is also subtracted, as it has no impact on overall public sector receipts;

- an adjustment is made for tax credits. In NTNIC, all tax credits are scored as negative tax to the extent that they are less than or equal to the tax liability of the household, and as public expenditure where they exceed the liability, in line with OECD Revenue Statistics guidelines. Although the ONS has adopted this treatment for the Working Tax Credit and Child Tax Credit they have continued to treat enhanced and payable company tax credits entirely as public expenditure in the National Accounts. Those parts of company tax credits that offset tax liability in NTNIC are added back into current receipts in Table C8;

- a similar adjustment is made for TV licences, which the ONS treats as tax receipts in the National Accounts. They score as non-tax receipts in NTNIC, in line with OECD Revenue Statistics guidelines;

- interest and other non-tax receipts, which are excluded from NTNIC, are added. This excludes oil royalties, as they are already included in NTNIC, even though the National Accounts treat them as non-tax receipts; and

- business rates paid by local authorities are included in the calculation of NTNIC but not PSCR. These are therefore deducted from NTNIC before this series enters the PSCR calculation.

Total Managed Expenditure

C114 Public expenditure is measured across the whole of the public sector using the aggregate Total Managed Expenditure (TME). TME is the sum of public sector current expenditure, public sector net investment and public sector depreciation. These aggregates are based on National Accounts definitions defined under ESA95.

C115 Public sector current expenditure is the sum of expenditure on pay and related costs, plus spending on goods and services, and current grants made to the private sector. Current expenditure is net of receipts from sales of goods and services.

C116 Public sector capital expenditure is shown in Table C14. It includes:

- gross domestic fixed capital formation (i.e. expenditure on fixed assets such as schools and hospitals, roads, computers, plant and machinery and intangible assets) net of receipts from sales of fixed assets (e.g. council houses and surplus land);

- grants in support of capital expenditure in the private sector; and

- the value of the physical increase in stocks for central government, primarily agricultural commodity stocks.

C117 Public sector net investment in Table C1 nets off depreciation of the public sector's stock of fixed assets.

C118 Public sector depreciation is the annual charge that is made in relation to the reduction in value of the public sector's capital assets over a particular financial year.

C119 For budgeting purposes, TME is further split into Departmental Expenditure Limits (DEL) and Annually Managed Expenditure (AME).

C120 DELs are firm three-year spending limits for departments. In general DELs will cover all running costs and all programme expenditure except spending that is included in departmental AME. DEL has distinct resource and capital budgets, as shown in Table C13.

C121 AME is spending that cannot be reasonably subject to firm multi-year limits. AME components are shown in Table C11 and are defined as follows.

C122 Social security benefits in AME expenditure covers contributory, non-contributory and income-related benefits for children, people of working age and pensioners. Broadly, benefits are paid in respect of retirement, unemployment, or disability, caring responsibilities and bereavement, as well as housing costs for all groups with effect from Budget 2004. Some expenditure on housing-related benefits is, however, covered by the locally financed expenditure category.

C123   Tax credits for individuals scored as expenditure includes spending on the Working Tax Credit and the Child Tax Credit that is classified as public expenditure under National Accounts definitions.

C124   Net public service pensions expenditure is reported on a National Accounts basis and represents the difference between the cash paid out during the year and any contributions received for the main unfunded public service pension schemes.

C125   National Lottery expenditures relate to the distribution of the money received from the National Lottery for good causes. Funds are drawn down by Distributor Bodies and directed towards Lottery funded projects.

C126   BBC domestic services includes the current and capital spending of the BBC home broadcasting service i.e. the BBC excluding the World Service and it's commercial subsidiaries.

C127   Other departmental expenditure aggregates all other expenditure made by departments that is not separately identified in the AME table.

C128   Net expenditure transfers to EU institutions include the AME spending component of the UK's contribution to the EU, comprising the Gross National Income (GNI) based contribution less the UK abatement. The other components of UK net payments to EU institutions are either included in DEL, or in public sector current receipts via the VAT based contribution. Some contributions, such as common agricultural policy expenditure and receipts, have no impact on public sector fiscal aggregates as they score as direct transactions between the EU and farmers in the National Accounts.

C129   Locally financed expenditure consists of local authority self-financed expenditure (LASFE) and Scottish spending financed by local taxation (non-domestic rates and, if and when levied, the Scottish variable rate of income tax). LASFE is the difference between total local authority expenditure, including most gross debt but net of capital receipts, and central government support to local authorities i.e. Aggregate External Finance (AEF), specific grants and credit approvals.

C130   Central government debt interest is shown gross, and only interest paid within the public sector is netted off. All other receipts of interest and dividends are included in current receipts. Interest payments also include the uplift on the capital value of index-linked gilts accrued each month of the gilt's life and an allowance (amortisation) over the life of a gilt not issued at par.

C131   Public corporations' own-financed capital expenditure is the amount of capital expenditure by public corporations that is not financed by general government.

C132   The AME margin is an unallocated margin on total AME spending and is included as a measure of caution against AME expenditure exceeding its forecast levels.

C133   The accounting adjustments reconcile the DEL and AME framework of departmental budgets to the National Accounts measure of TME, and are shown in Table C14.

C134   *Central government programmes* covers various items which relate to central government programme expenditure and where budgeting and National Accounts treatments differ, for example the depreciation costs of NHS Trusts and tax credits for companies.

C135   *VAT refunds* adds back refunds obtained by central government departments, local authorities and certain public corporations. DEL and AME programme expenditure are measured net of these refunds, while TME is recorded with VAT paid.

C136   *Central government non-trading capital consumption* (i.e. depreciation) as measured by the ONS for National Accounts is added.

C137   *Non-cash items in resource budgets and not in TME* includes cost of capital charge, write-offs, notional audit fee, take-up, movements in the value, and release of provisions, the subsidy and bad debt element of student loans, and movement in stocks.

C138   *Expenditure financed by revenue receipts* adds in certain receipts which are deducted from departmental budgets but which are not treated as negative expenditure in TME.

C139   *Local authorities* adds in local authority depreciation and subsidies paid to local authority trading bodies, and deducts capital grants from local authorities to public corporations, local authority receipts of investment grants from private sector developers and certain license fees collected by local authorities.

C140   *General government consolidation* adjusts for the fact that payments of certain taxes, grants and interest that are within the public sector do not score in TME, as TME is a consolidated public sector concept. The cost of over-75 TV licences in AME social security, as these represent payments within central government, from DWP to BBC.

C141   *Public corporations* adds receipts from public corporations of interest, dividends and equity withdrawals that are netted-off in budgets, interest paid by public corporations to the private sector and abroad (as property income paid by the public sector to the rest of the economy is in TME, but not in departmental budgets) and deducts the profit or loss of the Forestry Enterprise.

C142   *Financial transactions* deducts net lending, acquisition of securities and profit or loss on sale of financial assets.

C143   *Other accounting adjustments* deducts depreciation and impairments in AME. An adjustment is also made to reconcile to actual and expected National Accounts outturn. Differences can arise, for example, because of differences in the timing of data.

LIST OF ABBREVIATIONS

AEF	Aggregate External Finance
AEI	Average earnings index
AIDS	Acquired Immunodeficiency Syndrome
AMC	Advance Market Commitment
AME	Annually Managed Expenditure
AMS	Asset management Strategy
APD	Air passenger duty
ASP	Alternatively Secured Pensions
BBC	British Broadcasting Corporation
BNFL	British Nuclear Fuels Limited
BP	British Petroleum
BRE	Better Regulation Executive
BRTF	Better Regulation Task Force
CAP	Common Agricultural Policy
CC	Competition Commission
CCAs	Climate Change Agreements
CCL	Climate change levy
CCS	Carbon Capture and Storage
CCT	Company Car Tax
CERF	UN Central Emergency Relief Fund
CEO	Chief Executive Officer
CFC	Controlled Foreign Company
CGNCR	Central government net cash requirement
CNG	Compressed Natural Gas
CPI	Consumer Prices Index
CSR	Comprehensive Spending Review
CTC	Child Tax Credit
CVD	Cardiovascular disease
DCA	Department of Constitutional Affairs
DCLG	Department of Communities and Local Government
DCMS	Department for Culture, Media and Sports
DEFRA	Department for Environment, Food and Rural Affairs
DEL	Departmental Expenditure Limit
DfES	Department for Education and Skills
DfID	Department for International Development
DfT	Department for Transport
DH	Department of Health
DMA	Debt Management Account
DMO	Debt Management Office
DTI	Department of Trade and Industry
DWP	Department for Work and Pensions

ECAs	Enhanced capital allowances
ECFs	Enterprise Capital Funds
ECGD	Export Credits Guarantee Department
ECJ	European Court of Justice
ECOS	Employee car ownership scheme
ECOFIN	Council of European Finance Ministers
EEC	Energy Efficiency Commitment
EFA/FTI	Education for all fast track initiative
EPC	Economic Policy Committee
ERAD	Employment Retention and Advancement Demonstration
ESA	Employment and Support Allowance
EU	European Union
EU ETS	EU Emissions Trading Scheme
EYFR	End Year Fiscal Report
FDI	Foreign Direct Investment
FSA	Financial Services Authority
FTSE	Financial Times Stock Exchange
G7	Group of Seven. A group of seven major industrial nations (comprising: Canada, France, Germany, Italy, Japan, UK and US).
GAVI	Global Alliance for Vaccines & Immunisation
GCSE	General Certificate of Secondary Education
GDP	Gross Domestic Product
GNI	Gross National Income
GOs	Government Offices
GVA	Gross Value Added
HEFCE	Higher Education Funding Council for England
HEIs	Higher Education Institutions
HGVs	Heavy Goods Vehicles
HIPC	Heavily Indebted Poor Countries
HIV	Human Immunodeficiency Virus
HMRC	HM Revenue and Customs
IBAC	International Business Advisory Council
ICT	Information and Communications Technology
IFFIm	International Finance Facility for immunisation
IHT	Inheritance Tax
IMF	International Monetary Fund
IP	Intellectual property
IPCC	Intergovernmental Panel on Climate Change
IQ	IQ capital fund
ISA	Individual Savings Account
ISB	Invest to save budget
IT	Information Technology
IWC	In-work credit
JSA	Jobseeker's Allowance

LAA	Local Area Agreement
LABGI	Local Authority Business Growth Incentive
LASFE	Local Authority Self-Financed Expenditure
LBRO	Local Better Regulation Office
LDA	London Development Agency
LEA	Local Education Authority
LEGI	Local Enterprise Growth Initiative
LESA	Landlords energy Savings Allowance
LFS	Labour Force Survey
LHA	Local Housing Allowance
LPG	Liquefied Petroleum Gas
LTCS	Landfill Tax Credit Scheme
MDGs	Millennium Development Goals
MDRs	Marginal Deduction Rates
MIG	Minimum Income Guarantee
MPC	Monetary Policy Committee
MRC	Medical Research Council
MSC	Managed Service Company
MtC	Million tonnes of carbon
MTIC	Missing Trader Intra-Community
NAO	National Audit Office
NDDP	New Deal for disabled people
NDLP	New Deal for lone parents
NDP	New Deal for partners
NDYP	New Deal for young people
NGO	Non-Governmental Organisation
NHS	National Health Service
NICs	National Insurance Contributions
NICE	National Institute for Clinical Excellence
NIESR	National Institute of Economic and Social Research
NLF	National Loans Fund
NTNIC	National Institute of Health Research
ODI	Office for Disability Issues
ODPM	Office of the Deputy Prime Minister
OECD	Organisation for Economic Cooperation and Development
OFCOM	Office of Communications
OFT	Office of Fair Trading
OGC	Office of Government Commerce
ONS	Office for National Statistics
OPC	Optional planning charge
OPEC	Organisation of Petroleum Exporting Countries
OSCHR	Office for Strategic Coordination of Health Research

PEP	Personal Equity Plan
PFI	Private Finance Initiative
PGS	Planning Gain Supplement
PPPs	Public Private Partnerships
PSA	Public Service Agreement
PSGI	Public Sector Gross Investment
PSNB	Public sector net borrowing
PSPC	Public Sector Pay Committee
RAE	Research Assessment Exercise
R&D	Research and Development
RC	Research Council
RDA	Regional Development Agency
RPI	Retail Prices Index
RTFO	Renewable Transport Fuel Obligation
SBS	Small Business Service
SDRT	Stamp Duty Reserve Tax
SEEDA	South East England Development Agency
SET	science, engineering, technology
SFLG	Small Firms Loan Guarantee
SMEs	Small and medium-sized enterprises
SNA	System of National Accounts
SSC	Sector skills councils
STEM	Science, technology, engineering and mathematical
TB	Tuberculosis
TESSA	Tax Exempt Special Savings Account
TME	Total Managed Expenditure
UK	United Kingdom
UK-REIT	UK – Real Estate Investment Trusts
UKTI	UK trade and investment
UN	United Nations
UNITAID	UN unit on HIV and AIDS
UNRWA	United Nations Relief and Work Agency
VAT	Value Added Tax
VCR	Video Cassette Recorder
VED	Vehicle Excise Duty
WFI	Work Focussed Interviews
WFTC	Working Families' Tax Credit
WRAP	Work related activity premium
WTC	Working Tax Credit

LIST OF CHARTS

Economic and Fiscal Strategy Report

Financial Statement and Budget Report

LIST OF TABLES

Economic and Fiscal Strategy Report

Financial Statement and Budget Report

Cover photography:

Communities & Local Government

Westend61 / Alamy

image100 / Alamy

Michael Harder / Alamy

ImageState / Alamy

Mark J. Barrett / Alamy

Robert Harding Picture Library Ltd / Alamy

Mike Harrington / Alamy

Photofusion Picture Library / Alamy

Andrew Fox / Alamy

Paul Carter/reportdigital.co.uk

Third Avenue Ltd.

Printed in the UK by The Stationery Office Limited
on behalf of the Controller of Her Majesty's Stationery Office
ID5531150   03/07

Printed on Paper containing 75% fibre content minimum.